COMMUNIST REGIMES IN EASTERN EUROPE

Books by Richard F. Staar

Arms Control: Myth versus Reality (editor)

Aspects of Modern Communism (editor)

Communist Regimes in Eastern Europe

Future Information Revolution in the USSR (editor)

Long-Range Environmental Study of the Northern Tier of Eastern Europe in 1990–2000

Poland 1944–1962: Sovietization of a Captive People

Public Diplomacy: USA versus USSR (editor)

Soviet Military Policies Since World War Two (coauthor)

USSR Foreign Policies After Detente

Yearbook on International Communist Affairs (editor)

Hoover Press Publication 381

First printing, 1988

Manufactured in the United States of America
94   93   92   91   90   89   88   9   8   7   6   5   4   3   2   1

Library of Congress Cataloging-in-Publication Data

Staar, Richard Felix, 1923–
    Communist regimes in Eastern Europe / Richard F. Staar.—5th ed.
        p.   cm.—(Hoover Press publication; 381)
    Bibliography: p.
    Includes index.
    ISBN 0-8179-8812-2
1. Europe, Eastern—Politics and government—1945– 2. Communism—Europe,
Eastern.   I. Title.
DJK50.S7 1988   88-18121
320.9171'7—dc19   CIP

COMMUNIST REGIMES IN EASTERN EUROPE

FIFTH EDITION

RICHARD F. STAAR

HOOVER INSTITUTION PRESS
Stanford University, Stanford, California

For Jadwiga, Monica, and Christina

Contents

Tables

CHARTS

Preface

I have undertaken this fifth edition of my book to update earlier editions, which appeared during December 1967, April 1971, March 1977, and February 1982, all of which are now out of print. The six years since the fourth edition was published have witnessed many changes in Eastern Europe. The revised book continues to introduce the available source materials for studying this complicated part of the world. Besides changes in the text, the tables have been revised and the bibliography updated.

In large part, the data have been extracted from articles and books in the original East European languages. Albanian, Hungarian, and Romanian sources were used mostly in translation, as the footnotes indicate. Transcripts from monitoring by the U.S. Department of Commerce, *Foreign Broadcast Information Service* (abbreviated *FBIS* in the text) proved most useful, as did *Situation Reports* and other materials from Radio Free Europe (abbreviated as RFE in the text). Central Intelligence Agency *Directories* and *Handbooks of Economic Statistics* helped with some of the identifications, especially for purposes of establishing interlocking directorates and finding esoteric data.

Organized into eleven chapters the book's first eight chapters individually treat those countries of Eastern Europe now under communist party rule. Describing the governmental structure, each of these chapters includes the constitutional framework and the electoral system; the ruling party, which is called variously a communist, socialist, or workers' movement; domestic policies; and foreign relations. The last three chapters, incorporating an areawide approach, discuss military and economic integration through the Warsaw Treaty Organization and the Council for Mutual Economic Assistance, together with developments in intrabloc political relations.

Although errors in fact and interpretation remain my own, I wish to acknowledge with gratitude the assistance of Hoover staff members and especially reference librarians Miss Hilja Kukk and Ms. Linda A. Wheeler, as well as the assistant editor of the *Yearbook on International Communist Affairs,* Mrs. Margit

N. Grigory. To all of them I owe a special debt of gratitude. The laborious typing of text, footnotes, and tables, as well as the computation of statistics, is the work of Ms. Joyce Cerwin. I also wish to thank the following scholars who read and commented on separate chapters: Professor Jefferson Adams (Sarah Lawrence College), Professor John D. Bell (University of Maryland at Baltimore County), Professor Christopher D. Jones (University of Washington at Seattle), Dr. Robert R. King (Administrative Assistant to a Member, U.S. House of Representatives), Professor Bartlomiej Kaminski (University of Maryland at College Park), Professor Andrew A. Michta (Rhodes College), Professor Arthur R. Rachwald (U.S. Naval Academy), Dr. Miklos K. Radvanyi (Congressional Research Service, Library of Congress), Professor Robin Alison Remington (University of Missouri at Columbia), Professor Nikolaos A. Stavrou (Howard University), and Professor Zdenek Suda (University of Pittsburgh).

Finally, preparation of this latest edition of my book was made possible by the generous support of the Olin Foundation and, specifically, the John M. Olin Program for the Study of the Soviet Union and Eastern Europe at the Hoover Institution.

                                                      Richard F. Staar
                                                      July 1988

Chapter 1

People's Socialist Republic of Albania

Still a thorn in the flank of Yugoslavia and a shadow on what was formerly a Soviet sphere of influence, Albania no longer provides a window into Eastern Europe for the Chinese and enters the 1990s without communist allies. The People's Socialist Republic of Albania, bordering on Yugoslavia and Greece as well as the Adriatic Sea, has an area of about 11,100 square miles and a population of approximately three million. Yet this small, poor, and unproductive land of mountaineers, no larger than the state of Maryland, plays a role in international communist politics. From the days of the Greek and Roman empires, when traders plied its coasts, until well into modern times, Albania has remained aloof and detached from world affairs.[1] It was ruled by the Ottomans for nearly four hundred years, commencing in 1468 with the defeat of the Albanian national patriot Skanderbeg, who with his rugged mountain warriors had defended the country against the Turkish army for almost a quarter of a century.

Although the people of Albania have usually stood aside from affairs outside their borders, they found themselves overrun and engulfed by events of World War II. Enver Hoxha, a little-known schoolteacher and later a self-appointed army general, organized a clandestine group that became known as the National Liberation Front. When the Italians and Germans withdrew in 1944, Hoxha and his communist-dominated organization liquidated such Albanian anticommunist organizations as the Nationalist Front (Balli Kombetar) and the Legality Movement.[2]

In the absence of any effective opposition, Hoxha and his associates on 29 November 1944 established a new, revolutionary government at Tirana.[3] Up to this time they had been advised by Josip Broz-Tito's partisans in Yugoslavia. Although the Albanian communists could claim only 4 or 5 percent of the population as supporters, their spurious democratic front received 93.2 percent of the votes to elect a constituent assembly, which in January 1946 declared Albania a people's republic. The new dictatorial regime, supported by neighboring Yugoslavia, strengthened communist influence within the country not only through the physical liquidation of notable anticommunists but also by ruthless purges of its own ruling party.

Seemingly unimportant to the rest of the world, Albania began to move closer to Moscow, which was looking for a foothold on the Mediterranean. Afraid of impending annexation by his Yugoslav mentors, Hoxha severed relations with Tito in July 1948[4] but continued to maintain close ties with the USSR until Khrushchev's denunciation of the deceased Stalin, which in 1961 led to the public break. Left without a strong protector in Europe, Hoxha turned to the Chinese communists, who readily answered his request for assistance in the ideological dispute with the Soviet Union.

By the late 1970s, however, as post-Mao China embarked on a new course featuring technological modernization and improved contacts with the West, Sino-Albanian relations deteriorated. On 7 July 1978, the People's Republic of China notified the Albanian ambassador of a decision to "stop its economic and military aid and its aid payments to Albania and bring back its economic and military experts." Withdrawal of Chinese assistance, estimated to have totaled approximately $800 million during the seventeen years of cooperation, set back development plans by several years.[5]

After severing ties with the two largest communist-ruled states, Albania declared itself the only genuine Marxist-Leninist country in the world. For the first time since World War II, the regime had no protector or patron. In efforts to expand diplomatic, commercial, and cultural relations, Tirana turned increasingly to Belgrade. Fearing a Soviet invasion of Yugoslavia, which could lead to an attack on Albania, the Albanians pledged to support their neighbors. Although ideological differences still divide the two countries, relations were greatly improved until the March–April 1981 demonstrations by Albanians living in Yugoslavia's southern province of Kosovo, followed by seven years of accusations from Tirana concerning alleged repression of Albanian cultural life in Yugoslavia and demands that Kosovo be given the status of a republic rather than an autonomous region within Serbia. However, during 24–26 February 1988, an Albanian attended the first post–World War II meeting of Balkan foreign ministers in Belgrade.[6] The others came from Bulgaria, Greece, Romania, Turkey, and host Yugoslavia. (The previous summer, Greece had lifted the technical state of war with Albania.)

Albania also has sought to improve relations with Turkey and other European countries like West Germany and Great Britain. Any major expansion of trade is hampered, however, by Tirana's insistence on bartering merchandise and raw materials for badly needed Western machinery and technology. Nevertheless, young Albanians are being sent to study in Italy, France, and Scandinavia.

THE COMMUNIST PARTY OF ALBANIA

Sympathy for Marxist ideology in Albania dates back to the period from June to December 1924 under the revolutionary government of Premier Bishop Fan Stylian Noli.[7] An earlier affinity for Russia was evidenced after Soviet communists revealed the secret treaty of London (1915), which provided for Albania's partition. When Lenin, the leader of the Bolshevik Revolution, died in January 1924, the Albanian parliament observed five minutes of silence in tribute to the hero who had allegedly saved Albania from partition. Although a communist party was not founded until 1941, Albanian communists and fellow travelers were supported by the Comintern in the late 1920s and 1930s while they continued to agitate as a minority group both within their own country and from exile.

During the years 1924–1939, King Zog maintained an authoritarian regime. For twenty years no legal political parties existed in Albania except the fascist movement, which was organized after the 1939 Italian occupation. A communist party secretly established itself at Tirana in November 1941 under the supervision of two Yugoslav emissaries, Miladin Popovic and Dusan Mugosa, who advised the party until the end of World War II.[8]

The postwar system in Albania came into being without the assistance or presence of Soviet troops. Local communists organized and achieved power under the guidance of their Yugoslav mentors, who received directives from Tito. Leaders chosen by the Yugoslavs to head the party in Albania included Enver Hoxha—the intellectual first head of the Albanian Communist Party—and the proletarian Koci Xoxe, who was executed in 1949 as an "enemy of the people."[9]

Hoxha died on 11 April 1985 at age 77. Two days later the heir apparent, Ramiz Alia, became first secretary of the ruling Albanian Party of Labor. How will the new Gheg party chief handle the Tosk-controlled military and security forces? Hoxha selected Alia by virtue of his militant Marxism-Leninism and his support for policies based on national self-reliance.[10] The Hoxha personality cult continues under the direction of his widow, Nexhmije, who chairs the Albanian Democratic Front and also directs the Institute of Marxism-Leninism, which in mid-May 1988 published the 60th volume of Hoxha's collected works.

Organization. The structure of the party was sanctioned in 1948 at its first congress. A new name was also selected: the Albanian Party of Labor (APL). The statute adopted at this congress based the organizational hierarchy on the principle of democratic centralism, wherein full and free discussion is theoretically permitted. After a unanimous or majority vote, the minority must submit to the majority. The 1950 constitution of Albania recognized the special status of the party, as does the 1976 one.[11] The APL is organized along the country's territorial subdivisions, with a central apparatus in Tirana.

According to the party statute, the highest organ is the congress, which meets every five years. This supreme body is made up of delegates nominally elected by district, regional, and city conferences. Its functions include ratification of reports submitted by the Central Committee and other main organs, review and amendment of the party program and statutes, determination of tactics regarding current policy, and election of members to the Central Committee. In practice, the principal roles of the congress remain those of giving the impression of democratic rule and of providing an opportunity for deserving members to be elected as delegates.

The Central Committee, according to the statute, directs all party activities in the periods between congresses. It supervises lower-ranking organizations, elects members to central organs, administers funds, and represents the movement in its relations with other communist parties and mass organizations in foreign countries. In reality the Central Committee has little authority and power, owing to its size and the fact that it is not in continuous session. The day-to-day functions of this committee are delegated to the Politburo and the Secretariat, both of which are composed of persons elected by the Central Committee from its own membership.

The real locus of power is the Politburo, the policy-formulating body of the party. At the end of 1988 it consisted of thirteen full and five candidate members.[12] Through placement of these persons in top government offices and in the leadership of mass organizations, the Politburo can formulate policy that is certain to be carried out. The selection of Politburo members for the positions of premier and deputy premier represents a constant feature of policy, and this procedure assures continuity in power and control over the government. The system can be described as one of interlocking directorates, and it is patterned directly after that of the USSR, despite the suspension of relations between the two governments as well as between their respective ruling parties.

Regardless of this basic pattern, at one time the Albanian communists emulated the Chinese by temporarily assigning at least twelve high-ranking bureaucrats (including five Politburo members) to additional duties at the city or district level. An "Open Letter," released by the Central Committee to all party members on 4 March 1966, admitted that a chasm existed between the bureaucracy and the masses. Its dissemination probably reached the lowest organizational units, implementing the ideological and cultural revolution that had been inaugurated the previous month.

The lowest level in the party hierarchy is the basic unit, which corresponds to the primary party organization in the Communist Party of the Soviet Union. There are about two thousand such units in factories, transport and construction centers, various institutions, and towns and villages.[13] They can be formed only in places where at least three party members work, and they comprise a link between the masses and governing party organs. Their functions include recruitment of new members, administration of local party affairs, and close surveillance over every group living in the community or work center. The basic unit acts as an arm of the police state, but it remains subordinate to local party committees, which are formed successively at city, regional, and district levels.

Local committees meet once a month and are controlled by an executive agency, called the bureau, consisting of not more than eleven members. The bureau includes a first secretary plus two or more other secretaries, all of whom must be approved by the Central Committee. The first secretary is political boss over the committee and a trusted party member. Functions of local committees are to assure fulfillment of party directives, supervise implementation of these directives, administer party fiscal affairs, and approve enrollment of new members.

Membership and Composition.   The paucity of available information concerning the membership and social composition of the APL precludes a more than cursory and uncertain coverage of this subject. According to one author, who cites an official source, party membership in 1941 totaled about two hundred persons. Forty-six years later the regime provided a figure of about 147,000, not including candidates for membership. (See Table 1.)

Table 1
GROWTH OF THE ALBANIAN PARTY OF LABOR, 1941–1986

Year	Occasion	Membership
1941		200
1943		700
1944		2,800
1948	First congress (November)	29,137
1952	Second congress (March–April)	44,418
1955	Third congress (May–June)	48,644
1961	Fourth congress (February)	*ca.* 53,000
1966	Fifth congress (November)	66,326
1969		*ca.* 50,000
1971	Sixth congress (November)	86,985
1976	Seventh congress (November)	101,500
1981	Eighth congress (November)	122,600
1986	Ninth congress (November)	147,000

Sources: *Zeri i popullit,* 24 March 1954, as cited by Jani I. Dilo, *The Communist Party Leadership in Albania* (Washington, D.C., 1961), p. 10; Tirana radio, 1 November 1966; *Rruga e partise* (March 1969), p. 65; *Zeri i popullit,* 4 November 1971, 3 November 1976, 7 November 1981, 4 November 1986.

Data concerning the social composition of the party are of similarly dubious validity. In 1952 the membership could be classified by origin as 74.1 percent from the poorer class (mostly from rural areas), 22.2 percent from the middle class, and the remaining 3.7 percent from the former wealthy classes. In the words of one expert in 1955, "the Albanian Communist Party is fundamentally a party of poor peasants."[14] More recent statistics indicate that the proportion of industrial workers in the party had increased to 39.8 percent and the proportion of peasants on collective farms to 29.5 percent. The remaining 32.2 percent in late 1986 were probably for the most part government officials, intelligentsia, and members of the armed forces.

In recent years, there has been a concerted effort to bring more women into the party. Thus, in 1971 only 22 percent of the members were women, but in 1976 they made up 27 percent and in 1986, 32.2 percent. Recruitment also has been emphasized among the younger segments of the population. As of November 1986 about 70 percent of APL members were under 40, some 22 percent were between 40 and 50, and only 8 percent were over 51 years of age.[15]

The communist party of Albania still resembles that of the Soviet Union in many ways including organizational structure, widespread purges, and internecine rivalry. In Albania, as in other communist totalitarian states, the country is run by one man who also heads the party. Numerous front organizations operate to implement policies of the party-government. In early 1988 the total leadership cadre numbered 70,000 people, whereas 100,000 midlevel functionaries were serving just in agriculture.[16]

The Ninth Congress of the Albanian Party of Labor convened on 3 November 1986. Guidelines for representation at the congress consisted of one delegate with deliberative vote per 150 party members and one delegate with consultative vote per 150 candidates for membership. First Secretary Ramiz Alia presented a report on activities of the Central Committee; Premier Adil Carcani spoke on the directives for the eighth consecutive five-year plan (1986–1990).[17]

CONSTITUTION AND GOVERNMENT

The People's Socialist Republic of Albania currently functions under a fundamental law known as the 1976 constitution. It is the third such document adopted since the power seizure by the communists and the ninth since the Albanians won independence in 1912 from Turkey. Because the Albanian communists in effect represented an adjunct to the Yugoslav communist party, the first postwar constitution in March 1946 did not present much difficulty. Its verbiage is an almost direct translation from the then newly promulgated document in Yugoslavia, which, in turn, was based on the 1936 "Stalin" constitution of the Soviet Union.

The major difference was that the Albanian constitution provided for a single legislative chamber known as the People's Assembly, whereas Yugoslavia, owing to its federal structure, had a legislature composed of two houses. Other distinctions included omission of any reference to political supremacy of the Albanian Party of Labor, which already represented the locus of power. References to a regime monopoly over domestic trade and the socialist development of agriculture were also lacking. These deficiencies, however, came to be remedied in subsequent documents adopted in 1950 and 1976.

At the Sixth Congress of the Albanian Party of Labor in November 1971, it was announced that the 1950 constitution would be superseded by a new one. Almost four years later, approval for drafting a new basic law came at the eighth plenum of the Central Committee.[18] A constitutional commission of 51 leaders, elected by the People's Assembly the following month, included a majority of Central Committee members with Enver Hoxha as chairman.[19] In early 1976 a draft constitution of the People's Socialist Republic of Albania was made public so that it could be "widely discussed by the nation before being approved by the People's Assembly."[20]

Principal Features of the 1976 Constitution.   The new constitution[21] begins with a lengthy preamble that praises the regime's political-social order and emphasizes the need for protecting as well as strengthening that order, "promoting the construction of the socialist society in order to then progress gradually into a communist society." The body of the document consists of three parts, as did that of the 1950 constitution. The first part, which deals with the social order, defines political and economic foundations of the state as well as rights and duties of citizens. The second treats governmental structure, which includes the People's Assembly, Council of Ministers, armed forces, people's councils, and judiciary. The third part describes the state seal and flag, confirms Tirana as the capital city, and details procedures for making constitutional amendments.

The People's Socialist Republic of Albania is defined as having all powers derived from and belonging to the working people, who rule through people's councils (organs of local government) and the People's Assembly or national legislature. These bodies are elected by citizens allegedly on the basis of a universal, equal, direct, and secret ballot. Social and economic measures are stressed in the 1976 constitution, as they are in corresponding documents of other communist-ruled countries. Control over natural resources and industry, as well as other means of production, remains in the hands of the state. Private property is guaranteed protection, but it can be limited in amount or expropriated if it is used to the detriment of the state. Rights and duties of citizens resemble those affirmed by the basic laws of other East European countries. In fact, the outside observer may be led to believe that the 1976 constitution includes Western democratic principles that guarantee certain inalienable rights vis-à-vis the state. In reality, however, the constitution is superseded by the dictatorship of the proletariat or rather its vanguard, the communist party. Unrestricted authority of the state is upheld, and rights of citizens may be curtailed at any time.

According to the 1976 constitution, the 250-member People's Assembly is the highest and most important organ in the governmental structure (Article 66). The assembly is "elected" every four years by all citizens eligible to vote. It ordinarily meets twice a year, and at these times deputies are expected to approve all items on the agenda. Because the party selects all assembly candidates and presents them to voters on a single-slate ballot for election, the national legislature is merely a rubber stamp used to approve decisions made in advance by the party. Political rights, as they are known in Western democracies, are nonexistent. (See Table 2 for official election returns.)

Table 2
OFFICIAL ALBANIAN ELECTION RETURNS, 1958–1987

Date	Registered voters	Votes for regime	Percentage	Votes against regime
1 June 1958	780,061	779,935	99.98	126
3 June 1962	889,875	889,868	99.98	7
10 July 1966	978,161	978,158	99.99	3
20 September 1970	1,097,123	1,096,967	99.99	156
6 October 1974	1,248,530	1,248,528	99.99	2
12 November 1978	1,436,289	1,436,285	99.99	4
14 November 1982	1,627,968	1,627,967	100.00	1
1 February 1987	1,830,653	1,830,652	100.00	1

SOURCES: ACEN, *Survey of Developments in the Captive Countries* (March–October 1958), p. 6, and (January–June 1962), p. 53; Tirana radio, 11 July 1966; *Zeri i popullit*, 22 September 1970, 8 October 1974, 14 November 1978, 16 November 1982, 3 February 1987.

NOTE: Voting is mandatory, with universal suffrage beginning at age 18.

The People's Assembly elects fifteen of its members to form a legislative presidium, and powers are exercised between its sessions by this small group.[22] The presidium interprets and makes decisions concerning constitutionality of laws, ratifies international agreements, appoints and recalls diplomatic envoys, issues decrees, and promulgates legislation passed by the assembly. It also creates governmental commissions, proclaims elections, and convenes the assembly. Yet the presidium is said to be responsible to the assembly, which in theory may recall, replace, or dismiss any or all presidium members.

The Council of Ministers is considered the supreme executive and adminis-trative organ; it is formally appointed by the People's Assembly. Powers assigned by the constitution to the Council of Ministers include supervision of all social, economic, and cultural activities. In reality, the premier, his deputies, and various ministers[23] comprising the council are selected by the party's Politburo. The council's main function is to ensure that all Politburo decisions are carried out.

Local government organs consist of people's councils at district, regional, and city levels. These councils are directly elected for terms of three years and exercise authority over administrative, economic, and cultural matters within their own geographic areas. They also maintain order, enforce state laws, and are supposed to uphold citizens' rights. Executive committees are elected by people's councils and exercise the above functions between meetings of the councils.

According to the 1976 constitution, the highest judicial organ is the Supreme Court. Judges are elected by secret ballot in the People's Assembly. Courts at lower levels are formed similarly by corresponding people's councils and thus allegedly represent the "will of the citizens."

The Office of the Prosecutor General is yet another agency that is supposedly controlled by the People's Assembly. It supervises implementation of laws by ministries, other administrative bodies, all public officials, and citizens.

The 1976 constitution shows little difference or innovation from its 1950 predecessor and merely reflects previously enacted changes (for example, a 250-member limit in the People's Assembly) as well as emphasis on completion of socialist construction throughout the country.

Government. The typical Soviet-style relationship between communist movement and government is well established in Albania. The constitution of 1976 recognizes the privileged and controlling position of the APL, as mentioned above. Ramiz Alia, as first secretary of the Central Committee, holds the top party position.[24] He effectively controls the government from this office, even though he also is president of the Republic. Table 3 lists Politburo members and indicates the positions they hold in government. Alia (b. 1925) and other party leaders in top positions are not young, so it is likely that some of these men will retire from the political scene in the near future.

If free elections were to be held in Albania, the communists probably would not poll a majority. Such elections cannot be expected, however, because the ruling party will not permit them. Neither should one anticipate that Albania will supply strong enough indigenous leadership to bring the country out from under communist control in the near future.

DOMESTIC AFFAIRS

Economic and social transformation has come slowly to Albania, owing to its historic isolation from the mainstream of European affairs. More than 40 years of communist rule, however, have brought greater changes than the entire preceding

Table 3
ALBANIA'S INTERLOCKING DIRECTORATE, 1988

Politburo	Year elected	National Secretariat	Council of Ministers	Other positions
MEMBERS (13)				
Alia, Ramiz	1961	First secretary		Chairman, People's Assembly
Carcani, Adil	1961		Premier	
Bekteshi, Besnik	1981		Deputy premier	
Cami, Foto	1981	Secretary		
Cuko, Lenka	1976	Secretary		
Isai, Hekuran	1975		Deputy premier, Internal affairs minister	
Celiku, Hajredin	1981	Secretary		
Marko, Rita	1954			Deputy chairman, People's Assembly
Miska, Pali	1975			First secretary, Korce
Myftiu, Manush	1956		Deputy premier	
Mura, Prokop	1981		Defense minister	
Asslani, Muho	1981			First secretary, Shkoder
Stefani, Simon	1976	Secretary		
CANDIDATE MEMBERS (5)				
Mustaqi, Kico	1986		Deputy defense minister and chief of staff	
Gjegprifti, Llambi	1975		Industry and mining minister	
Cerava, Vangjel	1982		Deputy premier	
Mihali, Qirjako	1975			First secretary, Durres
Kondi, Pirro	1986			First secretary, Tirana

SOURCE: CIA, *Directory of Albanian Officials* (Washington, D.C.: June 1988), pp. 3–38.

four centuries of Ottoman domination and the 60 years of European influence. Progress in modernization has been considerable in relation to past backwardness, but it still leaves Albania far behind all other Eastern European countries.

Tradition.   Despite the communist philosophy of subordinating the individual to the state through contrived mass uniformity, certain parts of the Albanian population apparently have changed little and thus cling to prewar ethnic customs. In rural areas clan or feudal relationships still persist, and, as is usual in such sociological groupings, traditional norms are only altered at a slow rate. Although the clan may now call itself a village people's council, there is some question whether this is a fiction of communist terminology or a genuine sovietization of organizational forms. Almost five decades have brought changes in established mores and institutions, but these differences cannot be attributed exclusively to the nature of government. To a certain extent, customs keep pace with the social phenomena that accompany the modernization of any traditional society. The communist regime, of course, has done its utmost to mold and adapt these changes according to the Stalinist model.

Before World War II, Albania essentially comprised a two-class society of large landowners and peasant farmers. The smaller groups of artisans, government employees, and teachers formed the nucleus of a middle class, although their limited numbers rendered their influence insignificant. Under the present regime this basic social stratification still exists; only the occupations of the elite have changed. Party members immediately assumed the role formerly held by the *beys,* or landed aristocracy, to form what Milovan Djilas in neighboring Yugoslavia called the "new class."

Industrial progress and the rise of a government bureaucracy have fostered social mobility, and the Albanian "new class" (which is not recognized by communist definition) is increasing in size. Within this group, the rejection of tradition has been most pronounced. Although in one sense this break is designed to lead, under state guidance, to the formation of the patterns of a Marxist utopia, in another sense it creates the basis for some political objectivity.

The migration of labor, under government control, from agrarian pursuits to city industrial complexes represents another significant factor in the gradual diminution of Albanian traditionalism. During 1985 about 63 percent of the population still lived in rural areas and, therefore, was employed mostly in agriculture. [25] The urbanization of transposed peasants under a communist regime might seem to represent a potential source of unrest within the country, but in actual fact the problems are few. The inequity of living conditions, totalitarian rule, long working hours, and low pay of the new industrial worker are merely a continuation of his former agrarian existence. Substitution of local party leadership for feudal clan elders remains the essential difference.

During February 1966, the party and government launched an ideological and cultural revolution in part patterned after the one taking place in Mainland China at that time. This movement in Albania was designed to accelerate the pace of modernization and inculcate Marxist values throughout the country. The campaign has been reintensified periodically, and it continues as a permanent aspect of Albanian society, emphasizing ideological isolation from Western and revisionist cultural influences, antibureaucratism, and ideological indoctrination of the population.[26] The slogan, "holding in one hand a pick and in the other a rifle," is still popular.

Religion. Because communist regimes have been unable to eliminate religion, they have tried to "nationalize" it as a step to its control and eventual destruction.[27] In Albania this effort has been carried out with limited opposition owing to the sects of Muslim believers who comprise some 70 percent of the population. These sects are divided into Sunni, Bektashi, and other orders, which at first were recognized by the regime as "independent" religious communities. The rest of the population, about 20 percent Eastern Orthodox and 10 percent Roman Catholic, is insufficient numerically to register serious opposition.[28] A temporary accord appeared in the 1950 constitution that stated that freedom of religious practice would be guaranteed so long as churches did not utilize it as a political vehicle. Due to the basic intransigence of the Catholic Church vis-à-vis the tenets of communism, all ties with the Vatican were severed in August 1951 and a "National Albanian Catholic Church" was established.[29] Although the state could bring religious and even church officials under strict control, initially a more tolerant attitude was taken toward personal religious beliefs. Again, this represented expediency rather than relaxation of ideological imperatives. The principal tactic at first involved a subtle campaign to degrade religion to the level of superstition and slowly to eliminate places of worship. The thought seems to have been that, without the substance of organization and ceremony, the credence given to religious concepts would gradually become eroded.

After Hoxha's nine-hour speech at the November 1966 congress, however, the regime intensified its campaign to eliminate religion as an influence in Albanian public life. Places of worship were converted into "movie houses, garages, dance halls, stores. Over 2,000 mosques and churches underwent demolition . . . The beautiful Turkish mosque in the center of Tirana, adjacent to the Venetian clock tower, is a museum today."[30]

In 1967 Albania officially declared itself an atheist state, sanctioned by Articles 37 and 55 of the 1976 constitution. Hardest hit by the subsequent political repression has been the Christian population. The regime is much more tolerant toward various Muslim sects, however, and uses Albania's religious heritage to promote relations with the Middle East. According to Samuel Matathia, who escaped to Greece, the 2,000 to 2,500 Jews are also severely persecuted.[31]

Culture. Literature, the theater, music, and art are controlled by the party through various cultural organizations, such as the League of Writers and Artists, the Union of Albanian Women, and the Committee for Arts and Culture. Influenced by the Chinese communists,[32] Albania in 1966 launched a cultural revolution that called for production of a national and a socialist culture as well as selective rejection of classical Western culture and drama.

Intellectual revisionism of the type appearing in Poland, Hungary, or Czechoslovakia is almost nonexistent. Although the controls of the Alia regime are more than adequate for suppressing artistic deviation and nonconformity, it is probably the current scarcity of intellectuals rather than repression that accounts for the absence of substantial dissident sentiment after almost five decades of communist rule. However, cultural organizations and higher education have been undergoing an upheaval, with crackdowns on the ''bourgeois-revisionist life style'' among students and younger intellectuals. Ramiz Alia has acknowledged these problems of a young population, one-third of which is below the age of fifteen.

Education.   The objectives of the Albanian educational system vary little from those pursued by any standard communist thought-control program: development of technical skills, popular acceptance of Marxist ideology, and formation of a politically reliable intellectual elite. As with certain other less-developed East European countries, initial emphasis has been on the creation of technical competence in the vocational and engineering fields.[33] Each government ministry is responsible for such training through *teknikums* (vocational schools). Although a university was established in 1957, until the end of 1962 most students were sent to the USSR and other neighboring East European states for higher education.

Illiteracy represented the fundamental problem to be overcome by the communist government. By 1963 the prewar (1938) illiteracy rate of 90 percent reportedly had been all but eliminated in the population group up to age 40. Approximately 744,000 pupils and students were enrolled during the 1985–1986 academic year. The Enver Hoxha University has 12,500 full- and part-time students.[34] Claims by the regime regarding the effectiveness of its educational system are somewhat offset by frequent reforms. An elaborate description of one such reorganization, which appeared in the Albanian publication *Ylli,* noted that the new system would offer fresh incentive to the secondary-school graduate: a diploma qualifying him as a ''worker.''

Training in communist doctrine is conducted at all levels and in all schools, with adult education taking place through local party organizations. Outside observers indicate that the people have little interest in such efforts, and the supposed benefits are more than countered by day-to-day experiences of Stalinist communism in action.

An educational reform introduced in 1970 required students to work one year in a factory or on a farm before entering high school. The new curriculum foresees six and a half months of study, another two and a half months of physical labor, and one month of military training each year. Corresponding figures for university students are seven, one, and two months. During 1976, the school system was further revolutionized. More recently, education for science and technology has been emphasized in several speeches by Ramiz Alia and in the current five-year plan (through 1990).[35]

Security Controls. By democratic standards, Albania is unquestionably a police state. Leaders maintain power through an all-pervasive and powerful security organization. Police effectiveness may help to convince the people of the invincibility of the regime.[36] The hostility of the average Albanian toward the government, in whatever degree it may occur, stems from a basic dislike for the communist system and from the failure of the regime to fulfill its promises of "freedom, bread, and land."

It would be an error, however, to postulate that the communist nature of the regime per se is the only reason for this hostility. Albanians have a long tradition of dislike for central authority, particularly when it stems from an alien system. Control over popular disaffection and acts of protest, either passive or active, is vested with the police and security forces under the Interior Ministry. These forces include a directorate of state security called *Sigurimi* (secret police), border guards, and regular uniformed police.

The secret police employ standard communist techniques of population control, such as personal documentation, surveillance, and censorship. Paid or unpaid informants remain the principal source of information on antistate activities or sentiments. There is no apparent organized resistance,[37] and most instances of arrest or liquidation seem to result not from anticommunist activities but from disagreement with the Alia regime.

During the spring of 1973, more than three years before the seventh party congress, a purge began in the cultural sphere; it spread to the defense establishment and subsequently engulfed the economic bureaucracy of government. Two-thirds of all cabinet posts, one-third of the Politburo seats, and nearly half the Central Committee posts changed incumbents. Some ten thousand of the affected bureaucrats reportedly were exiled into rural areas. Few, if any, attempted to escape.

Border guards, primarily operating to protect frontiers against infiltration, also serve to prevent Albanians from clandestinely leaving the country. Entry and exit across the mountain borders, however, should not represent any substantial problem for the indigenous population, if so inclined. Regular police are charged with conventional tasks of keeping public order and safety. Close collaboration is maintained by the border guards with the directorate of state security and the uniformed police. Ramiz Alia in late 1986 emphasized, however, that the Interior Ministry must be "vigilant and fair."[38]

News. Daily papers and other media of mass communication are state or party controlled. *Zeri i popullit,* the official newspaper and the APL organ, and the Democratic Front's *Bashkimi* function as political instruments, with Tirana radio the broadcasting equivalent.[39] Despite claims to the contrary, there seems to be no jamming of foreign broadcasts. One observer has attributed this more to the technical inability of the regime to effect jamming than to any disregard for the effect of transmissions from abroad. A single television broadcasting station operates in Albania. Citizens prosperous enough to purchase TV sets can also receive Italian and Yugoslav stations, whose broadcasts appear to be preferred to local programs.

ECONOMIC AND MILITARY AFFAIRS

By any standard, Albania is the least-developed country in Eastern Europe. Modernization and industrialization are long-range objectives of the government, with the principal emphasis on extraction of mineral resources, agriculture, and light manufacturing. Under the communist regime substantial gains have been made in all economic areas, as the figures in Table 4 indicate. Although industrial production has expanded much more rapidly than agriculture, the differences remain

Table 4
SELECTED ECONOMIC INDICATORS IN ALBANIA, 1950–1986

Commodity	Unit	1950	1960	1970	1975	1986
Electricity	million kwhr	21.4	341.8	943.5	1,533	1,840
Petroleum	thousand metric tons	131.8	727.5	1,283.2	1,578	3,500
Coal	thousand metric tons	62.8	303.9	694.6	1,001	2,140
Cement	thousand metric tons	15.9	72.9	345.3	—	—
Bread	thousand metric tons	51.0	138.3	—	—	—
Sugar	thousand metric tons	0.5	13.3	7.6	—	—
Olive butter	metric tons	1,342.0	2,169.0	—	—	—
Fresh fish	metric tons	1,493.0	2,599.0	—	—	—
Cheese	metric tons	771.0	2,418.0	—	—	—
Sausage	metric tons	139.0	244.0	—	—	—

SOURCES: L. N. Tolkunov (ed.), *Sotsialisticheskii lager* (Moscow, 1962), pp. 41–42; Harilla Papajorgii, *The Development of Socialist Industry and Its Prospects in the People's Republic of Albania* (Tirana, 1964), p. 47; *Vjetari statistikor 1971–1972* (Tirana, 1973), pp. 66, 68, *Zeri i popullit,* 20 and 23 October 1976; Economist Intelligence Unit, *Country Profile* (1986–87), p. 32; CIA, *World Factbook 1987,* p. 3.

NOTES: The 1965 statistical yearbook gives only value in leks and percentage increase over the 1938 base year. *Vjetari statistikor 1965* (Tirana, 1965).

Since the early 1970s, Albania has issued only fragmentary statistical data. No percentages were released to the People's Assembly in a report for 1987 by the Planning Commission chairman. *Zeri i popullit,* 29 December 1987.

relative.[40] Industrialization by Western standards has just begun, and agriculture and mining contribute the most to the national product.

Economic policies are formulated by the party Politburo, and specific production goals are established by the State Planning Commission. The latter agency coordinates plans of national and local government, enterprises, cooperatives, and individual producers. All economic activity is state owned and operated, according to the 1976 constitution, and private entrepreneur property is forbidden (Article 16). Such private property as wages, homes, and "other objects serving to satisfy the material and cultural needs of the family and the individual" are permitted, according to Article 23 of the constitution.

Albania joined the Council for Mutual Economic Assistance (CMEA) in 1949. Since the break with Moscow in October 1961, however, it has not participated in council activities or sent representatives to meetings. The USSR had been the principal trading partner of Albania from 1948 to 1961, accounting for more than half of all exports and imports. During this period a consistently adverse foreign-trade balance of payments had to be financed with Soviet and other East European loans. These credits reportedly amounted to more than 1.6 billion rubles, as Table 5 shows. After the Albanian-Soviet rift, China assumed a major part of the trade formerly conducted by the USSR. In 1950 Tirana's deficit amounted to 779 million leks and in 1955 to almost 1.5 billion. In 1960 it surpassed that but dropped in 1970 to 1.3 billion and in 1978 totaled under 1.2 billion leks.[41] (See Table 8.) The 1976 constitution specifically prohibits Albania from obtaining credits from foreign capitalist and revisionist monopolies or states (Article 28).

Table 5
SINO-SOVIET BLOC CREDITS TO ALBANIA, 1945–1975
(in millions of rubles)

Country	Amount	Country	Amount
USSR	948	Poland	85
Czechoslovakia	222	Hungary	80
East Germany	152	Bulgaria	62
China	1,327		
Romania	92	Total	2,968

SOURCES: Ranko Banovic, *Posleratni razvoj privrede u Albaniji* (Belgrade, 1959), p. 14; Presseausschnitte und Radioberichte aus den osteuropaeischen Laendern, *Albanien und seine "Protektoren"* (Munich, 17 August 1966), pp. 10–11; Moscow radio, 1 August 1976, which claimed that 422 million rubles had been canceled from the total Soviet credits; CIA, *Handbook of Economic Statistics 1976* (Washington, D.C., September 1976), p. 71.

Industry. This sector of the Albanian economy comprises extraction of basic raw materials, processing industries, and food and textile plants but little else. The government has stressed development of mining, petroleum, and building materials. Only limited attempts have been made to establish other heavy industries, due to a limited market within the country and a lack of technical expertise.

Albania's industrial policy can be chronologically divided into two basic phases. The years 1944–1947 involved the reconstruction of factories destroyed by war and the nationalization of the sources of production. From 1947 to the present the industrial sector has been guided by the original Stalinist model and a succession of economic plans. The earliest plans were drawn up on an annual basis, followed by a two-year plan for 1949–1950.

By 1951 sufficient progress had been made to allow for reasonable planning over five-year intervals. This first five-year plan followed the Stalinist line of increasing heavy industrial output at the expense of agriculture and consumers' goods. With a great deal of Soviet technical aid, the objectives of this plan reportedly were reached. During the second five-year plan (1956–1960), industrial output again reportedly increased.[42] It has been asserted that before the break with Moscow a fifteen-year perspective plan (1961–1975) had been worked out to coordinate Albanian economic development with that of other East European countries.[43]

The third five-year plan (1961–1965) was proclaimed before completion as having been relatively successful, despite minor setbacks ensuing from the disagreement with the USSR. Official reports indicate that substantial economic difficulties, postulated by Western observers as resulting from the withdrawal of Soviet economic assistance, did not fully materialize, thanks primarily to the substitution of Chinese aid. One problem stemmed from the lack of spare parts for machinery of Soviet or East European origin. The Chinese, through extensive copying, were able either to provide necessary parts or to replace basic equipment.

Economic agreements with France, Italy, Austria, and Romania also led to significant (by Albanian standards) technical and material aid for Tirana's industrial efforts. The fourth five-year plan (1966–1970) goals reportedly were met and exceeded.[44] However, there were indications that industrial output from the fifth five-year plan (1971–1975) was less satisfactory, judging by the removal from office during 1975–1976 of the heavy industry and mining minister (Koco Theodosi), the State Planning Commission chairman (Abdyl Kellezi), and the trade minister (Kico Kgjela).[45] An important factor in this lower rate of achievement was Albania's basic problem with agricultural output. Although attainment of 1976–1980 goals still left the industrial sector far behind the rest of Eastern Europe, gains made, on a relative basis, served as evidence that a communist regime could create economic progress through totalitarian means over a limited period of time. Announced targets for 1981–1985 appear in Table 6.

Table 6

FIVE-YEAR PLAN TARGETS, 1980–1985 AND 1985–1990

Category	*Increase, 1985 versus 1980 (percentages)*		*1990 versus 1985 (percentages)*
	(plan)	*(actual)*	*(plan)*
Industry	36 to 38	26	
Agriculture	30 to 32		35 to 37
Investment total, including agricultural cooperatives	22 to 24	14	
Transportation	34 to 36		
Labor productivity industry	13 to 15		
construction	14 to 16		
Social product	34 to 36	18	31 to 33
Exports			44 to 46
National income	35 to 37	16	35 to 37
Real per capita income	21		5.8 to 12.7

SOURCE: Report by Premier Mehmet Shehu over Tirana radio, 5 November 1981; *Bashkimi*, 4 July 1986; *Zeri i popullit*, 4 July and 5–6 November 1986, 30 December 1987.

That five-year plan (1981–1985) was hailed as the first to be implemented without credits or economic aid from abroad. According to party secretary Hekuran Isai, industrial production for the period would increase by 40 percent. Albania is now first in the world in per capita and third in total production of chromium (880,000 tons of ore per annum). Annual extraction of oil is 3.5 million tons, much of it exported to the Federal Republic of Germany, Switzerland, and Romania. Other exports include electric power, minerals, construction materials, and light industry and food products as well as agricultural produce. Albania claims to conduct trade with 50 foreign countries, approximately two-fifths with Eastern Europe and the same proportion with Western Europe.[46]

Agriculture. In common with many other East European countries, Albania's agriculture has not kept pace with its industrial development. Although this can be attributed to a number of factors, it appears that the essential difficulty is the ideological foundation of Marxism. The millennium for the proletariat did not initially embrace the working peasantry. The Albanian standard communist doctrine regarding collectivization fails to recognize the traditional independence of farmers and their attachment to the land. The factory worker, deprived of his traditional orientations, can be molded according to socialist form; the peasant is less likely to adapt.

The drive to collectivize the agrarian sector has gone through the customary cycles. Unlike revisionist policies in Poland and Yugoslavia, the immediate objective in Albania had been full collectivization.[47] Hoxha reported to the party congress in February 1961 that 86 percent of all arable land had come into the possession of collective farms and that the peasantry had slowly begun to change its way of life by embracing a "new culture." No comparison was given of the level of production achieved on this high percentage of the land or on the remaining 14 percent, which was almost all independently owned at the time. A comprehensive book on Albania published in 1956 claimed that despite collectivization independent farmers working on less than 80 percent of the land raised some 94 percent of all agricultural products.[48] The years 1955–1957 seem to have been the time of greatest pressure by the regime because collectivization increased to 57 percent during that period. By February 1967 complete socialization of agriculture had been achieved.[49]

Policies of soil reclamation and cultivation of marginal land have helped to raise agricultural production. Although programs for expanding the amount of arable land are limited by topography, a target date of 1970 was selected for increasing the areas under cultivation by 89,000 hectares to a total of 540,000 hectares. State farms seemed to play a less significant role than collectives, which occupied 13.8 percent of all arable land and concentrated on animal husbandry, olive growing, and seed production. The data in Table 7 show the breakdown by type of farm in percentages. Food production during the latest five-year plan lagged behind industrial output. Earlier the regime had attempted to remedy the situation by procuring Chinese loans for agriculture, offering pension incentives to collective farmers, and merging collective farms.

Albania suffered two consecutive years (1977 and 1978) of heavy rain coupled with late summer drought, making it impossible to achieve planned increases in farm productivity. In 1978, the People's Assembly passed a law to protect the land that regulated the use of farm and grazing areas. During spring 1981, "new revolutionary initiatives" were undertaken by the peasantry to further limit cooperative farmers' personal plots of land and to herd together livestock from these plots. Also included was a drive to amalgamate agricultural cooperatives into larger units of the so-called higher type. Among the 421 cooperative farms, averaging 1,322 hectares in area, only 47 were classed in this higher category. They cultivated 23 percent of all land in the cooperative sector and employed more than one-fifth of all cooperative workers.[50]

Students of East European affairs have observed that communism does not appeal to the peasant and that, almost without exception, this element of the population is hostile to regime policies. The very independence that engenders such hostility, however, precludes any action in unison against the government.

Table 7
DEVELOPMENT OF AGRICULTURE, 1955–1983
(in percentages)

Year	State farms	Collective farms	Private entrepreneurs
1955	7.3	13.4	79.3
1960	13.1	73.8	13.1
1965	17.5	72.9	9.6
1970	23.0	77.0	—
1975	22.0	78.0	—
1976	13.8	*ca.* 86.0	0.2*
1983	**	**	0.0

SOURCES: *Vjetari statistikor 1963* (Tirana, 1963), p. 150, *1966–67*, p. 76; [Albania], *Republika Popullore e Shqiperise ne jubileum e 30 vjetorit te themelimit te PPSh* (Tirana, 1971), p. 101; Tirana radio, 3 September 1975; *Zeri i popullit*, 11 November 1976; [Albania], *40 Vjet Shqiperi Socialiste* (Tirana, 1984), p. 77.

*These are probably small garden plots for growing vegetables. According to Hoxha, they "are gradually fading into extinction." *Zeri i popullit*, 2 November 1981.

**All cultivated land is part of the socialist economy.

Consequently, it can be somewhat misleading to assume that the peasantry poses a substantial threat to any communist regime. The danger, if any, is indirect and stems from dissatisfaction among the more cohesive elements of the population when food is not in ample supply.

Labor. Workers in Albania have been strictly regimented, and rigid labor legislation provides penalities for those who do not fulfill state norms or who fail to appear for work. The work force is controlled partly by a Labor Directorate and partly by trade unions, whose organization is divided into three basic subelements: (1) industrial workers; (2) administration, public health, and educational-cultural employees; and (3) agricultural laborers on state farms.[51]

Compulsory work, freezing personnel in their jobs, and state control over mobility proceed along Stalinist lines. The principal difficulties involve a shortage of trained industrial workers and the lack of sufficient incentive to increase output. Stakhanovite and shock-worker methods have been copied from Soviet experience but have met with greater resistance than in the USSR. Many Albanians still tend to regard factory work as unmanly, and only intense indoctrination of the younger generation through contrived "youth action" programs has slowly dispelled this belief.

Armed Forces. The military in Albania is relatively insignificant by East European standards, consisting of approximately 54,000 men, with internal security and border guards.[52] In the 1960s the Chinese replaced the Soviets as advisers, although on a smaller scale, and a politicization of the armed forces along Chinese lines ensued. The 1974–1975 purge of the military high command seems to have stemmed from this politicization. Professional officers may have wanted to limit party influence among the troops and to downplay the Chinese people's war concepts. Firmer party control over the military was affirmed by the purge.

Departure of Soviet naval forces from the Valona base and Sasseno Island marked the end of Moscow's influence. One source has reported that the Albanians refused to allow the USSR to withdraw some of its submarines after the Tirana-Moscow break.[53] An armed engagement of limited scope allegedly took place between Soviet and Albanian military personnel. Subsequent negotiations resulted in the USSR's leaving four Class "W" submarines at Valona, along with support equipment. The Albanian armed forces pose little threat either to the North Atlantic Treaty Organization (NATO) or to Eastern Europe. In combination with internal security troops, they do comprise an effective element of control over the country.

The 1976 constitution requires universal military service "for defense of the socialist fatherland" and stipulates that the armed forces be led by the party, designating its first secretary as commander in chief. Out of a total budget of 9.45 billion leks, almost 1.1 billion leks (11.4 percent) were allocated during 1988 for defense.[54]

FOREIGN AFFAIRS

Although the postwar history of Albania's friendship and differences with the outside world has been shaded by overtones of political doctrine, there is little to indicate that ideological differences per se have predominantly influenced Albanian actions. As one expert has phrased it: "In the Communist world, conflicts have to take an ideological form even when the real motives may be the interests of individuals or groups or the power politics of countries."[55] Albania maintained diplomatic relations with more than 100 foreign countries in 1988.

Yugoslavia. Relations between Albania and Yugoslavia traditionally have been hostile, stemming from ethnic differences, territorial disputes, and the nature of Balkan politics. During World War II, common interests were generated by Axis occupation and the Marxist orientation of guerrilla groups in both countries. This collaboration became increasingly unilateral in favor of Belgrade: by 1947 it appeared that Tito's vision of Balkan unity involved less an independent federation of Balkan states and more a Greater Yugoslavia.[56] The link between Belgrade and

Tirana paralleled the master-satellite relationship of the Soviet Union vis-à-vis the other countries of Eastern Europe. The political opportunity for a break came with the expulsion by the Cominform of the Yugoslav communist party. Beginning in July 1948, Moscow replaced Belgrade as the protector of Albania.

During the remaining years of Stalin's life, Tirana radio supplied a prominent voice in the Soviet-inspired campaign of East European vituperation against Yugoslavia. Traditional animosities and the existence of the Kosmet (Kosovo and Metohija) enclave, in which some 1,730,000 (1987) Albanians resided within Yugoslavia, made it easier for the Tirana regime to maintain that close cooperation with the Soviet Union was a necessity for preserving its independence. The USSR in turn benefited from the arrangement through both the propaganda advantage and access to a military base on the Adriatic.

After the death of Stalin and the subsequent modification in Soviet policy toward Yugoslavia, the advantages of close Albanian cooperation with the USSR became more economic than military. The attempt by Tito to influence the politics of Eastern Europe, coupled with the geographic proximity of Belgrade to Tirana, created a threat to the party leadership in Albania. This danger, although not necessarily directed at territorial integrity, was sufficiently grave to cause concern for their personal security among Hoxha and his followers. It was apparent that, for them to remain in power, repressive methods of Stalinism had to be continued.

In recent years there has been détente between Albania and Yugoslavia, probably brought about by the threat of a possible Soviet invasion like the one in Czechoslovakia. Full diplomatic ties were re-established in 1971, and cultural contacts (mostly between ethnic Albanians of both countries) subsequently increased in frequency. During 1975 this rapprochement reached its peak with the exchange of cordial messages, an increase in Yugoslav-Albanian trade, and the virtual absence of ideological attacks. However, early in 1976 a serious rift occurred between the two countries, resulting in a return to polemics and border incidents, which seemed to stem from new unrest and Albanian irredentist activity in the Kosovo region of Yugoslavia. In 1987 almost two million Albanians lived in all of Yugoslavia.[57]

Despite these events, Belgrade took the lead in filling the vacuum caused by Tirana's 1978 break with Peking. Trade totaled only $170 million during 1976–1980. After the next five-year plan, it reached $80 million in 1986. Albania expanded trade relations with Yugoslavia, despite propaganda against Yugoslavia's "revisionism" and "the anti-Marxist self-management system." However, in March and April 1981 violent demonstrations, arising from complaints against living and working conditions among the 37,000 students at Pristina University, took place in Kosovo. These spread to other parts of the province. Demonstrators demanded freedom, democratic rights, and status as a republic for the autonomous province of Kosovo. Yugoslav army and militia units, sent from Serbia, killed many demonstrators and wounded others.

Relations with Yugoslavia continued to be strained because of allegations of restrictions on Albanian cultural life in Kosovo. Nevertheless, Tirana sent its foreign minister to participate in the first post–World War II ministerial-level meeting held at the end of February 1988 in Belgrade. It appears that the new leadership under Ramiz Alia is intent on opening the country and establishing better relations with other regimes in Eastern Europe. During 1987 almost 10,000 tourists from noncommunist-ruled countries were permitted to visit Albania.[58]

The Soviet-Albanian Rift.   Hoxha, during a speech to a 1957 plenum of his Central Committee in defense of Stalin, injected an ideological basis for the subsequent rift between Albania and the USSR. During the period 1957–1960 charges and countercharges of Marxist deviation were relatively subdued and conducted on a rather esoteric level.[59] Soviet military and economic aid to Albania continued, but ties between Tirana and Peking were already forming. The Chinese embassy in Albania enlarged its staff; translations of articles from *Pravda* were gradually replaced with translations from *Jen-min jih-pao,* the principal Chinese communist daily newspaper.

In 1960 the extent of discord between Albania and the Soviet Union became more apparent to the Western world. The absence of Hoxha and Mehmet Shehu from the East European summit meeting at Bucharest, the purging in September of Politburo member Liri Belishova and Audit Commission chairman Koco Tashko from the Albanian Party of Labor, and the ever-increasing shrillness of the academic debate on "revisionism" indicated that a serious split had developed.[60] These events were compounded by a growing divergence of views between the USSR and communist China.

Tirana did not receive an invitation to the twenty-second congress of the Soviet party in October 1961, an event of considerable significance for the international communist movement. At this congress, Khrushchev bitterly attacked the Albanian leadership. Chou En-lai, chief representative of the Chinese communists, departed from Moscow soon thereafter but not before indicating his support for Albania and his condemnation of certain USSR policies. It was alleged by Tirana that a Khrushchev-sponsored coup had attempted to overthrow the Hoxha regime. With words now reportedly translated into action, the split became irreconcilable. Albanians did not appear at the June 1969 international meeting of communist and workers' parties in Moscow or at any other Soviet-sponsored conference through the end of 1981.

Although Albania is of little current economic or military value to the Soviet Union, the fact of its successful defiance, its former position as an amplifier of internal discord within the communist bloc, and its previous use by the Chinese as an actual rather than a theoretical platform for influence throughout Eastern Europe do appear important. Tirana also has become the European gathering place for Maoist "Marxist-Leninist" party representatives from other parts of the world.[61] Albania condemned the twenty-sixth Soviet congress as "a congress of renegades from Marxism-Leninism, of a revisionist anti-Marxist party that stands at the head of a pseudorevolutionary, antisocialist, and imperialist state." It warned that Brezhnev sought "to cover up the ever-increasing aggressiveness of Soviet imperialism by presenting himself as the standard-bearer of world peace."[62]

Although there had been speculation about a possible reconciliation between Tirana and Moscow following the deterioration of Sino-Albanian relations, no such rapprochement has occurred. Albania consistently attacks the Soviet Union for its policies and displays no interest in normalizing relations. The USSR, however, has not given up hope that Albania will return to its sphere of influence. Each year on the anniversary marking establishment of diplomatic relations between Moscow and Tirana, the USSR publishes articles glorifying its assistance in consolidation of the Albanian government and declaring that a restoration of normal Soviet-Albanian relations would be beneficial to both countries and in the common interest of socialist states.[63]

Communist China. With the disappearance of Moscow's influence, Peking assumed the role of protector over Albania. Initially, the ability of distant China to support a European protégé appeared questionable. The USSR may have felt that this might soon become obvious to Tirana and that an accord might again be reached. This did not happen, if for no other reason than China's surprisingly effective program of assistance. The aid from Peking, which amounted to loans of $125 million during 1961–1965, some $215 million in the period 1966–1970, and approximately $400 million during 1971–1975, could not approach the previous Soviet effort in quantity, but the impetus earlier given Tirana by Moscow seems to have created a base sufficient to make the Chinese support adequate. Peking committed itself to supply assistance for the construction of some thirty industrial projects throughout Albania in 1976–1980. This program ended only two years after it had begun.

On 7 July 1978, an official note informed Tirana that the Chinese government would sever economic and military assistance to Albania and recall its economic and military experts. The latter condemned this as a "perfidious and hostile act" that "brutally and arbitrarily violated elementary international rules and norms and extended ideological disagreements to state relations."[64] This same source lists eight alleged facts used by Peking as reasons for the break. Upon departure, the Chinese took all blueprints with them.

Albania and China resumed diplomatic relations at the ambassadorial level in the spring of the following year. They remain cool, however, with Tirana continuing to criticize Peking's domestic and foreign policies. Competition between the two communist parties for control of the anti-Moscow Marxist-Leninist movement continues. The Chinese are apparent winners due, in a large part, to the minimum assistance the Albanians can offer these splinter groups. By the early 1980s Tirana had the support of only about two dozen Marxist-Leninist parties and groups, with a combined membership of about one thousand.[65]

Attitude to the West.   Despite its continuing hostility toward the United States, which is based to a large extent on ideology, the Tirana regime maintains varying degrees of diplomatic and economic relations with other Western powers. France, Austria, Italy, West Germany, Spain, and the Scandinavian countries have become increasingly active in its foreign trade. Britain has indicated a willingness to resume diplomatic relations, subject to a compensation settlement for the damage sustained by two British warships that in 1946 struck mines in the Corfu Channel.

Differences with Greece over its claim to part of southern Albania (northern Epirus), the abduction into Albania of about 25,000 Greek nationals by the communist-insurgent "Democratic Army" at the termination of the civil war in Greece, and the support given Greek communists by Albania during this conflict are gradually being forgotten. Following establishment of informal trade agreements between the two countries (in 1966 and 1970) and the re-establishment of electronic communications, after more than three decades of de facto belligerency, formal diplomatic relations were resumed in 1971. This came about after the Greek government had withdrawn claims to northern Epirus. Subsequent political changes in Athens have improved this new relationship. The technical state of war ended in August 1987.

Albania was the only European country that did not attend the Helsinki conference in July–August 1975 or the follow-up meetings in Belgrade (1978), Madrid (1980–1981), and Vienna (1986–1988); it charged that the conferences represented a tool of the superpowers for achieving a condominium over Europe.[66] Albania also stressed that peace could only come about in Europe after dissolution of both the Warsaw Pact and NATO.

Other Countries.   Most probably due to the common tie provided by their Muslim backgrounds, Albania has maintained friendly relations with Algeria, Egypt, and especially Libya. Since the break with Moscow, contacts with Turkey also have improved markedly. It is significant that several of the communist-ruled countries (while otherwise following the USSR) have maintained trade with Albania, although after 1961 they suspended diplomatic relations. That they have done so may mean that Moscow had second thoughts on the usefulness of a total economic blockade and even encouraged some of these countries, including Bulgaria, Cuba, Czechoslovakia, East Germany, Hungary, North Korea, Poland, Romania, and Vietnam, to maintain commercial relations.[67] The adverse balance of payments has been reversed, as shown in Table 8.

The position of Albania vis-à-vis the United States continues to be hostile, despite an improvement in Sino-American relations during the 1970s. Indications that Tirana would be favorably disposed toward some type of trade have not fully materialized. The United States continues to represent an important component in the Albanian world image of the superpowers in their alleged roles as Gog and Magog, which Hoxha spoke of at one of his last party congresses.[68]

Table 8
ALBANIA'S FOREIGN TRADE, 1960–1985
(in millions of leks)

Category	1960	1965	1970	1978*	1985
Imports	4,054	4,260	5,450	8,670	16,750
Exports	2,441	3,050	4,150	7,525	17,250
Deficits	−1,613	−1,210	−1,300	−1,145	+1,500

SOURCES: L. N. Tolkunov (ed.), *Sotsialisticheski lager* (Moscow, 1962), p. 47; *Vjetari statistikor 1965* (Tirana, 1965), p. 313; *Zeri i popullit*, 17 July 1969; *Rruga e partise* (August 1976), p. 12; CIA, *World Factbook 1981*, pp. 2–3, *1987*, p. 3.

NOTES: The figures in the table reflect the old (pre-August 1965) rate of 50 leks to the dollar. The current exchange is 4.14 leks to the dollar, as of 1987.

According to an editorial in *Rruga e partise*, cited above, exports were 75 percent greater and imports 77 percent higher during 1971–1975 than they had been in the preceding five-year period. These data are not precisely comparable with those obtained from earlier sources.

*Estimates.

Albania is a member of the United Nations, admitted in 1955 through the device of a trade-off and a U.S. voting abstention. Although Albania had not participated in Warsaw Pact matters since 1961, its membership in this treaty organization was not formally dissolved until 13 September 1968, after the Soviet invasion of Czechoslovakia.[69]

One school of thought contends that the verbal friction between the Soviet Union and Albania had evolved into a personal vendetta between Khrushchev and Hoxha. From this follows the conclusion that with the passing of one or both of these leaders from the political scene, Tirana and Moscow might again be brought together. Nevertheless, although Khrushchev was deposed in mid-October 1964 and Hoxha died in April 1985, the events of the past several years suggest that a rapprochement is likely only if it involves an advantage for the Albanian leadership.[70]

It would seem that Ramiz Alia is attempting to relax the tight control over the population that had been maintained by Enver Hoxha. The cautious opening to Western Europe, which includes sending students there for training, suggests a pragmatic approach to the shortage of indigenous expertise. At the same time, domestic economic reforms have begun, based on the realization that the Albanian regime can not continue to pursue autarky. Although Alia would not admit it, he is faced with problems that are similar to those in the Soviet Union.

NOTES

1. For good historical introductions see Stavro Skendi (ed.), *Albania* (New York, 1956), pp. 1–30 and Nicholas C. Pano, *The People's Republic of Albania* (Baltimore, 1968), pp. 13–43.

2. About fifteen thousand Albanians were executed and fifty thousand others imprisoned. *ACEN News*, no. 144 (January–February 1970), p. 26, and [Albania], *Twenty Years of Socialism in Albania* (Tirana, 1964), p. 12.

3. Names and offices in this ten-man regime are listed by Free Europe Committee, *A Chronology of Events in Albania, 1944–1952* (New York, 1955), p. 1. See also Mehmet Shehu, *Der Kampf um die Befreiung Tiranas* (Tirana, 1980).

4. On the eve of the break with Tito, Stalin suggested that Yugoslavia absorb Albania. Milovan Djilas, *Conversations with Stalin* (New York, 1962), p. 143. Yugoslav aid to Albania before that time is discussed by Harry Hamm, *Albania: China's Beachhead in Europe* (London, 1963), p. 50.

5. [Albania], *Letter of the Central Committee of the Party of Labour and Government of Albania to the Central Committee of the Communist Party and the Government of China: 29 July 1978* (Tirana, 1978), p. 1.

6. "Albania Joins Meeting," *New York Times*, 25 February 1988, p. 6. See also the articles from Tirana by Eric Bourne in the *Christian Science Monitor*, 27 January, 1 and 2 February 1988, as well as *FBIS*, 3 March 1988.

7. An exile since December 1924, Noli died in 1965 in the United States. An article in *Rabotnichesko delo*, 8 November 1976, published in Sofia, gives some details about communist activities in Albania during the 1920s and 1930s.

8. Vladimir Dedijer, *Jugoslovensko-Albanski odnosi, 1939–1948* (Belgrade, 1949), p. 5.

9. Jani I. Dilo, *The Communist Party Leadership in Albania* (Washington, D.C., 1961), pp. 7–8, provides names of others purged before and after Xoxe.

10. Nikolaos A. Stavrou, "Albania," in Richard F. Staar (ed.), *Yearbook on International Communist Affairs: 1986* (Stanford, Calif., 1986), pp. 255–56; henceforth, cited as *YICA*.

11. Article 21, as given in V. N. Durdenevskii (ed.), *Konstitutsii evropeiskikh stran narodnoi demokratii* (Moscow, 1954), p. 112; Articles 1 and 2 in [Albania], *Constitution of the People's Socialist Republic of Albania* (Tirana, 1977), pp. 7–8.

12. *Zeri i popullit*, 8 November 1987; *YICA:1988*, p. 237.

13. Pillo Peristeri, APL Control Commission chairman, in *Bashkimi*, 4 November 1986.

14. Skendi, *Albania,* pp. 84–85.

15. Ramiz Alia, *Report to the 9th Congress of the Party of Labour of Albania* (Tirana: 8 Nendori, 1986), p. 90.

16. Ramiz Alia, speech at Vlore, broadcast over Tirana radio, 22 March 1988; *FBIS-Eastern Europe,* 24 March 1988, pp. 2–6.

17. *Zeri i popullit,* 5 November 1986.

18. Ibid., 10 October 1975.

19. *Zeri i popullit,* 18 November 1975.

20. Tirana radio, 21 January 1976, broadcast the draft, which was three articles longer than the final version.

21. It was adopted by the People's Assembly on 28 December 1976. *Zeri i popullit,* 29 December 1976, printed the full text of this new constitution.

22. The chairman of the People's Assembly presidium, his three deputies, and the secretary are identified in RFE, *East European Leadership List* (Munich, 15 January 1988), p. 3.

23. Article 69 of the 1950 constitution had enumerated only ten ministries, according to Durdenevskii, *Konstitutsii,* pp. 121–22. There existed sixteen such offices by 1988. See RFE, *East European Leadership List,* p. 4, for names of incumbents.

24. In this post he is also commander in chief of the armed forces and chairman of the Defense Council, according to Article 89 of the 1976 constitution.

25. The economically active Albanian people include an industrial labor force (311,000), peasants on collective farms (677,000), and individuals in services (223,000). *Europa Yearbook,* vol. 1 (London, 1987), p. 298.

26. Nicholas C. Pano, "The Albanian Cultural Revolution," *Problems of Communism* (July–August 1974), pp. 44–57.

27. Kemal Vokopola, "Church and State in Albania," in U.S. Senate, Committee on the Judiciary, *The Church and State under Communism* (Washington, D.C., 1965), II, 33–47.

28. Peter A. Prifti, *Socialist Albania since 1944* (Cambridge, Mass., 1978), p. 250.

29. *L'Osservatore Romano,* 11 July 1967, reported that the last churches were closed by Red Guards, depriving 130,000 Catholics of public places in which to worship.

30. Rolf Italiaander, *Christ und Welt,* 16 January 1970.

31. *Zeri i popullit,* 29 February 1976; Amnesty International, *Albania* (New York, 1984); *New York Times,* 30 August 1986; Amnesty International, *1987 Report,* p. 280; *New York Times,* 20 June 1988, p. A3.

32. See Prifti, *Socialist Albania,* pp. 144–49, for a comparison between the Albanian and Chinese cultural revolutions.

33. John I. Thomas, *Education for Communism: School and State in the People's Republic of Albania* (Stanford, Calif., 1969), 131 pp.

34. The 1976 constitution guarantees eight years of schooling (Article 52). Figures are from *Europa Yearbook* (1987), p. 297.

35. Tirana radio, 5 July 1976; Albanian Telegraphic Agency, 2–5 December 1987.

36. A United Nations survey indicated that some 80,000 persons of the then 1.7 million population were being held in concentration camps during 1945–1956 and that more than 16,000 had died there.

37. According to a transcript from an espionage trial, at least four organizations as late as 1950 opposed the communists: the Nationalist Front, the Legality Movement, the Independent Bloc, and the Agrarian Party. Georges Fournial (preface), *Le Proces des Espions Parachutes en Albanie* (Paris, 1950), p. 23.

38. Louis Zanga, "Changes in Albanian Leadership Signify Struggle for Succession to Power," RFE, *Background Report*, 24 November 1975, p. 17; *Zeri i popullit*, 30 April, 8 and 14 November, 1976, 4 November 1986.

39. Tirana radio broadcasts 480 hours per week in seventeen languages. [Albania], *An Outline of the PSR of Albania* (Tirana, 1978), p. 147. This source also gave figures for newspaper circulation.

40. Between 1976 and the end of 1980, industrial output reportedly increased by 34.4 percent, whereas agricultural production grew by only 21 percent. Tirana radio, 3 and 5 November 1981. Albania's per capita income amounted to the equivalent of $740 in 1978. During the first four years of a recent five-year plan (1976–1979), industrial production increased 28 percent compared with only 15 percent for agriculture. *Zeri i popullit*, 11 April 1980. In 1980, industry reportedly registered a 7.1 percent gain over 1979, and agriculture, a 2.4 percent gain. *Albania Today*, no. 3 (1981), p. 3. Gross national product reached $2.8 billion, for a per capita income of $930 during 1986. CIA, *World Factbook* (1987), p. 3.

41. V. I. Zolotarev, *Vneshniaia torgovlia sotsialisticheskikh stran* (Moscow, 1964), p. 141 and [Albania], *Vjetari statistikor i Republika Popullore te Shqiperise 1965* (Tirana, 1965), p. 313; hereafter cited as *Vjetari statistikor*. See also *Rruga i partise* (August 1976), p. 12.

42. The USSR claims to have delivered 93 percent of the equipment needed by Albania for petroleum and mining industries, about 90 percent of its trucks, more than 80 percent of its tractors, and 65 percent of its other agricultural machinery during this period. *Izvestiia*, 28 November 1976.

43. E. B. Valev, *Albaniia* (Moscow, 1960), pp. 30–31.

44. Heavy industry increased twice as rapidly as production of consumer goods. The goals for overall industrial production were reportedly attained in four years and seven months. Tirana radio, 10 August 1970.

45. *Zeri i popullit*, 5 June 1975, and 2 November 1976.

46. Ibid., 15 April 1980; *Bashkimi*, 31 December 1980; *Quarterly Economic Review* (2d Quarter 1981), p. 28; *Albania Today*, no. 2 (57), 1981, p. 16; *Europa Yearbook* (1987), p. 297.

47. For basic documents, see N. D. Kazantsev (ed.), *Osnovnye zakonodatelnye akty po agrarnym preobrazovaniiam v zarubezhnykh sotsialisticheskikh stranakh* (Moscow, 1958), 4th ed., pp. 5–60, on Albania. See also Bernhard Toennes, *Sonderfall Albanien* (Munich, 1980), p. 499, for table.

48. Skendi, *Albania*, p. 170.

49. L. V. Tiagunenko, *Development of the Albanian Economy* (Washington, D.C., 1961), p. 42. Translated from the Russian. The victory of collectivization is described in *Probleme ekonomike* (January–March 1967), pp. 83–87.

Albania claims to have achieved self-sufficiency in the production of bread grains. Nicholas Pano, "Albania," in *YICA: 1980*, p. 6.

50. *Zeri i popullit*, 22 February 1978 and 13 March 1981; *Quarterly Economic Review* (1st Quarter 1981), p. 22. All cooperative farms ultimately will be transformed into state farms, according to *Rruga i partise*, no. 5 (May 1981), pp. 24–31. Figures for the five-year plan were broadcast over Tirana radio, 3 and 5 November 1981. Information on cooperative farms is from [Albania], *40 Vjet Shqiperi Socialiste* (1984), p. 77.

51. A party-government decision reduced the highest wages (more than 900 leks per month) from 4 to 25 percent, making the ratio between highest and lowest wages only two to one. *Zeri i popullit*, 2 April 1976. This was still the case three years later. *Gazeta zytare* (March 1979).

52. International Institute for Strategic Studies, *The Military Balance 1986–1987* (London, September 1986), p. 81.

53. Eight submarines and a modern Soviet supply ship reportedly did leave Albania in June 1961. Hamm, *Albania*, p. 23.

54. *Zeri i popullit*, 29 December 1987.

55. Stavro Skendi, "Albania and the Sino-Soviet Conflict," *Foreign Affairs* (April 1962), p. 474.

56. Yet the ruling party's Central Committee reportedly met at Tirana in February 1948 to discuss incorporation of Albania by Yugoslavia. Skendi, *Albania*, p. 24.

57. [Yugoslavia], *Statistical Pocket Book of Yugoslavia* (Belgrade, 1987), p. 37.

58. *Rilindja* (Pristina), 22 February 1981, and Economist Intelligence Unit, *Country Profile* (1986–1987), p. 36, for trade statistics; Tirana radio, 2 April 1981, and *Zeri i popullit*, 9 April 1981, on the riots; Nikolaos Stavrou, "Albania," in *YICA: 1987*, p. 272.

59. Hamm, *Albania*, pp. 11–23; Elez Biberaj, *Albania and China* (Boulder, Colo., 1986), p. 183.

60. Dilo, *Communist Party Leadership in Albania*, p. 8.

61. See individual profiles in *YICA: 1988* for activities of these groups.

62. *Zeri i popullit*, 17 March 1981.

63. *Pravda*, 12 January 1988. See, however, *Zeri i popullit*, 9 February 1988, on the Soviet ideology of revisionism. *New Times*, no. 21 (Moscow: May 1988), pp. 30–31.

64. [Albania], *Letter of the CC of the Party of Labour and the Government of Albania to the CC of the Communist Party and the Government of China* (Tirana, 1978), p. 1.

65. Nicholas C. Pano, "Albania," in M. M. Drachkovitch (ed.), *East Central Europe: Yesterday, Today, Tomorrow* (Stanford, Calif., 1982), p. 210.

66. *Zeri i popullit*, 30 November 1980, and 9 February 1988.

67. *Countries of the World and Their Leaders* (Detroit, Mich., 1988), p. 176.

68. On the other hand, trade with the United States during 1985 totaled $16 million. Economist Intelligence Unit, *Country Profile* (1986–1987), p. 36.

69. Hoxha provided an explanation in his 25th anniversary speech, broadcast over Tirana radio on 28 November 1969. See also Peter R. Prifti, *Albania Since the Fall of Khrushchev* (Cambridge, Mass., June 1970), p. 35.

70. See Elez Biberaj, "Albania After Hoxha," in *Problems of Communism,* vol. 34, no. 6 (November–December 1985), pp. 32–47.

Chapter 2
People's Republic of Bulgaria

In a geographic sense, Bulgaria occupies a special position among the communist-ruled states of Eastern Europe. Anchored on the southern flank of what would otherwise be a monolithic belt, it has just one other bloc neighbor (Romania to the north) and borders on three nonbloc states (Turkey and Greece to the south, Yugoslavia to the west).[1] Also, the Bulgarians share with the East Germans the distinction of remaining under Soviet influence without being contiguous to the USSR.

Slightly smaller than New York State, Bulgaria encompasses 42,818 square miles within dimensions of roughly 250 by 150 miles. Significant topographical features include the Danubian tableland across the north, the Balkan mountains in the center, the Thracian plains to the south, and the mountains in the southwest. The national language is Slavic, with touches of Turkish and Greek. The population in 1987 totaled 8,960,749 of which 65 percent was classified as urban and 35 percent as rural.[2]

HISTORY

For 500 years Bulgaria remained under Turkish rule; as the Turkish rulers declined their rule became oppressive, which seemed all the less tolerable because of new aspirations brought by the penetration of modern ideas from Western Europe.[3]

During the early nineteenth century a national awakening began to develop based on the writings of a monk named Paissi of Hildender, who recalled heroic deeds of the past and inspired people to fight for spiritual and political liberation. Bulgarians suffered setbacks in several minor revolts; in 1876 a major and widespread uprising failed and resulted in the massacre of about thirty thousand men, women, and children.

This insurrection generated an international protest over Turkish atrocities, evoked considerable sympathy for Bulgarians, and eventually became one factor in

Russia's taking up arms against Turkey. The following year a tsarist army crossed the Danube and, joined by Bulgarian volunteers, defeated the Turks. The terms of peace, which were signed in 1878 at San Stefano near Constantinople, provided for an autonomous Bulgarian state encompassing most of Macedonia and having access to the Aegean. This, however, proved unacceptable to Great Britain and Austria-Hungary. When the terms were renegotiated that same year under the Treaty of Berlin, the country's proposed size was reduced by two-thirds. Additional territorial gains were achieved at Turkey's expense, however, in 1885 and again in 1912.

During World War I, Bulgaria entered into a secret alliance with the Central Powers and subsequently declared war against neighboring Serbia. Not being on the winning side cost of the Bulgarians the loss of a part of Western Thrace to Greece and a part of the western frontier area to Yugoslavia.[4] When World War II broke out, Bulgaria repeated the mistake and in 1941 became an ally of Germany for the purpose of obtaining the territories envisaged at San Stefano. Initially things went well and, along with the Germans, Bulgaria occupied parts of Greece and Yugoslavia to which it felt it held legitimate claim. By 1944 defeat appeared inevitable, and Bulgaria sought to break away from the alliance. Its plea for an armistice with the Western powers was disregarded by the USSR, which, although not then in a state of full belligerency with Bulgaria, proceeded to declare war and occupy the country. Under the terms of the armistice Bulgaria was forced to evacuate the territories it had gained from Greece and Yugoslavia.

The Tirnovo Constitution.   Both treaties of 1878 at San Stefano and Berlin provided for the convocation of a national assembly to elect a prince and institutionalize a future government. An initial draft of the Bulgarian constitution, prepared by the temporary tsarist governor and elaborated on by a Russian professor of constitutional law, explicitly included the principles of a parliamentary monarchy. But the assembly, which was convened the following year at the ancient capital of Tirnovo, went further:

> [It] adopted the principles of extreme liberalism with the framework of a parliamentary form of government. Parliament was to be unicameral, elected on the basis of universal suffrage, and controlling the executive. Absolute political and civil liberty was explicitly guaranteed. Thus, the pure and spontaneous democratism of the Bulgarian people gave them what was then referred to as "one of the most democratic constitutions in the world."[5]

During the 65 years of its existence, the Tirnovo constitution was frequently violated through impulsive actions and personal ambitions. Probably some blame can be attributed to lack of experience and the general absence of a tradition of self-government. Nevertheless, this constitution represented one of the most advanced and democratic fundamental laws in the world at that time. It explicitly guaranteed broad political, civil, and social liberties. Significantly, "the Tirnovo constitution has remained the symbol of free government for all democratic Bulgarians."[6] Possibly with this in mind the communists, when they usurped power in World War II, disarmingly professed a return to its principles.

The 1947 Dimitrov Constitution.   After the Fatherland Front[7] seized the government and the Red Army occupied Bulgaria in 1944, the communists methodically undertook to consolidate their rule. Initially holding only the ministries of Interior (police) and Justice, they conducted widespread purges and trials to eliminate all opposition. As their control became more nearly absolute, an attack was launched on the old Tirnovo constitution and "popular requests" were trumped up for a new one. In September 1946 the results of a plebiscite eliminated the monarchy and declared Bulgaria a republic.[8] The following month, elections were held for a Grand National Assembly (*Sobranje*) that would enact a new constitution. After the legislature convened, Georgi Dimitrov formed his government.

Because Dimitrov was so closely associated with the new fundamental law of the People's Republic of Bulgaria, it is commonly called the Dimitrov constitution. Dimitrov, born in 1882 to a working-class Protestant family, became active as a young man through the trade unions in the socialist movement and instrumental in its transformation (1919) into the Bulgarian Communist Party. During the years 1920–1921 Dimitrov served as delegate to the second and third Comintern congresses at Moscow and subsequently as a member of the organization's executive committee.[9] In 1923 he fled Bulgaria after an unsuccessful coup. Ten years later, the Nazi government arrested him for alleged complicity in the Reichstag fire.

Through the intervention of the USSR, Dimitrov was released and deported to Moscow, where he became a Soviet citizen. From 1935 to 1943 he held the post of Comintern general secretary. He initiated the Fatherland Front and returned to Bulgaria, still as a Soviet citizen, in November 1945 to become at various times chairman (later general secretary) of the ruling party's Central Committee, Politburo chairman, and premier. Dimitrov went to the USSR for medical treatment at the beginning of 1949 and died in July of that year at a sanatorium near Moscow.[10]

Although the initial draft of the Dimitrov constitution, as it was prepared by an Assembly committee, looked like the Tirnovo document, it later underwent revision by a special group. When it was promulgated, the new law closely resembled the 1936 "Stalin constitution" of the USSR. During the period between drafts, all legal opposition within the Assembly had been silenced; moreover, the signing of a peace treaty eliminated further necessity for the Tirnovo facade. The new constitution received formal approval by the Assembly on 4 December 1947, the eleventh anniversary of the constitution named after Stalin.[11]

On 16 May 1971, to coincide with the new stage in the building of an advanced socialist society, a successor document was adopted. It defines collective ownership of the means of production by the state or cooperatives; indicates that the regime can nationalize any and all industrial, trade, transport, or credit facilities; affirms that ownership cannot be detrimental to the public interest; and specifically mentions that private property is subject to compulsory restrictions and expropriation. Furthermore, Bulgaria is referred to as a socialist state, although it remains a people's republic, and the communist party is named as the leading force in society and the state. The document also guarantees ties with the socialist camp and fidelity to the Soviet Union. [12]

The constitution defines the unicameral National Assembly as the "supreme organ of the state power" and stipulates that its 400 members, who are elected to five-year terms in constituencies that have equal numbers of inhabitants, shall meet three times annually as convened by the State Council. [13] The Assembly elects the State Council, Council of Ministers, Supreme Court, and chief prosecutor; amends the constitution; and performs a number of other legislative functions. The 27-member Council of State combines legislative and executive authority. [14] It exercises the prerogatives of a collective head of state by representing the country externally, legislating by decree, interpreting laws, and calling elections. In actual fact, however, these are not deliberative bodies; they merely serve to ratify communist party proposals.

The Council of Ministers is defined by the constitution as "the supreme executive and administrative organ of the state." After being reorganized following elections, in 1988 it consisted of a chairman or premier, a deputy premier, eleven ministers, and the chairman of the Committee on State and People's Control. [15] The present State Council chairman, Todor Zhivkov, also serves as general secretary of the Bulgarian Communist Party. The current premier, Georgi Atanasov, is also a member of the party's Politburo.

Local government is administered by people's councils that are elected for 2.5-year terms and that are primarily responsible for the implementation of the economic, social, and cultural policies laid down by superior organs of the state. These councils, which are equivalent to soviets in the USSR, exist at the district and commune levels. A total of 51,161 people's councillors and 3,953 mayors were elected on 28 February 1988.

The judicial organ at the highest level is the Supreme Court, supported by city, regional, and district courts. Judges and lay assessors are generally elected by citizens, people's councils, or the National Assembly. The chief prosecutor wields exceptional power in controlling observance of the law by government organs and officials as well as citizens. He is charged specifically "to attend to the prosecution and punishment of crimes which affect the state, national, and economic interests of the People's Republic, and crimes and actions detrimental to the independence and state sovereignty of the country." [16]

The longest chapter in the constitution deals with guarantees covering a wide range of civil liberties and economic and social rights. As in the corresponding

Soviet document, almost every desirable right is spelled out:[17] equality before the law, individual liberty, inviolability of domicile, and freedom of religion, speech, press, and assembly. There is the qualification, however, that these rights may be exercised only in the interests of the working people.

It would seem on the surface that the 1971 constitution provides Bulgaria with a democratically representative form of government. Although the document does not adhere to the principle of separation of powers, it nevertheless suggests a theoretical degree of responsibility. Against the objection that it is strongly fla: vored with the dominance of state over individual, the communists argue that the state represents the people who elect the government and that guarantees of individual rights and liberties are abundantly enumerated.

Constitution and Government in Practice.   Theory remains far removed from practice in Bulgaria, where the literal provisions of the constitution bear only faint resemblance to the actual operation of the government. The basic law amounts to little more than a facade behind which the ruling party wields tight control over all levers of national power. Hence, the constitution is merely an instrument that can be used or abused as need dictates. Bulgaria today is a dictatorship of the proletariat (that is, of the communist party) and, in Lenin's definition, "a power limited by nothing, by no law, directly based on violence."[18] Examples include replacement in 1978 of the Agriculture Ministry with a National Agro-Industrial Union, whose chairman is elected by the National Assembly and holds a seat on the Council of Ministers. Subsequent reorganizations took place in the Ministry for Industry (replaced with an Industrial Union) and the Ministry of Culture (superseded by a Cultural Committee). These moves were part of a process that Zhivkov described as "the state . . . handing over the tasks that it fulfilled in a centralized fashion to elected bodies that are more directly answerable to their grass roots."[19]

In practice, the constitutional provisions for a representative government remain a farce; only the views of the communist leadership become policy and law. Furthermore, only those persons who are ultimately approved by the party are allowed to participate in administering the government.[20] Assembly deputies are nominated in advance under party supervision and then elected without opposition. They convene a few times a year for periods of several days and rubber-stamp proposals of the Assembly presidium, the Council of Ministers, or the ruling party's Central Committee. The same electoral process applies to the judiciary. In all cases, officeholders who fail to adhere to the party line can be recalled. Despite the assertion of individual liberties and human rights in the basic law, freedom of speech, assembly, and press is permitted only when its exercise is consonant with communist policies. Deviation from the dictates and will of the party simply is not permitted.

THE COMMUNIST PARTY OF BULGARIA

Dimitur Blagoev, who was born in Macedonia and educated in Russia, introduced communist ideas into Bulgaria toward the end of the nineteenth century.[21] The movement, which received its inspiration at this time, failed to grow during its early years owing to a split into "narrow" and "broad" groups. In addition to the absence of a substantial urban proletariat, peasants on their small holdings were not susceptible to easy organization. The "narrow" fraction advocated policies based on an industrialized economy, while the "broad" group felt, more realistically, that the almost wholly agrarian economy in Bulgaria would be unable to support the classical Marxist approach. The communist party did not play any role in the government until the end of World War II.[22]

After 1944, defeated Bulgaria appeared in the plans of the Soviet Union. The Fatherland Front, including communists, left-wing agrarians, the Zveno group, and left-wing social democrats, came to power following the entry of the Red Army and a military coup, which resulted in the installation of Kimon Georghiev (Zveno) as premier. The new cabinet had four Zvenos, four communists,[23] four agrarians, two socialists, and two independents. Stalinization took hold in Bulgaria perhaps more aggressively than in any other East European country. Already in 1944 large numbers of persons who were considered threats to the regime were being tried as "fascists" or "traitors" and summarily executed.[24] Despite a renewal of this terror during 1945–1947, the main opposition party managed to hold one-third of the vote.

In a September 1946 broadcast to the Bulgarian people, communist party leader Georgi Dimitrov proclaimed,

> Bulgaria will be a people's republic, a factor for Slav unity and fraternity against any possible aggression. It will not grease the axle of any anti-Slav or anti-Soviet policy leading to enmity between the peoples. Bulgaria will be a people's republic which, together with other democratic and freedom-loving peoples, will represent a strong element of peace and democracy in the Balkans and Europe and not a tool for military adventures and aggressive wars.[25]

During a later speech, at the fifth congress of the Bulgarian Communist Party, Dimitrov stated that the foundation of the government involved collaboration and friendship with the Soviet Union and that Bulgaria belonged to the anti-imperialist camp.

Along with the purges, Dimitrov created 30 trade unions, replaced the former police organization with his own militia, and appointed trusted individuals from his party to positions of authority. The general election held in November 1945 to choose members of the new National Assembly was anything but free. After the count the Fatherland Front had won 364 seats, as opposed to 101 for the noncommunist opposition. Of those in the Front, a total of 277 were communists, who thus held an absolute majority.

Dimitrov, despite some vacillation (especially in his views on a Balkan federation), supported the Moscow line in opposition to certain nationalists who felt that Bulgarian interests should come first. After Dimitrov died in July 1949, Vulko Chervenkov assumed control of the party and promptly eliminated the nationalist group. The orthodox Bulgarian communists were so anxious to imitate the USSR that they found themselves making the same mistakes long after the Soviets had taken a new approach and attempted to rectify their errors.

Purges within the party had been so thorough that they left few people of stature who were willing or able to offer any effective opposition to Moscow's directives. Stalin was suspicious of all Bulgarian communists who had spent the war inside their own country rather than in the USSR, the more so after Tito of Yugoslavia came into conflict with the Cominform. Traicho Kostov, who had been the most obvious successor to Dimitrov, ended on the gallows as a Titoist. Chervenkov soon became the "little Stalin" of Bulgaria.[26] During his six years of rule approximately 100,000 persons were purged from a communist party of about 460,000 members.

After the death of Stalin in 1953, the Chervenkov group would have preferred to continue its hard line but was held in check by the milder "new course" in the Soviet Union. Although Chervenkov remained loyal to his mentors in Moscow, realignments within the USSR between 1953 and 1956 resulted in the rise of Soviet leaders who were patrons of his opponents in the Bulgarian party and in the demise of those who had supported him. In accordance with the collective leadership philosophy, which was current in Moscow after Stalin's death, Chervenkov gave up the highest party position in 1954 but continued to hold office as premier; he remained the dominant figure until 1956. The rise of Khrushchev in the USSR brought about promotion of Todor Zhivkov, and Chervenkov lost the premiership. Although he was gradually stripped of his party position, his purge did not come until 1962 amid the familiar charges of excess and error during "the period of the personality cult."[27]

Soviet support had been essential in resolving the intense struggle among Bulgarian party factions. The departure of Chervenkov, plus previous purges, left Todor Zhivkov more fully in control. He entered the Politburo in 1952, became first secretary in 1954, and, additionally, premier in 1962. His victory was assured when he obtained the support of a majority on the then nine-man Politburo and an enlarged Central Committee. (In 1962 the larger Committee had 101 full members and 67 nonvoting candidates. The party's twelfth congress, in April 1981, elected 166 members and 139 candidates.) The serious internal factionalism and infighting among Bulgarian party leaders left them susceptible to Soviet manipulation; hence, Bulgaria has been probably the most conservative East European state.

After a Central Committee plenum in December 1972, a series of measures were introduced to improve living conditions, and some progress has since been made. Zhivkov also took steps to reduce the use of terror and to bring the Interior Ministry under closer control.

The eleven-member Bulgarian Communist Party (BCP) Politburo, elected at the 1986 party congress, has a majority drawn from the older generation whose experience has been in party or military affairs but includes a younger group of specialists in administrative or economic areas.[28] The first group is represented by Defense Minister Dobri Dzhurov (73), Fatherland Front chairman Pencho Kubadinski (70), State Council member Milko Balev (67), National Assembly chairman Stanko Todorov (68), BCP Secretary Grisha Filipov (68), *Rabotnichesko delo* editor Iordan Iotov (67) and includes Todor Zhivkov (77). Those falling into the second category are Foreign Minister Petar Mladenov (52), BCP Secretary Chudomir Aleksandrov (51), economic specialist Ognian Doinov (53), and Prime Minister Georgi Atanasov (52). The younger generation is more heavily represented among the six candidate members: Petar Diulgerov (58), Andrei Lukanov (49), Stoian Markov (45), Grigor Stoichkov (61), Dimitar Stoianov (59), and Georgi Iordanov (56).

The current leaders around Zhivkov show a tendency toward continuity and unity. They are generally mediocre individuals who are willing to accede to the desires of Moscow. There are no groups or individuals of sufficient strength to suggest an independent course of action in the near future. In 1965, however, a plot was uncovered to overthrow the Bulgarian leadership. Of the ten men implicated, one committed suicide and the others were sentenced to prison terms.[29] About half of this group consisted of officers who had fought in guerrilla detachments inside Bulgaria during the war and may therefore have represented a more nationalist and independent way of thinking.

There has been no indication of disloyalty among the rank and file of the party, which in 1987 totaled 932,055 members and candidates organized into some 29,000 local units. This represents a net increase of more than 442,000 in membership since 1958, with bureaucrats and blue-collar workers accounting for most of the gain. Among those who joined the party between 1981 and 1986, about 70 percent were under 30 years of age, half were workers, and more than 90 percent had completed at least a high school education. In 1986 women comprised 32.7 percent of total party membership.[30] The intelligentsia seems frustrated by controls, whereas the younger generation is apathetic toward them. The family remains unreceptive to regime indoctrination, and peasants are hostile to programs imposed by the government.

Party members and candidates constitute 9.6 percent of the country's population. In 1987 workers still maintained the largest bloc within the party (some 44.4 percent), although not an absolute majority, and this group claimed the largest share of new members. The proportion of farmers in the party declined to 16.3 percent. White-collar intelligentsia membership expanded to some 27.9 percent.[31] (See Table 9.)

At the time of the twelfth congress, the BCP had 825,876 members. The class composition of the party was not revealed by Zhivkov in his 1 April 1981 report. He did state, however, that "the backbone of the party" is the working class, "with its 352,649 members" (42.7 percent of the membership). Zhivkov added that "the party nucleus in the agricultural sector, in sciences, education, and culture is also strongly represented." He stressed a change in criteria for new members: "We must recruit party members from the strata of working people who have already asserted themselves, people who have earned party and public recognition with their new qualities—such as high cultural standards, professional training, political maturity, and prestige among the people."[32]

Even though pressure may have eased against the noncommunist population since 1972, under the new policy the machinery of the Interior Ministry has been streamlined and its head, Dimitar Stoianov, controls only uniformed police and fire department personnel. On the 25th anniversary of this organization, his predecessor described one aspect of security as follows:

> In the same way as hundreds of institutes of the capitalist countries cultivate the bacilli of deadly diseases, so are the bacilli of ideological diversion cultivated in hundreds of institutes, radio and television companies, departments and publishing houses. Every day these bacilli penetrate our frontiers and look for a fertile soil.[33]

Security provisions remain, and their enforcement varies with the policy in effect at any particular time.

The people realize this, which is probably why they vote. In the election of 8 June 1986, it was claimed that 99.9 percent of the adult population had voted. According to official figures, some 99.9 percent of the qualified electorate cast ballots for candidates of the Fatherland Front. Despite the pressure to register an affirmative vote, a total of 4,968 persons (out of 6.6 million) voted against the regime, spoiled their ballots, or left them blank. All 20,483 voters in 26 polling stations of his district "unanimously" elected party leader Todor Zhivkov to a seat in parliament. (See Table 10.) Local elections held in February 1988 were conducted under a new system providing for multiple candidacies: in about one of every five constituencies voters had a choice of two or more candidates. According to official results, 99.15 percent of the electorate voted, with the winning candidates averaging 90 percent support.[34]

Table 9

COMPOSITION OF THE BULGARIAN COMMUNIST PARTY, 1971–1986

(in numbers of members and percentages of total)

Occupational class	April 1971 (tenth congress)		March 1976 (eleventh congress)		March–April 1981 (twelfth congress)		April 1986 (thirteenth congress)	
Industrial workers	280,480	(40.1)	326,974	(41.4)	352,649	(42.7)	413,832	(44.4)
Agricultural workers	182,563	(26.1)	181,655	(23.0)		n.a.	151,925	(16.3)
White-collar workers and others	236,433	(33.8)	281,167	(35.6)		n.a.	366,298	(39.3)
Total	699,476	(100.0)	789,796	(100.0)	825,876	(100.0)	932,055	(100.0)

SOURCES: *Rabotnichesko delo*, 22 April 1971, 30 March 1976, 1 April 1981, 6 April 1986.

Table 10

COMPOSITION OF THE BULGARIAN NATIONAL ASSEMBLY, 1962–1986

| Party | NUMBER OF REPRESENTATIVES | | | | | |
	1962	*1966*	*1971*	*1976*	*1981*	*1986*
Bulgarian Communist Party	197	280	266	272	271	276
Bulgarian National Agrarian Union[a]	80	99	100	100	99	99
Nonparty	44	37	34	28	30	25
Total	321	416	400	400	400[b]	400

SOURCES: *Rabotnichesko delo,* 26 February 1962, 30 June 1971, 1 June 1976; Sofia radio, 28 February 1966, 8 June 1981, 10 June 1986.

NOTES: [a]BNAU, a separate political party in name only, is maintained by the communists as a control device in the villages because of its past importance and for external propaganda. It held its 34th congress during 18–20 May 1981. BNAU's membership of 120,000 has not changed since 1957. Some 100,000 of these are directly involved in agriculture. However, only 2,000 members hold leading posts on cooperative farms and agro-industrial complexes. *Zemedelsko zname,* 19–21 May 1981; RFE, *Bulgarian Situation Report,* no. 6 (1 June 1981).

[b]All candidates, including those labeled "nonparty," run on the Fatherland Front ticket without any opposition. Nonparty also includes Komsomol members.

The influence of propaganda, apart from elections, permeates every field: education of adults and young people, trade unions, book publication and distribution, even dress and conduct. The regime attempts to mold completely the mind of every Bulgarian. Admittedly and openly,

> the party is the guiding political force in socialist [Bulgarian] society. As for public opinion, on the one hand, the party plays a guiding role in the creation of the conditions and forms which are necessary premises for the normal and efficient functioning of public opinion; on the other, it is the guiding subjective force in the formation of public opinion itself.[35]

According to an editorial in an official party publication: "Self-education becomes the basic method of Marxist-Leninist training of the cadres [and] depends most of all on the qualifications of the propagandist, who must have a thorough knowledge of the subject he will teach."[36] The Central Committee has called on Bulgarian women to treat friendship with the USSR as a sacred legacy and "to watch over that friendship as over the apple of their eye, convey it to their children with their mother's milk, and bequeath it from generation to generation as the dearest heritage." Party leader Todor Zhivkov subsequently stated that

"Bulgaria and the Soviet Union will act as a single body, breathing with the same lungs and nourished by the same bloodstream."[37]

Zhivkov emphasized his personal allegiance to the USSR when he addressed the 30th anniversary meeting to celebrate the seizure of power by the BCP:

> Once, the great Lenin called the Bulgarian left-wing socialists, "internationalists in deeds." Several decades later Comrade Brezhnev defined the relations between Bulgaria and the Soviet Union as "socialist internationalism in action." We are eternally proud of these two evaluations, because they define a straight and clear political line; the line of the BCP from the time of Dimitur Blagoev, through the time of Georgi Dimitrov, up to our time. Years and decades will go by, new generations will grow, new leaders will lead our parties, countries and peoples, but the line of loyalty to Marxism-Leninism and proletarian internationalism, the line of Bulgarian-Soviet fraternity will continue to be bright and unchanging, marching forward and upwards through decades and through centuries.[38]

The twelfth BCP congress, held during 31 March–2 April 1981, coincided with thirteen centuries of the Bulgarian state and the 90th anniversary of the movement. A change in the BCP statute restored the post of general secretary, which represented a symbolic recognition of Todor Zhivkov on the eve of his 70th birthday and 27 years in office. This change follows the pattern established by the Soviet, Czechoslovak, and East German parties, all of which are headed by general secretaries, while the leader in Poland holds the title of first secretary. The designation general secretary had been abandoned during the mid-1950s in most of the bloc as part of de-Stalinization.

Zhivkov praised the achievements of Soviet communists and especially the "decisions of the twenty-fourth, twenty-fifth, and twenty-sixth CPSU congresses, the new USSR constitution and the exceptional successes in economic and cultural construction, in developing science and technology, and in solving mankind's spiritual problems." He added that all this provides the "basic theoretical and practical landmarks of the new road that will be followed by other countries and peoples." In his discussion of the world situation, Zhivkov echoed the line presented at the 26th CPSU congress in February–March 1981. He praised "the victories of the peoples of Ethiopia, Mozambique, Angola, South Yemen, and Afghanistan," which have chosen a socialist orientation for development; condemned U.S. and Chinese imperialist aggression; and called for "strengthening the cohesion and unity of the socialist community."[39]

In advance of the thirteenth BCP congress, several changes were made within the leadership. Aleksandrov and Filipov transferred from government into the party Secretariat, replacing Atanasov and Doinov, who moved in the opposite direction. The Politburo composition also changed after the dismissal of Bonev and Bozhinov. The congress itself, during 2–5 April 1986, merely ratified the foregoing. Todor Zhivkov engineered a situation whereby the succession remains unclear. Aleksandrov has rivals in Atanasov and, possibly, Doynov.

The BCP convened a national conference on 28 January 1988. The 3,226 delegates, representing 28 district and nine regional party organizations, heard Todor Zhivkov report on restructuring and the new model of socialism, which he claimed has the people's well-being as its immediate goal. Four consecutive issues of the BCP daily newspaper carried statements made at the national conference by selected delegates.[40]

Although it may be difficult to identify the party's role in the government, it is obvious from the interlocking directorate that all major plans, programs, and policies of the regime originate with the party. (See Table 11.) It retains control over all important functions. Implementation of the communist program, however, is another matter and has come up against several obstacles.

First, Bulgaria is a farming country with few resources on which to base an industrialized economy. The emphasis on heavy industry has been supported by credits from the Soviet Union[41] and by capital extracted through forced collectivization of peasants. Considerable gains have been made in heavy industry, but production of consumer goods and investment in agriculture have lagged behind. The results of this policy are visible, and the peasants show little desire to produce for the government. Even according to official data the number of cattle and sheep has not changed much in almost four decades. (See Table 12.) A tribute to personal initiative can be seen on the part of the collectivized peasants, who, with their "acre and a cow" private plots occupying 14 percent of the arable land, in 1982 provided 25 percent of the agricultural output. Private plots produced 33 percent of all vegetables, 39 percent of fruit, 51 percent of potatoes, 40 percent of meat sales, 30 percent of milk, and more than 50 percent of eggs.[42]

Second, the workers' indifference and lack of enthusiasm have decreed harsh amendments to the labor codes. If an employee is absent without authorization during three consecutive days or for any five days in a calendar year, he loses the standard increments of pay, all leave in excess of fourteen days, and all indemnities for invalidism or sickness and retirement. Work contracts must be signed for a specific period of time, and employees are not allowed to break contracts without the consent of management. If an employee leaves without permission, he or she cannot be hired by another enterprise, remains subject to penalties for absence,[43] and must move out of government housing within one month.

Finally, poor discipline among the youth is mentioned time after time, indicating a problem of major proportions. Party leaders enumerate the absence of conscience, bad upbringing, the lack of proper guidance at home and school, negative attitudes toward the state, formalism and banalities in lecture programs, inadequate Komsomol[44] curriculum and organization, the degenerate influence of bourgeois culture, the consumption of alcohol, decadent music, vulgarity in

Table 11
BULGARIAN PARTY-GOVERNMENT DIRECTORATE, 1988

Politburo	Year of birth	Year elected	Secretariat	Council of Ministers	Other positions
FULL MEMBERS: (9)					
Zhivkov, Todor	1911	1950	General-secretary		Chairman, State Council
Atanasov, Georgi	1933	1986		Premier	Member, State Council
Balev, Milko	1920	1982	Secretary		Member, State Council
Doinov, Ognian	1935	1977			Member, State Council
Dzhurov, Dobri	1916	1974		National defense minister	
Filipov, Grisha	1919	1974	Secretary		
Kubadinski, Pencho	1918	1962			Chairman, Fatherland Front; member, State Council
Mladenov, Petar	1936	1976		Foreign affairs minister	
Iotov, Iordan	1920	1984	Secretary		Member, State Council
CANDIDATE MEMBERS (6)					
Diulgerov, Petar	1929	1981			Chairman, trade unions; member, State Council
Lukanov, Andrei	1938	1979		Foreign economic relations minister	
Markov, Stoyan	1942	1986		Committee for Science and Technology chairman	
Stoichkov, Grigor	1926	1984		Deputy premier	
Stoianov, Dimitar	1928	1984		Internal affairs minister	
Iordanov, Georgi	1931	1979		Culture, science and education minister	

SOURCES: John D. Bell, *The Bulgarian Communist Party from Blagoev to Zhivkov* (Stanford, Calif.: 1986), pp. 149–58; CIA, *Directory of Bulgarian Officials* (October 1986), p. 17; RFE, *East European Leadership List* (15 January 1988), pp. 5–6. Sofia Radio, 20 July 1988, for the ouster of Aleksandrov and Todorov.

Table 12
LIVESTOCK NUMBERS, SELECTED YEARS, 1948–1985
(in thousands)

Livestock	1948	1961	1972	1975	1980	1985
Cattle	1,783	1,452	1,379	1,554	1,787	1,706
(Cows)	(703)	(547)	(607)	(644)	(696)	(670)
Hogs	1,078	2,553	2,806	3,422	3,828	3,912
Sheep	9,266	9,333	10,127	9,791	10,538	9,724
Goats	720	246	318	299	—	460
Rabbits	128	470	350	345	—	354
Poultry	11,380	23,366	34,102	35,089	40,991	39,227

SOURCES: Eugene K. Keefe et al., *Area Handbook for Bulgaria* (Washington, D.C., 1974), p. 244; *Statisticheski godishnik 1974* (Sofia, 1974), p. 230; *Statistical Pocket Book 1976* (Sofia, 1976), pp. 55 and 94; *Quarterly Economic Review* (2d Quarter 1981), p. 23; *Statisticheski godishnik 1986* (Sofia, 1986), pp. 283–84.

dances, and a desire for cars and travel outside Bulgaria as some of the reasons for juvenile delinquency.

Bulgarian leaders have committed the people to full support of the Soviet Union, with concomitant restrictions on freedom and initiative. Party authority is absolute within itself; it is supported completely by the proximity of USSR military power. It does not seem likely that the regime will be overthrown in the near future, although disenchantment with the leadership seems widespread even at middle party echelons. In view of the successful October 1964 coup against Khrushchev in Moscow and the abortive conspiracy of April 1965 at Sofia, the possibility of a successful attempt cannot be discounted completely.

DOMESTIC AND FOREIGN RELATIONS

The Economy.   After World War II Bulgaria imposed currency reforms on three different occasions: 1947, 1952, and 1962. Each time, the revaluation was imposed to drain off excess purchasing power, curb existing inflation, and redistribute income. Following the currency reform of 1962, the low average wage has been the main reason for the depressed standard of living. To remedy this situation, wages and salaries (mainly for low-paid workers) were raised from 4 to 12 percent in three phases during 1970. The minimum wage increased to 80 leva per month in 1973, to 100 leva in 1979, and 120 leva in 1985 (with the average wage approximately 213 leva). The ninth five-year plan projected a rise to an average wage of 250–255 leva by 1990. The issue of wages and salaries has been under intensive scrutiny in the discussions on *perestroika*. The main proposal is to increase substantially the salaries of specialists even though this would create greater wage inequalities.[45]

Forced industrialization, almost complete socialization of the land, and heavy reinvestment have also caused the standard of living to suffer. The plan for the period 1961–1980, which was adopted by the BCP's ninth congress, envisaged an investment rate of 27 percent. This long-range plan was intended to raise the annual national income to approximately twenty billion leva, about five times the 1960 level. National income reportedly surpassed the twenty billion leva target, but investment totals have not been published. Failure to report investment data confirms the recent trend of reducing industrial investment, allocating more funds for consumer goods, and reflecting a desire to achieve industrial growth through greater labor productivity.

In an attempt to correct some of the serious deficiencies within the economy, Bulgaria began a reorganization of both government and economy away from the previous centralized lines. The so-called New Economic System, which was unveiled in April 1966 at a plenary session of the Central Committee, apparently did not work.[46] It has been superseded by a New Economic Mechanism, implemented during the 1976–1980 planning period. The main features included management by objective principle in the national economy, strengthening of centralized planning, and more authority for the national economic complexes, production units, and individual managers. In 1979 the government initiated a program to encourage foreign investment and establish joint enterprises in Bulgaria. The official news agency reported the following summer that more than 150 joint agreements had been signed with capitalist firms, including ten-year agreements with Shell and Occidental Petroleum. A new Commission for Energy and Raw Materials has coordinated national energy policy and promoted joint projects with foreign firms since mid-1980. Even with these expanding Western contacts, the Bulgarian economy still remains heavily dependent on the USSR.[47]

At the twelfth party congress, Zhivkov optimistically stated that the people of Bulgaria, "under the leadership of the BCP . . . are successfully implementing the party program to build a developed socialist society."[48] Official statistics for the seventh five-year plan (1976–1980) do not substantiate this optimism, however. Targets and percentages achieved (in parentheses) over 1971–1975 are national income 45 (35), industry 55 (35), and agriculture 20 (12). Targets for 1981, announced by Kiril Zarev, chairman of the State Planning Commission, but reduced a year later to the figures in parentheses by the National Assembly were national income 5.5 (5.1), industry 5.2 (4.8), and agriculture 6.1 (5.6). The new plan (1981–1985) foresaw a continuation of the economic slowdown, with percentages of increase being compared against the preceding five years: national income, 25 to 30; industry, 30 to 35; agriculture, 20 to 22; and real per capita income, 16 to 18 percent. The ninth five-year plan (1986–1990) projected a growth in domestic net material product of 30 percent; industry, 27 percent; agriculture, 8–10 percent; and real per capita income, 18 percent. These goals were more optimistic than for the preceding plan and reflected the belief that economic restructuring would lead to higher productivity.[49]

Collectivization.   Agricultural collectives expanded at a more rapid pace in Bulgaria than in any other East European country, even though collectivization moved through several distinct phases. The first of these phases involved persuasion, when the communists were consolidating their power. This step was followed, commencing in 1948, by a more aggressive policy. Only two years later, some 43 percent of all the land had been collectivized; by 1960, it was claimed that 97.4 percent of the land belonged either in this category or in that of agricultural enterprises directly operated by the state.[50]

The 1971 constitution of Bulgaria claims that "the land belongs to those who till it." As in the Soviet Union, the eventual desire of the Bulgarian communists is to bring all agricultural land into *sovkhozy* (state farms), although at present the greater part is in *kolkhozy* (collectives). Todor Zhivkov had ordered complete collectivization, despite the sometimes discouraging results. For example, in 1963 it became necessary to import some 100,000 tons of wheat from Canada, and a certain amount of food rationing had to be introduced. Although collectivization is pointed to with pride and declared to be irrevocable by officials, in practice measures are being taken to encourage production on private plots, a method that is more efficient. Bulgarian agriculture is not producing food stuffs in sufficient quantities to supply the population adequately. (See Table 13.) Hence some compromise must be reached between production and collectivization if the country is to deliver more than the basic necessities. Although collectivized farmers have been eligible for old-age pensions, accident and health insurance, vacations, and child allowances since 1976, these benefits may be inadequate to keep young people on the farm.[51]

At the twelfth party congress, Todor Zhivkov admitted the problem when he said that a "prompt increase in grain production . . . must be considered as the main strategic task of the agricultural sector during the eighth five-year plan period." He stressed "the necessity, with the assistance of agro-industrial complexes, to further develop and consolidate private plots and auxiliary agriculture, as a continuation and complement to the public sector." Zhivkov made an appeal "to overcome all economic, organizational, and psychological barriers, which are impeding better utilization of private plots and auxiliary farms for supplying the population."[52] He cautioned, however, that private plots are not to be favored over the public sector. The size of private plots is determined by the general assembly of the respective agro-industrial complex and, as a rule, cannot surpass

Table 13
ANNUAL CONSUMPTION LEVELS, 1970–1985

ITEM	MEASURE	CONSUMPTION LEVELS		
		1970	*1980*	*1985*
Meat and meat products	Pounds per capita	91.3	134.9	159.8
Fish	Pounds per capita	12.1	15.2	18.7
Milk and milk products	Gallons per capita	30.8	44.7	50.9
Vegetable oils	Pounds per capita	27.6	45.9	50.9
Flour and flour products	Pounds per capita	376.1	476.2	428.1
Sugar	Pounds per capita	72.5	76.5	77.4
Vegetables	Pounds per capita	196.0	206.8	226.6
Fruit	Pounds per capita	326.8	233.2	232.8
Eggs	Number per capita	122.0	204.0	256.0
Cotton fabrics	Square feet per capita	246.4	287.5	298.6
Wool fabrics	Square feet per capita	42.2	51.1	54.4
Shoes	Pairs per capita	1.7	2.0	2.3
Radio sets	Per 100 households	100.8	88.0	97.0
Television sets	Per 100 households	42.0	75.0	93.0
Telephones	Per 100 households	7.0	24.0	42.0
Washing machines	Per 100 households	50.0	71.0	89.0
Refrigerators	Per 100 households	29.0	76.0	94.0
Automobiles	Per 100 households	6.0	29.0	37.0

SOURCE: *Statisticheski godishnik 1986* (Sofia, 1986), pp. 95–96.

0.5 hectare. The secretary of the Fatherland Front reported that almost one-fourth of the total volume of farm production comes from these small holdings.[53]

Church-State Relations. The regime has been able to gain substantial control over religious life. This was accomplished in several distinct phases.[54] Minority faiths (Moslem, Jewish, Protestant, and Roman Catholic) were each handled separately but with great effectiveness. The majority of the people belong to the Bulgarian Orthodox church, and the government has capitalized on this fact:

> The Communists have patronized the church as the traditional national church of Bulgaria, not only to obtain support from the Church devotees, but also to unify national Orthodox Churches under the aegis of the Soviet-controlled Russian Orthodox Church. [Already] . . . Patriarch Kiril [had] clearly demonstrated his attitude . . . when he thanked the regime for the reestablishment of the Bulgarian Patriarchate and called on all the faithful to support the Government in its policies.[55]

Control over the Bulgarian Orthodox church and other religions was greatly facilitated by a 1949 statute whereby all denominations were required to register with the Committee for Religious Affairs, which was attached to the Council of Ministers, and to obtain approval for their bylaws. This statute also specified that the leadership of all religious organizations "must be responsible to the state" and that members of each hierarchy could not "take office or be dismissed or transferred without the approval of the Committee."[56] Religious organizations are authorized to operate schools if state permission is obtained, but they are not allowed the right to engage in secular education. Such restrictions have curtailed virtually all religious freedom and converted religious leaders into spokesman for the state.

Muslims of Turkish descent form the largest minority religious group and have fared less well than the Bulgarian Orthodox faithful. Approximately 150,000 Turkish Muslims were permitted to leave during 1950–1951, and the remaining 700,000 have been organized into communities numbering just over 1,000.[57] The Grand Mufti has repeatedly expressed his gratitude for the consideration shown to the Turkish minority; he undoubtedly retains his position under conditions that forbid any but favorable statements concerning the regime and the welfare of his group. Under a 1968 agreement with Turkey, Bulgarian Turks and families were allowed to emigrate. Repatriation commenced in 1969, but only 30,000 to 35,000 (those who had relatives in Turkey) appeared to be eligible. The number of those who had left apparently was smaller than this figure.

Between December 1984 and March 1985, approximately 900,000 Bulgarian citizens of Turkish ethnic extraction had been pressured to change their names to Slavic ones. At least 100 Turks were killed and more than 250 jailed during this assimilation campaign. A protocol between Bulgaria and Turkey, signed on 23 February 1988, specified a cessation of this inhumane treatment. The regime in Sofia allegedly has used this agreement for propaganda purposes.[58]

The position of the Roman Catholic church is even worse. In September 1952, 40 leading Catholics were tried at Sofia on trumped-up charges of spying. This action and the subsequent banishment of less important personnel sufficed to obliterate the church hierarchy in Bulgaria. The country still has about 56,000 Roman Catholics, but there are no church buildings or priests to conduct religious services for them.[59]

Protestants have suffered similar fates, although their denominations are still active to a limited degree. Five separate groups were forcibly combined into one United Evangelical church. All denominational schools were closed, and many clergymen faced trial for espionage. In March 1949, fifteen pastors were sentenced to prison and to pay heavy fines for allegedly spying on behalf of the United States and Britain. Protestant churches in Bulgaria exerted considerable influence on the educated class before the war, but now they remain under tight state control.

Another religious minority is the approximately 5,500 persons of the Jewish faith. The official leadership of this community has cooperated with the regime because the tenure of all recognized religious bodies depends on the will of the communist government. After surviving World War II, the Jews in Bulgaria were allowed to emigrate to Israel. Some forty-five thousand did so, mostly during the 1949–1950 period. Fourteen synagogues still exist in Bulgaria for worship.[60]

What effect the control exercised by the regime over churches has had on the younger minds is impossible to judge. Religion still remains a stronghold of anticommunist feeling, however, and is connected with a desire for genuine national independence. According to a Bulgarian expert on atheistic education, a survey of fourteen years ago[61] showed that more than one-third of the population was "religiously minded" to some degree.

Foreign Trade. Bulgaria became one of the original members of CMEA in 1949 when that organization was formed. Table 14 shows trade with the other East European states and the Soviet Union. By 1976 the bloc accounted for some 80 percent of Bulgaria's imports and exports.[62] East European states may now form temporary alliances or even subblocs within CMEA, and there is evidence that such arrangements had already occurred some time ago. On the other hand, the trade agreement for the period 1976–1980 involved transactions amounting to 24 billion rubles and increased Soviet-Bulgarian trade to four-fifths. By the end of 1975 the USSR had reportedly invested some two billion dollars in Bulgaria's economy.[63]

Table 14
BULGARIA-BLOC TRADE, 1968–1985
(in millions of leva)

Country	1968		1979		1985	
	Imports	*Exports*	*Imports*	*Exports*	*Imports*	*Exports*
Albania	6.6	4.9	8.6	7.8	12.6	12.6
Czechoslovakia	96.8	103.6	296.4	265.1	583.5	626.5
East Germany	176.1	141.5	486.7	444.8	712.0	700.8
Hungary	35.5	33.4	163.2	140.6	262.8	264.6
Poland	75.3	55.6	280.6	293.3	640.2	476.3
Romania	23.4	29.8	140.3	185.0	261.1	292.7
USSR	1,107.0	1,045.8	4,336.0	4,019.6	7,898.1	7,775.8
Total	1,520.7	1,414.6	5,711.8	5,356.2	10,370.3	10,149.3
All foreign trade	2,085.3	1,889.7	7,363.4	7,666.8	14,066.5	13,739.4

SOURCES: [Bulgaria], *Statisticheski yezhegodnik 1969* (Sofia, 1970), pp. 186–87; *Statisticheski godishnik 1980* (Sofia, 1981), pp. 385–86, *1986* (Sofia, 1986), pp. 367–68.

NOTE: One U.S. dollar equaled 1.17 leva and then 1.04 leva at official exchange rates before 1975, less than half the black market rate, but in 1981 it dropped to 0.85 leva, rising to 0.95 leva by July 1986.

During the 1981–1985 period, trade with the Soviet Union was expected to exceed 40 billion rubles. This will account for approximately 60 percent of Bulgaria's total foreign trade. Moscow has assisted with construction of more than 300 industrial projects, including the Kozlodoui atomic power station. More than 45,000 Bulgarian citizens work and study in the USSR, of whom 13,000 labor at extracting raw materials. Since 1977, there have been no reports about Soviet credits. A new *List of Facts, Information, and Subjects That Are State Secrets in the People's Republic of Bulgaria* (1980), approved by a Council of Ministers' decree, added a large number of subjects to the previous one (1964). Detailed foreign trade data, crude oil production figures, and civil defense information are a few of the areas considered secret. The new list also includes a ban of "summarized information on losses in economic activities on a nationwide level and analyses of the losses."[64]

Relations with Border Countries. Bulgaria is touched on the north by Romania, on the west by Yugoslavia, and on the south by Greece and Turkey. The country has not had particularly good relations with its neighbors, even communist-ruled ones. Its foreign affairs, however, are predicated on satisfying the Soviet Union, and in this respect have been conducted quite successfully. Foreign Minister Petar Mladenov has stated that "the basic goal of Bulgarian foreign policy is consolidation of the alliance with the USSR. . . . which is constantly moving forward and assuming ever increasing new dimensions."[65]

Bulgaria has a friendship and a mutual aid treaty, which was renewed in 1970, with Romania. Despite the maverick role played by Bucharest within the bloc, Sofia's relations with it have improved. During 1972 Nicolae Ceausescu and Todor Zhivkov exchanged visits, and plans for such joint projects as Danubian hydroelectric works were subsequently affirmed. In 1976 the two countries entered into a series of agreements involving joint enterprises and vastly expanded trade.[66] Bulgaria undoubtedly attempts to avoid a public airing of any intrabloc differences. In January 1981, Ceausescu met Zhivkov in Sofia for what was called "continuation of a good tradition" in top-level conferences between fraternal socialist states. The visit was repeated in October 1987.[67]

Relations between Greece and Bulgaria were initially hindered by Bulgaria's failure to pay reparations of 45 million dollars, which were assigned by the 1947 peace treaty, and by the fact that communist Greek insurgents were given sanctuary in Bulgaria during the ensuing civil war. The spring of 1964, however, witnessed talks to establish full diplomatic relations between the two countries. An agreement finally provided for payment of 7 million dollars in reparations as well as communications by telephone and air. A railroad linking Koulata in Bulgaria with the port of Salonika in Greece was scheduled for completion as an alternative to the port of Rijeka in Yugoslavia. The two countries signed a new trade and payments agreement covering the years 1970–1974.

From that time on, relations have steadily improved. Following the overthrow of the Athens military government in 1974, Bulgarian-Greek relations have included the expansion of economic and cultural exchange, culminating in visits by Premier Konstantinos Karamanlis to Bulgaria (in July 1975) and by Todor Zhivkov to Greece (in April 1976). The reasons for this rapprochement appear to be the need for Bulgarian neutrality in the event of a Greco-Turkish war and the Bulgarian wish to improve relations on a bilateral basis with its Balkan neighbors. There have been no fewer than six chief-of-state meetings in the 1976–1980 period between Zhivkov and his Greek counterparts. These regular contacts are regarded as essential in the current Bulgarian "good-neighbor" policy, with Prime Minister Andreas Papandreou visiting Sofia in July 1987.[68]

Relations with Turkey have never been especially good, stemming in part from the fact that the Ottomans represented the occupation power in Bulgaria for about five centuries. Bulgaria and Turkey have long had agreements for the mutual repatriation of nationals. During 1950–1951, as mentioned above, approximately one hundred and fifty thousand Bulgarian Turks were permitted to be repatriated to Turkey. Yet relations were strained. In 1973, a joint communiqué noted that the repatriation process had become regularized. During the preceding five years, more than forty thousand Bulgarian Turks had been repatriated.[69] (For a breakdown by nationality group, see Table 15.) In recent years, repression against the ethnic Turks in Bulgaria has aggravated relations between the two countries. The protocol of February 1988, mentioned earlier, reportedly involved an agreement on the level of Turkish emigration.

With regard to the Greco-Turkish dispute over Cyprus and the Aegean, Bulgaria (although it holds a basically pro-Greek position on Cyprus), like the Soviet Union, has been attempting to exploit Turkey's alienation from the Western alliance. In an effort to pursue this objective in the dispute, Bulgaria received Turkish premier Süleyman Demirel late in 1975 and BCP leader Zhivkov visited Ankara the following year.

Bulgaria's relations with Yugoslavia have been determined primarily by the degree of warmth or coolness between the USSR and that country. Macedonia province in Yugoslavia has been of prime concern and could become increasingly important if Bulgaria should ever break away from Soviet control. This border region, inhabited by 1.4 million persons, has been a bone of contention between the two states since before World War II. Yugoslavia claims that the Macedonians comprise a distinct nationality and has organized them into a federal republic. Belgrade would like Sofia to accord its own Macedonians (of the Pirin district) minority rights akin to those they enjoy in Yugoslavia. Bulgaria, however, views this population as Bulgarian. Because the Macedonians in Yugoslavia outnumber the relatively few Bulgarians listed as inhabiting Vardar Macedonia, the controversy could escalate into tension over a possible Bulgarian irredenta.[70] Apart from

Table 15
NATIONALITIES IN BULGARIA, 1987
(estimated)

Nationality	Number of persons (in thousands)	Percent of total
Bulgarians	7,643,519	85.3
Turks	761,664	8.5
Gypsies	232,979	2.6
Macedonians	224,019	2.5
Armenians	26,882	0.3
Russians	17,922	0.2
Others	53,764	0.6
Total	8,960,749	100.0

SOURCES: CIA, *The World Factbook 1987*, p. 35, for percentages that were used to compute absolute numbers. Approximately the same figures appear in Keefe, p. 65 (see Table 12 above).

NOTES: The Turks are called Muslims at times, that is, they are designated by religion, although they often feel themselves to be Turks. This is not true of the 160,000 Pomaks in the group, who are Bulgarian converts to Islam. About 200,000 repatriated Turks should be subtracted from the above table.

Population figures for 1980 were the first published since 1977. Available statistics show that a decrease in population of approximately 17,100 Bulgarians took place between 1977 and 1978. This decline is explained by the emigration of ethnic Turks to Turkey and by a small number (approximately 2,000 per year) of refugees. RFE, *Bulgarian Situation Report*, no. 1 (22 January 1981).

As of 1 January 1981, the nationality identification on Bulgarian internal passports has been eliminated. This complies with the policy of downplaying the national individuality of minority groups. Sofia radio, 20 November 1980.

this problem, relations with Yugoslavia have been correct in recent years, with more contacts between Sofia and Belgrade.

In 1978, Sofia celebrated the centennial of its liberation from Turkey and the Treaty of San Stefano, which ceded to Bulgaria almost all of Macedonia. These festivities created tension with Yugoslavia, in view of the latter's insistence that Macedonians be guaranteed their rights. Trade turnover between Sofia and Belgrade reached the equivalent of about 1.2 billion foreign exchange levas during the 1981–1985 period, and it was hoped that figure would increase during the current five-year period.[71]

Conclusions.   Over the past decade, there has been a marked upgrade in Bulgaria's standard of living. Zhivkov's policy of close alignment with the Soviet Union has brought a certain measure of security and stature throughout the

Balkans that size and indigenous strength would not otherwise warrant. Open crises, on the scale of the Hungarian, Czechoslovak, or Polish rebellions, have never occurred in Bulgaria and are not likely to occur in the near future. The leaders in Sofia undoubtedly will continue to go along with whatever policies Moscow professes and hope that those policies will not prevent the further expansion of economic and cultural contacts with the noncommunist world.

Politics in Bulgaria have always closely followed developments in the USSR, and thus *glasnost'* and *perestroika* can be expected to have a considerable impact. Moreover, Zhivkov's policy of seeking to bring the modern "scientific-technological revolution" to Bulgaria has produced a generation, now coming to maturity, that is much better educated and more sophisticated than any in Bulgarian history. Although not disloyal, they may—impatient with old ways of doing business and with the distrust the regime has shown toward the people—become a constituency sympathetic to real reform.[72]

NOTES

1. [Bulgaria], *Statisticheski godishnik na Narodna Republika Bulgariia 1986* (Sofia, 1987), p. 27.

2. CIA, *World Factbook 1987*, p. 34.

3. L. A. D. Dellin (ed.), *Bulgaria* (New York, 1957), pp. 6–7.

4. Ibid., pp. 16–17, for a useful summary of these events.

5. Dellin, *Bulgaria*, p. 85.

6. Ibid., pp. 86, 88–89, 118.

7. The Fatherland Front (*Otechestven Front*) was a communist-inspired coalition established secretly in 1942. The name is currently used for the umbrella front organization, which is quite different from the original movement. It now includes trade unions and the youth movement as collective members, communist party and the subordinate Bulgarian National Agrarian Union members, and also private citizens, who may join as individuals. Officers are listed in CIA, *Directory of Bulgarian Officials* (Washington, D.C., October 1986), pp. 72–73.

8. Robert Lee Wolff, "Bulgaria," in Stephen D. Kertesz (ed.), *The Fate of East Central Europe* (Notre Dame, Ind., 1956), p. 282. King Simeon and his mother went into exile.

9. He should not be confused with Dr. Georgi M. Dimitrov (nicknamed "Gemeto"), general secretary of the Agrarian Party, who resigned under communist pressure and was succeeded by Nikola Petkov (arrested and executed in September 1947). G. M. Dimitrov escaped from Bulgaria and died in the United States. See Chapter 5 in John D. Bell, *The Bulgarian Communist Party from Blagoev to Zhivkov* (Stanford, Calif., 1986), pp. 77–101.

10. Dellin, *Bulgaria*, pp. 390–91. An official biography by Nedelcho Ganchovskii,

Georgii Dimitrov (Moscow, 1979), appeared in two volumes, translated from the Bulgarian language.

11. V. N. Durdenevskii, *Konstitutsii evropeiskikh stran narodnoi demokratii* (Moscow, 1954), pp. 5–26, gives the text in Russian.

12. For the new constitution, see [Bulgaria], *Konstitutsiia na Narodna Republika Bulgariia* (Sofia, 1971), p. 64. William B. Simons (ed.), *The Constitutions of the Communist World* (Alphen aan den Rijn, 1980), pp. 34–67, provides an English translation; B. A. Strashun et al. (eds.), *Konstitutsii sotsialisticheskikh gosudarstv* (Moscow: Iurizdat, 1987), vol. 1, pp. 129–56, in Russian.

13. Ibid., Articles 66–89.

14. *Constitution*, Articles 90–97. Party leader Todor Zhivkov gave up the premiership in 1971 and became State Council chairman.

15. Ibid., Articles 98–108; the incumbents are listed in RFE, *East European Leadership List* (Munich, 15 January 1988), pp. 5–6.

16. Dellin, *Bulgaria*, p. 94. In addition, the regime has mobilized "volunteer" units of workers to preserve social order.

17. *Constitution*, Articles 34–65.

18. Quoted by Dellin, *Bulgaria*, p. 95.

19. Interview with *L'Humanité* (Paris), 24 November 1980, pp. 6–7.

20. Admitted by implication in B. Spasov and A. Angelov, *Gosudarstvennoe pravo Narodnoi Respubliki Bolgarii* (Moscow, 1962), pp. 82–83.

21. Two books on the subject of Blagoev's influence on Marxist ideology are Banko Ganov, *Dimit'r Blagoev* (Sofia, 1978) and Khristo S. Kabakchiev, *Dimit'r Blagoev i partiiata na tesnite sotsialisti* (Sofia, 1979).

22. The war period is covered in the Soviet version of the party history by L. Bidinskaia (ed.), *Istoriia Bolgarskoi Kommunisticheskoi Partii* (Moscow, 1960), pp. 345–83. See also John D. Bell, *The Bulgarian Communist Party,* Chapter 4, pp. 55–76.

23. The communists had only 25,000 members at this time and, because of their weakness, were forced to establish a coalition regime. See the interview with Todor Zhivkov in *Le Monde,* 4 August 1976.

24. An official statement issued in March 1945 admitted to 2,138 executions, some 1,940 prison sentences of twenty years, and 1,689 sentences of ten to fifteen years. Stanley G. Evans, *A Short History of Bulgaria* (London, 1960), p. 189.

25. Ibid., quoted in, p. 184.

26. Having become an "unperson" in the 1960s, Chervenkov is not mentioned in a party history covering this period. P. Kostov, M. Trifonova, and M. St. Dimitrov (eds.), *Materiali po istoriia na Bulgarskata Komunisticheska Partiia, 1944–1960* (Sofia, 1961), pp. 87–98. It appears that only the party leader can identify an unperson by name. Todor Zhivkov, in his report to the eighth congress, stated that the "personality cult of Vulko Chervenkov" had led to "incorrect, anti-Leninist methods of work and leadership." [Bulgarian Communist Party], *Osmi Kongres: stenografski protokol* (Sofia, 1963), p. 125. Chervenkov died on 21 October 1980. His obituary was not signed by any party official,

as is customary on the death of a prominent figure, thus further downgrading the former leader's status. *Rabotnichesko delo,* 24 October 1980.

27. L. A. D. Dellin, "Bulgaria," in Stephen D. Kertesz (ed.), *East Central Europe and the World* (Notre Dame, Ind., 1962), pp. 169–96. Chervenkov's party membership was restored on 19 May 1969.

28. Another member of this younger group, and daughter of the party leader, Lyudmila Zhivkova, died unexpectedly on 22 July 1981 after a brief illness. She had emerged in 1980 as head of the Committee on Culture at the Council of Ministers after becoming a full Politburo member in 1979 (without having served as a candidate member). From all appearances, Zhivkova was being groomed as a possible heir to her father. Others are listed by CIA, *Directory of Bulgarian Officials* (Washington, D.C.: October 1986), pp. 3–114.

29. Sofia radio, 19 June 1965; cited in RFE report, "Sentences of Bulgarians in April Conspiracy," 24 June 1965.

30. Bulgarian Telegraphic Agency, 4 April 1986; RFE, *Situation Report,* 22 April 1988. In 1986, only 11.9 percent of BCP membership was under 30 years of age; about 61 percent was under 50. RFE, *Situation Report,* 22 April 1986; cited by John D. Bell, "Bulgaria," in Richard F. Staar (ed.), *Yearbook on International Communist Affairs: 1986* (Stanford, Calif., 1987), p. 276; henceforth, cited as *YICA.*

31. Todor Zhivkov's report to the thirteenth party congress over Sofia radio, 5 April 1986; *FBIS,* 8 April 1986. See also *XIII s'ezd Bolgarskoi KP* (Moscow, 1987).

32. *Rabotnichesko delo,* 1 April 1981.

33. Speech over Sofia radio, 15 September 1969. Since the beginning of 1970, a trend toward greater secrecy has developed and less documentary material is being published.

34. *Rabotnichesko delo,* 10 June 1986; *Sofia News,* 2 March 1988.

35. *Novo vreme* (January 1964), in RFE, *Bulgarian Press Survey,* 20 February 1964. Ten years later, early in 1974, concern over ideology led to the establishment of a new Mass Information Media Department within the BCP Secretariat.

36. *Partien zhivot* (December 1963).

37. Sofia radio, 5 March 1964; *Rabotnichesko delo,* 20 September 1973.

38. *Rabotnichesko delo,* 9 September 1974. Note also that since early 1973, ambassadors to the USSR have held cabinet rank in the Bulgarian government.

39. Ibid., 1 and 5 April 1981. Bulgaria has concluded treaties of friendship and cooperation with seven Third World countries: Angola, Mozambique, and South Yemen (1978); Laos and Vietnam (1979); Ethiopia and Cambodia (1980). See [Bulgaria], *13th Centennial Jubilee of the Bulgarian State* (Sophia, 1981), for speeches by Todor Zhivkov and Lyudmila Zhivkova.

40. John D. Bell, "Bulgaria," in *YICA: 1987,* pp. 276–77, for the thirteenth BCP congress; Zhivkov's speech at the BCP national conference is in *Rabotnichesko delo,* 29 January 1988; *FBIS-Eastern Europe* (EEU), 9 February 1988, pp. 8–31. The other speeches were carried in *FBIS-EEU,* 29 January through 1 February 1988, 11 February 1988, pp. 6–9.

41. In recent years, most Soviet loans and credits to East European countries have remained unpublicized. USSR aid to Bulgaria during 1954–1979 totaled the equivalent of

almost two billions dollars, according to CIA, *Handbook of Economic Statistics* (1980), p. 110. The same source for 1987 gives $1.1 billion as Soviet economic aid for all of Eastern Europe, without any breakdown by country. (Table 85, p. 116).

42. Previous restrictions on private plots were removed by Council of Ministers' decrees issued in July and August 1973, obviously in order to raise production. Figures are from John R. Lampe, *The Bulgarian Economy in the Twentieth Century* (New York, 1986), pp. 210–12.

43. *Darzhaven vestnik,* no. 34 (29 April 1969) published a decree that the name "construction troops" should be applied to penal work groups formerly called the Labor Service.

44. According to the national Komsomol secretary, there were about 12,000 "parasites" among the 1.3 million members of that youth organization. *Washington Post,* 11 May 1976. By 1981 Komsomol membership had grown to 1.4 million, with an ever increasing number of students refusing to join. John D. Bell, "Bulgaria: The Silent Partner," in M. M. Drachkovitch (ed.), *East Central Europe: Yesterday, Today, Tomorrow* (Stanford, Calif., 1982), p. 229.

45. *Rabotnichesko delo,* 6 June 1981, 26 December 1986. See also the government decree on the three categories (worker, specialist, and leader) for the new wage scale, 9 February 1988.

46. L. A. D. Dellin, "Economic Reforms: Bulgaria," in *Problems of Communism* (September–October 1970), pp. 44–52. New Economic Mechanism regulations appeared in *Darzhaven vestnik,* nos. 98, 99, and 100 (1970), with subsequent amendments.

47. Sofia radio, 12 June 1980; *Quarterly Economic Review* (1st Quarter 1981), p. 28.

48. *Rabotnichesko delo,* 1 April 1981.

49. Ibid., 30 June 1981, 19 December 1979, 19 December 1980, 10 April 1981, 26 December 1986.

50. S. D. Sergeev and A. F. Dobrokhotov, *Narodnaia Respublika Bolgariia* (Moscow, 1962), p. 236.

51. Ivan Pramov interview with *Zemedelske noviny* (Prague), 17 March 1976.

52. *Rabotnichesko delo,* 1 April 1981.

53. *Darzhaven vestnik,* no. 25 (28 March 1980) for the law; Sofia radio, 2 April 1981, for the 24 percent output from private plots. See also *Statisticheski godishnik* (1986), pp. 117, 134, and 136, for specific production figures.

54. On the techniques, see Z. Oshavkov et al. (eds.), *Izgrazhdane i razvitie na sotsialisticheskoto obshchestvo v Bolgariia* (Sofia, 1962), pp. 266–76.

55. Dellin, *Bulgaria,* p. 187. Sofia radio, 17 December 1974, broadcast a message from the new Bulgarian patriarch (Maxim) to the United Nations and the World Council of Churches, protesting Israeli imprisonment of a "clergyman-patriot."

56. Dellin, *Bulgaria,* p. 189. See also Ivan Sipkov, "Church and State in Bulgaria," in U.S. Senate, Committee on the Judiciary, *The Church and State Under Communism* (Washington, D.C., 1965), II, pp. 21–32.

57. Joseph B. Schectman, *Postwar Population Transfers in Europe, 1945–1955* (Philadelphia, 1962), pp. 345–54.

58. RFE, *Situation Report,* 28 April 1976; John D. Bell, "Bulgaria," in *YICA: 1987,* p. 280, citing an Amnesty International report; "Sofia Can Not Be Trusted," *Milliyet* (Istanbul), 10 March 1988, p. 13, in *FBIS-Western Europe,* 15 March 1988, p. 28.

59. All priests, monks, and nuns were forced to leave the country in 1952, according to Sipkov, "Church and State," pp. 29, 32. However, in June 1976 Todor Zhivkov called on Pope Paul VI, and Agostino Casaroli, secretary of the Vatican Council, reciprocated the visit later that same year. Sofia radio, 8 November 1976.

60. Dellin, *Bulgaria,* p. 192; Sipkov, "Church and State," p. 32; Heinz Siegert, *Bulgarien Heute* (Vienna, 1964), p. 130. Some 3,500 Jews lived in Sofia and another 650 at Plovdiv, according to the *San Francisco Sunday Examiner & Chronicle,* 8 November 1970.

61. Nikolay Mizov in *Politicheska prosvita,* no. 10 (1974); cited by RFE, *Situation Report,* 6 December 1974.

62. Zhivkov interview, *Le Monde,* 4 August 1976.

63. *Rabotnichesko delo,* 26 December 1975.

64. Sofia radio, 29 January 1981, for trade figures; *Darzhaven vestnik,* no. 65 (19 August 1980), gave the decree.

65. *Rabotnichesko delo,* 17 May 1975.

66. RFE, *Situation Report,* 29 July 1976.

67. *Rabotnichesko delo,* 22 January 1981; *Scinteia,* 10 October 1987.

68. Sofia radio, 23 February 1988; *FBIS-EEU,* 24 February 1988, p. 17.

69. *Statisticheski godishnik 1975,* p. 66.

70. RFE report (by Robert R. King), "Macedonian Questions and Bulgaria's Relations with Yugoslavia," 6 June 1975. For a historical background, see L. A. D. Dellin, "The Macedonian Problem in Communist Perspective," *Suedost-Forschungen* (Munich), 1969, pp. 238–64.

71. *Statisticheski godishnik* (1986), pp. 367–68.

72. John D. Bell, "Bulgaria," in *YICA: 1988,* pp. 245–53.

Chapter 3
Czechoslovak Socialist Republic

Before World War II, Czechoslovakia was the most prosperous and most democratic country in Eastern Europe. Its government was based on a Western-style constitution, which was adopted in 1920. Two successive presidents, Tomas Masaryk and Eduard Benes, guarded and nurtured the democratic principles laid down in the constitution. Although much of the world did not appear to be apprehensive regarding Nazi Germany, the absorption of Austria by the Third Reich in early 1938 and the claims by Hitler to border territory within Czechoslovakia gave the government in Prague considerable reason for alarm. In September the agreement at Munich countenanced the transfer of this area to Nazi rule; thus began the process that would lead to the end of freedom for Czechoslovakia. The peace that the British prime minister thought he had purchased at Munich lasted only six months, and the remainder of Czechoslovakia fell under Nazi domination until World War II had almost ended.

From the moment that the Red Army crossed the Czechoslovak frontier in October 1944, indigenous communists began to move into key positions from which to assume control over the country. The Italian and French comrades were also making rapid gains, but Stalin may have been uncertain how the West would react to open seizure of power in Czechoslovakia. As a result, the communists used political means to fulfill a long-standing ambition: gaining control over a country through a coalition government.[1] This process took time and provided a brief respite for Czechoslovak freedom until February 1948; at that time the communists executed a bloodless coup and established a people's democracy.

CONSTITUTIONAL FRAMEWORK

Superficially the new regime, which was based on a constitution adopted in May 1948, was similar to those in other Soviet satellites because it combined Marxism with several features of the old "bourgeois" system. There were many reasons for this decision. The constitution was designed to mask the true nature of communist rule by providing a facade of democratic respectability.[2] The existence of a form of coalition government was also an important factor because many of the provisions in the constitution had been formulated before the communists seized power.

The Constitution of 1960. The draft of a new constitution received approval in July 1960 from the National Assembly, or legislature, only after it had been sanctioned by the Central Committee of the Czechoslovak Communist Party. Any attempt to explain why the party chose this particular time to adopt a new basic law would be difficult, although the rationale behind the step is fairly clear. The first and presumably main reason was ideological in nature. By adopting a new "socialist" constitution the party hoped to strengthen its position. The document also seems to have been intended to show that Czechoslovakia had successfully laid the foundations of socialism and to justify the policies that the communists had followed since gaining control. It thus represented an adaptation to the Soviet system.

Although the 1960 constitution has no more real meaning than its predecessor, it did have propaganda value among other communist regimes in Eastern Europe. The party could proclaim that Czechoslovakia was the second country in the world to have achieved socialism. The document summarizes various claimed achievements in legal form and outlines a program for the transition from socialism to communism. The preamble states that "people's democracy, as a way of socialism, has fully proved itself" and has brought Czechoslovakia "to the victory of socialism."[3] The country is allegedly "proceeding toward the construction of an advanced socialist society and gathering strength for the transition to communism."

The 1968 Constitutional Law. On 1 January 1969 a federal system with separate governments for the ten million Czechs and four million Slovaks went into effect in the Czech Socialist Republic and the Slovak Socialist Republic, respectively.[4] Federal authorities maintain exclusive jurisdiction over foreign policy, national defense, natural resources, and protection of the constitution. Joint control by the federation and the two republics is exercised over planning, currency, prices, industry, agriculture, transportation, communications and mass media, labor, wages and social policies, and the police. Education and culture are exclusively reserved for the governments of the two republics.

The ultimate success of the new arrangement will also depend on the USSR, which in general has been less than enthusiastic toward regionalism. Recent information seems to indicate that this negative attitude prevails, because the Soviets desire as little change as possible. The years since the Warsaw Pact invasion have seen an increased tightening of control and greater centralization, culminating in the May 1975 election of Gustav Husak, party leader and National Front chairman, as president of the republic. However, seven constitutional laws, adopted between 1969 and 1983, deal with specific additions such as a new Defense Council.[5]

The Government. Czechoslovakia is typical among communist-dominated states in that it has a real government (the communist party) and a formal government, a facade that carries out administration for the party, which alone makes policy. The formal government performs three functions: executive, legislative, and judicial. This artificial division is for only discussion purposes because no real separation of powers exists. Nor is there any genuine system of checks and balances that might prevent arbitrary abuse of governmental authority, which is subject only to party controls.

The executive branch of the formal government consists of the president of the republic and the cabinet. The president is elected by and is accountable to the Federal Assembly as the representative of state power. Although East Germany followed other satellites in installing a collective head of state, Czechoslovakia did not do so. Its constitution provides for a president having real executive functions; this is also the situation in Romania.

The Czechoslovak communists apparently decided to retain the one-man presidency rather than to adopt the standard presidium for two reasons. First, the party was trying to capitalize on the prestige and stature that the office had acquired under Presidents Masaryk (1918–1935) and Benes (1935–1938; 1945–1948). Second, the office represented a valuable political asset. Each of the five communist presidents (Klement Gottwald, 1948–1953; Antonin Zapotocky, 1953–1957; Antonin Novotny, 1957–1968; Ludvik Svoboda, 1968–1975; and Gustav Husak, 1975–to present) was eager to occupy Hradcany Castle and cloak himself with the mantle of respectability. Attempts to abolish the presidency have also been complicated by the fact that until 1968 the office had been occupied by the top leader of the communist party; this changed in December 1987, when Husak resigned from the latter position.[6] His term as president expires in 1991, although he may retire before then.

The duties of the Czechoslovak president include most of those discharged by chiefs of states that have parliamentary systems of government. He must sign all laws enacted by the legislature but may not veto legislation. He can declare a session of the Federal Assembly ended, although his authority to dissolve it is limited to cases in which the two chambers are in disagreement. The president represents the state in foreign relations, negotiates and ratifies treaties, and appoints and receives envoys. He has the right but not the obligation to submit a "state of the republic" message and recommend courses of action. He is supreme commander of the armed forces.

The president is "elected" by the Federal Assembly for a term of five years, and there is no provision for impeachment. In theory he is responsible to the Federal Assembly for the conduct of his office. There is no provision, however, for enforcing this accountability. In practice each communist president's power and prestige were derived not from the presidency but from his position in the ruling party. An exception to this rule was Ludvik Svoboda.[7]

The federal cabinet is composed of the premier, an unspecified number of deputy premiers, and the ministers. It is defined as "the supreme executive organ of state power" and is responsible only to the Federal Assembly. The president has the right to appoint and recall the cabinet. He must do the latter if the Federal Assembly votes the cabinet out of office (collectively or individually). The federal cabinet is organized into three distinct levels of authority: first, the premier; second, the government presidium, which is not mentioned in the constitution; and, third, the federal Council of Ministers. The federal cabinet safeguards the fulfillment of state tasks, directs and controls the work of ministers and other central organs of administration, and issues ordinances that are based on and implement the laws. The federal ministers issue binding regulations on the strength of government ordinances. Thus the constitution seemingly has assigned to the federal cabinet a decisive executive role. In practice, however, this organ is nothing more than a body of routine administrators. Issues of importance are decided in advance by the Presidium of the communist party before they are even considered by the cabinet.[8]

If the federal cabinet really exercised the authority granted it by the constitution, the premier would hold more political power than the president. As matters stand, the federal premiership is assigned to a second- or third-ranking communist, whose actual power is directly connected with his position in the party oligarchy.[9] It is apparent that the federal premier may never attain the same importance that other communist premiers enjoy as long as the presidency is filled by a man of top rank. The government presidium, which is composed of the premier and (at present) nine deputy premiers, is empowered to control the activities of the various ministries and agencies and to direct and control the entire work of the cabinet.

The federal Council of Ministers patterns itself after the Soviet model. In 1988 it had 16 members. The cabinet has never exercised the role of supreme policymaker that was assigned to it by the constitution. The federal ministers have so little real importance that the trend has been to appoint mediocrities to many of the cabinet posts. This has also provided a supply of scapegoats who can be sacrificed when difficulties develop.[10]

The Legislative Branch.   According to the 1969 constitutional reform, the Federal Assembly is the supreme organ of state power and the sole statewide legislative body. In theory, this gives it a lawmaking monopoly and, thus, considerable influence over all other central government agencies within areas of exclusive jurisdiction. The powers of the Federal Assembly would seem to be almost unlimited since only it has the power to amend the constitution, from which it draws its authority.

The Federal Assembly is headed by a chairman. If he is a Czech, the first deputy chairman is a Slovak, or vice versa. The chairman presides over the assembly and its presidium, signs all laws and legislative measures, and reports to the assembly on any action taken by the 40-member presidium (which includes deputies from each chamber, half Czechs and half Slovaks from the Chamber of Nations) while the full body is not in session. What looks like an "inner presidium" represents the second level of authority. The chairman of the Federal Assembly and the deputy chairman are elected from the members of the regular presidium. This inner group handles all important matters and is the directing organ of the assembly. It disposes of current business, drafts the assembly's agenda, and controls the work of all committees. It is charged with the task of directing the work of the Federal Assembly and has the power to enact laws when the assembly is not in session. It is explicitly accountable to, and can be recalled by, the assembly.[11] This is the group that would act as the collective head of state in a typical communist government.

The Federal Assembly has 350 members, 200 of whom are in the Chamber of the People. The Chamber of Nations consists of 150 deputies, 75 of whom are Czechs and 75 Slovaks. The assembly normally meets in the spring for one session and in the fall for another, although more than two sessions may convene annually. The near-perfect attendance record at these sessions before 1968 was surpassed only by the record of unanimity. Between 1948 and 1960, there was never one dissenting vote and no amendment of any type was offered from the floor. Thanks to this harmony, the assembly enacted legislation with amazing speed. The only incidents that slowed down the proceedings were the "spontaneous outbursts of enthusiasm" and "stormy applause"—carefully graduated according to the speaker's importance—that greeted even such dry reports as the one on the annual budget.[12] Since the Soviet occupation, there has been little or no evidence of parliamentary debates akin to those of the 1968 "Prague Spring." All parliamentary deputies who actively participated in that reform movement have been weeded out or silenced.

The Judiciary.   The prewar judicial system in Czechoslovakia was not unlike those of other Western parliamentary democracies. Judges were appointed to life tenure by the president of the republic or the cabinet, and their independence was guaranteed. The law represented the foundation of the judicial system, and justice was its goal.

The present organization bears no resemblance to the former one. It is a copy of the Soviet model, specifically designed to serve the will of the party and allegedly intended to protect the socialist state, its social order, and the rights and true interests of its citizens and of the organizations of the working people.

Courts are assigned the task of educating citizens so that they will be devoted and loyal to their country and to the cause of socialism and will observe the laws and the rules of socialist conduct. These principles include respecting socialist property, maintaining labor discipline, meeting production quotas, informing about hostile acts, and fulfilling obligations imposed by the state.

Constitutional courts were established for the country as a whole and for each republic separately in 1968. The judicial bodies now consist of three tiers: the supreme courts of the federation, the Czech Socialist Republic (which began its activities on 1 May 1970), and the Slovak Socialist Republic; below the latter two are regional and district courts. Only one appeal is permitted from a lower instance. Professional and lay judges have equal status.

Qualifications for a judgeship include being at least 24 years of age and being known for devotion to "the purpose of socialism."[13] Professional judgeships have the added requirement of legal training. Judges are expected to interpret the laws and regulations in accordance with the "socialist legal spirit," which means that civil and criminal cases are basically political in nature and must be decided accordingly. Judges are accountable for their actions and are subject to recall.[14]

The traditional roles of judge, public prosecutor, and attorney are not applicable to Czechoslovak courts. The defense lawyer must place the interests of society above those of his client, and lawyer-client communications are often not privileged. Many of the powers formerly held by judges have been transferred to the prosecutor, who is in effect a direct representative of the party.

The Office of the Procurator General exercises "supervision over the precise fulfillment and observance of laws and other legal regulations." Its primary duties include the enforcement and strengthening of socialist legality, the implementation of party policies, and the education of the people in socialism. The procurator general of the Czechoslovak Socialist Republic (CSSR) is appointed by the president. He is responsible only to the Federal Assembly and probably has more power than any court in Czechoslovakia. The following provision eliminates any possible misunderstanding with regard to the role and responsibility of the procurator: "The organs of the procurator's office form a coherent, centralized system, headed by the procurator general of the CSSR, where lower procurators are subordinated to the higher ones. They discharge their functions independently of local organs."[15]

Local Government. The units of local government are organized on three levels: regional (twelve units), district (more than one hundred units), and local (about fourteen thousand units). The cities of Prague, Bratislava, and Brno form additional territorial units with regional status. The local administrative agencies, known as National Committees, are defined as "the organs of state power and administration in regions, districts, and localities," working "under the leadership of the Communist Party." Each committee has from 11 to 130 members and even more for the districts, depending on the level and population of the area. Members normally serve terms of four years, after direct elections.[16] The organization on each tier is identical. The executive organ for any National Committee is a council composed of the chairman, his deputy or deputies, the secretary, and varying numbers of members.

These local councils, although nominally chosen by the committeemen and responsible to them, are indirectly subordinate to their respective republic-level governments. The councils perform some legislative functions by issuing decrees and ordinances. They "direct and control the activity of the National Committees." The local councils are assisted by commissions, elected or appointed by the National Committee, that are responsible for the operation of various administrative activities at the local level. Of the 147,409 National Committee members in the Czech Socialist Republic alone, some 12,721 (8.6 percent) either resigned or were recalled during the 1969–1970 purge[17] of pro-Dubcek representatives.

The National Committees have gradually been given more administrative authority, but they are not permitted to make policy. Their task is to organize and direct all economic, social, and cultural activity in the specific area. Regional and district administrations are organized into functional departments for planning, finance, agriculture, transportation, and so on. There is no mandatory departmentalization for the local levels; they are permitted to organize, with the approval of the next higher level, as the particular needs of the area dictate. Most of the effort expended by local government is devoted to the fulfillment of the state economic plan from indigenous resources and to the strengthening of the political system. As is generally true in East European countries, increasing agricultural production and protecting socialist property are two of the priorities.

Local administrations, despite the extensive theoretical power they exercise in areas ranging from national defense to recreation programs, do little more than carry out the directives of higher authority and have no self-government in the true sense. The principle of democratic centralism, with each level subject to the absolute authority of the next higher level, is strictly enforced. Members of the party dominate all levels of government and ensure that the party remains in fact "the leading force in the state and society."

The Slovak National Council, which was once a powerful organ of local government with its own executive Board of Commissioners, enjoyed unique autonomy under the 1948 constitution. (For a listing of national minorities see Table 16.) The 1960 constitution abolished the Board of Commissioners and described the council as "the national organ of state power and administration in Slovakia" (Article 73). Its legislative and executive actions may be repealed by the National Assembly. This loss of autonomy generated many problems and caused much resentment among Slovak communists and noncommunists alike. This dissatisfaction certainly contributed to the overthrow of Antonin Novotny in 1968, the establishment of the federation on 1 January 1969, and a separate Slovak Socialist Republic with its own government. However, centralized planning for the whole country has been maintained by the communist party. Some restrictions were imposed on the autonomous status of Slovakia in the wake of "normalization." The Soviet Union has been cool toward any kind of regionalism because of its possible effects on the Ukraine or Azerbaidjan.

Table 16
NATIONALITY COMPOSITION OF CZECHOSLOVAKIA, 1987

Nationality	Population	Percentage of total
Czechs	10,019,222	64.3
Slovaks	4,752,508	30.5
Hungarians	592,116	3.8
Germans	62,328	0.4
Poles	62,328	0.4
Russians	15,582	0.1
Ukrainians	46,745	0.3
Others (Jews, Gypsies)	31,164	0.2
Total	15,581,993	100.0

SOURCE: CIA, *World Factbook 1987*, p. 62.

The Electoral System. Voting in Czechoslovakia is direct and universal. Elections are normally held every five years to send representatives to all levels of the government. The "democratic" character of these elections is ensured by procedures that are typical throughout the communist bloc. At the latest election, in 1986, there was only one candidate per seat and no write-in names were permitted. The ballot was merely a formality. The communist-dominated National Front, which includes three subordinate political parties and representatives of the mass organizations, has complete control over the conduct of elections and the tallying of the ballots. It nominates the members of the electoral commissions on all levels from among the party faithful. As a final measure of control, the National Front is given the right to recall any "unworthy members" who might be elected.

In past elections the National Front has held the exclusive right to nominate candidates for the electoral list. This reportedly is to be changed. Henceforth the right to nominate candidates will allegedly extend to political parties, meetings of workers, social organizations, and like groups. It is doubtful that the voters will be given a greater choice as to who "represents" them since only one candidate acceptable to the National Front—and thus, in reality, to the communist party—can appear on the ballot for each office.[18]

The party in Czechoslovakia shares the passion for unanimity that prevails throughout the communist world. Although there is no legal obligation to vote, the force of the party and the governmental apparatus is brought to bear on the individual so that the "will of the people" shall be properly expressed in support of the regime. According to official statistics, which the communists have made public, almost perfect success has been achieved. In the most recent general elections a reported 99.34 percent of the eleven million eligible voters turned out at the polls. Some 99.94 percent of them supported National Front candidates on the single-slate ballot.[19] The Federal Assembly, like all lower-level legislative bodies, is elected by means of a unified National Front ballot with candidates chosen from a fixed key. Sixty-six percent of the seats are reserved for communist party representatives, with the remaining third divided among four noncommunist parties and the so-called mass organizations for youth, women, trade unions, and so on.

Elections to all representative bodies are held simultaneously. During the campaign, citizens nominate candidates through the intermediary of organizations grouped in the National Front. The latter is a coalition of political parties (Communist Party of Czechoslovakia, Communist Party of Slovakia, Czechoslovak People's Party, Freedom Party, and Revival Party in Slovakia) and social organizations (Revolutionary Trade Union Movement, women's and youth movements, physical education, and other organizations). National Committees at all levels include about 200,000 deputies.[20]

Government Controls. Tight controls are the essence of most totalitarian states that seek to maintain the masses in submission, and Czechoslovakia represents no exception. The communist party, of course, is in control. It has followed the Soviet model in establishing a firm grip on the administrative apparatus.

Perhaps the decisive power in Czechoslovakia is still external, for the Soviet Union can influence the communist leaders in Prague via official channels. This method might be likened to the surface current of a stream: the real power is in the invisible undercurrent that is represented by Moscow's network of native and Soviet agents. This network has proven to be an efficient device for keeping the native Czechoslovak rulers and party in line, although force had to be applied in August 1968. After that intervention, the presence in Czechoslovakia of Soviet advisers was openly admitted.

The police provide the most effective internal control device, and it is the secret, not the uniformed, police that generate fear in those who might be tempted to deviate. Secret agents have been infiltrated into every organization of the

Czechoslovak Socialist Republic. The efforts of police functionaries are augmented by the extensive use of informers. The role of the procurator general's office has already been discussed and requires little further amplification, except to note that it is in a position to accuse and is supported by its power of judicial prosecution. The Central Commission of People's Control[21] also represents a control device. This agency may investigate, recommend corrective action, and take disciplinary measures that include initiation of criminal prosecution against party members.

The state economic plan at one time represented yet another effective method of control. It worked as a yardstick by which all persons were measured. Fulfillment of a goal or a quota used to be of the utmost importance to the individual because, in the communist world, results were taken as an indication of personal effort and intent. Failure, regardless of the cause, could and did have dire consequences for the person responsible for it. This led to falsified reports, among other things. During the Dubcek era a new system for economic management was gradually introduced that was based in part on the law of value, the relationship between supply and demand, and certain principles of a traditional market economy. Since the August 1968 occupation by USSR troops, this development has been reversed. Nevertheless, the Soviet words "reconstruction," "openness," and "acceleration" have become slogans of economic management in Czechoslovakia, although none had been translated into a radical reform of the system through April 1988.[22]

Problems of Administration. Czechoslovakia has experienced the same administrative difficulties that plague most of the communist bloc: bureaucratism, disloyalty, incompetence, and dishonesty. The hard core of the communist party was small in 1945, but many opportunists were inducted during the rapid expansion that followed. The initial shortage of trustworthy communists was compounded by the rapid growth of governmental machinery, which was brought about by extensive nationalization of the means of production.

Although the communists obtained the necessary manpower, the government continued to be filled with what had been people of the middle class. After these "bourgeois" individuals had been purged, incompetent and frequently untrustworthy communists filled the vacancies. Further cycles of purge and reorganization have followed, but inefficiency and apathy still prevail. The average educational level of persons in high government positions is quite low. For example, among all of the leading officials in the state administration in 1965, some 61 percent had only acquired an elementary school education, about 10 percent had attended lower special school, approximately 9 percent had completed their secondary education, and only about 9 percent were university graduates.[23]

A cumbersome administrative machinery has resulted in overlapping and poorly defined areas of responsibility, which is advantageous to any bureaucrat who prefers to remain anonymous and escape responsibility. An organization that accepts no excuse for failure makes experimentation dangerous. Thus, it is easy to understand why initiative has been stifled. A massive bureaucracy is also an ideal breeding place for corruption, and the spoils system has flourished. Stealing from the state seems to be an accepted practice in most communist-ruled countries. In recent times, this situation has come under criticism by the media, which seek to emulate Soviet *glasnost'*.

In efforts to alleviate some of the discontent resulting from such difficulties and to respond to the popular demand for the correction of wrongdoings in the Stalinist era, President Novotny was forced to dismiss Premier Viliam Siroky[24] in August 1963 and to agree to the removal of several other old Stalinists from high positions. Certainly, one of the factors contributing to these changes was pressure by younger liberals who wanted to modernize the system and reverse the trend toward deterioration. The reorganization of the government did not seem to satisfy the liberal elements but instead raised their hopes for more freedom and a higher standard of living. They maintained their pressure on the regime, and the Stalinist leadership repeatedly had to give way.

Novotny resigned on 5 January 1968 and was replaced by Alexander Dubcek, the first time that a Slovak had become the political leader of the country. The so-called Prague Spring did not last long, apparently because the Soviets feared "contamination" in other parts of Eastern Europe and perhaps in their own country. Dubcek seemed to weather the invasion by Warsaw Pact troops in August 1968, but his days as party leader were numbered. On 17 April 1969 he was succeeded by another Slovak, Gustav Husak, who is an opponent of Novotny and a victim of Stalinist justice but a much tougher man who does the bidding of Moscow. Dubcek reportedly refused to engage in self-criticism. Recalled from political exile as ambassador to Turkey, he was subsequently expelled from the party and from all his posts. (See Table 18 for the 1988 leadership.)

This 1968 crisis is discussed in the 1988 self-serving memoirs of Vasil Bilak, who has unkind words about both Novotny and Dubcek. The Soviet attitude is reflected in a TASS dispatch from Prague as well as in a Vienna interview with the chief editor of *Ogonek*.[25]

THE COMMUNIST PARTY: ORIGIN AND ACTIVITIES

Although Czechoslovakia had been known for its political democracy, since 1948 it has been a communist one-party state. This reversal of political, social, and economic orientation resulted from international developments and domestic conditions that culminated in the February 1948 coup. Because it took place when Soviet armed forces were not in the country, a fundamental question arises. What were the contributing factors that enabled the Communist Party of Czechoslovakia (*Komunisticka Strana Ceskoslovenska*—KSC) to seize and maintain control?

World War I and the resultant independence of Czechoslovakia had an important effect on the realignment of political parties in that territory. The outward appearance of communist party growth and legality provided a facade behind which doctrinal struggles took place. In the aftermath of severe criticism in 1928 of KSC leadership by Moscow at the sixth congress of the Comintern, Klement Gottwald became the general secretary of the Czechoslovak party.[26] Immediately on taking office he instituted a large-scale purge.

From 1930 until 1938, after the completed bolshevization of the party that reduced the membership to a mere 25,000 individuals, Gottwald concentrated on recruiting young, unskilled workers. This program, however, was not successful in producing a mass party. Official figures indicate that the KSC had 350,000 organized followers when it was founded but that it continued to lose strength and had fewer than 50,000 card-carrying members in 1938. After the Munich crisis in September of that year, the party was banned from all political activity. By the time the Germans completed their occupation of Czechoslovakia in March 1939, the majority of the KSC leadership had fled the country. By what appeared to be a prearranged plan, they took refuge abroad: in Moscow, London, or Paris.[27] Some communists were apprehended while trying to escape and were later sent to Nazi concentration camps.

Hitler's invasion of the USSR brought the communists into superficial cooperation with the Benes government in exile. A portent of the future was the signing in Moscow of the Soviet-Czechoslovak agreement in December 1943. Benes regarded the treaty as "one of the links in the postwar system of security."[28] Article 5 precluded Czechoslovak participation in any alliances that were not acceptable to the USSR. For the KSC, this was the first step toward its ultimate goal: communist control of the country.

Penetration Tactics. Benes decided to negotiate with the representatives of various political parties about the establishment of a government in the liberated areas of the country on the occasion of the signing of the aforementioned mutual assistance pact between Czechoslovakia and the Soviet Union. The most fatal concession proved to be the restriction on the number of political parties permitted after the war, with an implicit ban on the formation of any new parties. When Benes arrived in the USSR in March 1945, establishment of a provisional government took place in an atmosphere of intimidation, with Gottwald pressing home "the tremendous psychological and political advantages accruing to them [the communists] from the Red Army's control over Czechoslovakia and the overt Soviet support of their cause."[29] Benes accepted a plan for a "government of the National Front of Czechs and Slovaks" in which communists were assigned 8 of 25 cabinet seats. The communists demanded and obtained the important government ministries of Interior, Agriculture, and Information, among others.[30]

At the national, regional, and local levels, communist-dominated National Committees were acting as organs of government. Because these committees had not been regularly elected but established under Red Army occupation and hence under communist control, they were of a revolutionary nature. From these bases the KSC began an intense drive, during which the party made rapid strides toward attaining political and economic power. The communist program was facilitated by the withdrawal of the Red Army at the end of 1945, for that action could be interpreted by many Czechs and Slovaks as evidence of Soviet nonintervention.

A historian of the KSC has described how the political, social, and economic structure underwent a revolutionary assault through the confiscation of property, the prohibition of certain "bourgeois" political parties, and the transformation of parliament, "actuating the further development and consolidation of the revolution into a direct instrument for the socialist building of the country."[31] Meanwhile, because it was necessary for the KSC to increase its voting base to achieve parliamentary control, a communist recruitment campaign strove for mass enrollment.

Opportunists saw real advantages in joining the party, and significant inducements and the lack of any ideological tests resulted in great success for the recruiting effort. At the end of the war the party had 27,000 members. A year later, just before the general election, there were 1,159,164 registered communists.[32] (See Table 17 for the party's subsequent growth.) The objective of the KSC was to gain an absolute majority in the May 1946 voting for a Constituent Assembly to establish the postwar government. The results were a disappointment to the communists because they polled only 38 percent during the balloting. The KSC had received more votes than any other party, however, so communist leader Gottwald became premier in a cabinet of 26 members, only 9 of whom officially belonged to his party. The communists, with 38 percent of the votes, and the Social Democrats, with 13 percent, together obtained 151 (114 plus 37) of the 300 seats in the Constituent Assembly. Clearly, Zdenek Fierlinger, a fellow traveler and the leader of the Social Democratic Party, looked like the key to KSC strategy.

Cooperation was encouraged by Fierlinger, but this attempt failed in November 1947 when he was ousted and anticommunists took control of the Social Democratic Party. Other political groups employed parliamentary maneuvers to impede the KSC programs. A plot to murder three noncommunists—the deputy premier, the foreign minister, and the justice minister (who had been sent packages with explosives)—was discovered by the organs of security and the judiciary. An investigation suggested that the conspiracy had originated with a local KSC organization in Moravia. In addition, the Soviet demand that Czechoslovakia withdraw from announced participation in the Marshall Plan conference at Paris served to undermine the KSC's prestige. The decline in communist strength also showed on a poll conducted by the Institute of Public Opinion Research, a branch

Table 17
CZECHOSLOVAK COMMUNIST PARTY MEMBERSHIP, 1949–1988

Date	Members	Candidates	Total
May 1949	1,788,383	522,683	2,311,066
February 1951	1,518,144	159,299	1,677,443
June 1954	1,385,610	103,624	1,489,234
June 1958	—	—	1,422,100
July 1960	1,379,441	179,641	1,559,082
October 1962	1,588,589	92,230	1,680,819
July 1963	1,624,197	55,286	1,679,483
January 1965	*ca.* 1,627,000	*ca.* 57,000	*ca.* 1,684,000
January 1968	—	—	1,699,677
December 1970	—	—	1,173,183
January 1974	*ca.* 1,200,000	*ca.* 124,000	*ca.* 1,324,000
April 1976	1,214,975	167,885	1,382,860
April 1981	1,325,150	213,029	1,538,179
April 1988	1,607,587	109,429	1,717,016

SOURCES: *Rude pravo*, issues of 2 July 1949; 23 February 1951; 12 June 1954; 22 June 1958; 8 July 1960; 5 December 1962; 26 January 1975; 8 April 1981; *Zivot stany* (October 1963 and May 1965); Prague radio, 14 December 1970 and 21 April 1976; *Rude pravo*, 9 April 1988.

NOTES: The thirteenth KSC congress abolished candidate status and provided that by September 1966 all should be full members. In February 1973 candidate membership was reinstated.

The communist party, which was undergoing a thorough purge in 1970, reportedly had a healthy core, or *aktiv*, of 200,000 members. Prague radio, 1 July 1970. In the period 1968–1975 about 460,000 members (nearly one-third of the party) were purged. *Rude pravo*, 13 September 1975.

of the KSC-controlled Information Ministry.[33] Independent of the government, the institute was abolished after the February 1948 coup d'état.

Seizure of Control. The coup of February 1948 followed the resignation of twelve noncommunist cabinet officers in protest over the refusal by the interior minister, a KSC member, to replace several ranking police captains who were guilty of violating the constitutional rights of citizens. Under normal conditions this action would have forced new elections. But the communists utilized key organizations, such as workers' councils, the Interior (police) and Information ministries, a workers' militia armed by the communists, and the "action committees," for the purpose of executing a coup d'état. These last groups, which had been operating clandestinely, revealed themselves and took over the direction of all government and industrial activities.[34]

Communist pressure on Benes, a sick man, was severe. Demonstrations, the loss of government control to action committees, and the threat of civil war caused him to accede to the demands presented by Gottwald. A former Czechoslovak diplomat described the situation as follows: "Once Benes had come to the conclusion that the only alternative to surrender was a bloody civil war, with strong likelihood of direct or indirect Soviet intervention, he was incapable of acting otherwise."[35]

In assuming control of the country, Gottwald enjoyed many advantages that had not accrued to Lenin after his seizure of power in Russia. Some of these centered on the experience that the communists had gained during their active participation in the government over a three-year period before the coup. Major industries had been nationalized, and no large segment of the population offered opposition to the regime.[36]

Transmission Belts.   All political organizations, including the two communist parties (a separate one exists for Slovakia), comprise the National Front. It actually represents a coalition of KSC-dominated political groups and mass organizations. The retention of subordinate organizations has been useful in preserving the fiction that a multiparty system and political freedom exist in Czechoslovakia. These groups also act as transmission belts to population segments that reject doctrinaire communism. They are large enough for their support to be required in achieving communist objectives.

Ever since the adoption of the 1960 constitution, which proclaimed the KSC as the leading force in society, the National Front facade has been retained. Communist control over the National Front at the highest level is exercised through the KSC Presidium. The chairman or a deputy chairman of the National Front has always been a member of that body. As of 31 March 1970, the Presidium discontinued its activities to rehabilitate the victims of the Gottwald and Novotny regimes.[37]

Mass organizations are also necessary under the communist concept of population control. The communists will exploit the help of nonparty elements so long as they work for KSC purposes and are subordinate to its leadership. Mass organizations transmit the party line in their particular spheres of activity. These groups parallel in structure the organization of the ruling party, and communist control is maintained by the appointment of important KSC members to key positions at all levels.

From a political and an economic point of view the Revolutionary Trade Union Movement (ROH), which has a membership of 5.5 million, is the most important of these organizations. The ROH is a symbol of the worker-KSC alliance. It is, however, more concerned with party goals than with traditional West European trade union objectives. There are thirteen unions in the ROH. The organization is headed by Miroslav Zavadil,[38] who is not a member of the KSC Presidium.

The Czechoslovak Socialist Youth League (SSMC), like the Komsomol in the USSR, serves as an apprentice organization for the party, with membership beginning at the age of fifteen. Its propaganda seeks to develop an early dedication to communism. Advancement in industry and higher education are practically impossible for those who fail to join. Yet, according to newspaper comments, apathy and indifference are the hallmarks of the SSMC. This organization was launched in 1970 to unify the eighteen youth organizations that, during 1968 and 1969, had proliferated over the country.[39]

The Union for Cooperation with the Army claimed more than one million members organized into almost 11,300 basic units in 1988.[40] It performs the same function as the Soviet DOSAAF in support of paramilitary-technical training and also serves as an umbrella for voluntary, including all kinds of hobbies and sports, organizations. Another of these mass organizations is the USSR Friendship Society, which sponsors cultural and social ties with the Soviet Union. Much of its propaganda effort emphasizes Soviet scientific and cultural achievements, together with USSR support for Czechoslovakia; the objective, of course, is the strengthening of ties between the two countries. Communist control over mass organizations from the national down to the local level is facilitated by the parallel structure of all organizations, in which both vertical and horizontal controls are utilized. The mass organizations are also represented in federal legislative bodies.

The Communist Party.   The KSC, or Communist Party of Czechoslovakia, in 1988 had more than 1.7 million members, approximately 11 percent of the total population.[41] By comparison, the Communist Party of the Soviet Union (CPSU) has in its ranks only 6.7 percent of the total population of the USSR. The organizational structure of the KSC is established by party statute. Its pyramidal system, in which final authority is held by a small group at the top, closely parallels that of the CPSU. In reality, the operating procedures and the locus of power are entirely different from the formal structure.

The Presidium (formerly called the Politburo) of the Central Committee determines policies for the KSC. A self-perpetuating body that is formally elected by the Central Committee and is insulated from rank-and-file party members by several layers, the Presidium holds supreme authority. It currently numbers twelve full members and five candidates. (See Table 18.) During September–October 1970, the rank and file underwent the greatest purge in KSC history when 326,817 members lost their party cards. Combined with those who left the party of their own will, membership was reduced by 473,731 people or 28 percent of the total membership of 1,690,000 recorded on 1 January 1968.

The Secretariat is allegedly the administrative arm of the Presidium, but in fact it is the party organ of real authority. Its activity is officially restricted to the implementation of policy, and it is nominally subject to review by the Presidium. The Secretariat transmits party orders from top to bottom and supervises the

Table 18

CZECHOSLOVAK COMMUNIST PARTY LEADERSHIP, 1988

Presidium	Year of birth	Year elected	National Secretariat	National Government	Other positions
MEMBERS (12)					
Jakes, Milos	1922	1977	General-secretary		
Adamec, Ladislav	1926	1986		Deputy premier	Premier, Czech government
Bilak, Vasil	1917	1964	Secretary		Chairman, KSC Ideology Commission
Colotka, Peter	1925	1968		Deputy premier	Premier, Slovak government
Fojtik, Jan	1928	1988	Secretary		Member, KSC Ideology Commission
Hoffman, Karel	1924	1971	Secretary		
Husak, Gustav	1913	1968		Republic president	Chairman, National Front
Indra Alois	1921	1971			Chairman, Federal Assembly
Janak, Ignac	1930	1988			Member, KSS[a] First secretary
Kempny, Josef	1920	1969	Secretary	Chairman, Czech National Committee	
Lenart, Jozef	1923	1970[b]	Secretary	Chairman, National Economic Commission	Chairman, Slovak National Front
Strougal, Lubomir	1924	1968		Premier	
CANDIDATE MEMBERS (5)					
Haman, Josef	1933	1986			
Herman, Vladimir	1929	1986			
Hruskovic, Miloslav	1925	1971			Chairman, KSC R&D Commission
Pitra, Frantisek	1932	1986	Secretary		Chairman, KSC Agricultural Commission
Zavadil, Miroslav	1932	1988	Secretariat member		Chairman, trade unions

SOURCES: RFE, *East European Leadership List* (15 January 1988), pp. 7–11; Zdenek Suda, "Czechoslovakia," in *YICA: 1988*, pp. 253–54; Prague radio, 9 April 1988, in *FBIS-Eastern Europe*, 11 April 1988, pp. 15–20.
[a]Communist Party of Slovakia.
[b]Lenart also had served on the KSC Presidium from 1962 to 1968.

selection and activities of secretaries at lower party levels. Together with the secretaries of the region, district, and city committees and other full-time functionaries, this staff comprises the *apparatchiki* of the party. Seven of the nine secretaries at the national level are also Presidium members and thus the most powerful persons in the country.

The current Central Committee, which was elected at the seventeenth party congress in March 1986, consists of 135 full members and 62 candidates.[42] Theoretically, it is the official ruling organ of the KSC when the party congress is not in session. In reality, its powers are in the hands of the Presidium and the Secretariat. The Central Control and Audit Commission, with 52 members, is responsible for making disciplinary investigations, screening KSC members, and hearing appeals against decisions of lower party organs. Another of its functions is to audit the fiscal records of all KSC organizations. About one-half million members were purged from the party after the Soviet invasion (see Table 17), and Husak announced to the 1976 congress that about 390,000 were technically eligible for readmission.[43]

The seventeenth congress, to a large extent a routine event, heard leaders praise successes and achievements under the party's guidance. The people were told to conserve, work harder, economize, and increase production. Difficult and complicated international conditions were to blame for economic problems.

Mikhail Solomentsev headed the most important foreign delegation. As member of the Politburo and chairman of the CPSU Control Committee, he spoke authoritatively for Moscow, revealing that the Soviet leadership is determined to improve economic planning radically.

KSC general secretary Husak's speech lasted three hours and suggested that ideological orthodoxy would be maintained. Federal prime minister Strougal discussed economic reform and announced ambiguous organizational/management changes.[44] A new version of the party statutes was adopted, with little change in how the KSC is ruled. The congress also approved resolutions on economic and social development through 1990 and a general outlook for the period until the end of the century.

The Communist Party of Slovakia (KSS) has a special position within the formal structure of the KSC. The 1968 plan to federalize the KSC and establish a separate party organization for the Czech provinces, a counterpart to the KSS, was abandoned three years later. In 1988 there were about 450,000 Slovak communists who made up 26 percent of the party membership in Czechoslovakia; in contrast, the population of Slovakia was about 33.4 percent of the total for the country. The retention of the KSS as an "independent" organization is a concession to Slovak nationalist sentiment and tradition. The KSS presumably cherished the fiction of its equality with the KSC, but it is definitely subordinate. Firm KSC control is maintained by an interlocking directorate in which three full members of the ten-member KSS Presidium are also members or candidates in the

Presidium of the KSC. Statements by Slovak communist leaders emphasize their subordination. For instance, Jozef Lenart,[45] until 1988 KSS first secretary, was premier of the Czechoslovak government from 1963 through 1968, the Novotny and Dubcek eras.

Connecting the top party organs with the broad base of primary units are the territorially graduated levels that correspond to the state administrative structure. Below the national level are the regional organizations, each of which in turn is broken down into districts. At the city, district, and regional levels the roles of committee, bureau, and secretary have ascending importance. Orders from above, conveyed through the secretaries at the regional and district committees who are appointed by the next higher level, outweigh the influence of the grass roots.

The primary party units form the base of the organizational pyramid. Some 48,000 of these units exist (about 12,000 in Slovakia), mostly on an individual plant and office basis.[46] A minimum of three members is prescribed for a basic unit, and its establishment must be approved by the appropriate district or city committee. The essential functions of such units are to

Improve training in the fundamentals of communism

Safeguard the security of the party dictatorship

Disseminate the party line on all domestic and foreign policy

Recruit and train new party members

Ensure that party economic goals are fulfilled and that workers' morale is strengthened.[47]

Because of its structure the party is able to control the government's activities on all levels and to direct all its economic, social, and cultural undertakings. This very power, however, poses significant problems. It is apparent that the communists consider party discipline to be the most important factor in this process. The concept of democratic centralism is invoked to compel discipline.

The party has difficulty in recruiting young blood. This condition is reflected in the Czechoslovak Socialist Youth Union, which held its fourth national congress during 2–4 October 1987. The Young Pioneers claimed 75 percent of all 7- to 14-year-olds as members. They convened their fourth national conference in June 1987.[48] The party is getting mostly young opportunists who are ready to buy personal advantage via the youth movement. It would appear that after more than four decades in power, the party holds little attraction for the younger generation. Despite efforts to recruit young persons, the average age of KSC members is high, with young party members and candidates for membership (25 years old and younger) comprising only one-fourth of the total.[49] Apparently the majority of the

Table 19
CZECHOSLOVAK COMMUNIST PARTY SOCIAL COMPOSITION, 1966 AND 1988

	JANUARY 1966		MARCH 1988	
Occupational status	*Number of members*	*Percentage of total membership*	*Number of members*	*Percentage of total membership*
Industrial workers	511,917	30.2	765,000	45.0
Agricultural laborers	46,062	2.7 ⎱	102,000	6.0
Collective farmers	91,109	5.4 ⎰		
Government officials	113,350	6.7		
Public workers	27,246	1.6		
Scientific workers	3,796	0.2		
Engineering and technical workers	293,277	17.3	544,000	32.0
Workers in arts and culture	9,218	0.5		
Teachers and professors	64,787	3.8		
Students	6,372	0.4		
Housewives	68,659	4.0	289,000	17.0
Pensioners	293,577	17.4		
Other	168,641	9.8		
Total	1,698,011	100.0	1,700,000	100.0

SOURCES: *Zivot strany* (September 1966), as reported in *Czechoslovak Press Survey,* 13 October 1966; RFE, May 1988.

NOTE: Although no complete figures have been released since 1981, the new KSC leader Milos Jakes claimed that 50.2 percent of the 1,717,016 members are workers. *Rude pravo,* 8 April 1988.

early postwar membership, on a national scale, joined the party between 1945 and 1949 (especially during 1948–1949), when it was expedient to do so.

Another effort of the party is to achieve a member ratio of approximately 60 percent industrial workers, 20 percent collective farmers, and the remainder in other categories. Its social composition for 1966 and 1988 is shown in Table 19. The party is weakest among farmers and young persons. Problems with recruitment in general have been encountered in Slovakia because the Slovaks are a strongly religious (primarily Catholic) people who are more conservative than the Czechs. The depredations of the Red Army during the immediate postwar period are well remembered. In addition, despite the facade of unity, the Slovaks resent the traditional centralism emanating from Prague.[50] Ironically, the Czechs now speak of a "Slovak mafia," that is, too many Slovaks in the federal government.

DOMESTIC AND FOREIGN AFFAIRS

The party's formerly solid grip on the populace has loosened, but there appears to be no alternative to the communist regime at present. The population has become less critical and outspoken, perhaps because of the "social engineering" that has altered the class composition (see Table 20) and the traumatic experience of August 1968. Czech and Slovak domestic resistance movements against the Nazi occupation, the valor of Czechoslovak armed forces abroad in World War II, and the uprisings toward the end of that conflict all indicate that the people will act against tyranny in the future. Withdrawal and apathy, which have been evident since the Warsaw Pact invasion, could be interpreted as pragmatism in the face of a situation that cannot be changed for the time being. However, 300 writers, journalists, scientists, politicians, and others active in the short-lived movement to liberalize communist rule had the courage to sign Charter 77 in January 1977, petitioning the Prague regime to uphold constitutional rights and United Nations convenants as well as the Helsinki declaration.[51] Many of those who signed were arrested.

Charter 77 members continue to monitor violations of human rights within Czechoslovakia. Members have been subjected to harassment, imprisonment, and forced exile. In 1979, six well-known leaders of the group were sentenced to long prison terms. Charter 77, though still active, lost much of its vigor over the next two years. Antiregime activities now take the form of increased samizdat publication and religious dissent. About thirty arrests of Charter 77 members occurred before the seventeenth KSC congress, including former Foreign Minister Jiri Hajek, who was charged with antistate activities.

Charter 77 celebrated its tenth anniversary in 1987 with a total of 1,300 signatory members. It continued to chronicle human rights violations by releasing bulletins (*Informace o Charte*) that included 197 documents over the first decade of its existence. A most unusual event occurred when the U.S. ambassador gave a dinner in September 1987 for Charter leaders. No arrests were made,[52] and all of the invitees attended.

Economic Planning.   The Czechoslovak communist regime, encountering difficulties, has found no effective means to facilitate the execution of its plans. Unforeseen circumstances forced the government to abandon its collapsing third five-year plan in 1962. An emergency one-year plan was subsequently introduced for 1963. Although its goals were eventually reported to have been attained, they were met only after various adjustments. Makeshift annual plans followed until 1966.

The fourth five-year plan in sequence was to guide the economy through 1970, and a different and more realistic approach could be seen in its details. Instead of setting rigid quotas or goals for the entire period, it planned for only twelve months at a time. Subsequent years had variable targets, with considerable

Table 20
CLASS COMPOSITION OF CZECHOSLOVAKIA, 1945, 1961, AND 1985

	1945		1961		1985	
Class	*Number*	*Percentage*	*Number*	*Percentage*	*Number*	*Percentage*
Factory workers	7,650,000	53.5	7,738,000	56.3	7,445,000	48.1
Office employees	1,810,000	12.7	3,834,000	27.9	6,301,000	40.7
Collectivized farmers	—	—	1,466,000	10.7	1,353,000	8.8
Cooperative workers	—	—	164,000	1.2	141,000	0.9
Private farmers	3,000,000	21.0	484,000	3.5	—	—
Craftsmen	960,000	6.7	51,000	0.3	33,000	0.2
Capitalists	880,000	6.1	—	—	—	—
Professionals	—	—	9,000	0.1	16,000	0.1
Others	—	—	—	—	189,000	1.2
Total	14,300,000	100.0	13,746,000	100.0	15,478,000	100.0

SOURCES: V. Srb, "Thirty Years of Population Developments in Socialist Czechoslovakia," *Demografie,* no. 2 (1975), pp. 97–105; *Statisticka rocenka CSR 1980* (Prague, 1980), p. 97, *1986,* p. 95.

latitude to allow for setbacks. Thus, the chances for a "successful plan" were increased, and the attendant propaganda value was enhanced.

The Czechoslovak economy has shown significant growth beyond the goals of the fifth consecutive five-year plan (1971–1975), although shortcomings in several sectors have become evident. Power, fuel, labor productivity, and agricultural problems still represent weaknesses.[53] With the success of the fifth five-year plan, ambitious goals were set for the sixth five-year plan. For example, industrial production was supposed to increase by 32–34 percent, industrial exports by nearly 50 percent, and market supplies by about 25 percent.[54] The prospects of attaining these goals became jeopardized by an adverse foreign trade balance, due particularly to the increase in Soviet and world oil prices. Petroleum imports from the USSR totaled 15.5 million tons during 1975, at a cost that had quadrupled since 1971.

With the exception of the years 1965–1968, Czechoslovak economic planning has been under the distinct influence of doctrinaire Marxist thinking. This adherence to the classics handicapped the communists with an overabundance of heavy industrial products and a consequent shortage of consumer goods.

Nonetheless, the Czechoslovak economy has proven beneficial to the economic growth of the Soviet Union and other East European countries.

A low population growth rate during the 1960s compelled the Czechs and Slovaks to take a closer look at their utilization of manpower.[55] By 1976 Czechoslovakia's birthrate was the highest in Europe, but it will take some time before this phenomenon affects the labor force. The economy has reached the limit of its labor potential, and further expansion will be predicated on greater efficiency in agriculture and industrial productivity. The latter has recently declined (see Table 21), and private enterprise has been thwarted by a continued purge over the years. In 1955 approximately forty-eight thousand private entrepreneurs remained within the economic system, but by 1959 their number had dropped to nine thousand. A limited revival of private enterprise was allowed after 1964, and by 1979 some seven thousand artisans were working. About 6 percent of the farmland was still in private hands as of 1985. (See Table 22.)

Table 21
DEVELOPMENT OF THE CZECHOSLOVAK ECONOMY, 1980–1990 (PLAN)
(Changes compared with the preceding year plan in percentages)

	1980		1985		1986–1990
Index	*Target*	*Fulfillment*	*Target*	*Fulfillment*	*Plan*
National income	3.7	3.0	3.2	2.7	18–19
Industrial production	4.0	3.2	3.0	3.2	15–18
Agricultural production	7.2	6.0	1.0	−1.6	6–17
Investments	2.4	1.2	1.1	4.9	10–12

SOURCES: *Rude pravo*, 23 January 1981; *Quarterly Economic Review* (2d Quarter 1981), p. 7; *Business Eastern Europe* 10, no. 15 (10 April 1981), p. 116; Economist Intelligence Unit, *Country Profile: Czechoslovakia, 1986–87* (London, 1986), p. 10; Radio Free Europe, May 1988.

Another weakness in the Czechoslovak economy is overspecialization, with a disproportionate emphasis on certain areas of the economy and a concurrent neglect of others. A prime example is found in the transportation system, wherein railroads have received the benefit of technological advances and improvements while roads and highways have been neglected. The economic situation in Czechoslovakia, as in most communist countries, reflects the imbalance in planning that results from a narrow and specialized approach.

During the fifth five-year plan, one of the seven principles of financing and monetary policy dealt with that problem in the same frame of mind. One expert called upon the authorities[56] to start regulation of investments and at the same time to ensure that the necessary financial means are available for projects included in the plan investments. . . . In contrast to the years 1967–1969, when the prevailing principle was that investments are made by those who have money, without there being an order of precedence as to how the means are to be expended, now the priorities are determined strictly by the State plan of investments.

During 1970, on the eve of the fifth five-year plan, federal subsidies were running at 38.5 billion Czechoslovak crowns (an increase of 2.7 billion crowns from 1969). By early 1981, about 15 percent of work time was being wasted overall, with levels in the construction industry reaching twice that.[57]

Czechoslovakia's sluggish economic performance during the mid-1970s has led to a program of economic reform, albeit of a limited nature. A pilot scheme, launched in March 1978, applied to a small section of the economy. Proposals were announced in 1980 for a comprehensive reform known as "Set of Measures for Improvement of the System of Planned Management in the National Economy After 1980," which was intended to encourage more cost-effective production and higher-quality products by rewarding skill or innovation and penalizing poor performance. Suggestions have circulated to eliminate the five-year planning cycles, replacing them with a more flexible ad hoc system. Two- or three-year cycles may be introduced in the future.[58]

During the mid-1980s, Czechoslovakia suffered from the same economic problems as the other bloc states. Statements by KSC leaders indicated disagreement, with older leaders apparently unwilling to introduce radical change. During 1987 performance of the economy remained substandard, with unsold merchandise increasing to 18 billion crowns ($3 billion). Gross national product grew by only 2 percent, compared with a target of 3.1 percent. Two Central Committee plenums of October and December 1987 adopted measures based partly on the Soviet reform model that do not promise any radical change in this situation.[59]

Table 22

AGRICULTURAL LAND DISTRIBUTION IN CZECHOSLOVAKIA, 1985

Type of unit	ARABLE LAND	
	Area in hectares	*Percent of total*
Collective farms	4,282,000	63.0
State farms	2,076,000	30.6
Private farms and others	436,000	6.4
Total	6,794,000	100.0

SOURCE: *Statisticheskii ezhegodnik stran-chlenov Soveta Ekonomicheskoi Vzaimopomoshchi* (Moscow, 1986), p. 168.

Industry. The extension of communist control over the country's vast industrial complex was facilitated through the nationalization policy started in October 1945 by the Czechoslovak coalition government. After this first wave of nationalization, about 40 percent of production (in certain exempted industries) still remained in private hands. A second wave beginning in 1948 brought nearly every type of industry and business under state operation. The seizure of wholesale and retail businesses and of all foreign trade occurred during this second period, after which only 5 percent of industrial production and 17 percent of the physical plants remained in private hands.[60]

Although Czechoslovakia's industrial output is a significant factor within the Soviet orbit, its products have failed to regain the prestige they once enjoyed on the world scene. The craftsmanship and skills of earlier days are not apparent today. The quantity of the output has remained significant, but its quality has deteriorated. One reason for this may be that bloc requirements were initially, and are even now, less stringent than those imposed by prewar customers. Another, certainly, is that the USSR has been exploiting all East European countries by paying lower than world market prices, and inferior products help to make up for this price reduction.

The importance of Czechoslovak industry to the bloc is most evident in its supplying of certain special requirements of the other countries. Eastern Europe, including the Soviet Union, has relied heavily on Czechoslovak machinery in building up its industrial sector. Entire plants are manufactured in Czechoslovakia for shipment and installation throughout the bloc. More than three-fourths of all types of machinery made in the world are available from Czechoslovakia. A considerable part of its industrial production involves armaments; as a result, Czechoslovakia has often been referred to as the arsenal of Eastern Europe. Also, arms captured from insurgent forces in many of the world's trouble spots have been found to have originated there.

A long-term objective involves replacement of energy from fossil fuels with hydroelectric and nuclear power, with the fossil fuel plant use declining by half and hydroelectric and nuclear power growing five-fold by 2020. Smoke stacks will disappear, and industry should change radically. During 1987, nuclear power plants produced 29 percent of the country's electricity.[61]

Agriculture. Nationalization has not been quite so thorough in the agricultural sector of the economy as it has in industry. Nevertheless, through expropriation of large landholdings the communists were able to exert influence and control over agriculture relatively easily. Six months before the 1948 seizure of power, private farms had already been limited to 50 hectares each. From this base, a collectivization program was initiated. When Stalin died in 1953, it came to a temporary halt; two years later the program had regained momentum.

To centralize control over agriculture further, many of the weaker and less successful collective farms have been amalgamated into a state farm system. In addition to communist ideological considerations, the idea of more profitably applying the advantages of large-scale production and improved methods of management may have been behind this policy. However, during 1960 to 1965 agricultural output in Czechoslovakia was actually below that of 1936. Cooperative farming has suffered a net loss of 224,000 workers since 1961, leaving in 1975 a labor force of 1,240,000 for this sector. By the end of 1984, it had grown to 1,353,000.[62]

In general, the agricultural economy has been beset with numerous difficulties. Output has fallen far short of established quotas and expectations. Up to World War II, Czechoslovakia was almost self-sufficient in food. During 1974 the country had a trade deficit of 2.5 billion crowns in agricultural commodities, and food products made up more than 10 percent of its total import trade, including more than one million tons of grain. In 1976 the agricultural production deficit totaled 16 percent. Agricultural production declined in 1979, with gross output 3.9 percent below that of 1978. However, for 1980, it was only 0.8 less than the planned increase of 6.8 points. During 1987, gross farm production increased by only 0.9 percent over the previous year.[63]

The total number of farm workers dropped from more than 3 million before the war to fewer than 1.2 million in 1979. Only about 11 percent of the population was engaged in agriculture.[64] Each farmer is permitted to cultivate a private plot of land that can be up to an acre in size, and he may have a cow to provide dairy products for his family. (For the distribution of agricultural land in Czechoslovakia, which is almost 94 percent collectivized or nationalized, see Table 22.)

Agricultural progress in Czechoslovakia and in the other communist-dominated countries is predicated on one of two developments. The first, and quickest, way to increase production is to return the land to individual farmers. The private entrepreneur, who owns his land and livestock, is concerned about erosion, weeds, waste, and the well-being and care of his animals and equipment. Pride in ownership, which is missing from the collective, stimulates the individual farmer into actions that rarely occur under the present system. Such a drastic measure, however, is unlikely to be adopted under a firmly established communist regime, although this did happen in Poland after October 1956 and even earlier in Yugoslavia.

A second development appears to be in consonance with theoretical policies in several communist-ruled states, but it would take many years to complete. It consists of achieving vertical integration by turning farms into factories, with agricultural workers being indoctrinated along the same line as their counterparts in the industrial plants. An essential prerequisite for this program is the passing from the scene of the current generation of farm workers, most of whom are becoming old (the average age is over 63) and have grown up on the land they are now forced to cultivate for the benefit of the state. The majority are women. Many are malcontents who long for the "good old days." The eradication of this group might lead to an atmosphere somewhat like that found in a factory. A wage system, patterned after that of the industrial program in theory, could provide incentives and bonuses. A scientific, technological, and impersonal approach to agriculture is envisioned, of course, under the current state farm system.[65]

Church-State Relations.   Roman Catholicism was the dominant force in Czechoslovak religious history until the Reformation, which established Protestantism throughout Bohemia and Moravia. Forcible re-Catholicization after 1620 again established Roman Catholicism as the dominant church in these two western provinces. At the same time, it stifled the religious zeal and devotion of the Czechs. Unlike some of the other East Europeans, the Czechs have been tolerant and even indifferent toward religion as a rule. In Slovakia, the Catholic church still plays a considerable role, especially in rural areas. But the Protestant minority there, which is larger than that in the Czech provinces, remains equally active. Throughout the Czechoslovak state, however, all religious schools, orders, and publications have been abolished. Suppression of the clergy has been intermittently relaxed as the tactics of party leaders have varied.

In 1952 relations with the Vatican were severed. Even before that date, the regime had imprisoned numerous high-ranking clergymen. In 1963, when the Soviet Union attempted to improve relations with the Vatican, the authorities in Prague released a number of those jailed. Yet there is no noticeable change in the basically hostile attitude toward any kind of religion, and an Institute of Scientific Atheism has been established in connection with Bratislava University. The church does not appear to have much potential for active resistance to the current regime because all its activities are effectively controlled. Negotiations with the Vatican brought about the departure from Czechoslovakia of Archbishop (later Cardinal) Josef Beran, who died in Rome, and the appointment of Bishop Frantisek Tomasek as apostolic administrator. By 1970, however, new restrictions had been imposed on religious activities.

Antireligious propaganda and efforts to suppress religion seemed to decline during the late 1970s but gained new momentum at the beginning of the current decade. About a hundred priests and clergymen are being held in prisons. Lay believers and many others have been placed in psychiatric clinics under police surveillance. For more than ten years, Jewish congregations have had no chief rabbi. Before the communists seized power, every Christian diocese operated its own institute of higher theological studies. Today, only two divinity schools exist in the entire country. Several times as many applicants as places allotted by the regime compete for admission. In the Prague archdiocese, each priest administers three or more parishes; in Moravia, the ratio is one to nine. Cardinal Tomasek commented in a pastoral letter[66] on the shortage of priests and the difficult conditions under which they work, even though 60 percent of the population is Roman Catholic.

Two government-controlled organizations for clergy have been established: Pacem in Terris (for Roman Catholic priests) and Christian Peace Conference (for Protestant and Orthodox clergy). Although both are ostensibly independent, they in fact serve the communist regime. Members willingly promote the party's policies within their church communities. As a rule, all church dignitaries are forced to take an oath of loyalty to the Czechoslovak Socialist Republic before joining either organization. Antichurch restrictions continued into 1988, the 40th year of harassment. The number of vacancies for bishops and archbishops increased as did delays in regime authorization for newly ordained priests, regardless of protests by Cardinal Tomasek. Despite such government policies, tens of thousands from among the faithful took part in annual pilgrimages to holy places.[67]

FOREIGN AFFAIRS

The Council for Mutual Economic Assistance (CMEA) and the Warsaw Pact provide the framework for the nature and extent of Czechoslovak activities within the Soviet sphere. Czechoslovakia was an original signatory to the statutes of both organizations, and it currently supports them in a comparatively wholehearted manner. The Soviet attempt to manipulate the controls of CMEA so that the other members will become increasingly dependent economically on the USSR has succeeded to some extent in the case of Czechoslovakia.

Almost all the petroleum (98 percent) used by the country comes from the Soviet Union, as do large proportions of the iron ore (83 percent) and cotton (57 percent) and a significant part of the nonferrous metals. During 1986 trade between the two countries represented more than 40 percent of Czechoslovakia's foreign trade.[68] Consequently the USSR is in a favorable position to exert economic pressure that should guarantee support by Czechoslovakia when and if required. Without petroleum and iron ore, Czechoslovakia would find it difficult to operate its industries and its transportation system. Strategically valuable uranium deposits also exist at Jachymov and Pribram;[69] these have been and may still be under Soviet control and supervision.

Intrabloc Relations. The substantial output of complete industrial installations by Czechoslovakia has assisted the expansion of heavy industry in the Soviet Union and other communist-dominated countries. As mentioned already, Czechoslovakia is the main supplier of machines and plants to the bloc. The specialization program of CMEA conflicts in many ways with the Czechoslovaks' new system of management. It is possible that this incompatibility will continue to grow rather than decrease.

Many of the East European communist leaders within the Soviet sphere are unhappy with CMEA because of certain features of the program and the resulting outside interference with what these men consider to be purely domestic matters. Czechoslovakia has also expressed dissatisfaction but for an entirely different reason. The Prague regime complains of lax enforcement procedures for CMEA decisions. Because of the country's heavy industrial output and contributions to CMEA, official Czechoslovak opinions must carry some weight. Still, the USSR holds the key to future economic success, and the leadership in Prague realizes this.

Since 1971 the CMEA International Investment Bank has granted credits to member countries for 73 projects, totaling 3.3 billion rubles. These concentrate on development of fuel and energy resources in the USSR as well as science and technology in general. Forty-five projects have been completed. The largest is the 2,750-kilometer-long Soiuz pipeline, which carries Soviet natural gas to Czechoslovakia and other East European countries.[70]

Czechoslovakia has been a member of the Warsaw Pact since 1955, and it apparently responds well to Soviet military directives. Like Hungary, Poland, and East Germany, Czechoslovakia has Soviet military personnel on its soil. Including security forces, the country is thought to have the equivalent of ten divisions available for deployment. These forces are well equipped with modern arms. The defensive capability of the Czechoslovak troops probably outweighs their offensive potential. The influence of the USSR is maintained throughout the armed forces by the placement of Soviet officers as advisers in the Prague high command.[71]

The production of arms and munitions makes Czechoslovakia a key member of the Warsaw Pact. With its industrial capacity and its relatively limited manpower, Czechoslovakia is an "ideal" associate of the Soviet Union. It is able to make a significant material contribution to the armed forces of the pact. Article 5 of the twenty-year treaty of 6 May 1970 even provides the basis for sending Czechoslovak troops to the Chinese border.[72]

Extrabloc Relations.   Foreign aid to countries outside the bloc has played an important part in Czechoslovakia's political and economic activities. Prague has spent more than all of the other East European states combined (except for the USSR) on foreign aid and technical assistance. The primary beneficiaries of its largess have been Egypt, Syria, Ghana, Guinea, Ethiopia, Sudan, Mali, India, Morocco, Cuba, Brazil, and Argentina. The political implications of the foreign aid and technical assistance programs have been repeatedly explained to the people by the Czechoslovak press to lessen internal resentment and resistance toward the program.

The regime in Prague follows Soviet policies throughout the Third World. Pronouncements of support, treaties of assistance and cooperation, trips abroad, and official visits by foreign dignitaries are orchestrated to harmonize with USSR initiatives. "Moral, material as well as political support for the Palestinian Liberation Organization, the Zimbabwe Patriotic Front, SWAPO in Namibia, and the African National Congress" all continue. Approximately three-fourths of the 5,000 foreign students studying in Czechoslovakia are from developing countries.[73] Trade with the People's Republic of China is modest but nonetheless important, representing virtually the only formal tie with that country. The 1981 agreement on trade and payments will supply Peking with metallurgical products, machinery, spare parts, motorcycles, and textile machinery in exchange for raw materials, canned food, and other consumer goods. The 1985 trade turnover amounted to 2.8 billion crowns, exports and imports almost balancing.[74]

The population has tended to blame the outflow of goods for the shortages experienced in certain commodities at home. Government officials have told the people that it has been necessary to conduct and continue the aid program for a number of reasons, the foremost being propagation of the socialist doctrine among neutralist or uncommitted countries. Another reason given has been the allegation that the West allegedly blocked Czechoslovakia from its normal channels of trade and that as a result new markets had to be found for the export of finished products and the import of needed raw materials. In recent years, however, economic aid to the developing areas has decreased considerably. This has especially been the case since August 1968.

During the 1960s Czechoslovakia also attempted gradually to reinstitute the trade ties with the West that had been so lucrative before World War II and that were cut off almost entirely immediately after the war by communist policy. The regime made important commercial agreements with Britain, France, Spain, the Scandinavian countries, and others.[75] Even the United States was approached by Czechoslovak officials. More recently, Czechoslovakia again has shown considerable interest in trade with the West. This trade has already resulted in a manageable adverse balance of payments, and that situation, in turn, makes the regime cautious about incurring debts that must be repaid either in hard currency or in quality exports. During 1987, the gross debt to the West had grown to $4 billion (net, $3 billion). It remained, nevertheless, the smallest in the Soviet bloc.

Conclusion. Aside from a possible replacement of the present leadership, other factors could intervene as agents of change in Czechoslovakia: eventual pressure from broad population strata or major difficulties in management of the economy. The lessons of Soviet military intervention have not been lost on the top party cadres. They realize the need for caution in conducting reform or independent policies. Domestic tranquility depends to a large extent on the comparison between expectations and realities. Any future party chief or collective leadership will need to assess soberly the domestic situation and weigh demands for change against the willingness of the USSR to allow what may become inevitable. If meaningful improvements are to take place in Czechoslovakia, these will have to go farther than just a change in the incumbent party general secretary[76] as occurred in December 1987.

NOTES

1. The basic agreement for a National Front government and an "action program" was announced in April 1945 at Kosice. For details of the Marxist view, see Ivan Bystrina, *Narodnaia demokratiia v Chekhoslovakii* (Moscow, 1961), pp. 196–205; translated into Russian from the original Czech.

2. H. Gordon Skilling, *Czechoslovakia's Interrupted Revolution* (Princeton, N.J., 1976), 924 p.

3. *Sbirka zakonu CSSR*, no. 100 (1960); English translation: [Czechoslovakia], *The Constitution of the Czechoslovak Socialist Republic* (Prague, 1964), 3d ed. Further references apply to this edition.

4. The constitutional law on the Czechoslovak federation, published in *Sbirka zakonu CSSR*, no. 143 (1968), was ratified on 31 October 1968. It supersedes most of the 1960 constitution except for Articles 1 through 38, which deal with the social order as well as the rights and duties of citizens. A Russian translation appears in B. A. Strashun (ed.), *Konstitutsii sotsialisticheskikh gosudarstv* (Moscow, 1987), vol. 2, pp. 173–217, together with later amendments.

5. Strashun, *Konstitutsii*, pp. 218–28.

6. *Frankfurter Allgemeine Zeitung*, 18 December 1987.

7. Svoboda commanded Czechoslovak troops in the USSR during World War II, and until March 1950 he served as defense minister. Arrested and jailed during 1952, he worked the next three years as an accountant on a collective farm and then returned to public life. Heinrich Kuhn (comp.), *Biographisches Handbuch der Tschechoslowakei* (Munich, 1969). On 20 April 1970, Svoboda received the Order of Lenin at a ceremony in Moscow. He died some ten years later. *Rude pravo*, 21 September 1979.

8. Edward Taborsky, *Communism in Czechoslovakia, 1948–1960* (Princeton, N.J., 1961), p. 200.

9. Since 1970, the federal premier has been Lubomir Strougal, who served during 1961–1965 as interior minister. His biography appears in Borys Lewytzkyj and Juliusz Stroynowski (eds.), *Who's Who in the Socialist Countries* (New York, 1978), p. 594.

10. Taborsky, *Communism in Czechoslovakia*, p. 201. Names of ministers are given by RFE, *East European Leadership List* (Munich: 15 January 1988), pp. 9–11. Four constitutional laws (1970–1983) deal with these ministries and are translated in Strashun, *Konstitutsii*, pp. 224–28.

11. RFE report by Henry Frank, "Czechoslovakia Becomes a Federation," 1 January 1969; Strashun, *Konstitutsii*.

12. Taborsky, *Communism in Czechoslovakia*, p. 256.

13. Same source as note 6 above. See also the interview with Justice Minister Jan Nemec in *Tvorba* (15 December 1976); translated in RFE, *Background Report*, 3 January 1977.

14. In this connection, see "Law on the Organization of Courts and Election of Judges," *Sbirka zakonu CSSR,* no. 19 (1970). On 27 May 1970, seven justices of the Supreme Court were dismissed.

15. Ibid., "Law on the Procurator's Office," no. 20 (1970). During that same year, a purge of public prosecutors took place.

16. "Constitutional Law on Extension of the Electoral Term for National Committees, National Councils, Federal Assembly, Supreme Court, Regional, District, and Military Courts," *Sbirka zakonu CSSR,* no. 117 (1969), extended the deadline for elections to 31 December 1971.

17. Deputy Interior Minister Antonin Balak in *Rude pravo,* 29 April 1970.

18. "Law on Elections to the National Assembly," in *Sbirka zakonu CSSR,* no. 113 (1967). This legislation had preceded the reform of 1 January 1969. An absolute majority (66 percent) of the candidates are members of the communist party. Zdenek Suda, "Czechoslovakia," in *Yearbook on International Communist Affairs: 1987* (Stanford, Calif., 1987), p. 286; henceforth, cited as *YICA.*

19. Radio Hvezda, 24 May 1986.

20. *Czechoslovak Life,* no. 5 (May 1981), p. 5.

21. "Law on the Commission of People's Control," *Sbirka zakonu CSSR,* no. 70 (1967); promulgated 29 June 1967. Modifications appeared in no. 85 (1968).

22. RFE report (by Harry Trend), "Return to Economic 'Normalcy' in Czechoslovakia," 20 June 1970. See "Principles of Restructuring" in *Rude pravo,* 1 March 1988, and interview with Jan Fojtik over Belgrade radio, 28 March 1988; *FBIS-Eastern Europe,* 8 April 1988, p. 6.

23. *Kulturni tvorba,* 9 September 1965. The remaining 11 percent presumably had not even completed elementary school.

24. His biography in Vladimir Krechler (ed.), *Prirucni slovnik k dejinam KSC* (Prague, 1964), vol. 2, p. 891, explains the dismissal on the basis of insufficiencies, unspecified errors, and poor health.

25. Prague radio, 26 June 1970. See the explanation in *Rude pravo,* 16 July 1970 and 11 December 1974 for Dubcek's ouster. Vasil Bilak, "Milestones of My Life," in *Nedelna pravda* (Bratislava), 4 and 11 March 1988; TASS dispatch in *Pravda* (Moscow), 5 January 1988; Vienna radio, 13 January 1988, in *FBIS-Soviet Union,* 25 January 1988, p. 36.

26. Josef Korbel, *The Communist Subversion of Czechoslovakia, 1938–1948* (Princeton, N.J., 1959), p. 28. Gottwald is eulogized in an article by Vasil Bilak, *Pravda* (Moscow), 23 November 1976.

27. For names see R. F. Staar, "Czechoslovakia," in Witold S. Sworakowski (ed.), *World Communism: A Handbook, 1918–1965* (Stanford, Calif., 1971), pp. 108–15.

28. Edward Benes, *Memoirs of Dr. Edward Benes* (London, 1954), p. 258.

29. Taborsky, *Communism in Czechoslovakia,* p. 13.

30. The separate communist parties of Czechoslovakia and Slovakia and four other political groups received three portfolios each. In addition, seven cabinet members qualified as "experts," including two communists and the left-leaning Defense Minister General Ludvik Svoboda. The communists also had two deputy premiers and the fellow-traveling

premier, Zdenek Fierlinger, who fulfilled Gottwald's directives. In this connection see Jozef Lettrich, "Czechoslovakia," in U.S. Senate, Committee on the Judiciary, *A Study of the Anatomy of Communist Takeovers* (Washington, D.C., 1966), pp. 17–25.

31. Jan Kozak, "How Parliament Can Play a Revolutionary Part in the Transition to Socialism," reprinted in U.S. House of Representatives, Committee on Un-American Activities, *The New Role of National Legislative Bodies in the Communist Conspiracy* (Washington, D.C., 1961), p. 17. See also his article on the years 1945–1948 in *Voprosy istorii KPSS* (Moscow), July–August 1962, pp. 72–91.

32. Paul E. Zinner, *Communist Strategy and Tactics in Czechoslovakia* (New York, 1963), p. 124. The author cites official party sources.

33. Taborsky, *Communism in Czechoslovakia*, p. 19.

34. Pavel Tigrid, "The Prague Coup of 1948," in Thomas T. Hammond (ed.), *The Anatomy of Communist Takeovers* (New Haven, Conn., 1975), pp. 399–432.

35. Edward Taborsky, "The Triumph and Disaster of Edward Benes," *Foreign Affairs* (July 1958), p. 684. The 40th anniversary of the coup was celebrated by 80,000 people, according to Prague radio, 25 February 1988; *FBIS-Eastern Europe*, 26 February 1988, p. 24. Milos Jakes spoke on television the day before.

36. During this initial period the communists applied the Leninist principle of "kto kogo?" (meaning "who will eliminate whom?"), according to Bystrina, *Narodnaia demokratiia*, pp. 263–64.

37. Prague radio, 7 April 1970. According to the same source, on 8 July 1970 the rehabilitation law was amended to prevent "acquittal of persons who had been justly sentenced under legislation valid at that [i.e., Stalinist] time."

38. His predecessor, Karel Hoffman, became a secretary of the KSC Central Committee.

39. Miloslav Dockal, chairman of the Youth Union, did not give new membership figures during his speech to the sixteenth KSC congress. *Rude pravo*, 11 April 1981.

40. Information from RFE, May 1988.

41. *Rude pravo*, 8 April 1988.

42. Ibid., 29 March 1986.

43. The KSS has been a separate organization theoretically since the 1939 occupation of Czechoslovakia, according to Krechler, *Prirucni slovnik k dejinam KSC,* 329–30. See *Pravda* (Bratislava), 21 March 1981, for statistics.

44. *Rude pravo*, 26 March 1986 for Solomentsev; *Rude pravo*, 25 and 26 March 1988, for Husak and Strougal.

45. His biography and those of other KSC Presidium and Secretariat members are given in Lewytzkyj and Stroynowski, *Who's Who in Socialist Countries*. KSS membership given on Prague radio, 14 April 1988; *FBIS-Eastern Europe*, 15 April 1988, p. 20.

46. Information from RFE, May 1988.

47. Party rules were published by Heinrich Kuhn, *Der Kommunismus in der Tschechoslowakei* (Cologne, 1965), pp. 275–99. Husak stated that these "organizations represent

an immense force in daily contact with the broad sections of the peoples. Fewer directives, less bureaucracy, more direct contacts with the people—this must hold true in party work as well." Speech to the sixteenth KSC congress, broadcast over Prague radio, 6 April 1981.

48. *Tribuna,* 10 and 17 June 1987; *Mlada fronta,* 22 June 1988.

49. Husak, *World Marxist Review* (June 1976), p. 12.

50. Communists in predominantly rural Slovakia also probably resent allegations in the official KSC history that the Slovak uprising against the Germans in August 1944 had been started "without sufficient political preparation" and that the Communist Party of Slovakia had been penetrated by right-wingers who "weakened the revolutionary nature of the movement." Pavel Reiman (ed.) *Dejiny Komunisticke Strany Ceskoslovenska* (Prague, 1961), p. 450. Reiman served as director of the KSC History Institute at that time.

51. For documents on the "normalization" in Czechoslovakia, see Skilling, *Czechoslovakia's Interrupted Revolution.* The text of Charter 77 appeared in the *New York Times,* 27 January 1977, reprinted from *The New Leader* (31 January 1977).

52. David W. Paul, *Czechoslovakia,* (Boulder, Colo., 1981), pp. 85–88; *New York Times,* 11 May 1981; Zdenek Suda, "Czechoslovakia," in *YICA: 1988,* p. 257.

53. For an official account of economic affairs, see "Czechoslovakia Between the 14th and 15th Congresses of the Communist Party of Czechoslovakia," *Czechoslovak Economic Digest,* no. 1 (January 1976).

54. Lubomir Strougal, "Report on the Main Trends in Economic and Social Development in the Czechoslovak Socialist Republic in 1976–1980," *Rude pravo,* 14 April 1976; English translation in *Czechoslovak Economic Digest,* no. 4 (June 1976), p. 22.

55. Increases of employment totaled 450,000 during 1961–1965, some 330,000 in 1966–1970, but only 120,000 for 1971–1975. About 800,000 persons, or 28.3 percent of the labor force, changed industrial jobs in one year. Interview with official in federal Labor and Social Welfare Ministry, published by *Svet hospodarstvi,* 17 April 1970, pp. 1–2. Because of a labor shortage, Czechoslovakia had to import foreign workers from Poland, Yugoslavia, Vietnam, and Cyprus. RFE, *Situation Report,* 10 March 1976.

56. Leopold Ler, "Financial Policy in the Fifth Five-Year Plan," *Nova mysl* (May 1975); English translation in *Czechoslovak Economic Digest,* no. 5 (August 1975), pp. 6–7.

57. Article by Finance Minister Rudolf Rohlicek, "About Financial Policy in Czechoslovakia," in *Pravda* (Bratislava), 3 March 1970. Guidelines for 1976–1980 stress expansion of the engineering industry, according to RFE, *Situation Report,* 8 December 1976. *Czechoslovak Newsletter* 6, no. 2 (February 1981), p. 4.

58. *Business Eastern Europe* 10, no. 26 (26 June 1981), p. 205.

59. *Hospodarske noviny* (Prague), no. 30 (24 July 1987); Suda, *YICA: 1988,* pp. 254–56.

60. Bratislava radio, 28 October 1965.

61. *Hospodarske noviny,* cited by Paris radio, 10 March 1988; *FBIS-Eastern Europe,* 10 March 1988, p. 12.

62. *Statistical Survey of Czechoslovakia 1976,* pp. 16 and 56; *Statisticka rocenka CSSR 1986,* p. 95.

63. Bratislava radio, 27 November 1976; *Quarterly Economic Review* (2d Quarter 1981), p. 6. Prague radio, 29 January 1988, in *FBIS-Eastern Europe,* 19 February 1988, p. 13.

64. *Statisticka rocenka CSSR 1980,* p. 97.

65. Information on agricultural plans appeared in "Main Lines of Economic and Social Development in Czechoslovakia in 1981–1985," *Czechoslovak Digest,* no. 5 (March 1981), pp. 8–12; see also no. 9 (May 1981), pp. 16–17. The percentage of farmers is from CMEA, *Statisticheskii ezhegodnik 1987* (Moscow, 1987), p. 13.

66. *Katolicke noviny* (11 March 1981), p. 3; *Christian Science Monitor,* 2 June 1981.

67. Zdenek Suda in *YICA: 1988,* pp. 259–60.

68. CIA, *Handbook of Economic Statistics 1987,* pp. 103–4; RFE, May 1988.

69. In November 1980, an agreement signed with the USSR obligated Czechoslovakia to build a nuclear power station equipped with a 1000-MW Soviet-type pressurized water reactor at Malovice in southern Bohemia. Furthermore, a similar 1760-MW installation, consisting of four 440-MW reactors, will be constructed at Mochovce in southern Slovakia. *Quarterly Economic Review* (1st Quarter 1981), p. 7.

70. *Czechoslovak Digest,* no. 2 (26 January 1981), p. 7.

71. This has been simplified by a 1958 agreement on dual citizenship. The complete text appeared in J. Cerny and V. Cervenka (comps.), *Statni obcanstvi CSSR* (Prague, 1963), pp. 199–202.

72. Text in *Pravda* (Moscow), 7 May 1970.

73. *Czechoslovak Digest* (March 1981), p. 30, for the quotation; *Czechoslovak Life,* no. 5 (May 1981), pp. 24–25, on students.

74. [Czechoslovakia], *Statisticka rocenka CSSR 1985,* p. 445.

75. Czechoslovak foreign trade in 1986 ran at the rate of about 80 percent with other communist-ruled countries. CIA, *World Factbook 1987,* p. 63.

76. See the essay by Zdenek Suda, in *YICA: 1988,* pp. 253–65.

Chapter 4
German Democratic Republic

In both East and West Germany, the initial postwar policies of the occupation authorities were directed more toward reparations than rehabilitation. The USSR pursued this goal with an almost exaggerated zeal. During its brief tenure as the sole power in Berlin, for example, the Soviet Union removed 75 percent of all capital equipment. Also in the first several months, machinery from about nineteen hundred industrial enterprises in the Soviet occupation zone was either partly or completely dismantled and shipped to Moscow. This practice, coupled with a policy of extracting reparations from current production, violated the letter as well as the spirit of the Yalta and Potsdam agreements and seriously hampered economic recovery throughout East Germany for many years. It is estimated that reparations to the Soviet Union in the postwar period amounted to 66.4 billion marks.[1]

The industrial property of "war criminals, national socialists [Nazis], and militarists" underwent expropriation. These categories received broad interpretation, with the result that private enterprise was eliminated from all large and most medium-sized industrial firms.[2] In addition, control over approximately two hundred large firms whose plants had not been dismantled was given to Soviet joint stock companies (*Sowjetische Aktiengesellschaft*—SAG). By 1948 only 8 percent of all East German industry had been socialized, but 40 percent of the country's total industrial output originated from these enterprises. Another 25 or 30 percent was produced by SAG units. "A comparison of these two figures shows clearly that only small plants and a few medium-sized enterprises, especially in the manufacture of consumption goods, like textiles, had escaped socialization."[3]

In other directions the Soviets proceeded more cautiously. During 1944 and 1945 they still looked forward to the eventual reunification of Germany and the extension of "socialism" over the whole country. Thus the sovietization of their occupied zone was accomplished under a facade of democratization and antifascist activity that was designed to mislead both the noncommunist East Germans and the Western powers. The following measures were undertaken by the Soviet Union during this initial period:

The *Laender* or provinces were allowed legislatures, based on free elections.
All private banks and insurance companies suspended operations.
Widespread seizure of agricultural and industrial property was justified on
antifascist rather than anticapitalist grounds.
Political activity was encouraged, and "antifascist" parties were licensed
much sooner than in the Western zones.[4]

From the early days of the occupation, the USSR encouraged the formation of
political parties. The Communist Party of Germany (*Kommunistische Partei
Deutschlands*—KPD), which was re-established in June 1945 throughout East
Germany, came first, of course. Within a month, the Christian Democrats, Liberals, and Social Democrats followed. Using the typical "people's front" tactics that
had been adopted in other satellite countries, all four East German parties in July
1945 joined the Antifascist Democratic Bloc, which was subsequently renamed
the Democratic Bloc of Parties and Mass Organizations. In October 1949 this
became the National Front.[5] The communists apparently believed that they could
win control over East Germany through free elections, and they wanted to maintain at least the pretext of separate parties.

At first many politicians regarded the Soviet reforms as a positive step. The
socialists, during the summer and fall of 1945, actually suggested a merger of
their party with the KPD but were turned down by the communists.[6] By November
1945, however, the KPD had come to regard the Socialist party as a serious
competitor because it had a large following in the industrial areas. Despite the fact
that most socialists now opposed the move, a forced merger with the KPD was
effected in April 1946 to form the Socialist Unity Party of Germany (*Sozialistische Einheitspartei Deutschlands*—SED).

In the fall of 1946 the last relatively free elections were held in East Germany.
An active SED campaign and interference with the activities of the other parties
(such as forbidding rallies and banning candidates) still did not bring the absolute
majority victory that the communists had wanted. However, SED candidates were
given key positions in all five *Laender.*[7] This was also the last time that voters were
given any choice of candidates. Subsequent national elections have presented only
a single list on the ballot, and the voter has had no option but to approve it.

In late 1947 the SED formed from among its own membership a People's
Congress. Despite the fact that it had no popular basis, this body assumed the task
of establishing a government for East Germany. In March 1948 the congress
named a 400-member People's Council. This group, in turn, appointed a committee to draft a new constitution; this assignment was completed by October.

To add an element of legality, national elections were held in May 1949 for
representatives to the People's Congress. The ballot, however, consisted of a typical "unity list" that was packed with communists. The draft constitution received
no mention during the campaign. After the election, a new People's Congress

convened and promptly approved the constitution. The German Democratic Republic (*Deutsche Demokratische Republik*) was thus established. Its administrative agencies are located at Pankow, a borough of East Berlin, which violates agreements among the four occupation powers.

The congress also appointed a new People's Council, which declared itself the provisional People's Chamber, or parliament, and promulgated the new constitution. Because the basic law envisaged the People's Chamber as a popularly elected representative body, the fact that this body actually appointed itself gave the German Democratic Republic (GDR) the unique distinction of starting with a government that had no legitimacy and was, in fact, unconstitutional.

CONSTITUTIONS OF 1949 AND 1968

It has been noted that "a good constitution may be the backbone of a state or it may be window dressing."[8] Nowhere was window dressing more evident than in East Germany. Its first constitution provided for a strong central government based on a multiparty, parliamentary system. The power of government was concentrated in an elected representative body, the People's Chamber. The concept of separation of powers, which was common to the United States and most Western democracies, did not appear in the document. In many ways, however, the GDR's constitution[9] looked like a remarkably liberal document and it could have provided the basis for a stable and representative government.

> The East German constitution of 1949 was phrased so that, if properly implemented, a genuine democracy, in which basic rights were preserved, could have functioned under it. However, the wording of the Constitution also was framed so that, once the Communists were in control, they could interpret and apply it to maintain their system of centralistic statism. This was more patently recognized by the even less "democratic" constitutional system of 1968.[10]

It should be mentioned that the 1949 constitution had been written for all of Germany and purposely resembled the Weimar Constitution, on the assumption that the East and West zones would eventually be reunited. In regard to this prospect of reunification, it paralleled also the Basic Law in the Federal Republic of (West) Germany.[11] With its seventeen sections and 144 articles, the 1949 constitution was also similar to the West German legislation in being long, thorough, and complex.

The 1968 Socialist Constitution. In typical communist fashion, only two months elapsed between the establishment of a constitutional commission and the publication of a draft document. Eight weeks later, the People's Chamber incorporated several minor changes and gave its approval. A national referendum in

April 1968 polled 94.5 percent in favor, and the new basic law for the GDR went into effect. In October 1974 certain amendments to this constitution were introduced; the following discussion reflects these changes.[12]

Article 1 proclaims the GDR to be "a socialist state of workers and farmers" (the 1968 terminology had been "German nation") and its capital to be Berlin. The so-called National Front of political parties and mass organizations, however, rather than the (communist) Socialist Unity Party, is identified as the "alliance of all forces of the people" (Article 3).

Elections held in the GDR have been neither free nor secret; thus, ultimate power over the government does not reside with the people, as the 1968 constitution proclaims. Other paradoxes and contradictions appear in the constitution's extensive listing of civil rights.

Every citizen allegedly may "express his opinion freely and publicly," and "freedom of the press, radio, and television is guaranteed" (Article 27). The right of peaceful assembly is also supposedly guaranteed: "The use of material prerequisites for the unhindered exercise of this right of assembly, such as buildings, streets, and places of demonstration, printing works, and means of communication, is guaranteed" (Article 28).

Nevertheless, there are between three and seven thousand political prisoners in the GDR at any one time. Many of them are incarcerated on charges of "slander against the state" for exercising their constitutional rights of free speech and public assembly.[13]

Perhaps also of questionable validity is Article 103, which states that "every citizen may submit petitions (proposals, suggestions, applications, or grievances)" and that these petitioners "may be exposed to no disadvantage as a result of exercising this right." The demonstrations at Erfurt, Dresden, Frankfurt/Oder, and East Berlin toward the end of August 1968 represented a vocal grievance against the invasion of Czechoslovakia. The regime's answer included arrest and prison terms of from 15 to 27 months for each defendant. Ten years later, would-be emigrants to the Federal Republic of Germany were being arrested and sentenced for up to one year in prison.[14]

THE GOVERNMENT

The regimes of East and West Germany seem, at first sight, to have much in common. Both evolved from an occupation status in 1949, achieved formal sovereignty during 1954–1955, and now have military forces integrated with their respective alliance systems.[15] In the West, the Federal Republic of Germany has developed into a free democratic country whose political and economic growth has been the envy of neighboring states. The GDR, on the other hand, remains under the strongman rule of Erich Honecker, who continues to coordinate indigenous requirements with the interests of the Soviet Union and in return can count on its support and protection. It should be noted that the East German standard of living is higher than that of other bloc countries, including even the USSR.

Abolition of the Laender. The provinces, or *Laender,* were the traditional basic units of German government. Evolving from the past, they served as centers of political and social life. The 1949 GDR constitution recognized this and established the provinces as semiautonomous entities that were represented in the central government through an upper chamber of parliament.

In July 1952 the governments of the *Laender* and their legislative bodies were abolished by law. This action was technically unconstitutional, for Article 110 provided that any change in territory required either an amendment to the constitution or a plebiscite in the *Land* concerned. The dissolved provinces were replaced by fourteen administrative areas, called districts, each of which had fifteen or more counties. A fifteenth district was established for East Berlin. This move completely eliminated local government as a source of potential opposition and increased the power of the central government, thus assuring greater control by the ruling communist party.

With the elimination of the *Laender,* the political basis for the upper chamber of parliament disappeared. It continued in existence for several years to fulfill such constitutional requirements as the election of the president. In December 1958 it, too, was formally abolished. With this move, the legislative body of the GDR became unicameral, and the last vestige of federalism disappeared.

Elimination of the Presidency. In October 1949, two days after the adoption of the constitution and the day after the nominal transfer of administrative powers from the Soviet Military Administration to the East German regime, Wilhelm Pieck became the first and, as it turned out, the only president of the GDR. In 1953 he won re-election, and in 1957 his tenure was extended for a third term. This last action should have been preceded by a change in the constitution in that Article 101 required that the president be elected by a joint session of the two parliamentary chambers. By this time, of course, the upper house had become relatively meaningless. Thus it is possible that the regime considered the formality of an election not worth arranging.

In September 1960 Pieck died in office. Instead of holding an election to determine his successor, the People's Chamber voted, without debate, to amend the constitution. A 26-member Council of State, which was elected by the People's Chamber to a four-year term of office, superseded the presidency. This new body not only assumed the duties of chief of state but also was empowered to issue orders and interpret the law.[16] This step established for East Germany a collective executive with fairly sweeping powers. Walter Ulbricht was elected the chairman of the new State Council by the People's Chamber. He thus became the head of the state in which he already held the supreme authority as SED first secretary. This type of arrangement, which ensures the domination of a country by a single trusted communist, has prevailed from time to time both in the Soviet Union and in other East European countries. Ulbricht assumed the honorary position of SED chairman in 1971, and after his death in 1973, Willi Stoph succeeded him as chief of state. On 29 October 1976 party leader Erich Honecker assumed the chairmanship of the State Council. (See Table 23.)

The National Defense Council.   Called into being by legislation in February 1960, the National Defense Council has a chairman and at least twelve members. It remains the only leading governmental organ whose personnel are appointed by the Council of State (although it was established before the council). A law in September 1961 empowered this body to direct the defense and security of the state. All government agencies were required to carry out regulations and orders issued by the Defense Council. It was given even wider powers by a 1978 law, including the authority to order "a total or partial mobilization" and to act as a de facto emergency government.[17]

According to the January 1962 law on universal military training, the Defense Council is authorized to issue rules implementing this legislation. These appear as regulations in the official journal of laws. The defense minister also remains subordinate to the Defense Council, which is chaired by Erich Honecker. Because Honecker is also the SED general secretary, perhaps the functions of the minister have been kept vague on purpose. It is possible that the Defense Council is intended to become fully operative only in time of hostilities, paralleling the Soviet organ that has a similar name.

Government Organization and Control.   According to the 1968 constitution of East Germany, final authority allegedly rests with the people. Control is supposed to proceed upward to various popularly elected assemblies and councils at each level of government. In practice, this flow is reversed. Ultimate authority rests with the SED control apparatus and is implemented by councils that appear at all levels of government. Much important legislation takes the form of executive orders issued by the State Council or the Council of Ministers.

The SED rules the state, and "the decisions of the communist party constitute the highest scientific generalizations derivable from political practice."[18] Control is applied indirectly. The Politburo makes decisions, and the Secretariat is responsible for carrying them out. SED members are detailed to governmental agencies and business enterprises, where they supervise and report. Periodic review and criticism are also conducted by party organs. East German political, social, and economic life is thus dominated by a single organization whose membership constitutes almost 13 percent of the population.

Table 23

EAST GERMAN COMMUNIST PARTY (SED) LEADERSHIP, 1988

Politburo	Born	Elected	National Secretariat	Council of Ministers	Other positions
FULL MEMBERS (22)					
Honecker, Erich	1912	1958	General secretary		Chairman, State Council; National Defense Council
Axen, Hermann	1916	1970	Secretary (foreign affairs)		
Boehme, Hans-Joachim	1929	1986		Minister, university and technical schools	First secretary, Halle
Dohlus, Horst	1925	1980	Secretary (party organization)		
Eberlein, Werner	1919	1986			First secretary, Magdeburg
Felfe, Werner	1928	1976	Secretary (agriculture)		Member, State Council
Hager, Kurt	1912	1963	Secretary (culture, science, and education)		Member, State Council
Herrmann, Joachim	1928	1978	Secretary (propaganda)		
Jarowinsky, Werner	1927	1984	Secretary (trade, supply, and church affairs)		
Kessler, Heinz	1920	1986		Minister, defense	
Kleiber, Guenther	1931	1984		Deputy premier	Permanent representative to CMEA
Krenz, Egon	1937	1983	Secretary (security affairs, youth, and sports	Deputy premier	Deputy chairman, State Council
Krolikowski, Werner	1928	1971		First deputy premier	

Table 23
(continued)

Politburo	Born	Elected	National Secretariat	Council of Ministers	Other positions
Lorenz, Siegfried	1930	1986			First secretary, Karl-Marx-Stadt
Mielke, Erich	1907	1976		Minister, state security	
Mittag, Guenter	1926	1966	Secretary (economy)		Deputy chairman, State Council
Mueckenberger, Erich	1910	1958			Chairman, Control Commission
Neumann, Alfred	1909	1958		First deputy premier	
Schabowski, Guenter	1929	1984	Secretary		First secretary, E. Berlin
Sindermann, Horst	1915	1967			Deputy chairman, State Council, and president, People's Chamber
Stoph, Willi	1914	1953		Premier	Deputy chairman, State Council
Tisch, Harry	1927	1975			Member, State Council; Chairman, Free German Trade Union Federation
CANDIDATES (5)					
Lange, Ingeborg	1927	1973	Secretary (women)		First secretary, Erfurt
Mueller, Gerhard	1928	1985			Member, State Council
Mueller, Margarete	1931	1963			Member, State Council
Schuerer, Gerhard	1921	1973		Deputy premier	Chairman, State Planning Commission
Walde, Werner	1926	1976			First secretary, Cottbus

SOURCE: CIA, *Directory of East German Officials* (August 1987), p. 3; RFE, *East European Leadership List* (15 January 1988), p. 17.

The continued existence of the communist regime in East Germany is guaranteed by the presence of approximately twenty Soviet divisions with 380,000 troops. The late Walter Ulbricht, in an article published in Moscow, referred to the circumstances of the installation of his government in these terms: "Protection and aid of the Soviet Union, which at that time had a military form, made it easier for the antifascist democratic forces of Germany to fulfill their historic task [and] deprived the class enemies of the possibility of resorting to measures of open violence."[19] The facts of the situation can be discerned behind these phrases. Even today, if the threat of Soviet military power were removed, the communist East German government might be in serious danger of collapse.

The USSR has always had a particular interest in East Germany not only as a buffer between the other East European states and the West but also as a source of industrial power. When the failure of the Berlin blockade stymied Soviet expansionist aims in Europe, the USSR turned its attention to integrating East Germany with the bloc. This goal was thought to have been accomplished, but the workers' revolt in June 1953 demonstrated that the situation had not become stabilized. Communist authority almost disintegrated and could be restored only by Soviet armed forces.

Elections. The formalities of nominating candidates and holding elections have been carried out regularly in East Germany despite the fact that these are meaningless exercises. Through mass organizations and subordinate political movements, the SED has been able to control most of the vote. Four subordinate parties are allowed to propose their candidates, but the choice of candidates is made in "consultation" with the SED. The communists have a veto power over any name that may be presented.[20] Until recently all ballots contained only a single "unity list," and voters were given no opportunity for a choice. In June 1965 the SED propaganda chief, Albert Norden, proposed that "more candidates be nominated than the number required for election" at regional levels; no similar proposal has been offered with regard to national voting.

Article 54 of the East German constitution, which was amended in 1974, stipulates that elections to the People's Chamber are to be held every five years. In 1962, however, merely through a vote by the Council of Elders in the legislature, elections required by the constitution were delayed for a year. This postponement may have been due to preparations for the sixth SED congress, which was held in January 1963.

Meetings of "electors" take place at which candidates are approved for inclusion on the ballot. The ballot then offers no choice to the voters, who turn out and record approval almost unanimously (although some do not vote). Ballots are constructed to assure a predetermined composition of the 500-member parliament. The current People's Chamber was elected on 8 June 1986, and the SED, with its affiliated organizations, holds the controlling number of seats. Of the 12,434,444 eligible voters, about 99.74 percent went to the polls. There were 2,407 spoiled ballots and 7,512 votes opposing the National Front ticket. All 703 candidates won: 500 deputies and 203 alternates. Honecker stated that the election "reflects the firm trust of the citizenry in our proven course of peace and socialism." He further said that "in our GDR the contrast between state and citizen, so typical of all exploitative systems, has been overcome once and for all."[21]

Loyalty.   Although East Germany celebrated its thirty-ninth anniversary as a separate state in 1988, it remains under the strong influence of the USSR. This provides stability for the regime and has produced an outward appearance of popular support. This domination is also responsible for such acts of subservience as the passive acceptance by the GDR of the Oder-Neisse Line as its eastern boundary. On 7 October 1975 East Germany signed an agreement[22] with the Soviet Union guaranteeing the inviolability of its own borders, while affirming its allegiance to the bloc. This special relationship is emphasized by the 1974 amendment to the GDR constitution: Article 6 of the amendment states that "the German Democratic Republic is forever an irrevocable ally of the USSR. The close and fraternal alliance with it guarantees the people of the German Democratic Republic further advance along the road to socialism and peace."

Agriculture.   One of the earliest actions by the East German regime, based on Article 24 of the 1949 constitution, involved the confiscation of all privately owned farms that were more than a hundred hectares in size. Some of these became cooperative enterprises (LPGs), and others became state farms. Collectivization continued, and by 1959 about 52 percent of the country's arable land had come under cooperative or state control.

In 1960 a new drive started and by the end of that year, agriculture was 98.7 percent socialized. Over a three-month period, about three hundred and forty thousand farmers had been forced to join LPGs or flee to the West. The German Democratic Republic's experience with collective farming, like that of most other East European states, has been less than satisfactory. The agricultural plight reached crisis proportions in 1969 when the grain harvest dropped 12 percent below that of the preceding year. Since 1964 the GDR has been purchasing more than one million tons of grain each year from the Soviet Union. With the exception of 1977 and 1979, Soviet grain deliveries were terminated in 1975, forcing East Germany to cover its imports on world capitalist markets, especially from the United States, and to pay in hard currency. Some modest gains in grain production have occurred since 1981. The current five-year plan aims "to achieve a grain output of 11.9 million tons by 1990 in order to render grain imports superfluous."[23]

Substantial improvement has occurred since then, chiefly due to efforts to operate farms along industrial lines, investments in chemical fertilizers, and the employment of modern technology. Another reason for agricultural growth has been the introduction of efficiency and production incentives, including the recent encouragement of private production. Nevertheless, the GDR is still forced to import food from abroad. Under a five-year agreement, the United States obligated itself to supply between 1.5 million and 2 million tons of grain to East Germany annually through 1980. During that last year, the GDR imported about 3.3 million tons of feed grain (including 3 million tons of corn and soybean meal) from the United States. In 1982, twelve full-time agricultural workers were required for every 100 hectares of cultivated land in the GDR, twice the West German average.[24]

Another serious problem involves the abandonment of the farm by the young East Germans seeking industrial employment in the cities. The average age on many collective farms is 65. Reportedly, fewer than 5 percent of the farm workers are under 25 years of age. The situation has deteriorated to such an extent that local government agencies are permitted to declare harvest emergencies and draft factory workers to help with the crops. Attempts to recruit students for summer work in agricultural production have failed during recent years.

Disaffection and Intellectual Ferment. The most striking indicator of dissent among East Germans toward their communist regime was the constant stream of refugees across the border until the last gap was sealed by construction of the Berlin Wall. In the period 1950–1961 an estimated three million persons fled from East Germany, making it one of the few countries in the world to have a declining population. Since that time, about thirty East Germans per week, on the average, manage to elude border guards and escape to the West. From the time the Wall was built in 1961 through 1983, some 196,924 persons are estimated to have left East Germany permanently.[25] Included were thousands of the aged and invalids who were granted exit permits because they were a burden to the GDR. But approximately half that total consisted of refugees who were outside the country when the border was sealed and refused the option to go home and later escapees who managed to foil the tight security along the East German frontiers. Since 1961 a total of 72 persons have died attempting to reach West Berlin, and another 110 were killed trying to cross the border into West Germany.[26]

The 857-mile-long border between the two Germanies had been fortified with more than one million land mines, some 45,000 self-firing machine guns, approximately one thousand watchdogs, and a large well-equipped border patrol, at an approximate cost to the East Germans of about $5 million per year. This barrier had been effective in decreasing the number of successful escapes to West Germany. In the first half of 1981, a total of 1,799 persons managed to flee across the border or by way of other East European countries. The landmines and self-firing machine guns were removed in 1984–1985 and replaced by a new system equipped with sophisticated electronic and acoustic alarms. The border troops number 48,000 to 50,000 men. During 1986 a total of 64 persons, 12 of them uniformed guards, managed to flee across the border despite these obstacles.[27]

The GDR has maintained generally close supervision over its intellectuals. One of the more vocal dissidents has been Robert Havemann, former professor of chemistry at Humboldt University in East Berlin. A lifelong communist, he maintained that the dogmatic SED leadership had replaced logic with authority and tradition. His thesis was that all mistakes and shortcomings should be discussed publicly, and he advocated "human socialism." Havemann was fired from his teaching position in 1966 and ousted from the SED because of "continued damage to the party and an outlook foreign to the party." Later he was attacked in an open letter by the Academy of Sciences; shortly thereafter his name was removed from the list of academy members.[28]

Despite this punishment, the mere fact that Havemann was not executed or even imprisoned could have been a sign that intellectual regimentation might be relaxed. This hope disappeared in 1968 when all dissent over the occupation of Czechoslovakia was quickly suppressed. Havemann's two sons, in fact, were at the time tried and sentenced to prison for "antistate incitement." Stricter curbs were reimposed on intellectuals in the wake of these developments. Another case involved the dissident poet-singer Wolf Biermann, who was deprived of GDR citizenship in late 1976, while performing at Cologne. In early 1988 several leading GDR peace and human rights activists, including singer Stephan Krawczyk and his wife Freya Klier, were forced to choose between a prison term or emigration to the West.[29]

From 1962 to 1985, according to West German sources, approximately forty thousand prisoners were purchased from the GDR at an estimated price of $20,000 to $60,000 in goods and services per person. The price in this human traffic varies according to education, profession, and "investment costs" charged by East Germany. In the fall of 1979, these transactions stopped but were resumed shortly thereafter and continue to the present day.[30]

East German political leaders apparently believe that economic prosperity and social benefits represent the best insurance against social ferment. Welfare programs cover virtually every aspect of daily life, including cradle-to-grave health and medical coverage, pensions, and a minimum ten years of free public education. State-operated day-care centers service 61 percent of preschool children at a cost of six dollars a month. In 1972 abortions were legalized, and women receive paid leave of fifteen to twenty days. Eighteen days of vacation a year are guaranteed for all workers; those in strenuous jobs, like mining and metal processing, have up to 30 days. These benefits are costly. Subsidies for food and consumer goods alone total almost $10 billion per annum. Housing in the form of low rents costs the government at least an additional $2 billion.

At the 1986 party congress General Secretary Erich Honecker announced the extension of several family benefits: the paid "baby year" now applies to women after the birth of their first child, all working mothers receive paid leave to tend to sick children, and loans to young married couples are available on more liberal terms. The following year the monthly child allowance was increased from 20 to 50 marks for the first, 20 to 100 marks for the second, and 100 to 150 marks for the third child. Honecker reckoned that this "important socio-political measure" would cost two billion marks annually.[31]

Ulbricht's Successor. With the death of Walter Ulbricht in 1973, leadership passed to Erich Honecker, who had already served for two years as SED first secretary; Willi Stoph, chairman of the State Council; and Horst Sindermann, premier. Honecker currently holds the most important post of party chief (general secretary); constitutional amendments in October 1974 made the post of State Council chairman a less significant position. However, as mentioned above, on 29 October 1976 Honecker became chairman of the State Council, with Stoph resuming his former position as premier.[32]

Born in Saarland in 1912, Erich Honecker, the son of a miner, became a roofer by trade and joined the communist children's organization at the age of eight. A decade later he was a student at the Lenin Academy in Moscow, but he returned the following year to become secretary of the Saarland youth movement. Arrested in 1935, he did not leave the penitentiary until the end of World War II. His early postwar activities centered on the youth movement. Then he became a candidate Politburo member from 1950 to 1958 (with one year of training in Moscow), and since that time he has been a full Politburo member and a member of the Secretariat.[33]

THE RULING PARTY

Although the Socialist Unity Party of Germany (SED) is farther geographically from Moscow than any other East European movement, it has been characterized by the greatest obedience to Soviet directives. During a decade of de-Stalinization and superficial liberalization, both in the USSR and to varying degrees throughout the bloc, the SED has retained its essential and original harshness.[34] Functionally, it is a mirror image of the Soviet communist party, operating through similar organs of control. Yet the nature of the East German people, the character of the leadership, and the conduct of the party congresses all give the SED its own peculiar form and character.

Party Membership. Of the approximately 16.6 million people in East Germany, only 2,324,386 were in 1987 either full members or candidates for membership in the Socialist Unity party.[35] Like other ruling communist parties, the SED originally assumed a mass form; this lasted from 1946 until 1948, when the order came to reorient it into a cadre-type organization. Since that time the requirements for membership have become more stringent, and some of the opportunistic elements have probably been removed in the process. Membership now comes only after acceptance as a candidate and a probationary period under the careful scrutiny of party functionaries. These functionaries derive largely from the white-collar and intelligentsia classes.[36]

Candidacy in the SED requires recommendation by other party members or, if the candidate is enrolled in the Free German Youth, by the local youth organization's functionary. The social composition of the SED once again shows a lower white-collar and intelligentsia component. (See Table 24.) Although the collectivized peasants in the German Democratic Republic numbered 863,650 in 1986, less than 5 percent of the SED membership belonged to that class.[37]

Table 24
EAST GERMAN COMMUNIST PARTY (SED) SOCIAL COMPOSITION, 1961–1986
(percentages)

Category	1961	1970	1981	1986
Industrial workers	33.8	47.1	57.6	58.1
Officials and intelligentsia	41.3	28.1	22.1	22.4
Farm workers	6.2	5.8⎫	20.3	4.8
Others	18.7	19.0⎭		14.7
Total	100.0	100.0	100.0	100.0

SOURCE: Eduard R. Langer, "Zum Bildungsstand der SED Funktionaere," *Die Orientierung,* no. 2 (1968), double issue, p. 7 (primary sources are given in a footnote by this source); *World Marxist Review* (August 1970), Supplement, p. 6; *Neues Deutschland,* 12 April 1981, 18 April 1986.

Party Organization.   The organization of the SED follows that of the Soviet communist party. The smallest unit is the primary party organization (96,006 of these existed in 1987), which permeates all activities on farms and in factories, government agencies, the armed forces, and so on. The next administrative level is the town, above this is the county, and then comes the district organization, which in turn reports to the Central Committee. This group is elected by the party congress once every five years and, in theory, evolves from its membership a Politburo and Secretariat. (The eleventh congress met 17–21 April 1986.)

In actual practice, the Politburo is a self-perpetuating body. Through the Secretariat it instructs lower levels on the accomplishment of goals; that is, the Secretariat oversees the implementation of policy decisions that are made by the Politburo. Instructors are assigned by the Central Committee apparatus to district headquarters; other instructors go from the district to the county, town, and primary organizations. These men and women are assigned either individually or, to assure the fulfillment of important plans, in teams.

The SED Central Committee in 1986 included 165 full members and 57 candidates. The Politburo consisted of 22 members and 5 candidates in that year, and the Secretariat had 11 persons who were designated as secretaries, including General Secretary Erich Honecker. There are 41 departments within the Central Committee's apparatus: cadres, agitation, foreign, women, youth, security, party organs, ideology, and so on. Some of these are duplicated in the fifteen district and 227 county organizations and remain under the supervision of district and county secretariats, which have five or six secretaries each.[38]

Organs of Control. Certain organizations through which the SED maintains control over the East German population are unique, whereas others can be found in one form or another either in the USSR or in other bloc countries. The ruling party itself is an organ of control, as are the four subordinate political movements already mentioned. During recent years, the National Front, which represents a concept that the Soviets have implemented with varying degrees of success throughout their orbit, has been upgraded in importance. The 1968 East German constitution declares in Article 3 that the National Front serves to unite all forces of the people to act jointly in accordance with the principle that each is responsible for all.

The Free German Youth (FDJ) organization is probably the most effective agent of SED control. It has affiliations with its Soviet counterpart, the Komsomol, and with other bloc youth organizations, as well as with the World Federation of Democratic Youth. Its 2.3 million members range from 14 to 25 in age, many of whom also belong to the Socialist Unity Party. The directorates of both organizations interlock. The FDJ first secretary, Eberhard Aurich, is a candidate member of the SED Central Committee.[39] The standard fare of Marxist-Leninist indoctrination is given to all FDJ members as preparation for membership in the ruling party. Admission to this youth organization takes place via a typical military ceremony.

The twelfth FDJ congress met in East Berlin from 21 through 24 May 1985. Eberhard Aurich reported to the delegates, whose ranks included 177 guests from 101 foreign countries, that "the goal of the FDJ's political and ideological work is to instill socialist class-consciousness in all youth." FDJ has 28,998 basic organizations and is structured in the same manner as the SED.[40]

East German youth brigades comprise 45,654 units and play a special role in regime attempts to organize and motivate youth. They are primarily designed to accomplish domestic economic tasks but also serve overseas in developing countries. An estimated 17 FDJ friendship brigades work in nine African and Latin American countries.[41] Party control over FDJ has increased in recent years.

The only person in East German history simultaneously to hold the rank of Politburo member and head the youth organization had been Erich Honecker.

Young children from the ages of six through twelve are urged to join the Pioneers. Membership in the Pioneers and in the older youth movement is promoted by monopolies over sports facilities[42] and education; these are controlled through FDJ cooperation with the trade unions. All vacations and entertainment, as well as entrance examinations for universities and educational scholarships, are administered by these regime organizations. Nonmembership or even poor performance as a member may deprive the young East German of an opportunity for advancement.

A particularly useful function of the FDJ movement for the SED is its activity in observing and reporting. Every school class has at least one FDJ member who reports on the teacher and on other students. These young informers are also used to watch older officials in government agencies, factories, and businesses. Consequently, the FDJ attracts many opportunistic and unprincipled youths to its ranks. It is not by any means a popular organization. Many young persons refuse to join despite its monopoly position.

The Free German Trade Union Federation (FDGB), like labor organizations in all communist-ruled states, has no real bargaining power for the improvement of wages or working conditions. It is an instrument of control, supervision, observation, and reporting. About 96 percent of East German workers (more than 9.5 million people) belong to one of the 250,848 trade union groups.[43] Most are employed in state-owned industries, where organizational control by SED activists is tight and well disciplined. Workers in the diminishing private sector represent only a small percentage of the population; here the FDGB exercises somewhat less influence.

The primary usefulness of a trade union to the regime is its ability to organize the labor force to increase productive efforts and fulfill national goals. For these purposes the East Germans have copied the Stakhanovite system from the USSR. Throughout the GDR the example for other laborers is a miner named Adolf Hennecke. In 1948 he supposedly became dissatisfied with his normal output of 6.3 cubic meters of coal during an eight-hour shift and surpassed this quota by about 400 percent. This achievement and similar efforts in other industries are held before workers as examples of efficient production.

Such "records" are usually produced under optimum conditions. Teams of workers with party activists as leaders challenge one another in socialist competition. Often those not engaged in such contests attempt to hold down the norms by resisting the incentives given for overfulfillment. Activists, on the other hand, have the task of obtaining more work out of one or two select squads in order to provide a justification for raising the norms.

In a typical case the activist is given a project with a team of fresh laborers and the best equipment to show that a rate of production significantly higher than the norm is possible. Then a union meeting is held to honor the team and to vote "voluntarily" for increasing the norm by a certain percentage. At times this is done in honor of a forthcoming event or even a prominent individual. It is considered unwise for a member to speak against an increase, abstain from voting, or vote negatively when one of these proposals is brought up at a trade union meeting. Other methods for increasing production include the payment of wages[44] on the basis of piecework and the encouragement of "volunteering" for extra shifts.

The Democratic League of Women has a membership of approximately 1.5 million. It allegedly works for the equal rights that are guaranteed by the constitution. These include the rights to perform all kinds of manual labor and to provide half of the support for a family. According to official statistics, nearly five million women comprise slightly more than half the total East German trade union membership. Nearly 81 percent of all women between the ages of 18 and 60 hold jobs in the GDR.[45]

The Fighting Units of the Working Class are militia groups that are recruited by local SED organizations and are politically responsible to the ruling party. Militarily, they report directly to the Interior Ministry's chief administration for the East German people's police. Politically reliable persons from 25 to 60 who work in industry, farming, or administration are sought out to become members. Training is conducted by SED members who are officers in the people's police and by the East German armed forces. These fighting units receive 136 hours of training each year in light arms, are uniformed, and number about 450,000 men organized into battalions that comprise three or four companies; there are about a hundred members in each company. One battalion out of four is given the heavy equipment that would be allocated to an equivalent army unit of motorized infantry. A number of autonomous mobile companies also exist, all heavily equipped for action outside their own districts in cooperation with the regular armed forces. The purpose of the other units is to suppress local disturbances and, in accordance with the oath taken by members, to protect socialist achievements with their lives.[46]

The Society for Sports and Technology is steadily gaining in importance both as a premilitary and a paramilitary organization; it has more than 500,000 young participants. The avowed purpose is to instill socialist soldierly virtues in members and to prepare them for service in the National People's Army.[47] Youngsters are attracted by free courses in auto mechanics, parachute jumping, driving, marksmanship, and so on.

Ideology. The habit of ideological mimicry, which requires quick adjustment to keep in step with the Moscow line, has been followed in East Germany with few signs of the independent developments that have appeared in other parts of the bloc. The party line corresponds with that of the USSR, and embarrassment over mandatory reversals of position seems to have been minimal.

In GDR economic theory, which is closely coordinated with Marxist-Leninist principles, centralized control and ideological aims usually supersede purely economic considerations. Even so, the ideas of Soviet economist Evsei Liberman, whose concept of "profitability" appeared rather un-Marxist, began to show up in East German writings after experimental application in the USSR. The SED sixth congress even reversed its positions by endorsing the concept of profit as well as the law of supply and demand. This led to the adoption of the New Economic System, which advocated economic planning based more on expediency than on ideological imperatives. Since its introduction, the New Economic System has gone through several modifications, with the "leading role" of the SED re-emphasized. In the 1968 constitution (Article 9), even after the 1974 amendments, the socialist planned economy is said to combine central state planning with individual responsibility by commodity producers and local state organs.

DOMESTIC AND FOREIGN POLICIES

The already mentioned October 1975 treaty of friendship between the Soviet Union and the German Democratic Republic was signed because the GDR allegedly "has become a sovereign, independent socialist state, a full member of the United Nations."[48] It would be difficult, however, to find instances in which East Germany has exercised any such prerogatives, even at the United Nations, which it joined in 1973. Under the leadership of Walter Ulbricht and Erich Honecker, the GDR has echoed every major Soviet policy since it came into existence. Even the introduction of visa requirements on 1 January 1977 must have received USSR approval, especially as it violates four-power agreements regarding Berlin.

Paradoxically, only in its reluctance to follow the Soviet lead in de-Stalinization has East Germany displayed some independence, or so it would appear. In response to Moscow's policy that was enunciated in early June 1953, Ulbricht promised an easing of some restrictions and a greater emphasis on the production of consumer goods. He failed, however, to modify a decision to increase work norms that had, in effect, brought about a reduction in wages. The result was an uprising during which workers demanded economic reform, free elections, and the release of political prisoners. The disorder spread throughout East Germany but was put down by Soviet troops. Ulbricht immediately fell back on the tried and trusted remedies of a purge in the SED hierarchy and reprisals against leaders of the rebellion.

In 1956 a period of liberalization again seemed to be in the offing after Khrushchev's secret denigration of Stalin at the twentieth congress of the Soviet communist party. The response in some of the bloc states was a turn toward national communism and attempts to gain limited freedom from total domination by the USSR. Ulbricht's reaction to these attempts took the form of purges, although he paid lip service to de-Stalinization and was, indeed, the first among East European leaders publicly to denounce Stalin. This did not prevent him from continuing to apply the old methods of repression.

As political tensions increased over the Berlin question in mid-1961, the number of refugees grew from more than thirty thousand during the month of July to more than forty thousand in the first ten days of August. On the night of 13 August the border was sealed on the orders of the German Democratic Republic, but some 3.5 million East Germans had already fled to the West. The Berlin Wall slowed the flow of refugees to a comparative trickle but condemned the GDR in the eyes of the world as a police state that retained control over its citizens primarily by physical means.[49]

Like the USSR, the East German regime limits the rights of free speech and assembly through its power of licensing. Nothing may be printed without a government permit. No meetings may be held unless official authorization is obtained. These devices are particularly important in the contest between church and state. In matters of religion, the regime is primarily concerned with Protestant churches rather than Roman Catholic ones, which remain in a minority. A religious census in 1965 showed that close to 80 percent of the population, or about 13.6 million East Germans, belonged to the Evangelical (Lutheran) church. The last official figures (1977) indicated only 7.9 million Protestants and 1.2 million Catholics. More recent estimates (1985) put the number considerably below 50 percent of the total population.[50]

After the final separation between East and West Germany at the end of the 1940s, pressure on the churches in the GDR increased. The regime made attempts to censor sermons of pastors and simultaneously to gain the political support of the Evangelical church. The basic position of the church was stated in a letter to the Soviet military governor, Marshal V. D. Sokolovskii, by the presiding bishops.[51] According to this document, Christians were obligated to obey the orders of the state as long as these did not contravene moral law. The church claimed the right to support or criticize governmental measures but only on moral and not political grounds. Despite the government's attempts to isolate the East German churches, close ties have been secretly maintained with their Western counterparts.[52]

Church and state have also come into conflict on the issue of education. Although the church accepted the removal of religion as a subject from the public school system after the war, it has registered opposition to the use of schools for preaching atheism. The church has also taken a stand against the regime's electoral practices, particularly the wording of referendum questions. It has aroused the anger of state officials by its refusal to grant a blanket endorsement to regime policies by way of a loyalty oath.

Over the years attacks against the church by the government have assumed various forms. Travel and contact between East and West are severely restricted. The church press and its meetings have been controlled through the licensing power. State subsidies have been withdrawn, and the right of the church to conduct door-to-door solicitation drives has been restricted. Church relief agencies have been closed and their leaders arrested. On the other hand, about sixty "progressive" pastors established a formal organization at Leipzig that is subsidized by the regime.

Probably the most successful mechanism the state has employed against the church has been the usurpation of rites and ceremonies. Government rituals now exist for such occasions as baptism, marriage, and death. The best known is the youth consecration (*Jugendweihe*), which is akin to the ceremony of church confirmation; in it young people between the ages of twelve and sixteen dedicate themselves to socialism rather than to Christianity. Failure to participate in this ceremony often closes the door to further education or favorable employment opportunities. An East German pastor, Oskar Bruesewitz, immolated himself in front of his church at Zeitz (Anhalt) as a protest against the regime's infringement on access to religious life by young people.[53]

The 1949 constitution still contained detailed regulations concerning the relationship between church and state. The 1968 document, as it was amended in 1974, severely limits the power of the church (Article 20) but does add that every citizen has the right to profess and practice a religion. For many years the Evangelical Church of Germany withstood numerous attempts to end its existence as the one remaining all-German organization and thus a bridge between East and West. In 1968, however, announcement was made of the pending amalgamation of the churches in the German Democratic Republic into a newly established Federation of Evangelical Churches in the GDR. The break was formalized in September 1969 when the first synod of this federation was held at Potsdam. SED leader Honecker and Bishop Schoenherr, head of the Evangelical churches, signed an agreement in March 1978 that allowed religious programs to be transmitted via radio and television in East Germany. Although a second top-level meeting between Honecker and Bishop Hempel, the new chairman of the Evangelical federation, took place in February 1985, the church continues to be subject to periodic raids and disruption of services by GDR security forces.[54]

Agriculture.   Life is also difficult on the economic front. In proper communist fashion, the economy has been oriented toward heavy industry at the expense of consumers' goods. Farm policies have been just as disastrous in East Germany as they have elsewhere in the bloc. Official food rationing was abolished in 1958, but each consumer was required to purchase his basic food supplies from a particular store. This requirement in effect continued rationing, but this policy was abandoned and reinstituted during the 1960s in accordance with the availability of supplies. Even in good times distribution remains a major problem. Two major reasons can be cited for the inability of the GDR to fill its agricultural requirements. (1) The cession of the lands east of the Oder and Neisse rivers to Poland resulted in the loss of one-fourth of the arable land possessed by all of prewar Germany. (2) Probably even more important, collectivization and communist mismanagement have stifled production.

Collectivization came rather slowly to East Germany. At the end of the war about one-third of the total agricultural land was seized from large landholders and redistributed to individual peasants and to collective farms. By the end of 1959 only half of all farms had been collectivized. Between February and April of 1960, however, the program was pushed through almost to completion in a manner similar to that employed during the early 1930s in the Soviet Union. The results were very much the same. An immediate decrease in grain production took place, and even today the annual deficit totals several million tons per year. Major shortages of meat and livestock products followed. Farmers are not interested in collective work and devote as much time as possible to their private garden plots. Remedial actions taken by the GDR have included the "industrialization" of agriculture, increasing political controls, and the pressing of communist youth groups into emergency service during crucial times of the year. However, this last device has failed, as mentioned earlier. (See Table 25.)

The Economy.   Elsewhere, the German Democratic Republic displays an economy that is seriously distorted by the demands of the Council for Mutual Economic Assistance (CMEA). East Germany, which became a member of that organization in 1950, today specializes in the production of machinery, chemicals, certain consumer goods, railroad rolling stock, ships, optical goods, and scientific instruments for the bloc. Raw materials are imported mainly from the other East European countries and from the USSR, and their rising prices have adversely affected the East German economy. Seventy percent of the GDR's foreign trade remains with other communist-ruled countries, and the Soviet Union is its principal trading partner.[55]

Despite the fact that it was looted of some ten to twenty billion dollars worth of industrial capital goods and production in the years following World War II, by the late 1950s East Germany could show a fair measure of economic vitality. In 1959 it adopted a seven-year plan that included the goal of surpassing West Germany by 1961 in per capita production. During 1959 a growth rate of 12.4 percent was claimed. This declined to 8 percent in 1960, then to 6.2 percent during 1961, and subsequently averaged close to 6 percent through 1969. Obviously the goal of overtaking the Federal Republic of Germany could not be achieved, although it was subsequently claimed that this would occur by 1975; this, of course, did not happen.

Table 25
EAST GERMAN GRAIN DEFICIT, 1966–1986
(in thousands of metric tons)

Production, imports, and consumption	1966	1968	1970	1972	1974	1979	1986
Total grain apparently available for consumption	7,688.5	9,468.1	—	—	—	12,471.4	13,765.9
Domestic production	5,917.5	7,829.1	6,456.5	8,563.2	9,703.2	8,857.4	11,664.2
Total imports	1,771.0	1,639.0	—	—	—	3,614.0	2,101.7
Imports provied by the Soviet Union	1,160.0	1,216.0	1,694.0	1,209.0	1,453.0	—	—

SOURCES: *Statistisches Jahrbuch der Deutschen Demokratischen Republik 1975* (East Berlin, 1975), pp. 194–95, 277, and 64 of appendix; Ibid., *1980*, pp. 178–79, 238; Ibid., *1987*, pp. 195, 246.

In the past East Germany's economic performance has not always been up to its optimistic forecasts, although in many ways the country is credited with its own "economic miracle." The seven-year plan for 1959–1965, with its ambitious goals, had to be abandoned two years early; by the middle of 1962 it became clear that the plan had been based on faulty estimates of capacity and costs. It was replaced by the 1964–1970 "perspective plan," which was revealed at the sixth SED congress. Fundamental changes in the economy, based on the socialist system, and preparations for a new 1971–1975 plan were next announced by the Council of State. The changes envisaged a combination of strong central planning for "structure-determining tasks" and the assignment of responsibility for production to individual enterprises and local state authorities. In fact this meant a curtailment of power at the factory level and the elimination of what previous reforms had hailed as "a certain self-regulation in the economic system." The current five-year plan (1986–1990) increases the integration of the GDR economy with the USSR and other CMEA member states. As CPSU general secretary Gorbachev stated at the eleventh SED congress, "The socialist countries are entering a period in which cooperation among them must be raised to a higher level, not just by several degrees, but, as the mathematicians would say, by a whole order of magnitude."[56]

There are several reasons for the economic difficulties East Germany has experienced. These include forced industrialization, which resulted in such errors as an expenditure of $600 million for construction of a huge steel combine at Stalinstadt that has been unable to produce anything except crude pig iron. Normal development was also hindered by Soviet and CMEA requirements. Plans for the development of Rostock as a major shipbuilding center and seaport were suspended because of competition with the Polish port of Szczecin. The aircraft industry was abandoned altogether. Automobile and textile plants were held back. An industrial complex for uranium mining that employs 140,000 workers is being maintained at the Wismut Aktiengesellschaft works simply to fulfill the needs of the USSR. There is no evidence that the East German regime has resisted CMEA policies as some of the other bloc countries have done rather successfully. Yet the GDR has attained the highest standard of living within the bloc, and despite all obstacles and demands it has achieved the rank of tenth most industrialized country in the world.

Ten key economic priorities were outlined by Honecker during his opening speech to the eleventh SED congress:

Accelerate scientific-technological progress

Improve labor productivity

More efficient use of raw materials and fuels

Improve quality of products, especially for export

More efficiency in human and material energy

Rationalization of labor based on microelectronics and computerization

Concentration of investment on projects with the maximum economic impact

Increased production of consumer goods

Growth in social production to achieve higher national income

High-quality management and planning[57]

Foreign Policy.   In the area of foreign policy, the GDR is vitally concerned about its own relationship with the Federal Republic of Germany. For years after World War II the division of Germany remained an emotionally charged and utterly unacceptable condition for both German states. Yet by 1969 it had become clear that bringing the two parts of the country together might be impossible because of various conflicting interests and that reunification was not a realistic goal. In the East the chances for reunification were limited by Soviet design and by the fears of GDR rulers for their socialist achievements; in the West they were circumscribed by Allied and NATO security requirements and concern over the status of West Berlin.

Moreover, the 1974 constitutional amendment defining the German Democratic Republic as a "socialist state of workers and farmers" implies that the maintenance of two separate German states is inevitable. This recognition had been underscored by long-standing verbal attacks that accused West Germany of revanchism, militarism, support for neo-Nazism, and the creation of obstacles to détente in Europe. Separateness had also been a clear factor in East German demands for full recognition of the GDR as a sovereign state under international law, the renunciation of the Federal Republic of Germany's (FRG) claims to sole representation abroad, and the acceptance of existing frontiers.

After years of diplomatic probes, an agreement between the two Germanies[58] on diplomatic recognition came into force in June 1973. The document, known as the Treaty on the Basis for Relations between the GDR and the FRG (Basic Treaty) included establishment of diplomatic relations and arrangements to facilitate transit by West German visitors. The new *Ostpolitik* of the FRG and this treaty have not effected an easing of tensions between East and West, however, but have delineated and intensified them. The East German government also reaped the benefits of wide international recognition, one of its basic objectives, through this treaty and the subsequent Helsinki agreement of 1 August 1975. The attainment of international status is being used by the GDR to affect the status of West Berlin vis-à-vis the FRG and to further enhance its position as the "other Germany."

The GDR regime has devised other obstacles to impair East-West contacts that had been guaranteed in the Basic Treaty. Vigilance has been intensified, including the intimidation of citizens and the placing of restrictions on their contacts with Western relatives and friends. Administrative devices such as increased fees and inspection times before entrance into East Berlin have also been imposed. In October 1980, the GDR doubled its currency minimum for tourists and foreign businesses in East Germany. Under the new rules, Western visitors must exchange 25 DM ($15.06) daily. The yearly revenue is estimated at nearly 500 million DM.[59]

Trade between the two Germanies has grown over the past decade. The Federal Republic is now the GDR's main Western outlet, and the East German debt to the FRG is about 3.6 billion DM.[60] This exchange, which has been considered internal German commerce since the 1956 treaty of Rome, has raised consternation among Common Market neighbors of West Germany. They are concerned about the free circulation within the European Economic Community of exports from East Germany, a country belonging to a different bloc. GDR firms have also been trying to capture West German markets by undercutting prices, a practice that has brought a reaction from FRG authorities. However, the latter provide annual contributions of 525 million DM in transit and maintenance fees for the highways, railways, and canals between the FRG and West Berlin. West Germany also pays for major improvements on the expressways to Berlin and for postal and communication fees.[61]

Another important aspect of foreign relations involves de jure recognition of the German Democratic Republic by states other than communist-ruled ones. With FRG agreement, East Germany has been able to obtain diplomatic recognition from all West European countries and the United States (4 September 1974) along with membership in the United Nations. It has since then entrenched itself in many international organizations and become involved in worldwide activities. By December 1983, the GDR had established diplomatic relations with 132 foreign countries.[62] Other contacts include national liberation movements, vis-à-vis which East Germany may be playing the role of proxy for the Soviet Union.

Honecker outlined the main GDR foreign policy objectives at the eleventh party congress as follows:

Strengthening alliances with the USSR and other socialist countries

Solidarity with national and social liberation movements

Improving relations with capitalist countries, on the basis of peaceful coexistence

Prevention of nuclear war and the militarization of space

Creation of a nuclear- and chemical-free zone in Central Europe[63]

East Germany, active mainly in Ethiopia and the People's Democratic Republic of Yemen, is moving into the Latin American arena. A June 1980 friendship and cooperation treaty provides Cuba with development assistance and military as well as civilian advisers. A key element is the pledge to support all peoples in Latin America in their fight against imperialism. The GDR established diplomatic contacts with the Sandinistas the day they overthrew Somoza. Two months later (September 1979), Foreign Minister Oskar Fischer visited Nicaragua, Colombia, and Ecuador. The only states East Germany has no relations with are Chile, Guatemala, Paraguay, El Salvador, and some of the Caribbean islands. The GDR maintains a diplomatic presence in 87 countries of Africa, Asia, and Latin America. By 1984, the GDR had concluded economic agreements with 63 of these countries, establishing joint economic commissions with 15 of them. An estimated 200,000 East German experts were working in the Third World, while the GDR was educating nearly thirty thousand students from developing countries.[64]

Conclusion.   The Honecker regime remains solidly in power. Domestic dissent is effectively suppressed and workers' discontent controlled to prevent strikes like those in Poland. Yet underneath the relatively submissive facade of East German society lie the same seeds of rebellion that stirred the Polish events. So long as the communist regime maintains the ability to satisfy its citizens' physical needs and keep pace with growing expectations, the threat from within should remain dormant.

The close relationship between East Berlin and Moscow undoubtedly will continue, perhaps with even further integration in the military, economic, and technological fields. This partnership, based on mutual dependence, is a necessity without which absolute SED rule would surely break down. The question of reunification for East and West Germany is infrequently touched upon by SED leaders and then only in terms of a united "socialist" Germany. During his address at the eleventh party congress, Honecker did not mention reunification. During the foreseeable future at least, the German Democratic Republic will play a vital role in the Soviet bloc as well as in the world arena.

NOTES

1. Stephen D. Kertesz (ed.), *The Fate of East Central Europe* (Notre Dame, Ind., 1956), pp. 160–61; [Federal Republic of Germany], Bundesministerium fuer gesamtdeutsche Fragen, *A bis Z* (Bonn, 1969), p. 530.

2. Elmer Plischke, *Contemporary Government of Germany* (Boston, 1969), 2d ed., pp. 182–83, describes the overall economic organization of East Germany.

3. Kertesz, *The Fate of East Central Europe,* p. 154.

4. For an official East German chronology of events from April 1945 to June 1964 see Stefan Dornberg, *Kurze Geschichte der DDR* (East Berlin, 1964), pp. 513–47.

5. Five political groupings operate in East Germany. For the names of key members in the four subordinate movements see [Federal Republic of Germany], Bundesinstitut fuer gesamtdeutsche Aufgaben, *Der Staats- und Parteiapparat der Deutschen Demokratischen Republik* (Bonn, 1 June 1986), p. 35.

6. [Federal Republic of Germany], Bundesministerium fuer gesamtdeutsche Fragen, *SBZ von 1945 bis 1954* (Bonn, 1961), pp. 10, 21, 23–27.

7. They took four out of five *Laender* premierships, the same ratio in the Interior Ministry, three out of five in Economics, and all five in the Education Ministry. Kertesz, *The Fate of East Central Europe*, p. 158.

8. U.S. Office of the High Commissioner for Germany, *Soviet Zone Constitution and Electoral Law* (Washington, D.C., 1951), p. 1.

9. For the text with amendments through 1960 see Siegfried Mampel (ed.), *Die volksdemokratische Ordnung in Mitteldeutschland* (Frankfurt/Main, 1963), pp. 56–79.

10. Plischke, *Contemporary Government of Germany,* p. 210.

11. The Basic Law (*Grundgesetz*) for the Federal Republic of Germany specifically states that it is temporary, makes provision for ratification by other *Laender,* and proclaims that it will be superseded when a "constitution adopted by a free decision of the German people comes into force." See Article 146 in Amos J. Peaslee (ed.), *Constitutions of Nations* (The Hague, 1956), 2d ed., vol. 2, p. 59.

12. [Federal Republic of Germany], *The Constitution of the German Democratic Republic* (Leipzig, 1968), p. 37. The German text appears in *Deutschland Archiv,* vol. 1, no. 2 (May 1968), pp. 166–81. Amendments are discussed and the complete text given in Dietrich Mueller-Roemer (ed.), *Die neue Verfassung der DDR* (Cologne, 1974), p. 12.

13. Amnesty International, "GDR," *Briefing,* no. 18 (February 1981), p. 16.

14. *New York Times,* 30 October 1968; *Bild* (Hamburg), 10 March 1988, gives 50,000 as the number who wish to leave the GDR.

15. Arnold J. Heidenheimer, *The Governments of Germany* (New York, 1966), 2d ed., pp. 182–83.

16. For a discussion of the Council of State, see I. P. Ilinskii and B. A. Strashun, *Germanskaia Demokraticheskaia Respublika* (Moscow, 1961), pp. 133–39.

17. Lech Janicki, *Ustroj polityczny Niemieckiej Republiki Demokratycznej* (Poznan, 1964), p. 156. The new law on civil defense in *Gesetzblatt,* no. 20 (1 October 1970), pp. 289–90 and no. 35 (19 October 1978), pp. 377–78 for broader powers.

18. Speech by a Central Committee functionary, quoted in Heidenheimer, *The Governments of Germany,* p. 184. All 11 members of the Secretariat elected at the eleventh SED congress in April 1986 also serve on the Politburo and, thus, consolidate decision-making and implementation within the latter body.

19. *Pravda* (Moscow), 30 December 1961.

20. The 1963 electoral law appears in Otto Gotsche, *Wahlen in der DDR* (East Berlin, 1963), pp. 17–21.

21. *Neues Deutschland,* 14 June 1986, for the Honecker quotation; [German Democratic Republic], *Statistical Pocket Book 1987* (East Berlin, 1987), p. 18; *Die Volkskammer* (East Berlin, 1987), p. 26.

22. This treaty of friendship, mutual assistance, and cooperation appeared in *Pravda* the day after it was signed. Article 7 stipulates that West Berlin "is not a part of the Federal Republic of Germany and also in the future will not be governed by it."

23. L. N. Tolkunov (ed.), *Sotsialisticheskii lager* (Moscow, 1962), p. 163; Mike Dennis, *German Democratic Republic* (London, 1988), p. 143.

24. *Washington Post,* 24 April 1981; *Handbuch DDR-Wirtschaft* (Reinbeck bei Hamburg, 1984), 4th ed., p. 192.

25. A total of 38,661 risked their lives to escape. Hartmut Zimmermann (ed.), *DDR Handbuch* (Cologne, 1985), 3d ed., vol. 1, p. 419.

26. Ibid., vol. 2, p. 1136.

27. *New York Times,* 13 August 1981; *Innere Sicherheit,* no. 1 (3 April 1987).

28. See the article about Havemann in *Der Spiegel* (22 November 1976), pp. 49–50.

29. Interview with Biermann published by *Der Spiegel* (22 November 1976), pp. 36–46; *Frankfurter Allgemeine Zeitung,* 8 February 1988.

30. Commission on Security and Cooperation in Europe, *Five Years after Helsinki* (Washington, D.C., 1980); *New York Times Magazine,* 16 February 1986.

31. *Washington Post,* 15 April 1981; *Neues Deutschland,* 18 April 1986.

32. *Die Welt,* 30 October 1976.

33. His biography appeared in *Neues Deutschland,* 17 April 1981.

34. Note, for example, the article by Bozidar Dikic on the Nazi pasts of certain SED theoreticians that appeared in *Politika* (Belgrade), 21 February 1970.

35. CIA, *World Factbook 1987,* p. 88; *Neues Deutschland,* 3 July 1987.

36. See Hermann Weber, *Die Sozialistische Einheitspartei Deutschlands, 1946–1971* (Hannover, 1971).

37. *Statistical Pocket Book* (1987), p. 72; *Neues Deutschland,* 18 April 1986.

38. *Staats- und Parteiapparat der DDR,* p. 35; *Neues Deutschland,* 6 May 1987; Dennis, *German Democratic Republic,* p. 96.

39. *Staats- und Parteiapparat der DDR,* p. 29.

40. *Neues Deutschland,* 22 May 1985.

41. Ibid., 6 May 1987; *DDR Handbuch* (1985), vol. 1, p. 361.

42. The monthly journal *Sports in the GDR,* published in four languages, illustrates the emphasis given sports in creating a new socialist society. See the article by Rudi Hellmann in no. 2 (February 1981), pp. 2–6.

43. Jefferson Adams, "German Democratic Republic," in Richard F. Staar (ed.), *Yearbook on International Communist Affairs: 1988* (Stanford, Calif., 1988), p. 266.

44. The minimum wage was increased by 50 marks to 400 and differentiated wages to 500 marks per month. *Neues Deutschland,* 12 April 1981.

45. *Statistical Pocketbook of the GDR 1987* (East Berlin, 1987), pp. 20, 38, 246.

46. Thomas M. Foster, *Die NVA* (Cologne, 1983), 6th ed., pp. 173–80.

47. Ibid, pp. 180–86.

48. Preamble, as given by *Pravda*, 8 October 1975.

49. Between 1961 and 1969 arrests for political reasons in the GDR involved 10,090 persons. *Sueddeutsche Zeitung,* (Munich) 8 August 1969. According to one West German authority, between 200,000 and 500,000 exit applications had accumulated by the end of 1983. Karl Wilhelm Fricke, *Opposition und Widerstand in der DDR* (Cologne, 1984), p. 171.

50. *DDR Handbuch* (1985), vol. 1, p. 715; CIA, *World Factbook 1987,* p. 88.

51. Richard W. Solberg, *God and Caesar in East Germany* (New York, 1961), p. 59.

52. *New York Times,* 4 April 1976, 13 November 1980.

53. *Der Spiegel* (30 August 1976), p. 36.

54. *Die Welt,* 25 March 1978. Only about 4,000 Protestant ministers and 1,200 Roman Catholic priests remained in the GDR, according to the *New York Times,* 2 August 1981. See *Die Welt,* 26–28 November 1987, and *Sueddeutsche Zeitung,* 7 March 1988, for recent events.

55. Half of all machine tools and instruments plus over one-third of the heavy engineering machinery exported by CMEA to the USSR during 1976–1980 came from East Germany, which undertook most of the work on several large projects in the Soviet Union: a gas pipeline, a pulp plant, an asbestos combine, and an electric power grid. *Christian Science Monitor,* 5 November 1976. For details on the 1981 GDR-USSR trade agreement, totaling ten billion rubles, see *Pravda,* 16 January 1981.

56. Quoted in *Neues Deutschland,* 19 April 1986.

57. Erich Honecker, *Report of the Central Committee of the Socialist Unity Party of Germany to the 11th Congress of the SED* (Dresden, 1986); also published in *Neues Deutschland,* 18 April 1986.

58. Ruediger von Wechmar (introd.), *Der Grundvertrag* (Hamburg, 1973), p. 224.

59. RFE/*RL Research,* no. 217 (10 November 1987).

60. *FS-Analysen,* no. 4 (1986).

61. RFE/*RL Research,* no. 217 (10 November 1987).

62. *DDR Handbuch* (1985), vol. 1, p. 121.

63. *Neues Deutschland,* 18 April 1986.

64. *Horizont,* no. 17 (1984).

Chapter 5
Hungarian People's Republic

During the so-called liberation of Hungary, and under Soviet tutelage, a provisional government was established in December 1944 at Budapest while that capital was still occupied by the Germans. A temporary legislature also came into being based on five political movements, including a small but highly disciplined communist one.[1] The leader of the coalition was the Smallholders' party, a popular and moderate group. The provisional assembly included a plurality of communists, however, and the police force came under their direction. Real power remained with Red Army occupation forces, specifically Kliment Voroshilov, the (Soviet) chairman of the Allied Control Commission.

Despite universal suffrage and the fact that the November 1945 elections were unencumbered by direct pressure from the USSR, the Hungarian communists still felt that they could win a plurality. To their surprise, they received only 17 percent of the vote.[2] During the ensuing struggle over the allocation of ministries, USSR influence successfully placed a communist, Imre Nagy (and shortly afterward Laszlo Rajk), in the position of interior minister. This gave the Soviet advisers control over the police.

By early 1948 the communists had penetrated every department of the government and actually dominated the Hungarian state apparatus.[3] The approach used by Matyas Rakosi, the leader of the Hungarian communist party, during this period has been described as follows:

> With the famous "salami tactics" he first went into a coalition with the Smallholders, Peasant, and Social-Democratic parties to crush the Conservatives, then annihilated the Smallholders' party with the help of the remaining two parties. Then he suborned the Peasant party and absorbed the Social-Democrats, killing off or imprisoning their party leadership. Politicians were bribed, blackmailed, driven to exile, imprisoned, or sentenced to death.[4]

As a prerequisite for a complete takeover and the promulgation of a new constitution, the so-called Hungarian People's Front for Independence came forth with a single list of candidates before the elections of May 1949; after that full communist control was established.

CONSTITUTION OF 1949

The principal feature of the constitution that was adopted after the takeover in 1949 was provision for the inauguration of a people's democracy[5] on the Soviet pattern. Like all satellite constitutions adopted subsequent to the expulsion of Yugoslavia from the East European bloc in June 1948, this one also mentions the prominent role of the USSR in making possible Hungary's development toward socialism. The preamble declares that

> A new era of our history began when in the course of her victories won in the Second World War, the Soviet Union liberated our country from the oppression of Fascism and opened the road to democratic development for the Hungarian people. With the friendly support of the Soviet Union, the working people rebuilt the country . . . in national unity, the Hungarian people are busy in the complete building of socialism.[6]

A comparison between the Soviet and Hungarian constitutions shows that most of the latter was inspired by the former. Variations exist, but these all emanate from the theoretical assumption that the USSR has achieved socialism, while Hungary has not. This difference appears in a number of instances, as in the articles dealing with the status of workers, the ownership of the means of production, and citizenship.

The USSR is said to be a socialist state, whereas Hungary still unofficially admits the existence of classes other than those of industrial workers and working peasants. The Hungarian constitution uses the term small-commodity producers in Article 12, which recognizes their "socially useful economic activities." The new intelligentsia remains a distinct class; industrial workers and peasants may become transformed into intelligentsia by means of appropriate education.

In Hungary, also, a degree of private enterprise is permitted.[7] The Soviet constitution allows private ownership by its citizens "based on their labor and precluding the exploitation of the labor of others," meaning that no one outside the family may be hired. Hungary is still working to "dislodge capitalist elements," whereas in the USSR the capitalist system has allegedly been liquidated already.

Because the Soviet Union claims to have achieved socialism in 1936, it is assumed that all persons in that country are instilled with the collectivist spirit. In the USSR, either a citizen will work or he will not eat. Hungary, which is still at the lower stage of a people's democracy, has not worded its constitution so strongly in this respect. As Article 14 of the basic law clearly states, Hungary only strives to apply the socialist principle "From each according to his ability, to each according to his work."

In Hungary, higher education was at first guaranteed only to every worker. The right to an education for all citizens, even for those with a "class alien" background (meaning persons whose parents were neither industrial workers nor peasants), was not established until 1963. Faith in the "socialist order"—in other words, the regime—continues to be a prerequisite for all university applicants.[8] In the USSR each citizen allegedly has the right to an education. Again, the difference can be ascribed to the level of socialist achievement. Hungary admits to the existence of classes other than workers. On the other hand, exploiters theoretically have been eliminated from the Soviet Union.

Parliament.   Hungary has a unicameral system, with the parliament designated the highest organ of state authority. The constitution charges parliament with responsibility for passing laws, determining the state budget, deciding on the national economic plan, electing the Presidential Council and the Council of Ministers, controlling ministries, declaring war and concluding peace, and exercising the prerogative of amnesty. Despite these official duties, this "highest organ" is actually a constitutional fiction whose work is carried out by the Presidential Council[9] between sessions of parliament.

"The members of parliament . . . are elected by the constituents by universal, equal, and direct suffrage, by secret ballot," says the Hungarian constitution; like the constitution of the USSR, it provides for direct election of representatives to all legislative levels. Needless to say, the slate of delegates is nominated and controlled by the Hungarian Socialist (communist) Workers' Party, although a few multiple candidacies have been allowed.[10]

Parliament meets in regular session three or four times a year. Its speaker, two deputies, and six recorders are chosen from the membership. All issues are decided by a simple majority, except for constitutional changes, which require a two-thirds vote. Laws are signed by the chairman and the secretary of the Presidential Council and then are published in the official gazette.

Presidential Council.   At its first sitting the parliament elects from its membership a Presidential Council consisting of a chairman, two deputies, a secretary, and sixteen members. According to the constitution, the functions of the Presidential Council include calling general elections; convening parliament; initiating legislation; holding plebiscites; concluding treaties, appointing diplomatic representatives, and receiving foreign diplomats; appointing civil servants; and performing the duties of parliament when it is not in session.

The chairman of the Presidential Council is the nominal chief of state.[11] A member of the cabinet, that is, the Council of Ministers, is ineligible for election to the Presidential Council. Article 30 of the constitution provides the Presidential

Council with the authority to dissolve local organs of government "whose activities infringe [upon] the constitution or gravely imperil the interests of the people."

Council of Ministers. The third part of the national government, the Council of Ministers, is referred to in the constitution as the highest organ of state administration. In mid-1988 it comprised a chairman or premier, two deputy premiers, and the heads of thirteen ministries and three agencies.[12] Article 24 of the constitution established 26 ministries, but changes since that time, effected primarily by combining ministries, have reduced this number. Eight other agencies are chaired by state secretaries. The Council of Ministers exercises administrative powers involving the enforcement of parliamentary laws and decrees issued by the Presidential Council, the fulfillment of economic plans, the promulgation of decrees that do not infringe on parliamentary legislation or that emanate from the Presidential Council, and the supervision of subordinate, local organs. Article 39 states that "the Council of Ministers is responsible to Parliament for its activities. It is bound to render regularly account of its work to Parliament."

Local Organs of State Power. For the purpose of administration Hungary is divided into nineteen counties, with the capital of Budapest given separate county status. In addition, five other cities (Debrecen, Miskolc, Szeged, Pecs, Gyor) are designated principal towns. Some larger towns or cities are divided into precincts.[13] Local organs of state administration exist at the county, city, and precinct levels. Members of these councils are elected to four-year terms by voters in the areas they represent.

Local councils are given authority to supervise all state organs (except the armed forces) that deal with maintenance of social, cultural, health, and labor regulations. Although civil police organs are directly under the national government, they are theoretically required to submit reports concerning public security conditions to council meetings and to their executive committees.

The councils functioned in essentially the same manner at all levels, with each receiving instructions directly from Budapest until in 1971 local government underwent a reform that provided the councils with greater policy autonomy and financial independence. This system allegedly provides an efficient administrative structure by assuring the implementation of directives as they filter down from the top to the lowest levels of government.[14]

The most important part of any local council is its executive committee, which is elected at the first organizational session. It is presided over by a chairman, who is assisted by one or more deputies and a secretary. The executive committee exercises control over the local administrative apparatus. Its relation to the local council approximates that of the Council of Ministers to parliament: theoretically subordinate but actually dominant. On the county and district levels, the executive committee is supported in its work by a secretariat and a number of specialized administrative organs. One party device for supervising the work of executive committees is the establishment of permanent committees. These units report via the communist party chain of command to Budapest.

The Judiciary.   Justice in Hungary is administered by the Supreme Court and county and district courts. The highest tribunal supervises the judicial activities of all of the lower ones. Specifically, according to the constitution, the courts "protect and guarantee the political, economic and social order of the state, the rights and lawful interests of the citizens, and inflict punishment on the perpetration of criminal acts." The National Assembly (parliament) elects the Supreme Court chief justice from among candidates proposed by the Presidential Council.

In April 1984 legislation established a Constitutional Law Council "to oversee the constitutionality of legislative regulations and directives." Members are elected by the National Assembly from among its own deputies and nominees of the Patriotic People's Front. "Authorized entities" may submit cases, or they can be selected by the new Council itself.[15] However, this is not a judicial organ.

Government in Practice.   Constitutionally, the Presidential Council has a list of functions that appears most impressive. In reality, it does not play any policy-making role in government. The fact that Istvan Dobi, who was the nominal chief of state between 1952 and 1967, had formerly been a leader in the Smallholders' Party is indicative of his subservience to the communists.[16] Because the leading members of the ruling party are concentrated in the Council of Ministers, and the members of the Presidential Council may not be appointed to ministries, the Presidential Council is composed mostly of people who have limited influence.

It is likely that parliament has even less actual power and influence than the Presidential Council. In practice, all policies are formulated by the communist party hierarchy and sent to the Presidential Council for rubber-stamp approval while parliament is not in session. Because parliament is rarely in session and approval by the Presidential Council is binding, the requirement that all enactments by the Council be submitted to parliament is purely academic.

A list of individuals in government shows that the premier, the minister of state as well as the minister of health and social affairs also sit on the Politburo. (See Table 26.) According to the constitution, the Council of Ministers is subordinate to both the Presidential Council and the parliament. However, in practice, it is subordinate to the Hungarian communist party, which controls all political, economic, social, and cultural activities.

Participation by nonparty members in responsible positions of the People's Patriotic Front once led some observers to conclude erroneously that this organization might become an opposition party. Janos Kadar, the communist party's first

Table 26
COMMUNIST LEADERSHIP IN HUNGARY, 1988

Politburo (11)	Year of birth	Year elected	National Secretariat (responsibility)	Council of Ministers	Other positions
Grosz, Karoly	1930	1988	General Secretary	Prime Minister	
Berecz, Janos	1930	1987	Secretary (agitprop)		
Csehak, Judit	1940	1987		Minister of health and social affairs	
Hamori, Csaba	1948	1985			First secretary, Communist Youth League
Ivanyi, Pal	1942	1988			Mayor of Budapest
Lukacs, Janos	1935	1988	Secretary (Communist party organizational affairs and youth)		
Nemeth, Miklos	1948	1988	Secretary (economic affairs)		
Nyers, Rezso	1923	1988		Minister of state	Director, Economic Institute, Academy of Sciences
Pozsgay, Imre	1933	1988			
Szabo, Istvan	1924	1985	Secretary (cooperatives policy)		Chairman, National Council of Producers' Cooperatives
Tatai, Ilona	1935	1988			Director General, Taurus Tire Factory

SOURCE: *New York Times*, 23 May 1988, p. A5. Budapest radio, 29 June 1988.

secretary, in a speech before the Front, clarified this point by presenting official government policy as follows:

> In the service of determined political purposes the Western bourgeois papers publish quite often articles about the liberalization, the loosening of the Kadar regime. The writers of such articles and the politicians standing behind them are taking their wish-dreams for reality . . . They would like to promote and bring about our weakening; this is why they write that the détente of international atmosphere makes possible such a People's Front movement which can lead to the revival of the coalition parties.[17]

At the Front's seventh congress, Kadar issued a similar warning to all the "muddleheaded people" who might have the "desire to create a stir" in Hungary. He declared, "Nobody will be permitted to fool around with the fate of the people and the nation. We have a social contract, and it must be honored by everybody." The Patriotic People's Front held its eighth congress during 13–15 December 1985. Imre Pozsgay called for more active involvement by members in sociopolitical policy development. He was re-elected general secretary, and Gyula Kallai, chairman.[18] Pozsgay gave up that post for minister of state on 27 June 1988.

HUNGARIAN SOCIALIST WORKERS' PARTY

Bela Kun, the leader of the Hungarian communist party in the aftermath of World War I, in 1919 attempted to establish a communist republic. After the collapse of his regime, the communist movement almost disappeared. Many of its members fled to the USSR and continued to work there under Soviet direction. Others stayed behind to engage in revolutionary activities. Some of the émigrés formed the nucleus for a new communist party of Hungary as World War II was approaching its end. Matyas Rakosi, Erno Gero, Imre Nagy, and others returned to Hungary in 1944 to assume the leadership of the party at Debrecen, the temporary government capital on "liberated" soil. Another group of indigenous communists, headed by Laszlo Rajk, Janos Kadar, and Gyula Kallai, had been active during the war at Budapest. In February 1945 these two groups merged.

The party remained small at the end of the war. Under a policy of rapid expansion that was adopted at that time, the usual high degree of selectivity with regard to membership was disregarded in an effort to attract recruits. As a result, the number of members grew from 2,000 in 1944 to more than 1.4 million by 1949. Part of the increase was achieved through a merger with left-wing Social Democrats in 1948, and at that time a new name was adopted: the Hungarian Workers' Party.[19] Discipline became tighter as the party gained more power.

Matyas Rakosi's wing of the communist movement, which was known as the Muscovites, received support from the USSR and the Red Army. This man controlled the party and ruled Hungary from 1945 to July 1956, although his power was temporarily lessened when Imre Nagy held the premiership. Rakosi fell out of step with the de-Stalinization program, however, and Khrushchev had him removed. He was succeeded by Erno Gero, but the Hungarians associated Gero with Rakosi's policies.

No discussion would be complete without some comment about the 1956 uprising and its effect on the people. This event not only left its mark on the participants but also colored subsequent internal and external policies. There is no doubt that one reason the revolt spread in Hungary was the brutal intervention by Soviet armed forces. The seeds of revolution, however, go back to the Stalinist hard line of Rakosi. Between 1953 and 1955 Hungarians enjoyed the more moderate policies of Premier Imre Nagy.[20] This occurred because Moscow had dictated that Rakosi give up the premiership, although he retained the position of communist party leader.

In early 1955 the line shifted, Rakosi returned to full power, and Nagy was expelled from the party. As the government became more and more tyrannical, dissident elements (primarily students and the intelligentsia) began discussing open revolt. Although Rakosi was ousted by the Soviet Union in mid-1956, as mentioned above, by then the Hungarian communist party and the pro-Soviet government had lost control: they could neither effectively govern nor even rely on the armed forces. Great sympathy existed among the military for the revolutionary movement. The secret police (AVH) had become too weak to defend the regime alone.

The uprising in Hungary was to be short-lived; it became doomed to failure when its Freedom Fighters[21] were opposed by superior Soviet military power. The leaders of the USSR could not allow one of their satellites to defect from the bloc or even become neutral, let alone Western-oriented, because of the impact this might have on other East European states. Current Hungarian policies must be viewed against such a background. Details of the rebellion and its suppression are well known.[22] Janos Kadar, who was chosen by the Soviet Union to be the new premier and party leader, took over both posts on 4 November 1956. The movement as it exists today has been shaped by Kadar. Its name, the Hungarian Socialist Workers' Party (*Magyar Szocialista Munkaspart*—MSZMP), is the one he gave to the new organization.[23]

Membership and Support. The only relatively free elections held in Hungary since World War II took place in November 1945. The communists suffered a defeat—83 percent of the votes went to other parties—but they obtained representation in the government because of pressure by the Kremlin and the physical presence of Soviet troops in the country. In fact, the USSR gave permission for the elections only after receiving promises from the noncommunist parties that they would include communists in the future government.[24]

Following the 1956 revolt, the Kadar regime did not attempt to reconstruct the party along its former lines. The leaders became more selective and allegedly brought into membership only those who genuinely supported the communist movement; they hoped thus to develop a new hard core. During this period Kadar gradually purged the Rakosi and Gero elements. Starting with local and county organizations and ultimately moving to the top echelon, he eliminated dogmatic officials from responsible positions. In several cases diehard Stalinists at the highest levels even found themselves expelled from the party.

By the fall of 1962 the strength of the Hungarian Socialist Workers' Party had risen to more than half a million members.[25] This number amounted to about 5 percent of the population. With the passage of time, the composition of the party has also changed. For example, in 1966 the party claimed that more than 40 percent of its membership consisted of workers or former workers (at desk jobs, presumably) and 37.3 percent of the intelligentsia.[26] This would indicate that educated Hungarians were no longer boycotting the party. Because the leadership remained dissatisfied with the number of new members, ideological indoctrination had to be stepped up to increase the proportion of white-collar workers in the party (see Table 27 for recent figures on social composition).

Table 27
HUNGARIAN SOCIALIST WORKERS' PARTY SOCIAL COMPOSITION, 1980–1985

CATEGORY	TWELFTH CONGRESS (MARCH 1980)		THIRTEENTH CONGRESS (MARCH 1985)	
	(Number)	*(Percentage)*	*(Number)*	*(Percentage)*
Industrial workers (including farm workers)	340,159	41.9	371,043	42.6
Intelligentsia (white-collar workers)	278,459	34.3	369,301	42.4
Retired	133,140	16.4	67,937	7.8
Others (armed forces, students, etc.)	60,075	7.4	62,711	7.2
Total	811,833	100.0	870,992	100.0

SOURCES: *A Magyar Szocialista Munkaspart XII. kongresszusanak jegyzokonyve* (Budapest, 1980), pp. 9–10; Bennett Kovrig, "Hungary," in Richard F. Staar (ed.), *Yearbook on International Communist Affairs: 1986* (Stanford, Calif., 1986), p. 296.

NOTE: The first source (p. 92) gives a class breakdown of Hungarian society. Of all economically active persons, workers comprised 59 percent, cooperative farmers 13 percent, intelligentsia 25 percent, and private businessmen 3 percent.

Local and factory organizations provide lower-level courses in communist policies and principles, townships offer intermediate instruction, and county and major city organs conduct advanced training. In addition to the Hungarian Socialist Workers' Party, mass organizations such as the Communist Youth League (KISZ) and the Women's Association assist the communists in indoctrination work among the population. KISZ, for instance, has about 720,000 (1987) nominal members organized into some 30,000 primary units. They are used by communist leaders to spread propaganda or to inform on nonmembers. Although increasing somewhat in total membership, KISZ is losing support among students. Membership among youth in secondary and vocational schools declined by some 20 percent over a one-year period. This trend apparently has affected all strata of students.[27]

Party Organization. The structure of the communist party is a familiar one that in general emulates the Soviet model. At the bottom of the pyramid are 25,402 primary party organizations.[28] These include members in all types of work. The next level up consists of county party organizations in towns and cities. Members of primary party organizations send representatives to county conferences. There is no democracy in this procedure, however, as the delegates are handpicked by county committees. Regional party organizations correspond to the nineteen major political subdivisions of the country and are run by regional committees elected at county conferences.

The national party congress meets every five years (the thirteenth congress was held 25–28 March 1985) and elects a Central Committee to carry out policies. It now consists of 108 members and no alternates. From the Central Committee in turn comes the Politburo, which has eleven members and no candidates; its chairman is the party leader. The Secretariat of the party, which is also part of the Central Committee, has six members who no longer supervise the implementation of Politburo decisions. Janos Kadar was replaced as general secretary by Karoly Grosz on 22 May 1988 at the end of the three-day national party conference.

After the revolt in 1956, the Kadar regime encouraged the development of a more relaxed political atmosphere. Probably because of this official attitude, party organization at the lower echelons is rather poor. The general level of schooling among rural party leaders remains inadequate. Up to 1960 national party leaders were interested above all in political reliability, and they cared little about formal education. Hence most villagers have gradually reached educational levels that are superior to those of the rural party chieftains. Kadar saw the danger in this development and began emphasizing the selection of nonparty experts for government work. Knowledge of particular fields is apparently held to be more important than blind adherence to communist ideology. There have been complaints about this trend, even though sensitive posts (such as in foreign affairs, police, and defense) cannot be held by nonparty members.

Party Leadership.   Most of the men who built up the party during 1944 and 1945 have died or gone into semiretirement because of disfavor. Of those who formally re-established the movement toward the end of the war, none remains in power today. (See Table 26.) Five of the older party cadres (Istvan Huszar, Bela Biszku, Jeno Fock, Dezso Nemes, and Antal Apro) were not re-elected to the Politburo at the twelfth congress. Age was probably the reason in the last two cases. The remaining three (including Kadar's former deputy, Biszku) have been excluded from higher party office, undoubtedly in an attempt to establish an ideologically balanced leadership within the Politburo. Today the highest posts in the party are held by a younger group than has been the case at any other time. The average age in the present Politburo is 52.7 years. During 1945–1956 most of these men had worked in lower-level party organizations, in the mass movements, or within government agencies.

Kadar, as leader of the party, had been assisted by nine national secretaries (of whom five did not have Politburo status). Gyorgy Lazar (64) was considered to be Kadar's deputy, though no such title exists. Janosz Berecz (48), head of agitprop, had broad support within the top and middle levels of the party. The youngest member of the Politburo, Csaba Hamori (40), was elected first secretary of KISZ on 25 May 1986. Other names mentioned as possible successors to Kadar included Berecz (above), Premier Karoly Grosz (58), and Secretary for foreign affairs Matyas Szuros (55). The last man was not a Politburo member as of mid-May 1988. As mentioned earlier, a national party conference replaced Kadar (who became party Chairman although not a Politburo member) and seven others with six newcomers to the Politburo on 22 May 1988. This reduced that policymaking body from fourteen to eleven members.[29]

Policies.   At the eighth congress of the Hungarian communist movement in November 1962, Kadar placed emphasis on policies that suggested the party had broken with its Stalinist past. One of these policies, involving amnesty for the 1956 revolutionaries, has had international significance. It removed a main obstacle to the acceptance of the Kadar regime by the West in general and by the United States in particular.[30]

Speaking about his type of communism, Kadar later stated, "If anybody stands today to the left of the socialist order of the state, the order of building socialism, then he actually stands for nothing but petty bourgeois radicalism and a great many confused ideas."[31] However, his chief ideologist warned against the West as the enemy who plays the old tune "according to which the personality cult [Stalinist-type terror] is the logical product of the socialist system." This man added that for many persons, even in Hungary, this conclusion had been "confirmed by the way in which Comrade Khrushchev was relieved of his duties."[32]

Although the party has liberalized some of its policies, provided the population with more freedom of action, and even restricted secret police activities, it still rules Hungary. If the regime considers it necessary, it can and will institute tighter and harsher controls. Although Kadar stated that "he who is not against us is with us," this does not mean that persons who express themselves openly against the regime will go unpunished. The security police are powerful and ready. Even for a Kadar, there was no possibility of bridging the ultimate ideological gap and allowing an opposition party to function.

DOMESTIC AND INTRABLOC AFFAIRS

In Hungary, as in much of Eastern Europe, agriculture had fallen into a state of crisis during the years just before World War II. A catastrophic slump in farm prices, coupled with an uneconomic division of the land, had created a chaotic farming situation.[33] In 1945, with the approval of Soviet authorities, communist Agriculture Minister Imre Nagy ordered the expropriation of large landholdings and their distribution as small allotments to the peasantry. Some collectivization was introduced immediately because the communist party wanted to assist the "inevitable development" of *kolkhozy*, but the major drive was launched only after 1948.

Agricultural Policies. The five-year plan covering 1950–1954 set extremely ambitious goals for the population. Statistics reveal that no governmental approach can so mismanage agricultural production as one based on a communist philosophy. The production of bread grain for this period totaled less than it had during 1911–1915, when the population had been nearly 25 percent smaller.[34] One of the former breadbaskets of Eastern Europe became an importer of grain.

The headlong rush by communists to collectivize after their 1948 takeover caused widespread dissatisfaction and antagonism. Agricultural production showed a decline because of poor organization and the use of coercion by regime leaders. Abortive means to stimulate production included compulsory deliveries, high taxes, fines for alleged violation of administrative regulations, and penalties ranging from admonition to death.[35] Table 28 details the rapid increase in collective farms throughout Hungary during a period of less than four years (1959–1962); this expansion was due to the new policy under Kadar that, after initial excesses, avoided terror and stressed methods of persuasion as well as indirect pressure. It is apparent that one criterion for judging the effectiveness of any communist leadership is its ability to promote collectivization, which frequently occurs in direct proportion to the amount of pressure applied. By the end of 1986

Table 28
AGRICULTURAL PRODUCTION COOPERATIVES, 1958–1986

Year	Number	Active members	Family workers (As of December 31)	Employees	Arable land (As percentage of total, as of May 31)
1958	2,755	—	—	—	11.1
1959	4,158	—	—	—	28.1
1960	4,507	653,000	—	—	59.9
1961	4,204	815,000	—	—	75.1
1962	3,721	811,000	—	—	75.5
1965	3,278	684,000	171,526	62,612	76.5
1970	2,441	637,951	127,993	120,687	76.6
1972	2,314	578,233	112,890	121,911	76.7
1974	1,917	529,473	—	124,469	77.1
1975	1,598	514,884	—	120,599	77.6
1979	1,350	454,000	—	645,000	74.3
1985	1,279	623,400	57,800	933,100	78.0
1986	1,267	557,700	—	—	81.8

SOURCES: *Statisztikai evkonyv, 1958*, p. 157, *1959*, pp. 139 and 165, *1960*, p. 151, *1961*, p. 134, *1962*, pp. 164 and 182, *1965*, pp. 54 and 142, *1970*, p. 232, *1972*, pp. 243 and 273, *1974*, p. 250, *1975*, pp. 205, 207, and 221, *1979*, pp. 40 and 133; *Statistical Yearbook* (1986), pp. 139 and 155.
NOTE: Retired members of agricultural production cooperatives are not included.

some 96.3 percent of all arable land had been organized into collective or state farms. (See Table 29.)

By the end of 1980, half-hectare household plots and ancillary farms covered 14 percent of the agricultural area but produced 35 percent of the total output, including about 75 percent of all potatoes, half of the fruit, and most of the vegetables.[36] Due to an 8 percent increase in Hungarian agricultural production between 1975 and 1980, other communist-ruled states have begun adopting the Hungarian method of small-scale farming. At the 26th CPSU congress, Brezhnev even mentioned "how skillfully the work of agricultural cooperatives and enterprises in Hungary has been organized."[37] All this has led the Hungarian government to give even more attention to this aspect of agriculture. One inference is that despite massive government efforts to promote collectivization, the profit motive still remains an important aspect of peasant psychology. Recent communist pronouncements seem to encourage intensive cultivation of existing household garden plots. The party also appears to recognize the importance of incentives in agriculture. One reason for this recognition is the fact that total employment in farming, especially of young people, has declined over the years. In 1986, only 9 percent of the rural population engaged in agriculture as its main occupation; the remainder were urban workers, retirees, or students who farmed part-time. This translates into 724,500 persons employed in agriculture.[38]

As in other communist-ruled countries, the government in Hungary had been facing the problem of putting into effect impossible agricultural policies. A Budapest newspaper reported in 1969 that 2,840 collective farms had been studied for purposes of classification. These farms covered 28.5 percent of the country's arable land and employed about one-fourth of all collectivized farmers, yet they contributed only 20 percent of gross agricultural production.[39] A shortage of meat during the past several years was caused by a lack of incentives for fattening cattle. Comparative figures released by the regime indicate that in 1935 Hungary had 1,911,000 cattle; in December 1985, the livestock census showed that this number had decreased to 1,766,000, with 222,000 head on household plots or small ancillary farms.[40]

The country is again self-sufficient in food, as it was before the war. Hungary suffers, however, from a shortage of fertilizer, a situation that is prevalent throughout the bloc. Although production has recently received great emphasis, Budapest still depends on Moscow for many of its agricultural chemicals. Moreover, production alone will not solve the problem. Fertilizers that are already available have been inefficiently used because of inadequate storage facilities, transportation bottlenecks, and peasant indifference.

The wheat harvest in Hungary grew from 5.1 million tons in 1976 to 6.6 million in 1985. It is hoped that agricultural output will increase 12 to 15 percent

Table 29
HUNGARY'S FARM AREA BY SECTOR, 1986

	ARABLE LAND	
CATEGORY	*Percentage*	*1,000 hectares*
Cooperative sector	81.8	3,845.3
State sector	14.5	679.8
Private sector	3.7	172.4
Total	100.0	4,697.5

SOURCE: [Hungary], *Statistical Yearbook* (1987), p. 174.

NOTES: In 1980, there were 131 state farms with 143,000 workers in Hungary and 1,350 cooperative farms with 618,000 workers. A Ministry of Agriculture and Food survey in July 1980 revealed that 283 of the agricultural cooperatives operated in localities where conditions were unsuitable for agriculture. *12th Congress of Hungarian Socialist Workers' Party: 24–27 March 1980* (Budapest, 1980), p. 41; *Magyar hirlap*, 29 July 1980. No such figures were released by the thirteenth congress at the end of March 1985.

during the seventh five-year plan (1986–1990). (See Table 30.) The latter emphasizes increasing production of corn to export to the West for hard currency. In addition, food exports can earn convertible money even from certain CMEA countries that must pay in that manner for any commodities imported above existing interstate agreements. Hungary is the only major consistent net exporter of wheat and corn in the bloc.[41]

Table 30
COMPARISON OF ECONOMIC TARGETS IN HUNGARY, 1976–1990
(percentages)

Category	1976–1980 Achieved	1981–1985 Achieved	1986–1990 Planned
National income	19–20	7	14–17
Industrial production	21–22	12	13–16
Agricultural production	13–14	−0.9	12–15
Real per capita income	8–9	7	10–13

SOURCES: *Nepszabadsag*, 1 February 1986; Economist Intelligence Unit, *EIU Regional Review: Eastern Europe and the USSR* (1986), p. 72.

In general, the doctrinaire approach of communism fails to recognize that East European peasants are traditionally attached to the land. The soil is viewed by those who work it with a sense of affinity that is difficult to erase by regime decree. These psychological attitudes have brought about a paradoxical situation: some peasants have been willing to join the party in Hungary but not to work on collective farms. Notwithstanding such problems, the regime encourages mechanization and has improved the standard of living for agricultural workers. All of this has had a favorable impact on productivity.

Industrial Development.　　By March 1948 all large industrial enterprises (those having a hundred or more employees) had been nationalized in Hungary.[42] The development of heavy industry was fostered with even more fanatical zeal than the transformation of agriculture. The initial five-year plan, covering the years from 1950 through 1954, was actually intended to transform Hungary first from an agricultural to a balanced agricultural-industrial economy and then to change it into an "iron and steel" country.[43] This attempt took place at the expense of farm production and the manufacture of consumer goods. Progress toward developing heavy industry could be achieved only at considerable sacrifice by the population, whose standard of living would be lowered.

Even before Stalin's death in 1953, a slowdown occurred in the rate of industrialization throughout the East European bloc. The slackened pace could be attributed to an unrealistic basis for the forced drive to achieve industrialization and to pressure by the people for a decent standard of living. The declining rate of industrial output in the bloc countries during this period is reflected in the following comparisons, where production of the previous year is given as 100 percent: 130 percent (1951) and 108 percent (1955).[44]

As was the case in agriculture, there appeared to be a direct relationship between industrial output and the amount of pressure exerted on the workers. After an unsuccessful five-year plan ended in 1954, a one-year plan was adopted that stressed an increase of consumer goods. With the removal of Imre Nagy from the premiership in April 1955, however, heavy industry again became emphasized. Such vacillations in the economy took their toll in both human motivation and resources.

The effects of the 1956 rebellion and the Soviet reoccupation exerted an incalculable influence on Hungary. Large credits had to be granted by the USSR[45] and other East European states to aid in the recovery from the damage to physical assets, the reduced productivity of workers, and the loss of skilled technicians who had been killed or had taken refuge abroad. Because the country is relatively deficient in raw materials but experienced in the manufacture of certain commodities, the CMEA "division of labor" had great appeal to Hungarian communist leaders. The adoption of this concept gave every indication of completely reorienting Hungary's industrial development, which was to become compatible with and complementary to that of other member economies. During the period 1957–1965, however, Hungarian trade with the bloc resulted in a foreign exchange deficit of almost 3.5 billion forints. In a single year (1986), Hungary's positive balance of payments in all foreign trade totaled $394 million.[46]

Industrial development in Hungary suffers from the same problems that beset the Soviet Union and the other East European states. There is widespread popular dissatisfaction with a living standard that remains low in comparison to that of Western Europe. As of 1 January 1980, the Labor Ministry modified wage limits, marking the third change over a ten-year period. The new wage modification should facilitate payment in accordance with actual contributions to production. Subsequently, the labor minister announced a change in the labor code. Beginning on 1 July 1981, Hungary joined other Soviet bloc countries in instituting a five-day workweek.[47] (Only Romania still has a six-day workweek.)

During 1980, the deficit in trade with the USSR alone totaled more than 2.2 billion rubles. Imports from the United States have become stabilized since 1978, when Hungary received most-favored-nation status, whereas exports increased by 53 percent during 1977–1979. About 58 percent of all trade as of 1986 was conducted with other bloc countries, almost 32 percent with the Soviet Union alone.[48] Communist leaders have made it clear, however, that increased investment in Hungarian industry, the need to repay credits granted by the USSR, and high expenditures for the armed forces militate against any substantial or rapid increase in consumer goods. In Hungary, as in the other Soviet dependencies, politically expedient economic measures (such as the purchase of Cuban sugar at artificially high prices, submission to Moscow's import requirements, and compulsory aid to underdeveloped countries) limit economic development.

New Economic Mechanism.   An enlarged Central Committee plenum met in May 1966 to adopt a new economic reform that became part of the five-year plan. Six months later, the ninth congress of the ruling party approved two basic decisions: a change in economic management and the introduction of a New Economic Mechanism (NEM). The reform went into effect on 1 January 1968. It maintained central direction over long-range tasks, yet provided for implementation by individual enterprises based on market demand. Each factory prepared its own plan. The state established credit, price, and interest policies to influence effectiveness indirectly. Even wages were established by individual factories, within certain limits that depended on profits. The government provided financial assistance to plants that incurred additional costs because of technological improvements. On the other hand, tax penalties were levied against industries that turned out goods of inferior quality. Enterprises that reduced costs by 1.2 percent were authorized to give their workers twelve to thirteen days' pay as a bonus, with an extra day's wages added for each reduction of 0.1 percent below this target. A new quota bonus was fixed at 70 percent of the bonus paid the previous year. It could be increased to 100 percent or even 130 percent depending on the extent of profit-plan overfulfillment.[49]

The decisive feature of NEM was a new price system that attempted to reflect the true value of each article. By mid-1970, the number of prices fixed by central planners had dropped from approximately one million to about one thousand. Production could be planned better, and the ratio of consumer goods could be increased. Official data, however, indicate that productivity improved only slightly, labor efficiency remained unsatisfactory, and the economic situation in general was uneven. To eliminate these difficulties, the government's Economic Committee issued new guidelines on the further development of economic regulators. The aim is to achieve greater differentiation on the basis of quality work, managerial responsibility, and improved manpower utilization.

NEM radically changes the economic picture and also inevitably affects various parts of society. The coordinating role of central organs, however, assures firm party control. For this reason, the Soviet Union probably considers that the NEM represents economic reorganization rather than a basic reform that might bring major social change or even undermine communist rule in Hungary.[50]

In recent years, some capitalism has been introduced into the economic system. It enjoys a large degree of success but is criticized by hard-line party members. Some of the more controversial measures include leasing to private entrepreneurs of retail shops, small restaurants, and bars that had operated at a loss. These small enterprises (five to twelve employees) remain the property of the state. Managers receive no salary but may dispose of profits after paying a fixed fee, salaries, taxes, and maintenance. In response to arguments that managers of small businesses could earn too much money, the senior political editor of the party daily replied that whatever is earned by the fruit of the individual's labor corresponds to socialism.

Second jobs, private artisans, and small ancillary farms also come under attack by those who fear that the private sector is becoming too strong in Hungary. In each case, the party daily provided official counterarguments to the effect that socialism benefits from workers who can take on a secondary activity and place their skills to greater use for society. Moreover, under current economic conditions, many people cannot live on one salary and need to earn more. Private artisans, who numbered around 48,000 as of 31 December 1986, perform useful work for which they earn an honest income. Small-scale farming has become an integral part of socialist agriculture. More dangerous would be barren lands, abandoned fruit gardens, and shortages of meat, vegetables, fruit, milk, and eggs.

At the fall 1987 session of parliament, premier Karoly Grosz introduced austerity measures in the form of an economic program. Approved unanimously, it comprises two phases: the first phase involves three to six years of stabilization to balance the budget, cut the $16 billion foreign debt, increase productivity, and alleviate social tensions. A full development stage of ten to fifteen years would follow. The initial stage envisages 6 to 8 percent reduced consumption, an annual inflation rate of more than 15 percent, and introduction on 1 January 1988 of a value-added tax as well as a comprehensive personal taxation system.[51]

Church-State Relations. In the mid-1960s there were indications that government restrictions on clerical activity were being relaxed. Five bishops and one apostolic administrator traveled to Rome and were received by the pope. The leader of the Hungarian delegation, Bishop Endre Hamvas, told the Vatican Council that there were signs of a "growing understanding" between Roman Catholics and other Christians who were faced with "the common danger of atheism."[52] On 15 September 1964 the Vatican signed an agreement with the regime in Budapest that was the first of its kind to be negotiated with a communist-ruled state.

Of all the forces at work in a society, probably none is more annoying to communists than well-organized religion. This is particularly true of a church that owes its loyalty to a center outside the Soviet bloc. Religion works on the mind, and it is the mind that must be made subservient to the state or neutralized as a center of resistance to communist ideology. In addition, religious influence on the young must be eliminated just as ties with foreign countries must be severed.

Taking exception to any tolerance vis-à-vis the Roman Catholic church, the initial Hungarian postwar regime under Rakosi recognized that religion posed a serious threat to communism. In early 1949 Jozsef Cardinal Mindszenty was arrested and, after "confessing," sentenced to life imprisonment. Rakosi miscalculated the effect of this move, and the cardinal-primate became a martyr. The churches soon filled with both the "religiously" religious and the "politically" religious.[53]

During the 1956 rebellion churches were among the first to shed the restrictions placed upon them by the regime's control apparatus. By attending religious services, people manifested their deep-seated love of liberty. After the revolt had been crushed, state control over the churches was reinstituted. Several new policies were developed, and although the government refused to grant complete freedom to the churches, it did recognize the influence of religion on the population.

Late in 1957 the government resumed the payment of subsidies to the Catholic Church,[54] and the communist-sponsored "peace movement" of priests disbanded. Although these steps indicated a temporary desire to "coexist," the state continued to exercise considerable control over the church and its leaders. This situation continued until after the 1958 elections, the results of which apparently made the regime feel strong enough to drive what it considered to be a lasting wedge between the people and their religion. Catholic as well as Protestant bishops were required to take oaths of allegiance to the state, and the Office for Religious Affairs was re-established.

Ten years after the Vatican-Budapest agreement mentioned earlier, Pope Paul VI retired Cardinal Mindszenty, who had already left Hungary after more than two decades in prison and a period of self-imposed exile at the United States legation. He died in Vienna. Appointment by the pope of Laszlo Lekai[55] as the new primate and later as cardinal finally filled all three positions of archbishop and eight of bishop in Hungary. Bishops recently have been granted greater freedom to travel abroad. In 1979, nursing homes for elderly Catholics and a spiritual retreat center for laymen were established.

Cardinal Lekai traveled to Poland in June 1979 during Pope John Paul II's visit to that country. He served as presidium member at both the sixth (1976) and seventh (1981) Patriotic People's Front congresses. In his address to the latter, Lekai commented that "as our religious ancestors carried out invaluable work by laying foundations of the Hungarian language and culture, so in our day religious Hungarians peacefully cooperating with their nonreligious countrymen are employing their hands and minds in the building of a socialist Hungary."[56] The cardinal, however, did call for precise implementation of constitutional laws, specifically the guarantee of freedom of religion, and for teaching catechism in elementary and high schools. After the death of Lekai, Laszlo Paskai, the new primate, received his investiture on 25 April 1987 at Esztergom. He promised to support improved relations with the state, which are complicated by the existence of "basic communities" in the church and by increasing religious opposition to military service.

Dissent. The party leadership has a high level of tolerance for internal dissent, and repression is not as brutal as it has been in Czechoslovakia. Intellectual ferment has increased somewhat in recent years, following similar developments in other bloc states. Samizdat literature is more widely disseminated but has not received popular support. Most of the citizens appear to be resigned to the status quo and accept the limits of freedom imposed by the regime, so long as the latter satisfies their material needs.

Rising expectations are becoming a more difficult problem for the government. It has been estimated that between 8 and 15 percent of the population lives below a "comfortable level," that is, on less than half the per capita average income.[57] Growing economic deficiencies could stir up internal discontent, causing a confrontation between regime and people. The country, however, has no organized group of human rights activists like Czechoslovakia's Charter 77 or a united worker-intellectual movement of the kind in Poland. A growing number of critics within Hungary are willing to break the silence, express discontent, and openly discuss current problems.

An officially sanctioned political discussion forum, known as Polvax, was permitted during 1976–1979 at Karl Marx University. Among the participants were Politburo member Gyorgy Aczel, then Foreign Minister Frigyes Puja, then Culture Minister Imre Pozsgay, and economist Rezso Nyers.[58] Discussions eventually began to center on controversial issues, such as human rights, questions of leadership, socialist democracy, and communications policy. As might be expected, the meetings were soon attacked by hard-line communists, who called the discussants "Eurocommunists." These discussions, in light of the distinguished participants, serve as an example of how the regime attempts to create channels for dialogue in order to diffuse tension.

A secret Politburo document, leaked to the West in July 1987, analyzes the domestic political opposition and calls for more repression against both individuals and organizations. The anniversary of the 1848 revolution against Austria witnessed 10,000 Hungarians peacefully walking through Budapest on 15 March 1988. The police conducted raids at dawn that day, arresting leaders and confiscating samizdat publications. They used clubs and tear gas to put down a smaller demonstration three months later.

FOREIGN RELATIONS

For all intents and purposes, Hungarian foreign policy follows the Soviet line. Intrabloc relations remain the dominant forum, while support for liberation movements and friendly developing countries proceeds after Soviet initiatives. For example, in September 1980 Hungary signed treaties of friendship and cooperation with Mozambique and Ethiopia, several years after the USSR had done so. Relations with neighboring Romania are strained, due to the large Hungarian minority living in Transylvania.[59] As a matter of fact, one-third of all Hungarians live outside the country in Romania, Slovakia, Yugoslavia, and several Western countries.

Diplomacy in general suffers from subservience to the Soviet Union, and yet Hungarian foreign trade has developed along different lines. Despite an $18 billion hard-currency debt to the West, as of June 1988, the leadership is optimistic about future international economic endeavors. During 1986, exports accounted for 17 percent of the national income. New experiments in foreign trade are being carried out on an impressive scale. One such is the Central-European International Bank at Budapest. Founded in 1979, it represents the only joint venture with a Western majority ownership in Eastern Europe. The purpose is to promote Western trade with Hungary and other CMEA member states as well as to establish joint projects within these countries. At the end of its first year of operation, the bank showed total assets of $165 million.[60] As of the end of 1985, total assets were $385.7 million. In August 1980, Budapest radio announced formation of a new venture in foreign trade. Called Interinvest, it has the objective of increasing exports and decreasing hard-currency imports. Thirty-eight Hungarian foreign trade companies joined together to form Interinvest, which operates as an independent enterprise. It can solicit trade with foreign companies and negotiate agreements on a larger scale than individual enterprises would be able to handle.

Relations with the West continue to be dominated by economics. During 1987 Matyas Szuros, the party's foreign affairs expert, visited the United States and stressed commitment to political reform. Hungary and Israel established interest sections in their respective foreign embassies, a diplomatic link broken two decades earlier. The Federal Republic of Germany seems to be cultivated most, with Premier Karoly Grosz visiting there in October. Other ranking party government leaders traveled to Sweden, Spain, Italy, and Norway, as well as Brazil.

Conclusions.   Under the leadership of Janos Kadar, Hungary had become the bloc's showplace of liberalism and tranquility. Keeping the population content while fostering a policy of individual initiative for the purpose of building socialism may prove to be a difficult task for Kadar's successor. The structure of Hungarian society cannot avoid being affected by the country's economic policy, which in Kadar's words consists of "the socialist planned economy, based on social ownership in conjunction with the independence of enterprises and cooperatives and endorsing group interests and individual financial interests."[61] It remains to be seen just how much independence will be granted to the new-style enterprises and private entrepreneur businesses. Furthermore, any measure of true decentralization in the economic sphere sooner or later will have repercussions on society as a whole. This is the task of Kadar's successor, Karoly Grosz,[62] whose biographic sketch appears in Chapter 11.

NOTES

1. The five political parties (communist, social-democratic, citizens-democratic, smallholders, and people's peasant) organized themselves into a National Independence Front. Sandor Balogh, *Parlamenti es Partharcok Magyarorszagon, 1945–1947* (Budapest, 1972), chaps. 2 and 3.

2. Ibid., pp. 98 and 525. During the next election in August 1947, the communists resorted to various kinds of fraud and intimidation but could increase this figure to only 22.3 percent.

3. Ernst C. Helmreich (ed.), *Hungary* (New York, 1957), p. 81.

4. George Paloczi-Horvath, *The Undefeated* (Boston, 1959), p. 246.

5. Zbigniew K. Brzezinski, *The Soviet Bloc* (New York, 1961), rev. ed., p. 78. Actually, the third congress of the Hungarian communist party, in September 1946, had already announced a "people's democracy."

6. [Hungary], *The Constitution of the Hungarian People's Republic* (Budapest, 1972), consolidated text with amendments through 19 April 1972. For a brief background and text of the constitution, with amendments through 12 April 1975, see William B. Simons (ed.), *The Constitutions of the Communist World* (Alphen aan den Rijn, 1980), pp. 192–213.

7. For example, a total of 43,530 private entrepreneur retail shops and catering units still exist. [Hungary], *Statisztikai evkonyv 1986* (Budapest, 1987), p. 890.

8. Professionals who graduate from universities must compete for listed positions and must work at least three years in jobs for which they are qualified. Decree in *Magyar kozlony,* 15 July 1976.

9. Note, for example, the Presidential Council's decree on the expropriation of private agricultural land that came into force on 1 January 1977. Budapest radio, 27 August 1976.

10. Article 71, *Constitution*, p. 55. In the last five elections, more than one candidate ran in 9 (1967), then 49 (1971), then 34 (1975), only 15 (1980), and finally in all (1985) of the 352 constituencies.

11. He is nonparty Bruno F. Straub, charged with environmental conservation in the parliament. Budapest radio, 29 June 1988.

12. RFE, *East European Leadership List* (1988) p. 23, lists the incumbents.

13. CIA, *World Factbook 1987*, p. 110.

14. See Article 43, *Constitution*, p. 34, for the specific responsibilities of the people's councils.

15. Ibid., Article 50, p. 40, for provision from constitution; Bennett Kovrig, "Hungary," in Richard F. Staar (ed.), *Yearbook on International Communist Affairs: 1985* (Stanford, Calif., 1985), p. 297; henceforth, cited as *YICA*.

16. Helmreich, *Hungary,* p. 85.

17. Kossuth radio, 19 March 1964. Proceedings of the Front's sixth congress were broadcast over Budapest radio, 17–19 September 1976.

18. *Nepszabadsag,* 14 March 1981; *Magyar nemzet,* 16 December 1985.

19. For a study covering the early postwar period see Bennett Kovrig, *Communism in Hungary* (Stanford, Calif., 1979), especially Part II, pp. 69–149.

20. Subsequently, however, Nagy was accused by a Soviet writer of "left-wing errors" and "revisionism" during this period. M. A. Usievich, *Razvitie sotsialisticheskoi ekonomiki Vengrii* (Moscow, 1962), p. 132.

For a discussion of the subsequent period in Hungary, see Bennett Kovrig, "Hungary under Communist Rule," in M. M. Drachkovitch (ed.), *East Central Europe: Yesterday, Today, Tomorrow* (Stanford, Calif., 1982), pp. 287–301.

21. The name "Freedom Fighters" *(szabadsagharcosok)* originated during the 1848 insurrection led by Lajos Kossuth against Hapsburg rule. Russian troops aided the Austrians in putting down the insurrection. For the part played by the United States in allegedly "fomenting" the 1956 revolt see I. I. Orlik, *Vengerskaia Narodnaia Respublika* (Moscow, 1962), pp. 51–53.

22. See, for example, Ferenc A. Vali, *Rift and Revolt in Hungary* (Cambridge, Mass., 1961), p. 590. Some 32,000 refugees (including 1,800 students) came to the United States. *New York Times,* 31 December 1976. During the aftermath, about 63,000 Hungarians were deported to Siberia. Reportedly, 463 participants still remained in the central prison at Budapest; another 143, who were under eighteen in 1956, were executed as they came of age. Rev. Bela Fabian and Imre Kovacs, "Kadar's Hungary," *New York Times Magazine,* 24 January 1965, p. 6.

23. A decision taken allegedly on his own initiative, according to a Soviet biography. Iu. Egorov (ed.), *Ianosh [Janos] Kadar* (Moscow, 1960), pp. 622–23.

24. Jozsef Koevago, "Establishment and Operation of a Communist State Order," in Robert F. Delaney (ed.), *This is Communist Hungary* (Chicago, 1958), p. 197.

25. Ianosh [Janos] Kadar, *Otchetnyi doklad Tsentralnogo Komiteta Vengerskoi Sotsialisticheskoi Rabochei Partii na VIII sezdu partii* (Moscow, 1964), p. 75. It was admitted that some 38 percent of these joined after May 1957, that is, following the revolt.

As of 1 January 1980, a total of 74 percent of the membership had joined the party after 1956. *The 12th Congress of the Socialist Workers' Party: 24–27 March 1980,* p. 10 (English translation of the first source in note 27 below).

26. *Nepszabadsag,* 29 November 1966.

27. *A Magyar Szocialista Munkaspart XII kongresszusanak jegyzokonyve* (Budapest, 1980), p. 24; *The Economist* (6 June 1981), p. 52; *Kozneveles,* 22 May 1987.

28. [Hungary], *The 13th Congress of the Hungarian Socialist Workers' Party* (Budapest, 1985), p. 14, where they are called branch organizations.

29. *New York Times,* 23 May 1988, p. A-5; *Izvestiia,* 30 May 1988, p. 3.

30. The United States raised its diplomatic relations with Hungary to the ambassadorial level on 28 November 1966. Subsequently, agreement on the repayment of debts for U.S. goods purchased after World War II and on U.S. pensions to certain Hungarians was

reached, according to Press Release no. 242, U.S. Department of State, *Bulletin* (15 August 1969), p. 214. See also U.S. Congress, Subcommittee on Europe, Committee on Foreign Affairs, "Hungarian Claims Legislation," *Hearing* (Washington, D.C., 4 April 1974) and *New York Times,* 5 December 1976, about the crown of St. Stephen as well as other treasures held at Fort Knox, Ky. The crown, a symbol of Hungarian nationalism, was returned by the U.S. government. *New York Times,* 6 January 1978.

31. Quoted in *East Europe* (April 1964), p. 42.

32. Istvan Szirmai in *Tarsadalmi szemle* (April 1965); translated by *Hungarian Press Survey,* 20 April 1965.

33. Hubert Ripka, *Eastern Europe in the Post-War World* (New York, 1961), p. 9.

34. Vali, *Rift and Revolt in Hungary,* p. 87.

35. Even in 1957 there were no more than 3,000 kulaks or wealthy peasants who "exploited" the labor of others. G. V. Barabashev, *Gosudarstvennyi stroi Vengerskoi Narodnoi Respubliki* (Moscow, 1961), p. 21, n. 2.

36. *Magyar nemzet,* 28 November 1980.

37. *Pravda,* 24 February 1981.

38. *Nepszabadsag,* 22 January 1981. *Statistical Pocket Book of Hungary 1986* (Budapest, 1987), p. 30.

39. *Nepszabadsag,* 2 August 1969.

40. *Statisztikai evkonyv 1979* (Budapest, 1980), pp. 250–51; *Statistical Yearbook 1985* (Budapest, 1987), p. 186.

41. *Statisztikai evkonyv,* p. 247; *Nepszabadsag,* 4 January 1981; *Statistical Yearbook 1985,* p. 180; CIA, *Handbook of Economic Statistics* (1986), p. 105.

42. Kovrig, *Communism in Hungary,* pp. 233–84, discusses the 1948–1955 period in detail.

43. Vali, *Rift and Revolt in Hungary,* p. 82.

44. Edward Taborsky, "The 'Old' and the 'New' Course in Satellite Economy," *Journal of Central European Affairs* (January 1958), p. 383.

45. Reportedly credits totaled $320 million during 1956–1958. Lucjan Ciamaga, *Od wspolpracy do integracji* (Warsaw, 1965), pp. 39–40.

46. CIA, *World Factbook 1987,* pp. 103 and 104.

47. *Magyar kozlony,* no. 94 (18 December 1980); *New York Times,* 26 April 1981.

48. *Vneshniaia torgovlia,* no. 3 (March 1981), insert; *Statisztkai evkonyv 1979,* pp. 304–5; CIA, *World Factbook 1987,* p. 110; CMEA, *Statisticheskii ezhegodnik* (1987), p. 305.

49. Article by Jozsef Balint in *Pravda* (Moscow), 27 March 1970. Note also the experiment with "direct democracy," subsequently conducted at 50 enterprises. Budapest radio, 22 September 1976.

50. Some 3.7 percent of the employed population works as artisans or small private shopkeepers. *Statistical Yearbook* (1987), p. 28.

51. Zoltan Barany, *YICA: 1988,* pp. 279–81.

52. "Hungarian Bishops Abroad," *East Europe* (January 1964), p. 42.

53. Vali, *Rift and Revolt in Hungary,* p. 65.

54. Resumption marked a step in an attempt by the state to regain financial control over the church. U.S. Senate, Committee on the Judiciary, *The Church and State Under Communism* (Washington, D.C., 1965), vol. 6, pp. 10–11.

55. *Nepszabadsag,* 28 April 1976. Lekai had served as Cardinal Mindszenty's secretary in 1945 at Veszprem.

56. *Magyar hirlap,* 15 March 1981.

57. *Esti hirlap,* no. 22 (August 1979).

58. Chief architect of the 1968 economic reform, Nyers has called for a continuation of these measures. *Nepszabadsag,* 30 November 1980.

59. Bennett Kovrig, "Hungary," in *YICA: 1979,* p. 48, *1981,* pp. 265–66. Some 30,000 citizens marched to the Romanian embassy in Budapest in protest over plans to destroy 7,000 Hungarian villages in Transylvania. *Nepszabadsag,* 28 June 1988. p. 9.

60. *Business Eastern Europe* 10, no. 6 (6 February 1981), p. 44. *Insight,* 20 June 1988, p. 39, for the debt.

61. *A Magyyar Szocialista Munkaspart XII. kongressusanak jegyzokonyve,* p. 10.

62. Grosz was received by M. S. Gorbachev in Moscow on 5 July 1988.

Chapter 6
Polish People's Republic

The USSR accomplished a classic operation when it installed a puppet communist regime at Warsaw. All odds were against such a transformation.[1] The countries of Eastern Europe seemed more receptive to democracy after World War II than they had been after World War I. The populations had become completely disenchanted with semidictatorships and disgusted by ruthless Nazi and Soviet occupation forces. The Poles, in particular, with their homogeneity and intense nationalism, craved such basic democratic attributes as self-government, freedom of speech, and private ownership. They also sought freedom to practice their Roman Catholic religion, an ideology that was diametrically opposed to the atheistic communist system soon to be imposed upon them from the outside.

Given the foregoing factors, and assuming that it had freedom of choice, Poland would have been the East European country least likely to fall under Soviet domination. Yet it did, and even today it remains under the control of a communist regime. The governmental structure is patterned, in all important aspects, after that of the USSR. Although two subordinate political organizations exist, there is no doubt as to who rules in Warsaw: the Polish United Workers' Party (*Polska Zjednoczona Partia Robotnicza*—PZPR).

Historically, Soviet leaders have maintained a belief that whoever controls the East European countries will ultimately dominate all of Europe. A corollary is that the power that holds Poland will be in a key position in Eastern Europe. At the Yalta conference, Stalin agreed in February 1945 to a formula for establishing a Polish government through "free and unfettered elections as soon as possible on the basis of universal suffrage and secret ballot."[2] But the Soviets interpreted the words "free" and "unfettered" in a totalitarian manner. Their understanding of a government friendly to the USSR, which the formula also proposed, meant only a regime that would act in blind obedience to the Kremlin. Therefore, they quickly exploited the early postwar situation and pushed ahead with typical Trojan-horse tactics. These consisted of infiltration, subversion, purges, and terrorism, all directed toward obtaining control over communications, elections, and sensitive government positions—particularly the Interior Ministry and its security police.

ELECTORAL PROCEDURES

In the years since World War II there have been ten occasions on which the communist leadership asked the people of Poland to decide on the composition of government by means of parliamentary elections. The first, in 1947, came during an intermediate stage in the subjugation of Eastern Europe by the USSR. The goal was clear: to eliminate all opposition by any means necessary (including violence, deception, and falsified results). The campaign was directed primarily against the Polish Peasant Party[3] and the Roman Catholic church. Despite widespread dissatisfaction and disillusionment on the part of the population, a ruthlessly conducted campaign rewarded the communists with success.

By 1952 there was little need to fire bullets or falsify ballots. The communists were in full control. Statutes had been promulgated that made it impossible for an opposition candidate to be considered for election. All of the unopposed 425 United Front candidates for parliament (including the communists, candidates from two bogus political parties, and a few independents) received overwhelming majorities. As might have been predicted, it was announced that more than fifteen million persons, or 95 percent of the electorate, had voted.

The characteristics that distinguished the elections that took place between 1957 and 1980 included (1) an apparent but superficial relaxation of the dictatorial stranglehold on the population, (2) a real yet subtle and sophisticated communist totalitarianism, and (3) public awareness of these conditions, resulting in widespread apathy.

In 1957 the elections were somewhat modified when the communists allowed more candidates to run than there were seats available in parliament (a total of 750 candidates for 459 seats). In view of the fact that all genuine opposition parties had been liquidated in 1947 and none had been allowed to come into existence in the ten years since then, the ruling party presumably considered this a safe concession. Even so, the communist leadership had misgivings about the turnout at the polls and about the possibility of widespread crossing-out of communist-proposed names from the ballot by voters.

To eliminate these doubts, the communist first secretary, Wladyslaw Gomulka, delivered a major speech to the nation shortly before the election. "Deletion of our party's candidates," he warned, "is synonymous with obliterating Poland from the map of Europe."[4] The implication was that unless support appeared to be overwhelming, Poland might suffer the fate of Hungary. The voters heeded the warning.

However, in 1961 support was noticeably less overwhelming. For example, in Warsaw only 55 percent of the eligible voters bothered to register. The emotion of the electorate could best be described as apathetic. There was no hope for outside help other than the aid that had been provided by Western radio broadcasts. The tragedy in Hungary had offered proof that an uprising would be crushed by Soviet armed forces.

In the 1965 elections there were 617 candidates for the 460 seats in parliament. The formality of voting took place on 30 May with the results shown in Table 31. In only one way could the population manifest its discontent—by crossing out the names of persons belonging to the communist elite. Among districts with large populations and thus several seats, a candidate whose name had been crossed off by numerous voters could still be elected if he received more than half the ballots. However, his ranking within the district would drop below those of other successful candidates who received larger numbers of votes. This kind of ranking can serve as a basis for judging the public image or popularity of each candidate.

Table 31
POLISH PARLIAMENTARY ELECTIONS, 1965–1985

| | SEATS WON | | | | 1985 | |
PARTY OR OTHER GROUP	*1965*	*1969*	*1972*	*1976, 1980*	*Seats*	*Percentage*
Polish United Workers' Party	255	255	255	261	245	53.3
United Peasant Party	117	117	117	113	106	23.0
Democratic Party	39	39	39	37	35	7.6
Nonparty	36	35	36	36 ⎫	74 ⎫	16.1
Catholic activists	13	14	13	13 ⎭	⎭	
Total	460	460	460	460	460	100.0

SOURCES: *Trybuna ludu*, 3 June 1965, 5 June 1969, 21 March 1972, 25–26 March 1980. RFE, *Situation Report*, 26 March 1976; *Polityka* (3 April 1976), p. 4; [Poland], *Polska: dane statystyczne* (Warsaw, 1987), p. 19.

NOTES: For the background of the above political groups, see R. F. Staar, *Poland 1944–1962* (Westport, Conn., 1975), pp. 227–40.

The 1972 electoral campaign involved 625 National Unity Front candidates running for 460 seats. Two-thirds of those elected were newcomers. Although the voters could not influence the outcome, they rearranged the order of preference in all eighty constituencies; in only seven of these constituencies did the top-listed candidates keep that position.[5] Four years later the electorate returned only 15 of the 71 candidates at the top of the list with a majority, and six of the nine Central Committee secretaries dropped in the final ranking. Voter turnout in 1976 was lowest in Gdansk, Gdynia, central Lodz, and Szczecin, the cities in which most of the December 1970 rioting had occurred.[6]

Results of the 23 March 1980 elections were identical with those of March 1976. A reported 98.8 percent of those eligible went to the polls, and National

Unity Front candidates received 99.5 percent of all valid votes. Subsequent events in Poland would prove to have an impact on the composition of the *Sejm,* or parliament, including the dismissal of three consecutive premiers: Piotr Jarosze-wicz replaced by Edward Babiuch (18 February 1980); Babiuch by Jozef Pin-kowski (24 August 1980); Pinkowski by Wojciech Jaruzelski (9 February 1981). This last man gave up the premiership to Zbigniew Messner in November 1985, after national elections.

In contrast to all preceding ones, elections held in October 1985 attracted less than 79 percent of those eligible to vote, according to the regime. Independent estimates suggest that only 60 percent of the electorate went to the polls. The final results in parliament did not differ substantially from earlier ones. (See Table 31.) Arrests and intimidation, combined with heavy propaganda, had not brought out a heavy vote.[7]

THE 1952 CONSTITUTION

The farce of the Polish people's democratic governmental structure extends to its very foundation, namely the constitution. On the surface this basic law possesses all the elements of a progressive instrument written by the people to serve the people. In actual fact, it was prepared by a hard core of Soviet-trained communist party leaders. In most respects it derives from the 1936 ''Stalin'' constitution, which still remained applicable to the USSR at the end of 1977.

The preamble to Poland's basic law provides an opening clue to the unreality of the democratic facade. Unlike its 1921 and 1935 predecessors, this docu-ment expresses no religious dependence. References to God have been replaced by verbiage about allegiance and gratitude to the Soviet Union. A second clue can be found in the obvious alignment with the governmental structure of the USSR, which at the time claimed to be centered on the proletariat. The Polish constitution of 1952 avowedly relates itself to ''the historical experience of the victorious socialist constitution in the USSR, the first state of workers and peasants.''[8]

Following the preamble, the document consists of three principal segments divided into ten chapters and 91 articles. The opening and closing chapters de-scribe in general terms the political, social, and economic structure of the people's democracy. Aesopian language comes into full play throughout Chapters 1 and 2 in the descriptions of free elections, social and economic equality, and a govern-ment operated by and for the peasants and workers. The middle section, Chapters 3 through 6, deals with principal state organs: the legislature, the executive, and the judiciary.

The 1952 constitution was amended in February 1976 but in a modified form because of a wave of protest that had begun the previous December in response to a draft. As a result, statements about the leading role of the PZPR, Poland's unbreakable ties with the Soviet Union, and the need to make civil rights dependent on the performance of duties were removed from the phraseology. The amendments[9] proclaim Poland to be a socialist state, urge friendship with the Soviet Union and other socialist states, and finally exhort citizens to fulfill their obligations.

Legislature. The parliament, or *Sejm,* is described as the supreme organ of state authority. Its 460 members are elected to four-year terms. Full sessions are held once every six months. Theoretically, the *Sejm* makes laws, controls other state agencies, and appoints and recalls the government. It formally elects the Council of State. In actual practice, this body merely gives official approval to drafts of laws proposed by the executive organs of government and also rubber-stamps Council of State decrees. In recent years, however, there has been considerable debate in the *Sejm.* Although regime proposals always pass, some of the deputies have recorded negative votes on legislation.

At the ninth extraordinary PZPR congress (14–20 July 1981), Premier Jaruzelski presented proposals to revitalize the Council of Ministers and also entrust more "real" power to the *Sejm.*[10] This has not yet happened.

Council of State. This body, which is elected from and by parliament to four-year terms in office, consists of a chairman who acts as chief of state, four deputy chairmen, a secretary, and twelve other members.[11] The Council of State possesses the authority to call elections, summon parliament, interpret laws, appoint and recall diplomatic representatives, supervise local people's councils, and issue decrees during the intervals between *Sejm* sessions.

In general, the Council of State performs most of the functions formerly assigned to the presidency. It is not a vitally important policymaking body, but it remains useful to the ruling party as a vehicle for issuing decrees. The elimination of the presidency and the transfer of its functions to the Council of State aligned the government structure more closely with those of the Soviet Union and other East European countries.

Up to 1952 the post of president was filled by Boleslaw Bierut, who also headed the Polish communist party. During the next fourteen years, Aleksander Zawadzki served as chairman of the State Council. After his death in 1964, Edward Ochab became chief of state. (It was Ochab who stepped down from the party leadership in October 1956 in favor of Wladyslaw Gomulka.) He resigned from the Council of State because of poor health in 1968. Former Defense Minister Marian Spychalski and former Premier Jozef Cyrankiewicz each served two years in succession. In March 1972 the titular chief of state was former Education Minister Henryk Jablonski, succeeded in November 1985 by junta leader Wojciech Jaruzelski.[12]

Council of Ministers.   This body is defined as the highest executive and administrative organ of state authority. Its duties include the coordination of ministries, the preparation of the budget and economic plans, the supervision of public law and order, and the control of foreign and defense policies. In 1988 the Council of Ministers consisted of 28 members headed by a chairman or premier.[13]

This instrument of the government is supposedly the key policymaking agency. Following the ninth PZPR congress in July 1981, an attempt was made to simplify the Council of Ministers in order to improve its efficiency. At a meeting of the *Sejm,* Premier Jaruzelski announced that eight ministers had been replaced, five new ones appointed, and four others reassigned.[14] All the changes occurred in the economic sector, except for replacement of the higher education minister. In a further move to streamline the government, parliament created four ministries out of the eight previously dealing with agriculture, food, energy, mining, chemicals, metallurgy, machinery, and heavy machinery. At the same time, the Maritime Economy Office was separated from the Foreign Trade Ministry, in order that the latter could more effectively handle its responsibilities.

The People's Councils.   These organs are similar in all respects to the soviets in the USSR. They comprise local administrative units existing in each of the 2,120 communes, 813 towns, and 49 provinces.[15] The term of office for all councils is four years and coincides with that of the *Sejm.* Their main functions include the adoption of local economic plans and budgets, the supervision of local law enforcement, the maintenance of public services and, in general, the linking of local needs to state tasks. Executive organs called presidia are responsible to the next higher echelon, with the provincial level presidia subordinated in turn to the Council of State.

The activities of the people's councils are defined in a law of 25 January 1958. They have jurisdiction over the protection of public order, agriculture, local industry and handicrafts, local building and the development of towns and villages, communal housing arrangements and policy, domestic trade, government purchases, public transportation and the construction and maintenance of roads, the management of waterways, education and culture, health and tourism, unemployment, social welfare, and finances. The law was amended in June 1988.

The Judicial System.   This area of government is administered by the Supreme Court for the country as a whole. Provincial, county, and special courts operate at successively lower levels. Justices on the Supreme Court are elected to five-year terms by the Council of State. Lower-ranking judges receive their appointments from the justice minister.[16] The makeup of the judicial system shows the absence of any separation of powers. No provision exists for judicial review, and the interpretation of laws belongs to the Council of State, which is a body theoretically created by parliament. A prosecutor general investigates offenses that are deemed harmful to the safety and independence of the Polish People's Republic. He is assisted by a militia (regular uniformed police) and a secret police.

Constitutional Practice. In any discussion of the governmental structure, it would be a serious error to overlook a concept adopted by the communist hierarchy known as "constitutional practice." Under this practice, directives are issued that supposedly interpret the real meaning of provisions in the constitution. Changes are made in the content of some provisions, while other provisions are rejected. New regulations or institutions that were not envisioned by the constitution are introduced.

There were several examples of "constitutional practice" between the adoption in 1952 of the fundamental law and its 1976 amendments. By passing an ordinary resolution, for instance, it is always possible for the *Sejm* to expel members. This concept has also enabled members of parliament to ignore constitutional provisions forbidding them to hold government posts and preventing government officials from holding more than one post simultaneously. In effect, there is no binding constitutional law. The constitution can be manipulated and reinterpreted in any manner that the ruling party sees fit and that will best serve its needs.

Democratic Centralism. A key principle in communist governmental systems is designated by the term "democratic centralism," which refers to an organizational theory developed by Lenin and also to a technique that he first put into practice. The principle, in both aspects, arose for Lenin's demand for tight, centralized control that would at the same time allow for flexibility of execution and mass participation in administrative activities. The principle is thus used vertically in centralized control and horizontally in mass participation. This system has also been called "dual subordination."

All policy decisions and directives emanate from the top and filter down vertically to the lowest echelons of the governmental structure. There is little room for interpretation and none for interference or disagreement. At the same time, a horizontal line of activity is carried on by the various territorial units. Each of these performs specific administrative tasks within its own limited sphere. It is apparent that once again the Aesopian language needs interpretation. What the propaganda statements allude to as "local democratic autonomy" is not in fact local, democratic, or autonomous. Such statements merely signify that the implementation of centralized directives is locally administered.

THE COMMUNIST PARTY

The population of Poland is just over 38.5 million. Of this number, approximately 2.1 million belong to the ruling political movement, which represents about 5.5

percent of the population. (See Table 32.) Like the Communist Party of the Soviet Union, the Polish United Workers' Party—the PZPR—maintains a dictatorship in the name of the working class,[17] which itself has only minority representation in the party. How is it possible that a few men in control of an organization that has only a minority of the people as members can maintain such regimentation over a nation? The answer lies in the structure of the party and in the principle of democratic centralism.

General Organization. The Polish communist party is organized along five distinct levels: the primary party organization (PPO) at the bottom, then the

Table 32
GROWTH OF THE POLISH COMMUNIST PARTY, 1942–1988

Date	Number of members	Date	Number of members
1942 (July)	4,000	1966 (June)	1,848,000
1943 (January)	8,000	1967 (May)	2,000,000
1944 (July)	20,000[a]	1970 (October)	2,296,000[c]
1945 (January)	30,000	1971 (December)	2,270,000
1946 (July)	364,000	1975 (November)	2,453,000
1947 (July)	848,000	1976 (December)	2,500,000
1948 (December)	1,500,000[b]	1980 (September)	3,158,000
1950 (December)	1,360,000	1981 (April)	2,942,000[d]
1952 (June)	1,129,000	1982 (June)	2,488,000
1954 (March)	1,297,000	1983 (January)	2,327,349
1956 (January)	1,344,000	1984 (May)	2,327,349
1959 (March)	1,067,000	1985 (June)	2,112,000
1961 (July)	1,270,000	1986 (July)	2,125,762
1963 (January)	1,397,000	1987 (May)	2,130,000
1965 (January)	1,640,000	1988 (May)	over 2,000,000

SOURCES: R. F. Staar, *Poland, 1944–1962* (Westport, Conn., 1975), p. 167 (citing various Polish sources for the years 1942–1961); Tadeusz Galinski (ed.), *Rocznik polityczny i gospodarczy 1963* (Warsaw, 1963), p. 98; *Trybuna ludu*, 31 October 1965, 14 August 1966, and 17 May 1967; Warsaw radio, 3 November 1970; *VI zjazd* (Warsaw, 1972), p. 67; *Polish Perspectives* (November 1975), p. 5; Warsaw radio, 1 December 1976; *Glos wybrzeza*, 9 July 1981; Warsaw radio, 12 June 1982; *Polityka*, 30 July 1983; *Nowe drogi* (May 1984); *Trybuna ludu*, 13 June 1985; *Polityka*, 5 July 1986; *Sueddeutsche Zeitung*, 25 May 1987; *Polityka*, 14 May 1988, p. 6.

NOTES: [a]Some eight thousand of these returned from the USSR with the advancing Red Army. *Nowe drogi* (January–February 1951), p. 235.

[b]After the fusion congress with the socialists.

[c]Includes 206,640 candidates for membership or 9 percent of the total.

[d]Between 1 July 1980 and 30 April 1981, approximately 28,100 new members were accepted into the party while 253,600 left. Of the latter 164,800 had resigned. *Glos wybrzeza* (Gdansk), 9 July 1981.

commune, county, province, and national levels. With the exception of the 20,270 PPOs, each of the lower levels includes a body of delegates to the next higher echelon. At the intermediate levels these bodies are called conferences; when delegates are assembled on a national scale, they form the party congress. Conferences and congresses are too large for handling routine party business. Therefore they form committees for day-to-day activities. The committees then elect bureaus and even smaller organs, secretariats, to handle party affairs. In effect this system represents a duplication of the government's administrative structure, but it costs more than the state bureaucracy because of the higher salaries paid to party officials.

These units and the individual secretaries theoretically are responsible to the parent group on the same level, reporting to it on the implementation of tasks.[18] All meetings, committees, organs, and individual secretaries also remain sensitive to direction coming from higher levels and report to them. In this horizontal and vertical network of responsibility, the principle of democratic centralism, or dual subordination, manifests itself. The tripartite division of authority at each level (meeting, committee, organ) is in reality a device used to create the feeling among rank-and-file party members that they are involved in decisionmaking. The real authority rests with the occupant of the key post at each level, the secretary or first secretary who heads the executive organ.

During the first half of 1981, provincial committees underwent a sweeping change. Before the extraordinary party congress in mid-July, the first secretaries of 30 of these 49 regional organizations had been fired, and nine others lost elections. Eighty percent of the officials in city party committees had been replaced. In Krakow alone, fourteen of the top sixteen apparatus workers were voted out of office.[19]

Relationships among the five party levels are governed by a statute issued at the third PZPR congress in 1959 and amended by subsequent congresses through the tenth in July 1986. This document defines the principle of democratic centralism. Relations among the various levels are guided by the following rules, which appear under Chapter 2, paragraph 17, of the statute:

All directing authorities from the lowest to the highest are elected in a democratic manner.

All party resolutions are passed by a majority vote.

All party authorities are required to report to the party organizations [that elect them].

Maintenance of party discipline [is required], and the minority is subordinate to the resolutions of the majority.

Resolutions and directives from higher party authorities must be carried out by lower ones.[20]

Significant changes in the statute were proposed and accepted by the ninth extraordinary party congress in mid-July 1981. Reportedly they will "strengthen the role of basic party links and introduce considerably broader rights for the party's elective organs as opposed to executive bodies." The new statute also introduced genuine control by voters over elective bodies, "as the mandates are supposed to remain valid throughout the term of office," meaning the delegates to the ninth congress will retain their powers until the tenth congress. Under these changes, a congress can be convened on consent of more than 50 percent of all delegates.[21]

Seven years after his election as first secretary in October 1981, Jaruzelski appears firmly in control; his list of Politburo and Secretariat members was accepted without question. The only candidate for the post of first secretary, Jaruzelski's nomination was greeted with "enthusiastic applause." Of the 229 Central Committee members, 228 cast their votes for Jaruzelski (the one abstention was probably Jaruzelski). The Politburo is packed with Jaruzelski's cronies (Kiszczak, Siwicki, Baryla, Messner, Czyrek), the first three of whom are military officers. Mikhail Gorbachev expressed strong support for the PZPR first secretary in his speech to the tenth congress.[22]

Theoretically, ultimate control in the party rests with the meetings of members—at the highest level, the congress; at intermediate levels, the conferences; at the bottom level, the primary party organization meeting. In actual practice, these bodies are little more than rubber-stamp organs whose consent serves to legalize, in the eyes of the rank and file, the actions taken by the party leaders. Some 20,270 primary party organizations (PPOs) represent the base of this vast facade for the few who actually make decisions in Poland today. There are three types of primary party organizations:

Institutional, for those working in factories, mines, railroad yards, government agencies, hospitals, or universities

Village, in rural areas for peasants, artisans, teachers, and doctors

Territorial, in urban areas for those employed by small shops that do not have a primary party organization and the unemployed (e.g., housewives)[23]

Of the three types, the institutional is normally the largest. If the organization has more than a hundred members it can be subdivided into brigades, aggregate units, work areas, or shifts, according to the specific production links of the industry involved. General meetings of the primary party organizations are being replaced by institutional, village, and territorial conferences of delegates from the smaller units. These conferences avoid convening at the lowest party level, so they provide much tighter control over the participation of individual members.

Whether it occurs at the level of the primary party organization, the commune, the county, or the province,[24] all activity and work is theoretically handled in accordance with the principle of democratic centralism. The concentration of power in the hands of a small elite is perpetuated through this procedure.

All meetings, conferences, commission sessions, and the like, supposedly expressing the attitudes of Polish United Workers' Party's rank-and-file members, remain open to influence from above. Itinerant groups from higher authority attend meetings to see whether all is proceeding in accordance with the first secretary's wishes. A good example of this principle on an international scale occurred during the eighth plenary session of the party's Central Committee. The meeting had just begun when the chairman announced the arrival of Nikita Khrushchev, Viacheslav Molotov, Lazar Kaganovich, and Anastas Mikoyan, among others. The top hierarchy in Moscow, having learned that standard operating procedures were not being observed in Poland, had come to investigate. This took place in October 1956 and was accompanied by simultaneous Soviet troop movements in the direction of Warsaw. After an all-night discussion, the Soviet leaders agreed to the election of Wladyslaw Gomulka as first secretary.

The National Congress.   The ruling party's first postwar congress[25] convened at the end of 1945. There have been ten congresses since that time. The "fusion congress" of 1948 involved a forced merger of left-wing socialists with communists; for that reason it is known as the first. Party congresses have been convened as follows:

First postwar (PPR) congress	6–12 December 1945
First PZPR (unification) congress	15–21 December 1948
Second PZPR congress	10–17 March 1954
Third PZPR congress	10–19 March 1959
Fourth PZPR congress	15–20 June 1964
Fifth PZPR congress	11–16 November 1968
Sixth PZPR congress	6–11 December 1971
Seventh PZPR congress	8–12 December 1975
Eighth PZPR congress	11–15 February 1980
Ninth (extraordinary) PZPR congress	14–20 July 1981
Tenth PZPR congress	29 June–3 July 1986

At first the party congresses were scheduled to meet at least once every three years, but this interval was changed to four years in the new statute adopted by the third congress and extended at the seventh congress to five years.[26] The meeting held in June 1964 was fifteen months overdue. This postponement probably resulted from uncertainty regarding the control exercised by Gomulka. Extraordinary national party conferences may be called by the Central Committee or by application of a majority of the province committees. So far only two extraordinary conferences have been held, in October 1973, to discuss a socioeconomic development program for the country, and in March 1984 after the ninth congress.

A total of 1,811 delegates attended the seventh congress in December 1975. Present were representatives from 65 other communist parties, including a Soviet delegation headed by Leonid I. Brezhnev. It was here that the CPSU general secretary gave strong endorsement to the policies of Edward Gierek. Nothing ever happened at any of these congresses that had not been arranged in advance down to the smallest detail. Elections were rigged with one candidate for each post, and a rubber-stamp balloting or acclamation registered approval to the actions of the party leadership.

The eighth PZPR congress in February 1980 has been overshadowed by subsequent domestic turmoil and by convening of the ninth extraordinary congress only seventeen months later. It became apparent even before the ninth congress opened that it would be an unprecedented event in the history of communist party congresses. Delegates had been elected by secret ballot, not handpicked in the usual manner by party leaders. Of the 1,955 representatives, all but 121 were attending a congress for the first time. Approximately 22.5 percent of them were members of the autonomous Solidarity trade union or Rural Solidarity.[27] In a break with tradition, the congress opened with the Polish national anthem, which preceded the customary "Internationale."

On opening day of the ninth PZPR congress, delegates refused to vote party leader Stanislaw Kania back into office before a new 200-member Central Committee had been elected. That body would then choose a first secretary. In his address on opening day, Kania leveled criticism at both dogmatism and revisionism. He warned of the danger from counterrevolutionary forces in society at large. Kania insisted, however, that reform would continue and include changes in the party's own statutes. Deputy Prime Minister Mieczyslaw Rakowski told the congress that any retreat from *odnowa* (renewal) would lead to a bloodbath.[28]

Kania continued as PZPR leader about thirteen and a half months, until his resignation at a Central Committee plenum in mid-October 1981. During that session, he suggested that the one million PZPR members who belonged to Solidarity would have to choose one organization or the other. The sole woman Politburo member, Zofia Grzyb, promptly resigned from Solidarity, and party control commissions in the provinces began purging prominent trade union spokesmen from the PZPR.

The tenth PZPR congress, the first held since martial law and the ban on Solidarity, took place during the summer of 1986. Delegates adopted a resolution to increase the standard of living based on the premise that national income would grow 16 to 19 percent during the five years through the end of 1990.[29] Jozef Czyrek's report to the congress included generalities about accelerating economic development and supporting USSR foreign policy objectives. He emphasized that the new program outlined long-range goals for the first time since World War II.

The Central Committee.   This organ is chosen by the party congress. The Central Committee is supposed to meet at least once every four months in plenary session. It has the following functions: to represent the party externally with other communist parties, to establish party institutions and direct their activities, to nominate the editorial boards of party newspapers, and to control party cadres that are sent into the field.

At the ninth congress, 275 nominees ran for the 200 Central Committee seats and 105 for the 70 candidate posts.[30] In all, 618 names appeared on the ballots to fill 430 positions in the Central Committee, Audit Commission, and Control Commission, meaning that every third delegate to the congress ran for one of these offices. Of the 200 members on the new Central Committee, only 18 had served previously.[31] This Central Committee included 80 workers; 28 farmers; thirteen first secretaries of factory committees; eleven technical specialists; nine professors; eight first secretaries of province committees; eight medical doctors; six teachers; six directors or deputy directors of industrial, construction, and farming enterprises; six army officers; five ministers and deputy ministers; five pensioners; two farmhands; three Central Committee secretaries from previous terms; a premier; a deputy premier; a journalist; an actor; a chief forester; a seaman; the head of and an activist in the Polish Scouts' Union (leaving two unaccounted for).[32] This was undoubtedly the most representative of the rank and file for any Central Committee in the Soviet bloc at that time.

However, following the tenth PZPR congress, no multiple candidates were allowed. A single slate of 231 Central Committee members and 58 candidate members was offered to the delegates, who voted unanimously to elect all of them. Formally the secret ballot has been retained, although only for the Politburo and Secretariat. Candidates for these positions are "approved" by the Central Committee through an open vote.[33]

The Political Bureau.   According to the party statute, a Politburo is elected by the Central Committee from among its own membership and is entrusted with directing the work of that body between plenary sessions. This agency parallels in importance the position of the Soviet communist party's Political Bureau. It is the most powerful among all the organs and represents the summit of the party hierarchy. All of its members can be found on a 1988 list of the power elite. (See Table 33.)

It is in the Politburo that one sees the principle of interlocking directorates at work. As members of the Politburo, the hierarchs make policy; as Secretariat members, certain of them see to it that policy is carried out by the party apparatus; and as government officials, they legalize policy in the form of laws and decrees

Table 33
POLISH COMMUNIST PARTY LEADERSHIP, 1988

Politburo (15)	Year of birth	Year elected	Secretariat	Council of Ministers	Other positions
Jaruzelski, Wojciech	1923	1971	First secretary		Chairman, State Council; National Defense Council
Baka, Wladyslaw	1936	1988	Secretary		Deputy chairman, State Council
Barcikowski, Kazimierz	1927	1971	Secretary		Chairman, Internal Affairs and Party Activity Commission
Baryla, Jozef	1924	1986	Secretary		
Czyrek, Jozef	1928	1981	Secretary		Chairman, International Commission and Foreign Affairs Commission of Sejm
Glowczyk, Jan	1927	1981	Secretary		Chairman, Propaganda Commission
Kiszczak, Czeslaw	1925	1986		Internal affairs minister	
Messner, Zbigniew	1929	1981		Premier	
Miodowicz, Alfred	1929	1986			Chairman, National Confederation of Trade Unions; Suggestions and Complaints Committee
Muranski, Zygmunt	1952	1986			Chairman, Mining, Raw Materials and Energy Commission
Orzechowski, Marian	1931	1986	Secretary		Chairman, Ideology Commission
Porebski, Tadeusz	1931	1981			Chairman, Science and Education Commission; deputy speaker, Sejm
Rakowski, Mieczyslaw F.	1926	1987	Secretary		Chairman, Socioeconomic Council
Siwicki, Florian	1925	1981		Defense minister	Deputy chairman, National Defense Council

Name					
Stepien, Zofia	1939	1986			Chairman, Family Affairs Commission
CANDIDATES (5)					
Ciosek, Stanislaw	1939	1988			General secretary PRON
Gorywoda, Manfred	1942	1988	Chairman, Planning Commission		Deputy chairman, Economic Reform Commission; Economic Policy, Reform and Worker Self-Management Commission
Kubasiewicz, Janusz	1938	1986			First secretary, Warsaw City
Michalek, Zbigniew	1935	1986		Secretary	Chairman, Agriculture, Food Economy and Forestry Commission
Rembisz, Gabriela	1937	1986			

SOURCES: CIA, *Directory of Polish Officials* (April 1987). FRE, *East European Leadership List* (15 January 1988), pp. 33–36. *Trybuna ludu*, 15 June 1988, pp. 1 and 3; *Pravda*, 19 June 1988, p. 4.

that become effective throughout the country. The internal operations of the Politburo are cloaked in secrecy. The chief of this organ is Wojciech Jaruzelski, who also serves as first secretary of the Central Committee.

At the ninth congress, for the first time a party leader was elected by secret ballot from among two candidates: Stanislaw Kania, the incumbent first secretary, and Kazimierz Barcikowski, Politburo member and secretary. On 18 July 1981, results of voting that had taken place in closed session of the congress were announced: with 1,939 delegates casting valid ballots, Barcikowski received 568 votes to Kania's 1,311 (60 votes went against both candidates).[34] The fifteen-member Politburo elected at the congress included only four out of eleven former members. Among the newcomers were a pro-Moscow hardliner, Albin Siwak; a member of Solidarity, Zofia Grzyb, who was also the first woman to sit on that body; a miner, Jerzy Romanik; and four first secretaries of regional party committees.

The Secretariat, which is considered the hub of party activity, is nominally elected by the Central Committee in plenary session, just as the Politburo is. There are currently nine national secretaries, including Jaruzelski. Under the direction of these men, about fifteen departments, one bureau, and fifteen commissions operate at this top level.[35] The Secretariat maintains a constant check on local party officials throughout the country. It also remains in permanent contact with the Politburo, since seven of the secretaries are Politburo members or candidates for membership on that policymaking body. (See Table 33.)

Composition of the Party. The social composition of the party is shown in Table 34. What does not appear is the quality of membership. The proportion of intellectuals (including white-collar employees) rose from less than 10 percent to almost 43 percent within three decades, then dropped to 34 percent (1981), and went back up to 53 percent. Many of these persons are probably opportunists. On the other hand, the hard core of the party consists mainly of those members who were activists and functionaries during the 1940s. Few of these are left on the current leadership list, although some 22,000 PZPR members in 1976 belonged to the pre-1938 Polish communist movement and its youth affiliate or to the socialist party's left wing.

Since 1942, when the party was reconstituted,[36] its membership has grown almost steadily (see Table 32). This growth, however, has been accompanied by the purging of considerable numbers. The main reasons have been theft, bribery, embezzlement, misuse of official positions, and drunkenness. Table 35 shows the party's losses since 1955.

There has been condemnation by the party's leadership of the trend toward an increasing percentage of intelligentsia in the party. This shift toward control by the better educated is more than just a trend; it is in reality a current problem. Only about 38 percent of the PZPR membership belongs to the proletariat or industrial

Table 34

POLISH COMMUNIST PARTY SOCIAL COMPOSITION, 1945–1986

Category	December 1945		September 1957		October 1970		July 1986	
	Number	Percentage	Number	Percentage	Number	Percentage	Number	Percentage
Industrial workers	130,620	62.2	511,917	39.9	939,064	40.9	807,789	38.0
Peasants	59,220	28.2	164,224	12.8	266,236	11.6	191,319	9.0
Intellectuals	20,160	9.6	497,804	38.8	975,890	42.5	1,126,654	53.0
Other (artisans, retired, housewives)	—	—	109,055	8.5	114,810	5.0	—	—
Total	210,000	100.0	1,283,000	100.0	2,296,000	100.0	2,125,762	100.0

SOURCES: *Nowe drogi* (January–February 1947), p. 29, and (May–June 1948), p. 29; *Zycie Warszawy*, 25 October 1957; *Trybuna ludu*, 18 November 1957; Warsaw radio, 3 November 1970; *Polityka*, 5 July 1986. Absolute figures computed.

NOTE: Only 15 percent of the members had complete or incomplete university educations and only another 26 percent had high school diplomas at the time of the seventh PZPR congress in 1975. PZPR members hold about 900,000 of the 1.2 million managerial positions in the public sector. *Polityka*, 14 May 1988, p. 1.

Table 35
PURGES IN THE POLISH COMMUNIST PARTY, 1955–1986

Year	Number of members purged	Year	Number of members purged
1955	55,000	1969	52,300
1956–1964	400,000	1970	53,600
1965	41,900	1971	163,900
1966	44,100	1972–1975	206,000
1967	117,100	1976–1981	253,600
1968	40,100	1982–1986	816,000*

SOURCES: *Nowe drogi* (December 1958), p. 87; *Trybuna ludu*, 16 January and 16 June 1960, 16 March 1961; Warsaw radio, 15 April 1964; *Trybuna ludu*, 26 February and 14 August 1966; *Zycie Warszawy*, 18 April 1968; *Zycie partii* (March 1970), p. 2; *VI zjazd PZPR* (Warsaw, 1972), p. 68; *Nowe drogi* (February 1971), pp. 79–94; *Trybuna ludu*, 26 June 1974; *Zycie partii* (May 1975), p. 25; *Glos robotniczy* (Lodz), 5 December 1975; *Glos wybrzeza*, 9 July 1981.

NOTE: *This number includes resignations. Between mid-December 1981, when martial law was proclaimed, and mid-March 1982, about 129,000 members were purged. *Zycie partii*, 31 March 1982, p. 3. The 1981–1986 figure has been derived from the decline in membership between April 1981 and July 1986, given on Table 32.

labor force in Poland. The goal set by Gomulka reportedly had been 90 percent industrial workers and 10 percent "mental" workers. (See Table 34.)

Despite these problems, temporary stability has been achieved within the party leadership. Acceptance of many younger provincial secretaries and workers from large factories into the Central Committee after the ninth PZPR congress possibly could become a threat to Jaruzelski. These individuals, who have grass-roots contacts, desire an increased living standard for the workers. Among them may be a dark-horse candidate for party leadership, one who will combine support from the intellectuals and the young people. This represents a long-range proposition, although developments during the latter half of 1981 may have brought it closer.

A possibility that should not be excluded is intervention by the Soviet Union; the USSR may decide that Jaruzelski must be sacrificed to avoid even more serious disturbances among a population that has never been noted for its procommunist and especially its pro-Russian sympathies. The two precedents, in December 1970 and September 1980, which saw the rise and fall of Gierek, are probably on the minds of those who make decisions both in Warsaw and in Moscow.

Regardless of any differences among party factions, the winner will always be a communist. The PZPR can be expected to continue to be patterned after its counterpart in the Soviet Union. The goal of the party still remains that of a "socialist" state, and the maintenance of control over the nation by a self-perpetuating elite considered a prerequisite for the attainment of this objective. Even the so-called de-Stalinization and "liberalization" have not changed this fact of life. Whether or not the renewal process undertaken by the party since mid-1981 will be able to change this basic reality remains a question for the future.

During the eleven months before the ninth extraordinary PZPR congress, Poland experienced a series of crises. They began on 2 July 1980, with strikes protesting the price increases for meat, and continued during that summer.[37] Commencing at Gdansk on the Baltic coast, work stoppages extended throughout the country. An agreement between the government and Gdansk dockworkers on 31 August 1980 seemed to end Poland's domestic problems. It included the following essential points:[38] the right to establish independent trade unions, submission of a new censorship bill to the *Sejm* by the end of the year, radio broadcasts of Sunday mass, and release from jail of political prisoners, pending review of their cases. Elements of this revolution from below included (1) Solidarity, the ten million-member independent trade union that had weakened the party-dominated labor organization to the point that the latter had practically ceased to exist; (2) Rural Solidarity, a union of 3.5-million private entrepreneur farmers; and (3) the powerful Roman Catholic church.

DOMESTIC AFFAIRS

Poland remains unique among East European countries within the Soviet power bloc. This is not only due to the remarkable success of the communists in fettering the people and establishing a regime despite the seemingly insurmountable socio-religious and political barriers. There are other reasons for its uniqueness, among which perhaps the most interesting remains the "deviationist" manner in which Poland's agriculture has been permitted to develop. The unusual modus vivendi between church and state would be another. This arrangement permits such incompatible ideologies as those of the Roman Catholic church and of communism to coexist within the country.

The Agricultural Program. Even before the cessation of hostilities in World War II, radical land reform was introduced by the communist-dominated provisional government. It consisted principally of expropriating large landholdings and redistributing them among the peasantry and the new Polish settlers in the so-called Recovered Territories to the west of the 1939 Polish-German boundary. Little was done toward the collectivization of agriculture, as the communists were concentrating on the consolidation of their control over the government during the early years. This postponement of collectivization represented in Poland, as in some of the other "people's democracies," merely a tactical divergence from the traditional Soviet path toward the so-called socialist state. Deferment was permitted by Moscow during the formative years of the bloc as a temporary means toward the desirable end of solidifying communist control.

By 1947, however, Stalin had decided that the time was ripe for establishing more uniformity within the diverse East European satrapies. The organization of the Cominform[39] was the signal for the beginning of this conformity drive. Gomulka, nominally the leading communist in Poland at that time, reportedly indicated his coolness toward establishment of this international organization and, by implication, objected to forced agricultural collectivization, which had not given brilliant results elsewhere. He was removed as party leader at a September 1948 plenary session of the Central Committee. By the following year, collectivization patterned after the Soviet model had been launched in Poland.

This forced process was conducted by such coercive devices as compulsory state deliveries, heavy land taxes, and punitive visits by party activists and police to farm areas where opposition to the program had been encountered. Between late 1949 and the fall of 1956, some 10,600 collective farms came into being. The resentment of the peasants against the abrogation of their property rights mounted. The farmer in Poland not only considers this land to be a source of income but he also attributes to it sentimental and traditional values.

The growing discontent finally came to be recognized by communist authorities. It was probably this fact more than any other that tempered the degree of force and violence subsequently used in Poland to achieve the aims of the program. A much more severe campaign of terror and coercion was applied in the other East European satellites. As a result, collectivization of farms in Poland showed only a 3 percent growth between 1950 and 1958, in contrast with increases of 48 percent in Bulgaria and 52 percent in Czechoslovakia.[40]

Production figures that have subsequently been released indicate that Polish farms remaining in private hands outproduced those in the socialist sector (both collective and state operated) by a considerable margin. This led Gomulka, after his return to power in 1956, to suggest the dissolution of the collective units that were operating at a deficit.[41] He also announced more liberal regulations pertaining to organizing production cooperatives, as collective farms are euphemistically called. The reaction probably represented a barometer of peasant attitudes toward collectivization. Taking the speech of Gomulka literally, the peasants began to dissolve the cooperatives. By the summer of 1957 more than 8,500 of the 10,600 previously existing collectives had been disbanded.[42] Further liberalization of control over agriculture resulted in the reduction of compulsory deliveries to the state, increases in the prices paid for agricultural commodities, and more autonomy within rural areas.

What is the current situation? After almost four and a half decades of communist rule, Poland is a country of gross food and fuel shortages, low industrial and agricultural productivity, and $28 billion in debt to the West. Once ranked among Europe's most fertile centers, it now imports meat and grain, including corn to feed livestock. Sizable grain deliveries (ten million tons in 1980 at a cost of over one billion dollars) have continued from the USSR and the West.[43] During that same year, agricultural production fell to its lowest level since 1970 (see Table 36), although meat did not do as poorly. Premier Jaruzelski announced that a harvest of 21 million tons of grain was expected in 1981, compared with the 18.3 million target for the previous year. This result was not achieved until 1986, however. It is problematical whether enough usable machinery exists to cope with a large harvest, in view of the fact that 60,000 tractors and 3,000 combine harvesters remain idle for lack of spare parts. Poland's agriculture has long been tied to central planning through product determination, fertilizer supplies, and land allocation. New reforms proposed releasing private entrepreneur farmers from day-to-day control, more advantageous purchasing prices, and improved supplies.[44]

Table 36
POLISH AGRICULTURAL PRODUCTION, 1970–1986

Category	1970	1975	1980	1986
	(in million tons)			
Four grains	15.4	18.0	16.4	21.5
Potatoes	50.3	46.4	26.4	39.0
Sugar beets	12.7	15.7	10.1	14.2
	(in thousand tons)			
Slaughter animals	2,187.0	3,067.0	3,147.0	3,135.0
Meat	1,699.0	2,405.0	2,560.0	3,016.0

SOURCE: RFE, *Polish Situation Report*, no. 12 (3 July 1981), p. 8; *Polska: dane statystyczne* (1987), pp. 59 and 62.

Although Poland is the only country within the Soviet bloc in which collectivization has not been actively pursued since 1956, the communist regime there did not ignore the idea entirely. It instituted "agricultural circles" to inculcate collectivist attitudes among the peasantry. These state-controlled organizations are designed to favor members over strictly private entrepreneur farmers in the procurement of agricultural supplies and in arrangements for distribution and sale of produce. Apart from the introduction of these circles, heavy taxes were reimposed on individual nonaffiliated farms.

With a membership of more than two million, agricultural circles cultivate about 99,000 hectares of their own land.[45] Six years earlier, they had farmed

264,000 hectares.[46] Agricultural circles are now literally fighting for survival in the wake of the popular Rural Solidarity movement.

Officially called the Independent Self-Governing Trade Union for Individual Farmers, Rural Solidarity had a membership of approximately 3.5 million (about one-fourth more than the agricultural circles) and was growing. Formal recognition of the union was announced on 12 May 1981, following an eight-month struggle by approximately 71.4 percent of Poland's private farmers. Under its national chairman, Jan Kulaj, the new organization demanded increased pensions for private farmers, review of regulations on press censorship, and restoration of religious instruction.[47] One demand, ending subsidies to the state agricultural sector, was put into effect as of 1 July 1981. Enormous power is available to the private farmers of Rural Solidarity, who can use the threat of withholding products from the market. In 1979 private farmers produced 93 percent of all eggs, some 90.8 percent of the potatoes, 85 percent of the milk, and 73.4 percent of all cattle.[48] (See Table 37.) During 1986, they contributed 84 percent of all agricultural products.

At the ninth party congress, the first secretary for Gdansk province, Tadeusz Fiszbach, assessed the economic conditions as follows: "The situation is not improving; it is constantly deteriorating." He briefly described the conditions in Lodz province as being typical of the entire country. People wait in front of shops for up to 24 hours, due to shortages of cigarettes, soap, and washing powder. Rationing of meat, butter, and grain products began during the first months of 1981 and has continued despite nationwide demonstrations and warning strikes.[49]

Industry suffers from absenteeism and malingering. Approximately one-fourth of all production capacity was idled during mid-1981. Although exports bring in an estimated twelve billion dollars annually, almost nine billion is used to service the huge foreign debt. Economic forecasts for the 1981–1985 period were vague and often contradictory, but one message is clear: Poland requires several years of hard work to bring the debt problem under control and to streamline the economic infrastructure after decades of mismanagement. Growth indicators portray the failure of past policies and lend dramatic significance to the necessity of economic reform. (See Table 38.) At the close of the extraordinary congress, an appeal to the population appeared in the press. It stated, in part: "Fellow countrymen! The homeland is in need. A profound economic, social, and political crisis is tormenting our country. There is danger to the secure existence of the nation and to the future of the state. Let us join forces to avert the danger that hangs over Poland." The appeal stressed that the crisis had not resulted from the socialist system, laying blame on deviations from principles and on "men who, while standing at the helm of the party and the state, betrayed the ideals they voiced."[50]

Officials in Warsaw are weighing the advantages of rejoining the International Monetary Fund (IMF). Among communist-ruled states in Eastern Europe,

Table 37
CHANGES IN THE OWNERSHIP OF ARABLE LAND, 1970–1986
(in hectares)

Type	1970		1975		1979		1986	
	Area	Percentage	Area	Percentage	Area	Percentage	Area	Percentage
Individual farmers	12,636,500	83.7	12,000,300	81.3	11,108,500	75.8	13,551,000	71.4
State farms	2,198,600	14.6	2,373,700	16.1	2,737,500	18.7	3,518,000	18.5
Collective farms	193,500	1.3	225,400	1.5	503,600	3.4	678,000	3.6
Other state land	61,300	0.4	164,700	1.1	302,100	2.0	1,188,000	6.0
Agricultural circles	—	—	—	—	—	—	99,000	0.5
Total	15,089,900	100.0	14,764,100	100.0	14,651,700	100.0	19,034,000	100.0

SOURCES: *Maly rocznik statystyczny 1970*, pp. 163–65; *Rocznik statystyczny 1975*, p. 245; Warsaw radio, 5 December 1976; RFE report (by Roman Stefanowski), "Agricultural Perspectives," 20 January 1976; *Concise Statistical Yearbook of Poland 1980*, p. 139; *Rocznik statystyczny* (1987).

Table 38
POLISH GROWTH INDICATORS, 1980 AND 1986
(percent of increase over previous year)

Indicators	1980	1986
National income	−4.0	2.0
Industrial production	−1.3	4.2
Agricultural production	−9.6	−3.0
Investments	−10.5	5.1
Trade turnover	4.8	4.6
Coal production	−3.9	0.0

SOURCES: *Business Eastern Europe* 10, no. 18 (1 May 1981), p. 139; *Zycie gospodarcze*, no. 12 (20 March 1988).

Hungary, Romania, and Yugoslavia are members. Poland had joined IMF at its inception in 1944 but was forced by the Soviet Union to withdraw six years later. In 1957 the regime in Warsaw requested readmission, but the application was blocked by the United States. In view of the economic chaos today, membership would be a positive step toward normalization. To quote an unidentified Polish economist: "Had we been a member of the IMF five years ago, we would not be in the state we are today."[51] Poland rejoined the IMF in 1986.

Poland's debt to other East European countries (mostly to the USSR) totals 6.6 billion transfer rubles, which amounts to 62 percent of annual exports to these CMEA members. The hard-currency debt, based on $47.5 billion in credits between 1971 and 1987 from the West, in 1988 had reached $39.2 billion, five times the annual revenue from exports to hard-currency markets.[52]

Church-State Relations. The prewar Roman Catholic population of Poland numbered about 23 million out of a total of almost 34 million inhabitants. In addition to more than three million Jews, the remainder included Ukrainian (Uniate), German (Lutheran), and Belorussian (Eastern Orthodox) minorities. Now, after the Nazi holocaust and the annexation of Polish territory in the east by the USSR,[53] the minority groups consist of fewer than half a million individuals, less than 2 percent of a population totaling almost 38 million, some 95 percent of whom adhere at least nominally to Roman Catholicism.[54]

In 1945 the new, communist-dominated Council of Ministers declared null and void the twenty-year-old concordat between Warsaw and the Vatican. This agreement had regulated church activities in Poland. In abrogating the concordat, the regime charged that the church had allegedly violated its provisions by favoring

Germany during the war. From that time on, a slowly intensifying campaign against the church was waged, beginning with press attacks against the hierarchy and the teaching of catechism in public schools. It gradually expanded to include the arrest and trials of clergy and the suppression of the Catholic news media.

In January 1949 Archbishop Stefan Wyszynski was appointed primate of Poland. He immediately opened negotiations with regime authorities to clarify the position of the church in relation to the state. These talks became seriously hampered by a Vatican decree ordering the excommunication of all Catholics who actively supported communism. The regime in Warsaw, claiming that this constituted interference in the internal affairs of the country, retaliated by announcing that priests who attempted to enforce the excommunication order would be punished under Polish law.

Despite these difficulties, a modus vivendi was signed in April 1950 between the church and the regime.[55] In essence, the church agreed to abstain from all political activities and to restrain its clergy from opposition to the government. The state, in turn, guaranteed freedom of worship, permission to conduct religious education in public schools, and noninterference with the Catholic press. The wording of the agreement, however, appeared flagrantly one-sided and provided the basis for subsequent government interference. In almost every case where specific guarantees of freedom were given, the regime carefully qualified them with restrictive phrases.

The communists took advantage of this terminology and reverted to their campaign against the church almost immediately. In the following years, persecution by the government mounted in intensity. The new Polish constitution (1952) omitted any mention of safeguards for religion. In the fall of the next year Cardinal Wyszynski was secretly arrested and forbidden to carry out the functions of his office. Arrests of other clergy followed. The state even went so far as to require, and insist on obtaining, its own approval whenever changes in clerical assignments or new appointments were contemplated.

In 1956, immediately after Gomulka's return to power, Cardinal Wyszynski and the other arrested clergymen were released. Persecution of the church halted temporarily. A new, more liberal church-state agreement[56] was announced whereby religious instruction could once again be provided on a voluntary basis in the schools, government control over certain appointments was relaxed, and other concessions were made. At this time communist control had weakened throughout the country because of the October upheaval, and there was fear of a revolt.

Subsequent events showed that the new church-state agreement represented more a political expedient to gain temporary church support than a sincere intention to liberalize former restrictions on religious activities. Once the communists had gained sufficient strength, persecution in one form or another followed and, indeed, persists to this day. It is apparent that the communists want not only to separate church and state but also to eliminate religion totally from the lives of the people.

The large Catholic population is still a powerful factor in domestic politics. The church hierarchy remains well aware of communist desires to rid the country of religion. It continues to fight for religious freedom despite nearly continuous oppression during the postwar years. In the fall of 1965 Cardinal Wyszynski and Archbishop Antoni Baraniak of Poznan were attacked by the regime media for making speeches at the Ecumenical Council meeting in Rome without mentioning "the avoidance of war, disarmament, and worldwide cooperation by states and peoples on behalf of peace."[57]

Shortly afterward the cardinal and 35 Polish bishops, who had participated in the sessions at Rome, sent a letter inviting the Catholic bishops in all of Germany to attend the forthcoming celebration of the millennium of Poland's conversion to Christianity at Czestochowa. The letter reviewed relations between the two countries, made a plea for a "dialogue," and offered forgiveness and asked for it in return. The regime in Warsaw reacted vehemently by accusing the church hierarchy of meddling with foreign affairs. On 15 December 1969 Cardinal Wyszynski gave Pope Paul VI a memorandum from the Episcopate requesting the appointment of regular bishops in the Oder-Neisse territories. The Vatican finally recognized the former German territories as de jure part of Poland on 28 June 1972, when it confirmed the appointment of six Polish bishops who had been officiating there as apostolic administrators.[58]

Church-state relations deteriorated to the extent that an episcopal letter was read on 28 November 1976 in all churches throughout the country. It mentioned that the government continued to wage a "hate-filled and brutal campaign against religion" and that "one can constantly feel a secret conspiracy against God." Then came a detailed indictment listing discrimination against believers, limits placed on new church buildings, atheism in schools, and even use of the legal system against religious persons.[59] During the first half of December, Cardinal Wyszynski in two different sermons criticized the government for having used force against demonstrators during the June 1976 food riots.

Two years later, an outburst of national pride greeted the news that Krakow's former Bishop Karol Wojtyla had been elected pope. John Paul II visited his native country during 2–10 June 1979. Reports described the trip as a significant political event in Poland. The purpose of the pope's visit was religious, although he met with PZPR leader Gierek and other officials. During his address to the episcopal conference of Polish bishops on 6 June, he commented that the dialogue between church and state "cannot be easy, because it takes place between two world views that are diametrically opposed; but it must be possible and effective for the good of the individuals, and the nation demands it."[60]

Pope John Paul II appointed Bishop Jozef Glemp as archbishop of Gniezno and Warsaw as well as primate of Poland, succeeding Stefan Cardinal Wyszynski who had died on 28 May 1981 after a serious illness. Archbishop Glemp, 52 years old, is a specialist in both canon and civil law. He had served as an aide to the cardinal since 1967 and, thus, received good training to lead the church during uncertain times. Pope John Paul II has made visits to his native country in both 1983 and 1987. An immediate benefit following the second visit came from acceptance by the regime of a U.S.-funded program that allows the church to import farm machinery for private farmers. The funds totaled some $28 million at that time.[61]

Youth. Organizations for Polish youth and students did not escape the ferment overtaking the country. By the end of 1986, the three groupings forming the Federation of Socialist Unions of Polish Youth claimed the following memberships: Union of Polish Socialist Youth, almost 1.5 million; Socialist Union of Polish Students, about 93,000; and Union of Polish Scouts, almost 2 million.[62] At an earlier period, the independent Polish Student Association began to operate at institutions of higher learning in the country, posing a threat to the party-backed youth movement. By the time of its third congress in May 1981, the official Union of Polish Socialist Youth had lost more than one-third of its membership. The other two organizations experienced similar defections during early 1981. Officially, registration of the autonomous youth association (called Independent Students' Union) by the Ministry of Science, Higher Education, and Technology took place on 17 February 1981.[63]

Another autonomous youth organization is the Democratic Youth Union, composed of young people either connected with the Democratic Party (SD) or simply interested in the kind of ideology officially espoused by it. It met for the first time on 13 February 1981 at Krakow but has antecedents in the underground Movement of Young Democrats that participated in the 1944 Warsaw uprising. The successor Democratic Youth Union, resurrected during the first years after World War II, was forcibly incorporated in 1948 by the regime-sponsored Polish Youth Union. In 1956, under Wladyslaw Gomulka, a Union of Young Democrats was formed; it did not outlast the brief thaw. During the early 1960s youth circles began developing from within the ranks of the Democratic Party, but again these ceased to exist by 1964. Under Edward Gierek, all attempts at pluralism in the youth movement were officially suppressed. According to the new organization's chairman, Piotr Wallo, branches operated in 30 of the 49 provinces and had about two thousand members.[64] After the introduction of martial law in December 1981, all such independent organizations have been forced to operate underground.

The Media. Due to the anticipated relaxation of mass media censorship, a number of new nationwide newspapers began publication. The independent union

Solidarity had its own paper, *Solidarnosc,* a weekly with a 500,000-copy circulation. A paper for conservatives, *Rzeczywistosc,* emphasized nationalism, egalitarianism, and communist orthodoxy yet sold only about 150,000 copies. Even the communist party newspapers changed. *Trybuna ludu,* the main PZPR daily organ, regularly printed information on activities of Solidarity and openly reported on economic difficulties. The communist newspaper in Krakow, *Gazeta Krakowska,* made full use of relative press freedom to publish investigative reports on corruption by party officials and detailed stories of other official abuses of power. It had a press run of only 220,000 and a black-market price of 300 zlotys.[65]

Since the ban on Solidarity more than 80 publications, with runs between 1,000 and 10,000, have been published by underground presses in Poland. In addition, estimates of videocassette recorder ownership range from 100,000 to 600,000, which suggests that the regime has lost control not only over the dissemination of newspapers but also over video films.[66]

INTRABLOC AFFAIRS

Poland belongs to those treaty organizations that are sponsored by the Soviet Union. Among them, the Council for Mutual Economic Assistance (CMEA) is perhaps the most consequential, owing to the effects of its program of economic integration within the bloc. Involvement in this group has proven rather expensive to Poland, as it has to several other bloc countries. Large capital investments have been diverted to long-range CMEA economic improvement projects. This capital has been badly needed for shorter-range domestic programs that have been delayed or remained abortive. Heavy expenditures for construction of the Polish section of the Danube-Oder canal and exploitation of brown coal deposits in the Turoszow area are two examples of such large investments. The best illustration, perhaps, is the *Druzhba* (friendship) oil pipeline, the northern spur of which crosses Poland from the USSR and ends at Schwedt in East Germany. An expensive refinery has been constructed at Plock to process this Soviet crude petroleum. Part of the cost of the construction of the pipeline itself has also been borne by the government in Warsaw.

Polish economists, however, seem to recognize the problems that the long-range investments required by CMEA are generating in their domestic economy. They apparently no longer follow blindly the dictates of Moscow. For example, on the fifteenth anniversary of the CMEA, then Deputy Premier Piotr Jaroszewicz admitted that economic differences existed within the organization: "Even a husband and wife who love each other are not always of the same opinion about investments. It is hard to imagine that eight countries are also of the same opinion. In Comecon [CMEA] the only method is to use persuasion through economic arguments."[67]

It seems likely that Poland's membership in the CMEA has been one of the factors contributing to a faltering economic development. It may be, however, that when large investments in CMEA projects begin to provide a return, the government will be able to invest more funds in the domestic economy. This might conceivably remove some of the current economic weaknesses that beset the country. One attempt to improve the system has involved a cautious change that has led to some decentralization by transferring planning and responsibility down to the intermediate level of industrial unions for similar plants, though not to the level of the individual factory.

Between 1971 and 1979, the Soviet Union extended the equivalent of $2.4 billion in credit to Poland, the largest amount publicly reported to any East European country. Only USSR aid to Cuba during the same period exceeded that amount ($3.1 billion went to Havana). During the period July 1980 to July 1981, Moscow reportedly gave Warsaw about $4.5 billion in soft- and hard-currency credits.[68] In calendar year 1980, Poland failed to fulfill obligations amounting to $39.4 million in supplies to other East European trading partners. This included three-fourths of contracted coal deliveries and more than half of the promised sulfur, coke, machinery, and other products.[69]

Aside from the purely organizational aspects of intrabloc relations, a geographical issue loomed large among the postwar problems concerning Poland and other countries. This issue involved the ratification of the country's new western boundary along the Oder and Western Neisse rivers.

The Oder-Neisse Line. The origin of the problem pertaining to the boundary between Poland and Germany dates back to the latter part of World War I. Roman Dmowski, the chairman of the Polish National Council that was then recognized by the West as the government of Poland, defended Poland's right to the Oder-Neisse river line as a frontier. Wladyslaw Sikorski, who was premier of the Polish exile government at London early in World War II, suggested the Oder River as the future boundary between the two countries after the war. In 1943 the Polish communists living in Moscow echoed the same proposal and further indicated that this extension of the boundary to the Oder River in the west should be considered compensation to Poland for the territories annexed by the USSR in the east (as a result of the 1939 Nazi-Soviet nonaggression pact).

The "Big Three" discussed Germany's future boundaries in the course of three conferences during and immediately after the war. At Teheran, in November 1943, Stalin proposed the boundary along the Oder River. The other two participants, Churchill and Roosevelt, agreed in principle, but no firm agreement was reached. Later, at the Yalta meeting during early February 1945, the border question again came up. The final communiqué after this conference specified that Poland would receive accessions of territory in the north and west, that the Poles themselves were to be consulted before a final settlement, and that the ultimate demarcation of borders would be determined at the peace conference after the war.

During the Potsdam meeting, in August 1945, the three heads of government agreed that

> Pending the final determination of Poland's western frontier, the former German territories east of a line running from the Baltic Sea and thence along the Oder River to the confluence of the Western Neisse River and along the Western Neisse to the Czechoslovakian frontier [should] be under the administration of the Polish State.[70]

A procedure was also agreed upon for the removal of German citizens from these Recovered Territories, as they have come to be known. This implied that Poland was to repopulate the vacated area.

Despite the provisional nature of the Potsdam agreement, the USSR in that same month signed a treaty of friendship with Poland that included an agreement for the demarcation of the Polish-Soviet frontier.[71] In June 1950 a Warsaw communiqué issued at the close of negotiations between East Germany and Poland announced agreement over their existing frontier and established cultural cooperation between the two countries. Finally, the new Brezhnev leadership in the Soviet Union traveled to Warsaw in April 1965 and reaffirmed the 1945 pact, signing a twenty-year extension[72] that specifically guarantees the inviolability of the Oder-Neisse border.

The regime has consolidated its hold over the Recovered Territories. Besides asserting legal and historical rights to these lands, the Warsaw government has repopulated them with more than eleven million citizens of Polish nationality. Reconstruction efforts have been so successful that more than a third of the country's annual gross national product is attributed to production from these former German lands.[73] Many countries had apparently come to regard Poland's hegemony over the territories as a fait accompli, and most states in the West gave it tacit recognition.

Regardless of the earlier Western stand that Warsaw only administered the territories, it would seem that Poland's sovereignty over the area indeed represented a fait accompli. Only a major conflict or a significant shift in the world balance of power could result in a revision of the present boundary between Germany and Poland. During 1970 it appeared that the government of Chancellor Willy Brandt would recognize the border de jure, the Soviet-West German treaty in August of that year removing the main obstacle to recognition.[74] A visit by Foreign Minister Walter Scheel to Poland during early November solved certain problems and Chancellor Willy Brandt was invited to initial a treaty, which he signed on 7 December 1970 at Warsaw.[75]

Despite this agreement, it was not until after the foreign ministers of the two countries met again at Helsinki on 31 July 1975 (during the conference on security and cooperation in Europe) that a comprehensive settlement of the issues could be agreed on. A nineteen-article treaty[76] specified that Poland would receive 1.3 billion marks ($543 million) in pension claims as indemnity to Polish victims of Nazi concentration camps and one billion marks ($416 million) in low-interest credits.

In return, Poland obligated itself to issue between 120,000 and 125,000 exit visas over the next four years to individuals of German extraction who wished to join their families in the Federal Republic. More than one-half million people had been resettled in this manner during the preceding two decades.

Conclusion. Poland's future depends on internal as well as external considerations: (1) on the determination of people from all strata of society to carry out reforms and implement innovative production programs and (2) on massive economic assistance from the West and Soviet bloc countries. Whether the ferment during 1980–1981 will lead Poland toward a decentralization of political and economic power or to greater repression and tighter controls cannot be known as yet. However, one thing is clear: the communist party will never be the same. Indeed, it now faces a particularly difficult predicament coping with an indigenous force (Solidarity) that professes to be only an economic organization and denies any competition for political power in a country where economic power *is* political power. On 13 December 1981, Premier Jaruzelski invoked marshal law and established a 21-man Military Council (eighteen generals and three colonels) to run the country.

In an effort to co-opt noncommunists, the Warsaw regime established the Patriotic Movement of National Rebirth (PRON). In mid-July 1983, it received official recognition. Less than one-third of the PRON national council were PZPR members, some 20 percent belonged to the two subordinate political parties, and half of the total had no affiliation. However, the original secretary came from the top PZPR leadership.[77] This front organization still exists, although it probably has little credibility among the population at large.

Three weeks of strikes at Bydgoszcz, Nowa Huta, Stalowa Wola, Gdansk, and other locations through 10 May 1988 proved that the Jaruzelski regime's economic policy had failed. Prices of food and other basic goods rose between 40 percent and 200 percent, while the inflation rate ran at 45 percent; these impelled the strike action. The regime also showed bad faith by encouraging mediation efforts of the church and then unleashing riot police to attack the Nowa Huta steel workers at night.[78] Although these events did not repeat what had happened in 1980, they may be a prelude to upheavals in the future. Gorbachev's visit to Poland during 11–16 July 1988 only showed his support for the Jaruzelski regime.

NOTES

1. Susanne S. Lotarski, "The Communist Takeover in Poland," in Thomas T. Hammond (ed.), *The Anatomy of Communist Takeovers* (New Haven, Conn., 1975), pp. 339–67. See also Jan B. de Weydenthal, *The Communists of Poland* (Stanford, Calif., 1986), rev. ed., 272 pp.

2. U.S. Senate, Committee on Foreign Relations, *A Decade of American Foreign Policy* (Washington, D.C., 1950), p. 30. The Yalta agreement did not provide for international supervision of elections in Poland.

3. Other prewar political parties had already been banned. For an account of this election by an eyewitness, the leader of the Polish Peasant Party, see Stanislaw Mikolajczyk, *The Rape of Poland: Pattern of Soviet Aggression* (New York, 1948), pp. 180–202.

For subsequent political developments, see R. F. Staar, *Poland, 1944–1962* (Westport, Conn., 1975), 300 pp., which also discusses the so-called United Front.

4. Wladyslaw Gomulka, *Przemowienia 1956–1957* (Warsaw, 1957), p. 193.

5. RFE, *Situation Report,* 24 March 1972.

6. Ibid., 26 March 1976.

7. *Trybuna ludu,* 25–26 March 1980; Arthur Rachwald, "Poland," in Richard F. Staar (ed.), *Yearbook on International Communist Affairs: 1986* (Stanford, Calif., 1986), p. 319; henceforth, cited as *YICA*.

8. *Dziennik ustaw,* 23 July 1952. See also Kazimierz Gosciniak, *Czym jest, a czym nie jest Konstytucja PRL* (Warsaw, 1969), p. 155.

9. For an English translation of the constitution as amended, see William B. Simons (ed.), *The Constitutions of the Communist World* (Alphen aan den Rijn, 1980), pp. 283–310.

10. His speech appeared in *Trybuna ludu,* 20 July 1981.

11. For members on the Council of State, see RFE, *East European Leadership List* (15 January 1988), p. 34.

12. CIA, *Directory of Polish Officials* (April 1987), p. 21.

13. RFE, *Leadership List* (15 January 1988), pp. 34–36, gives the new lineup.

14. *New York Times,* 4 July 1981, provides names and posts affected.

15. [Poland], *Rocznik statystyczny 1987* (Warsaw, 1987), pp. xlvi and 45–48.

16. An evaluation of the new penal code was provided by the then justice minister, Stanislaw Walczak, over Warsaw radio, 27 December 1969.

17. *Contemporary Poland* (February 1976), p. 8.

18. Names of provincial-level incumbents appear in CIA, *Directory of Polish Officials* (Washington, D.C., 1987), pp. 57–80.

19. *Wall Street Journal,* 28 May 1981.

20. Polish United Workers' Party, *III zjazd PZPR* (Warsaw, 1959), pp. 1213–27. The amendments did not change these principles. See *IV zjazd PZPR* (Warsaw, 1964), pp. 783–802; *V zjazd PZPR* (Warsaw, 1968), pp. 863–74; *VI zjazd PZPR* (Warsaw,

1972), pp. 207–24; *VII zjazd PZPR* (Warsaw, 1976), pp. 201–11, and *IX nadzwyczajny zjazd PZPR* (Warsaw, 1983), pp. 701–34. Apparently no changes in the statute were made by the eighth PZPR congress in 1980 or the tenth (*Trybuna ludu,* 28–29 June–4 July 1986).

21. Announced over Warsaw radio, 19 July 1981, and printed in *Trybuna ludu* the following day. The new statute contains 88 articles compared with 62 in the previous one.

22. *Trybuna ludu,* 4 July 1986.

23. Article 38 of PZPR statute in *IX zjazd PZPR* (1983), p. 719.
Pay scales within the party during 1980 ranged from 5,700 to 11,300 zlotys for secretaries of lower-level committees to a high of 28,100 zlotys for the first secretary of the Central Committee. The average wage was 5,300 for industrial workers. *Glos wybrzeza,* 9 July 1981; Warsaw radio, 4 February 1981.

24. The number of provinces was increased from 22 to 49, allegedly to streamline administration. *Trybuna ludu,* 13 May 1975. In actual fact, this caused fragmentation of the regional PZPR power structure.

25. Wladyslaw Gomulka-Wieslaw, *Ku nowej Polsce* (Katowice, 1945), 108 pp., gives Gomulka's four speeches and the final resolution of the congress.

26. Chapter 4, Article 28, in *III zjazd PZPR,* p. 753; and *VII zjazd PZPR,* p. 206.

27. *Trybuna ludu,* 15 July 1981.

28. Ibid., and also 16 July 1981. See also *IX zjazd PZPR,* pp. 513–18.

29. Rachwald "Poland," in *YICA: 1987,* pp. 313–14.

30. Interview with PZPR congress spokesman Wieslaw Bek over Warsaw radio, 16 July 1981; *U.S. News & World Report* (3 August 1981), p. 21; names of those elected are listed in *IX zjazd PZPR,* pp. 740–43.

31. *Trybuna ludu,* 17 July 1981.

32. Ibid., 18–19 July 1981.

33. *Trybuna ludu,* 28–29 June, 1 and 4 July 1986.

34. Ibid., 20 July 1981.

35. CIA, *Directory of Polish Officials* (1987), pp. 10–13.

36. The prewar Polish communist party was dissolved by the Comintern in 1938, and most of its leaders (who had taken refuge in Moscow) were executed or sent to Soviet forced-labor camps. Their posthumous rehabilitation by the USSR Supreme Court came after October 1956. *Polityka,* 21 August 1965. See also *Zycie partii,* no. 1 (1988), p. 11, for information on the January 1942 re-establishment of the party.

37. R. F. Staar, "The Opposition Movement in Poland," *Current History* (April 1981), pp. 149–53, 180–81.

38. Krajowa Agencja Wydawnicza, *Protokoly porozumien Gdansk, Szczecin, Jastrzebie; Statut NSZZ "Solidarnosc"* (Warsaw, 1980), pp. 2–9.

39. Eugenio Reale, *Nascita del Cominform* (Rome, 1958), 175 pp., gives an eyewitness account of the establishment of the Cominform.

40. Zbigniew K. Brzezinski, *The Soviet Bloc* (Cambridge, Mass., 1960), p. 98.

41. *Nowe drogi* (October 1956), pp. 24–25 (complete issue on the eighth plenum of the PZPR Central Committee).

42. *Trybuna ludu,* 28 August 1957.

43. *U.S. News & World Report* (27 July 1981), p. 24; Richard Portes, *The Polish Crisis* (London, 1981), p. 14. The United States agreed to supply Poland with 4,000 metric tons ($80 million worth) of corn for poultry feed, to be paid in zlotys. *New York Times,* 19 July 1981, 19 August 1981, on the debt.

44. *The Economist* (25 July 1981), pp. 65–66; *Business Eastern Europe* 10, no. 11 (13 March 1981), p. 82.

45. *Rocznik statystyczny* (1987), p. 323.

46. [Poland], *Concise Statistical Yearbook of Poland 1980* (Warsaw, 1980), p. 139.

47. For background on the new farmers' union, see RFE, *Polish Situation Report,* no. 8 (14 May 1981), pp. 34–37. The text of acts passed by the *Sejm* on 6 May 1981 regarding the private farmers' trade union is printed in *Contemporary Poland,* no. 12 (June 1981), pp. 42–43.

48. [Poland], *Concise Statistical Yearbook of Poland 1980* (Warsaw, 1980), p. 135.

49. *Trybuna ludu,* 20 July 1981, for Fiszbach; *Contemporary Poland,* no. 10 (May 1981), p. 5, and *Christian Science Monitor,* 30 July 1981, on demonstrations.

50. For the text, see *Trybuna ludu,* 21–22 July 1981.

Details on corruption and names of those involved from 24 August 1980 through 30 May 1981 appeared in *Frankfurter Allgemeine Zeitung,* 11 July 1981, p. 6. Two high-ranking officials committed suicide. *Trybuna ludu,* 17 July 1981, gave the PZPR commission report.

51. *Business Eastern Europe* 10, no. 25 (19 June 1981), p. 193. See also *New York Times,* 19 August 1981, for a discussion of possible IMF membership for Poland.

52. Warsaw radio, 24 and 26 February 1988; *FBIS-Eastern Europe,* 25 February and 1 March 1988. See also Adrian Karatnycky in *Wall Street Journal,* 10 May 1988.

53. In 1964, there were about 1.4 million Poles in the USSR, scattered as follows: Belorussia (539,000), Ukraine (363,000), Lithuania (230,000), the Russian Soviet Federated Socialist Republic (118,000), Latvia (60,000), Kazakhstan (53,000), and other republics (17,000). *Polityka,* 30 October 1965, p. 10. The latest Soviet census gave the total as 1,151,000, which represents a substantial decline. [USSR], *Naselenie SSSR: po dannym Vsesoiuznoi perepiski naselenia 1979 goda* (Moscow, 1980).

54. CIA, *World Factbook 1987,* p. 199.

55. The text of the agreement appears in Henryk Swiatkowski (ed.), *Stosunek panstwa do kosciola w roznych krajach* (Warsaw, 1952), pp. 132–37.

56. Published in *Trybuna ludu,* 8 December 1956.

57. An article whose title can be translated as "Pig-Headed and Intolerant" appeared in *Zycie Warszawy,* 16 October 1965; excerpts were reprinted in the PZPR daily, *Trybuna ludu.*

58. See R. F. Staar, "Poland: Old Wine in New Bottles?" *Current History* (May 1973), p. 227.

59. Vatican radio, 28 November 1976, broadcast the letter.

60. Quoted by Jan B. de Weydenthal, "Poland," in *YICA: 1980,* p. 56.

61. Rachwald, "Poland," in *YICA: 1988*, p. 291. *Argumenty i fakty*, no. 25 (1988), p. 6.

62. *Polska: dane statystyczne* (1987), p. 20.

63. RFE, *Polish Situation Report*, no. 8 (14 May 1981), p. 20; no. 4 (13 March 1981), p. 26 gives the text of the agreement.

64. *Gazeta Krakowska*, 17 February 1981; *Kurier Polski*, 14–15 March 1981.

65. *New York Times*, 28 June 1981, 19 August 1981. A two-day strike of printers, called by Solidarity, closed down almost all newspapers in Poland.

66. Rachwald, "Poland," *YICA: 1985*, p. 313; Owen Johnson, "East European Glasnost'," *Wilson Center Reports* (April 1988), p. 1.

67. Warsaw radio, as cited in the *New York Times*, 28 April 1964.

68. CIA, *Handbook of Economic Statistics 1980*, p. 110; *The Economist* (25 July 1981), p. 65.

69. *New York Times*, 3 July 1981; *Wall Street Journal*, 17 July 1981.

70. U.S. Senate, Committee on Foreign Relations, "The Berlin (Potsdam) Conference, July 17–August 2, 1945," in *A Decade of American Foreign Policy: Basic Documents, 1941–49* (Washington, D.C., 1950), pp. 43–44.

71. Text in S. M. Maiorov (ed.), *Vneshniaia politika Sovetskogo Soiuza v period Otechestvennoi Voiny* (Moscow, 1947), vol. 3, pp. 386–87.

72. Text published in *Trybuna ludu*, 9 April 1965.

73. See R. F. Staar, "Poland: Myth Versus Reality," in *Current History* (April 1969), pp. 218–23. *Rocznik statystyczny 1987*, pp. xlvii and li.

74. This treaty recognizes the inviolability of borders, "including the Oder-Neisse line." Article 3, as given in *Krasnaia zvezda* (Moscow), 13 August 1970.

75. Text broadcast over Warsaw radio, 20 November 1970; i.e., in advance. See also Arthur Rachwald, *Poland Between the Superpowers* (Boulder, Colo., 1983), pp. 64–71.

76. Published in *Trybuna ludu*, 10 October 1975.

77. Rachwald, "Poland," in *YICA: 1984*, pp. 345–46. See also Table 33.

78. *Wall Street Journal*, 10 May 1988, p. 34 and 12 May 1988, p. 18; *New York Times*, 12 May 1988, pp. 1, 5, and 12 (letter from R. T. Davies); *Pravda*, 7 May 1988, p. 7, for the Soviet and Polish regime's version of events.

Chapter 7
Socialist Republic of Romania

The history of Romania has indelibly affected the makeup of its population. Although the communists seek to create a new world in Eastern Europe, the path of their type of ''socialism'' is no longer the same for all countries. The roots of the past not only affect the attitudes of the great masses of people whom totalitarian regimes hold captive but also lock into the attitudes of the current leaders.

These men lay claim to an infallible interpretation of Marxism-Leninism, but what they practice is far removed from ideological purity. The contemporary Romanian dictatorship may have as firm a hold on the nation as any previous regime had. Impeding the road to a national variety of socialism and a new world, however, are historical influences that express themselves in a variety of ways.

From the background of this land emanates the strong influence of a Latin heritage. Romanians point to it with pride today, claiming that they are Latins and not Slavs. As proof they cite the fact that more than 60 percent of the words in their language have Latin roots, while only 20 percent are of Slavic derivation. Because of this heritage, among other reasons, the views of the people have generally been pro-Western. Perhaps this is why much of the leadership of the Romanian communist party in the past came from ethnic minorities that felt no compunction about aligning their goals with those of Russia and other Slavic groups.[1]

Because of Romania's alliance with the Axis powers until August 1944, the USSR took steps early to press for a government that would be essentially pro-Soviet. Even so, provisions regarding the organization and functioning of central and local agencies contained in the communist-inspired constitutions of 1948, 1952, and 1965 have been applied only when it has been convenient for the rulers. The postwar regime in Romania has generally shown a discrepancy between its professed theory of constitutional government and its actual practice.

In February 1945 the USSR's political representative, Andrei Vyshinskii, peremptorily ordered King Michael to appoint Petru Groza, a communist-selected front man, as premier. The cabinet proposed by Groza included representatives from a number of different political parties. Communists were placed in the key

Interior, Justice, and Public Works ministries. They soon expanded their power from these important positions. The monarchy lasted two more years acting as a passive restraint, but it remained powerless to prevent this consolidation.[2]

The war crimes trial of Romanian leaders who were held responsible for supporting the Axis assisted in immobilizing all opposition and prevented the establishment of a liberal and peasant coalition. In addition, the USSR seemed to favor Romanian claims to that part of Transylvania taken away by the Axis Powers in 1940, and this generated some support for the communist program. Opposition groups were intimidated by the use, or even threat, of violence. From a base of fewer than 1,000 members in 1944 through a rapid recruitment up to 217,000 by September 1945, the Romanian Workers' (communist) Party soon attained the numbers to staff its regime.

During the consolidation period, the essential features of the prewar government were retained. The Grand National Assembly was reinstated in 1946, though as a unicameral parliament. Suffrage was extended to women, and the voting age was lowered to eighteen. Parliament experienced a purge of noncommunist deputies and underwent transformation into a rubber-stamp type of legislative body. In December 1947 King Michael was forced to abdicate. Soon thereafter parliament passed Law 393, illegally abolishing the existing constitution of 1923 and calling for a constituent assembly to decide upon a new basic law. A draft constitution actually appeared before the constituent assembly could be elected; it was published by the People's Democratic Front (the front, as in other bloc countries, represented an electoral organization for the communist party and its ancillary groups). The new constitution, which introduced the designation "Romanian People's Republic," was adopted in April 1948. Communist rule now superficially appeared to have a legitimate basis.[3]

NEW CONSTITUTIONS

The basic law of 1952 represented a modification of the one introduced four years previously. Like the 1936 Stalin constitution, after which it was closely patterned, the Romanian document appeared to grant all fundamental rights to the people. These rights, however, were subordinated to the interests of achieving socialism. The interpretation of "interests" rested with the ruling party. The Romanian Workers' Party gained its official mandate in Article 86, which proclaimed it to be the "vanguard of the working people" and the "leading force of organizations of the working people as well as of the State organs and institutions."[4]

Therefore, as in the USSR, the ruling party interpreted the constitution, made laws, and maintained complete dictatorial power. Judicial prerogatives also transcended constitutional rights. From the standpoint of the individual citizen, as no judicial review over the constitutionality of government acts existed, the articles of the constitution pertaining to basic rights remained unenforceable. The constitution prescribed the various organs of government, including the ministries, but even these frequently did not correspond to the written outline and were in a constant state of change.

The subsequent constitution, which was adopted on 21 August 1965, did not substantially change the system.[5] It merely proclaims in Article 1 that Romania is now a socialist republic, meaning that the country has reached the level of development previously attained by the USSR (1936), Yugoslavia (1958), and Czechoslovakia (1960). In keeping with Article 1, the name of the country no longer included the reference to a people's republic; it became the Socialist Republic of Romania.

Governmental Structure.   The present governmental system is similar, both structurally and functionally, to the one established by the 1952 basic law. The fundamental difference is that Article 3 of the 1965 constitution proclaims the entire regime to be led by the "Romanian Communist Party."[6] This control is most direct at the administrative level because party members hold key positions in executive and legislative organs as well as in the judicial arm of government. Although the organizational provisions of the constitution are generally upheld, the composition and action of the various agencies follow the directives of the party.

The central government consists of the Grand National Assembly or parliament, the Council of State, the Council of Ministers, and the court system. Functions are not clearly defined because the communists reject the concepts of separation of powers and checks and balances. The Grand National Assembly is theoretically supreme. It remains essentially a legislative branch, although its function is to provide approval rather than to act in a deliberative capacity. The Council of State, which was formerly called the presidium of parliament, plays the role of a collective presidency for the country. The Council of Ministers is the supreme administrative and executive organ.[7] The courts are in charge of administering justice.

Grand National Assembly.   According to Article 43 of the 1965 constitution, the Grand National Assembly has 23 specific powers that range from adopting and amending the constitution to appointing and recalling the supreme armed forces commander. This legislature is elected every four years and has one representative for each 60,000 citizens. The balloting on 17 March 1985 resulted in election of 369 deputies, all of whom were nominated by the Socialist Unity Front (comprising the communist party and mass organizations). Reportedly, some 99.99 percent of all registered voters went to the polls. Of these, about 97.8 percent voted for the official candidates and only 2.2 percent against, up from 1.5 percent in 1980. Candidates for the Grand National Assembly are selected to reflect an appropriate representation of women, ethnic minorities (principally Hungarians and Germans), and various social, cultural, and economic groups.[8] Laws are adopted by a simple majority and are signed by the president and the secretary to the Council of State. The Assembly convenes twice a year for ordinary sessions. Extraordinary meetings may be called when one-third of all Assembly members or the Council of State considers it necessary.

The Assembly elects a chairman and four deputies to preside over sessions and guide the flow of business. All members are entitled to inquiries to the government and to individual members of the Council of Ministers. They are immune from arrest or prosecution and can not be held legally responsible without the consent of the Grand National Assembly or, between its sessions, the Council of State. Such privileges, however, do not alter the fact that the Assembly is merely a facade that helps to perpetuate the appearance of democracy. It is unlikely that the new rules will change this situation, although they do call for more activity on the part of the members.

State Council and the Presidency. The Council of State presently consists of 20 members elected by the Grand National Assembly who, from among themselves, elect a chairman and his four deputies. Theoretically accountable to the Assembly under the constitution, the State Council functions more like a legislature than does the Assembly. It exercises power through decrees that are subsequently approved by the Assembly. This fact is evident from the small number of laws passed by the legislature itself and from the large number that are officially enacted only after having originated with the Council of State. Lawmaking, however, is a secondary matter. The primary function of both bodies, like that of the USSR Supreme Soviet and its Presidium, is their joint role in the ratification of decrees issued by the government's executive branch.

At the end of a legislative term, the Council of State orders elections to be held within three months, but it remains in power until the new Assembly has had an opportunity to elect another council. In an emergency the Grand National Assembly may extend the mandate of the council for the duration.

Until 1974 the chairman of the State Council was ex officio the titular head of state, that is, the president. In 1948 and again in 1952 a noncommunist was elected chairman for tactical reasons. In 1961 the party leader Gheorghiu Gheorghiu-Dej was elected to this post, and on his death in 1965, Chivu Stoica became chairman. He was replaced on 13 March 1969 by Nicolae Ceausescu.[9] Five years later the constitution was amended to provide for the position of president of the Socialist Republic of Romania. Although the State Council continues to exist, the president is now ex officio also its chairman. He has additional prerogatives by virtue of the office of the presidency, being entitled to issue decrees and to take other measures on his own initiative without State Council approval.

The Executive.   The administration of the government is centered where the ruling communist party can best exert its influence and control, in the Council of Ministers. It is significant that more members of the party's Executive Committee serve there than on the Council of State. All key positions are filled by trusted communists.

The Council of Ministers is elected by the Grand National Assembly; theoretically it is responsible to that body and, between its sessions, to the Council of State. Decisions by the Council of Ministers are formulated as orders that are binding throughout the country. A good example is the decree authorizing public meetings to decide on contributions in money and labor to works of "public interest," such as schools, maternity homes, roads, and bridges. A summary of the Council's eleven official prerogatives appears in Article 70 of the new constitution.[10] This document also fully describes the functions of the ministries.

The large number of ministers and agencies under them reflects the specialization as well as the centralized nature of the economy and the extensive administrative apparatus of the government. The exact number of ministries and agencies is in constant flux, with fusion or separation reflecting current needs. In 1988 there were 35 units.[11]

Local Government.   The administrative subdivisions of Romania include 40 counties and the municipality of Bucharest. Within these units there are 237 towns and 2,705 communes. According to official estimates, the total population of 22.9 million is about 46.9 percent rural and 53.1 percent urban.[12]

The local instruments of state power are called people's councils; they correspond to soviets in the USSR. These operate under the principle of democratic centralism, with a downward flow of guidance that limits the initiative of subordinate units. People's councils operate at county, municipal, district, town, and commune levels. More important administrative organs within the councils are called executive committees. It is noteworthy that while the constitution proclaims the supremacy of the councils, the executive committees are packed with trusted party members who exercise the real power.

Elections in counties and municipal districts are held every four years, in towns and communes every other year. Upon the expiration of its term, the executive committee retains power pending the election of a new council, in direct parallel with the State Council and the Grand National Assembly at the top of the organizational pyramid. The latest elections at the local levels were held in mid-November 1987, and approximately 57,584 deputies were chosen.[13] There were 114,349 individuals running for the positions involved, which meant multiple candidacies in 80 percent of the races. All candidates, however, had been officially approved in advance.

Under the electoral provisions in the constitution, suffrage is universal for all persons eighteen and older. Candidates for the people's councils must be at least

23. The right to nominate candidates is reserved to the Socialist Democracy and Unity Front. Article 25 of the constitution denies suffrage to citizens who are considered unworthy and unreliable, including "mentally alienated and deficient people."

Judicial System. The fundamental tasks of the judiciary, as they are defined in the constitution and subsequent laws, include, since 1965, defending the regime of socialism, the rights of the working people, and the interests of state agencies and institutions. Theoretically the judiciary must ensure the observance of justice, and, furthermore, it must educate the people in the spirit of devotion to the fatherland and to the construction of socialism. Here, as is usual under communist regimes, politics becomes the basis for law. Legal rules must be interpreted in the light of the class struggle, and justice is deemed to be the will of the working class.

The task of administering justice is carried out by the *procuratura* (office of the prosecutor general)[14] and by regular and special courts. Regular courts, which are known as people's tribunals, hear civil, penal, and any other cases within their competence. The jurisdiction of each court is graduated in accordance with the level of government at which it functions. Military courts hear cases and announce the penalties provided by the law to punish such enemies of the people as traitors, spies, those sabotaging the construction of socialism or committing "crimes against peace and humanity," warmongers, embezzlers, and those who destroy socialist property. Courts in the city of Bucharest and at the county level hear cases that are on appeal from the people's tribunals. The supreme court, theoretically, is entrusted with control over the judicial activities of the other courts; it meets for this purpose at least once every three months. Soviet practices are copied here also, for the supreme court has no power to review the constitutionality of statutes. Judges of all courts are nominated exclusively by the Romanian communist party. People's tribunal judges play a larger role than is specified in the constitution. For example, the justice minister can move them from court to court to meet exigencies.

The prosecutor general possesses the highest supervisory authority over the observance of the law by all central and local government organs. Naturally he must be a trusted member of the party. He is "elected" by the Grand National Assembly for a term of five years. He then designates his deputies and prosecutors to serve at lower levels for periods of four years. All prosecutors are independent of local government organs because they are formally responsible to the Assembly or, between its sessions, to the State Council. However, the *procuratura* is really an organization that is directed exclusively by the party.[15] It is modeled closely after the corresponding agency in the USSR. The prosecutor general enjoys a "consultative" vote in the Council of State and in the Council of Ministers.

Education.   The structure of Romanian education is founded on three basic enactments. These are the August 1948 educational reform law, the July 1956 joint decree of the party's Central Committee and the Council of Ministers that implemented the resolutions of the party's second congress, and the October 1961 decree transforming into law the resolutions of the third party congress.

Since October 1961 compulsory education has encompassed the first eight grades, a change that was made to parallel the system in the USSR. This period comprises elementary school grades one to five and intermediate grades six through eight. Four additional grades, from nine through twelve, provide a complete secondary education. These upper grades are oriented toward either the humanities or the physical and mathematical sciences. If they are complemented by two years of employment and practical experience, they can lead to a higher education.

Admission to the six universities and to some 36 other institutions of higher learning in Romania is based on both successful completion of an entrance examination and political reliability, with the latter requirement generally certified by the communist party or the youth organization unit at the applicant's place of residence.[16] The aims of the educational system, thus, include political conformity. Vocational training is provided at special schools. Technicians who teach at these schools have both specialized training and practical experience.

ROMANIAN COMMUNIST PARTY

A communist movement was established in 1921, only to be outlawed three years later. The party continued its agitation underground, but effective government police harassment prevented the maintenance of a viable political organization. Determined action in 1936, which led to the arrest and conviction of nearly all the communist leaders, virtually eliminated the party as a political force. The movement had little or no war record of partisan activity to give it prestige, and in 1944 its reduced leadership included a large number of Jews, Ukrainians, and Hungarians.[17]

In August, King Michael forced a change of government and took Romania out of the war it had been fighting as a German ally. Hitler responded by bombing Bucharest, following which the king formally declared war on Germany and brought in his fifteen divisions on the side of the Red Army.

> Romania's change of front, together with the Teheran decision not to open a front in the Balkans, decided the fate of Central Europe, decided that the Soviet Union should dominate the whole region, that its new order should be a communist new order. Generalissimo Stalin therefore had good reason later to award to King Michael the highest Soviet decoration, the Order of Victory.[18]

In most of the other countries within the USSR's orbit, communist-dominated "front" governments assumed power immediately after Red Army occupation. In Romania, however, a so-called bourgeois government (although it included communist party representation) was tolerated for a short time. In March 1945 the USSR ordered the king to install a People's Democratic Front regime. This was done, and the communists received the three ministries they had demanded: Interior, Justice, and National Economy. They sought mass support by redistributing confiscated land to peasant smallholders and promising improved working conditions to factory workers. National and local government administrations were controlled by placing trusted personnel in key positions.

In February 1948 the communists and the left-wing social democrats merged to form the Romanian Workers' Party. A new Central Committee and Politburo drew a majority of their members from the previous communist organization, and the new party, from its inception, clearly came under the leadership of the old communists. Thus, in the period between 1944 and 1952, an initially insignificant communist movement, working with the assistance of Soviet advisers and supported by the presence of Soviet troops, ousted and destroyed all political opposition to make itself the sole ruler of Romania.

Central Organization. The supreme organ of the Romanian communist party is the congress, to which delegates are elected by regional conferences. Congresses are to be called at least every five years; at these times delegates hear and approve reports by central organs, adopt programs, and establish basic policy. They elect a Central Committee and a Central Audit Commission, which controls party finances. After performing these functions, the congresses then delegate their authority to the Central Committee until the next session.[19]

As the seat of power between congresses, the Central Committee provides a rostrum for publicizing the party program, directs and controls party as well as government organs, and also administers party finances. It has the responsibility for electing the Political Executive Committee and the Central Committee Secretariat. These bodies are not elective but actually consist of leading party personalities who are chosen by an inner group and then rubber-stamped by the Central Committee.

As the foremost consultative body of the party, the Central Committee tends to include the top stratum of government after the familiar model of interlocking directorates. (See Table 39.) Of the 46 persons listed as members of the Council of Ministers in 1988, the majority hold membership or candidate status on the Central Committee of the party. According to an excellent but dated analysis,[20] in 1961 half the Central Committee was made up of hard-core party professionals, with 80 percent of this half being drawn from the inner circles of government or industry and the remaining 20 percent from lesser positions of power.

Table 39
ROMANIA'S INTERLOCKING DIRECTORATE, 1988 POLITICAL EXECUTIVE COMMITTEE

Members (19)	Year of birth	Year elected	Secretariat/ PermBuro	Council of Ministers	Other positions
Ceausescu, Nicolae	1918	1954	General secretary/ member		President, State Council; chairman, Defense Council, Supreme Socioeconomic Development Council, Socialist Democracy and Unity Front
Bobu, Emil	1927	1974	Secretary/member (org. section)		Chairman, Economic and Social Council
Cazacu, Virgil	1927	1979	Secretary (foreign relations)		
Ceausescu, Elena	1919	1977	Member	First deputy premier	Chairman, National Council of Science and Technology; chief, Communist Party and State Cadres Commission
Ciobanu, Lina	1929	1973		Deputy premier	
Coman, Ion	1926	1976	Secretary (military and security)		Member, Defense Council
Constantin, Nicolae	ca. 1929	1979			Chairman, Central Collegium
Dascalescu, Constantin	1922	1978	Member	Premier	Member, Defense Council
Dinca, Ion	1924	1979		First deputy premier	Chairman, National Council for Agriculture
Dobrescu, Miu	1920				Chairman, Central Council of Trade Unions
Fazekas, Ludovic	1920	1979		Deputy premier	Chairman, Coordination and Production of Consumer Goods
Manescu, Manea	1916	1983			Vice-president, State Council
Niculescu, Paul	1923	1965	Member		Chairman, CENTROCOOP

Name					
Olteanu, Constantin	*ca.* 1926	1983	Secretary (propaganda)		Member, State Council
Oprea, Gheorghe	1927	1969	Member	First deputy premier	
Pana, Gheorghe	1927	1969			Chairman, Committee on the Affairs of the People's Councils; member, State Council
Patan, Ion	1926	1972			
Popescu, Dumitru	1928	1969			Rector, Stefan Gheorghiu Academy
Radulescu, Gheorghe	1914	1965	Member		Vice-president, State Council; chairman, Higher Council for Financial Control

SOURCES: RFE, *East European Leadership List* (15 January 1988), pp. 37–42, CIA, *Directory of Romanian Officials* (June 1986); Bucharest radio, 28 June 1988.

As has been mentioned previously, the locus of party power rests with the Political Executive Committee. It functions as the primary policymaking body and also reviews work of the Secretariat and the Central Collegium (formerly known as the Party Control Commission), which maintains party discipline.[21] (The collegium has been downgraded in recent years; it now performs only control and investigative functions.) The Political Executive Committee selects a Permanent Bureau, which is at present composed of seven members. Although this small group is concerned with day-to-day matters of high-level significance, it is not equivalent to a Politburo in the other East European ruling parties or to the former Standing Presidium, which had existed until spring 1974 in the Romanian party. The Political Executive Committee now appears to be the policymaking body. Those who decide policy are, as often as not, the ones who implement it. The ten-member Secretariat sees to it that policies are executed. Although the Secretariat is nominally elected by the Central Committee, it is really appointed by the party leadership and represents one of the main power centers.

Decisions and policies established by the leaders and checked by the Secretariat and the Central Collegium are supposed to be reviewed critically and then approved by plenary sessions of the Central Committee at least four times a year.[22] This procedure, however, merely provides a forum through which the party leadership can submit to the Central Committee for its rubber-stamp approval the party line as established by the Political Executive Committee.

Regional Organization.   The county is the intermediate organizational echelon within the party.[23] Committees at this level are near duplicates of the Central Committee at the top both organizationally and functionally, although they are smaller in size.

The supreme organ of the county is the conference, which is called to meet by its respective committee every two years. It reviews and approves reports, debates problems connected with party activities, and elects a new party committee as well as delegates to the conference of the next higher party organization or to the national party congress. Conferences are basically sounding boards, and the policies and directives issued by the Central Committee are implemented by lower committees and secretariats that are subordinate to them.

The county committee is supposed to meet every three months. It always remains in contact with the party apparatus at the center through the county first secretary, who is usually a member of the Central Committee. The town or commune meets every two months and represents the immediate superior to the basic party organizations that comprise the bottom of the pyramid. In 1987 the Romanian communist party had 40 county; 237 municipal and city; 2,705 commune; more than 8,500 enterprise, institute, and agricultural; and about 70,000 basic party organizations.[24]

Basic Party Organization. By statute, these units constitute the party's foundation as they are the ultimate executors of the policies and directives issued by the Central Committee. They exist in government, industry, agriculture, schools, and military units. Their size can vary from a minimum of 3 to a maximum of 300 members. The larger ones are headed by bureaus. If they contain fewer than 10 members, the leadership comprises a secretary and one deputy. These lowest-ranking organizations play a dual role; they are the executors of party and government policies and directives and supervisors over the activities of local administration and other nonparty organs. This arrangement is indicative of the manner in which party and government functions overlap and of the fact that the party and its organs are placed above the government and its institutions.

Party Membership. Probably the most astonishing aspect of the communist movement has been its growth during the postwar years, due to different kinds of pressure. Its size is estimated to have increased from about a thousand members[25] in 1944 to almost a million only four years later. Over the next several years it fluctuated between 600,000 and 900,000 members. In 1964, when the party had 1.2 million members and candidates, about 16 percent, or 200,000, of these were classified as activists. In 1988, total membership was reported to be 3,709,735, or some 15.8 percent of the population.[26]

Like the communist parties in the other East European countries, the party in Romania has had difficulty maintaining a proper representation of factory workers in its ranks. Even with mass recruitment during 1947 the proletarian component made up less than 40 percent, with the majority of the members coming from white-collar employees and the intelligentsia. This emphasis on derivation from the industrial workers follows from the glorification of the proletariat in communist doctrine and from a conviction that the leaders within this class—the competitive Stakhanovite types who have a zeal for surpassing production goals—are generally more reliable, more susceptible to indoctrination, and easier to control. Recruitment procedures were relaxed for this group, and by 1960 the party could claim an increase in the percentage of factory workers. By 1975 the total in this category had not quite reached the 1960 level. (See Table 40.) Lack of verification for these figures and the uncertain definition of a worker make such regime statistics questionable. A 1976 report on cadre policy states that the party now has more members with a higher education than it had two years before.[27] Of course, those with a working-class background are given preference in promotion.

Mass Organizations. The Union of Communist Youth (UTC), which was originally founded in 1922 and reorganized in 1948 as a junior branch of the party, comprises a mass organization of some four million members.[28] It is patterned after the Komsomol in the Soviet Union. The UTC is organized similarly to the party, and party rules indicate that those aged eighteen to twenty must belong to

Table 40
ROMANIAN COMMUNIST PARTY SOCIAL COMPOSITION, 1970, 1980, AND 1988

CATEGORY	MARCH 1970		JULY 1980		APRIL 1988	
	Number	*Percent*	*Number*	*Percent*	*Number*	*Percent*
Workers	867,290	43.4	1,622,788	54.0	2,042,951	55.07
Peasants	531,447	26.6	540,930	18.0	575,751	15.52
Intelligentsia	481,083	24.0	861,446	28.0	757,157	20.41
Pensioners and housewives	119,900	6.0	—	—	333,876	9.00
Total	1,999,720	100.0	3,005,164	100.0	3,709,735	100.00

SOURCES: *Scinteia,* 20 March 1970, and 19 July 1980; 2 April 1988, p. 2.

NOTE: Composition of the party by nationality was 90 percent Romanian, some 8 percent Hungarian, and only 2 percent German. *Scinteia,* 20 November 1979.

the UTC to be eligible for party membership. Apart from providing the core of the future party members and cadres, the UTC has the responsibility for carrying out and supervising the execution of party policies as they affect the whole of Romanian youth within and above its age range.

Until April 1966 the UTC supervised the introductory Pioneers for children, whose membership of 1.3 million encompasses about 70 percent of the nine-to-fourteen age group. The inspiration provided by a similar organization in the Soviet Union can be noted in the Pioneers' former motto: "In the fight for the cause of Lenin and Stalin, forward." They are under the direct control of the party. A cultural-ideological program approved on 2 November 1976 established a new organization called "Fatherland's Falcons" for children in the four-to-seven age group. Political indoctrination, henceforth, will include the entire population.

The General Confederation of Trade Unions is one of Romania's largest mass organizations. With a membership of more than seven million, it covers the complete spectrum of workers and professional people.[29] Like the party, it is organized according to the principle of democratic centralism. The sixteen component trade unions maintain county councils that are superimposed on some 11,600 basic units. Instead of representing workers, factory committees, and professional groups, the trade union apparatus has the primary purpose of ensuring the successful fulfillment of the government's economic plans. It exercises the additional responsibility of raising the cultural level, and especially the political consciousness, of its members. Indoctrination is generally carried out at the lowest level by party or UTC members who belong to the local trade union council. At the latest trade union plenum Miu Dobrescu was chosen as chairman.[30]

The Socialist Democracy and Unity Front, which in 1968 replaced the People's Democratic Front, is open to those who are eligible for membership in other mass organizations. In order to maintain the fiction of representative government, the party has chosen to consider all candidates in parliamentary and local elections as representing the Socialist Democracy and Unity Front. The Front accepts these nominees as its own, promotes the election, and presents a political program that is identical with the program of the ruling party. The activities of the Front are limited to election periods occurring every two and four years, that is, at both local and national levels.

DOMESTIC AND FOREIGN POLICY

The history of the people dates back to the second century, when Roman legions were stationed in what is today Romania. The language, a Romance tongue of Latin origin, can also be traced to this period. Somewhat modified by Slavic, Albanian, Hungarian, Greek, and Turkish influences in the centuries that followed, it still has today a majority of word elements that are derived from the Latin once spoken in the Eastern Roman Empire. This fact (noted earlier) continues to be important in the current situation, perhaps as important as the demographic and geographic features of the country.

Losses of territory occurring in the early part of World War II included parts of Transylvania, Bessarabia, Northern Bukovina, and Southern Dobruja. Transylvania was eventually recovered from Hungary; Bessarabia[31] and Northern Bukovina, however, were annexed in 1940 to the Soviet Union, recaptured by the Romanians in 1941, but lost again in 1944; Southern Dobruja has been kept by Bulgaria. The various modifications in borders have contributed to animosity between Romania and her neighbors, including the USSR.

National Minorities. Although the population is principally of ethnic Romanian origin, some 10.9 percent comprise minorities. The largest minority groups are the Hungarians (in 1987 they numbered almost 1.8 million or 7.8 percent of the population) and the Germans (just over 345,000 or 1.5 percent of the population), but there are also smaller groups of Jews, Ukrainians, Russians, Bulgarians, Gypsies, Turks, Tatars, and others.[32]

The treatment of the Hungarian minority after 1948 represented an important issue and one with which the government in Budapest was concerned. In 1952 a Hungarian Autonomous Region was established under the provisions of the Romanian constitution adopted that year. After unrest arose among the people in this autonomous region during the 1956 Hungarian revolution just across the border, however, the Romanian government began to restrict the rights of this

Table 41
ETHNIC GROUPS IN ROMANIA, 1966, 1980, and 1987

	1966		1980		1987	
Nationality	*Number*	*Percentage*	*Number*	*Percentage*	*Number*	*Percentage*
Romanians	16,746,510	87.7	19,402,740	87.0	20,436,424	89.1
Hungarians	1,619,592	8.5	1,784,160	8.0	1,389,047	7.8
Germans	382,595	2.0	446,040	2.0	344,048	1.5
Jews	42,888	0.2	35,000	1.0	—	—
Ukrainians	54,705	0.3				
Russians	39,483	0.2				
Bulgarians	11,193	0.1				
Gypsies	64,197	0.3	634,060	2.0	366,984	1.6
Turks	18,040	0.1				
Gaugauzi (Tatar)	22,151	0.1				
Others	101,809	0.5				
Total	19,103,163	100.0	22,302,000	100.0	22,936,503	100.0

SOURCES: Bucharest radio, 18 September 1966. (Cited by Robert R. King, *Minorities Under Communism* [Cambridge, Mass., 1973], p. 267, from which the above data were taken); RFE, *Romanian Situation Report*, no. 12 (29 June 1981), p. 14; CIA, *World Factbook 1987*, p. 205.

minority. In 1959 the Hungarian-language university of Cluj was merged with the Romanian-language university in the same city. During the following year the boundaries of the Hungarian Autonomous Region were redrawn to exclude a large homogeneous Hungarian population and thus to provide a mixed population that included a larger number of Romanians.

Since the advent of Nicolae Ceausescu to the party leadership in 1965, a more conciliatory policy toward minorities has been followed. However, limitations still restrict minority activity, and links with Romania are emphasized. Although schooling in their mother tongues is permitted, minority youths are expected to learn Romanian. In the territorial reorganization of 1968, the Hungarian Autonomous Region was abolished, as were all fifteen other regions. Among the 40 new counties that were created, however, 2 had Hungarian majorities and several others had large Hungarian minorities.[33] Table 41 shows the ethnic composition of the country together with the extent of change over the 1966–1987 period, the latest period for which census data or estimates are available.

The 1965 constitution also makes special provision for minority groups. Article 22 states the following:

In the Socialist Republic of Romania, the coinhabiting national minorities are ensured the free utilization of their native language as well as books, papers, magazines, theaters, and education at all levels in their own language. In districts also inhabited by a population of non-Romanian nationality, all the bodies and institutions use the language of the respective nationality in speech and in writing and appoint officials from its ranks or from the ranks of other citizens who know the language and way of life of the local population.

At one time, 2,000 Hungarian elementary schools and 1,000 Hungarian high schools existed in the former autonomous province.[34] By December 1960, however, the southern part had been transferred to the ethnically Romanian province of Brasov. Hungarian archives and libraries were destroyed and buildings torn down to provide stone for new construction. In education, a system of ''parallel sections'' added a Romanian curriculum, and after a period of time, the Hungarian curriculum was eliminated. However, in 1969 some 240,000 students were being taught Hungarian, German, and other minority languages.[35] The situation since that time reportedly has deteriorated considerably.

The Economy. In the past Romania was primarily an agricultural country. More than half the population is still classified as rural. Some 64 percent of the total labor force is employed in industry and nonagricultural work, but a manpower shortage persists. Although the rate of population increase declined from 10 per thousand in 1959 to 5.2 per thousand in 1966, it rose again to 9.7 per thousand during the 1970–1975 period. Romania is expected by 1990 to have 24 million inhabitants.[36]

In the years just preceding World War II agriculture and forestry contributed more than half the national income. This proportion dropped to one-third in 1961, which was a good harvest year. During the period 1971–1975, Romania's industrial production reportedly expanded at an annual rate of more than 13 percent, and the total national income grew at the rate of 10 percent a year. The production growth rate planned for 1976–1980 was 30 percent for agriculture and only 11 percent for industry. Agriculture remains a problem, in part because of the low motivation of the farmers.

It should also be emphasized that in the 1976–1980 five-year plan much more concern was shown than in the past for increasing the amount of consumer goods. Three new bodies were established to coordinate the production and sale of these commodities. It should also be mentioned that per capita income in Romania was only about one thousand dollars a year, compared with an average that is four times higher in developed countries. As a corollary, foreign trade targets were drastically raised, from 72 to 80 percent in the 1976–1980 planning period.[37] Hence, the government had to place considerable emphasis on controls and work discipline.

Investment has been concentrated in industry since the communists gained control. The Soviet party program emphasized heavy industry in "creating the material and technical basis for communism," and similarly the leaders in Romania have sought to develop and expand this sector of the economy. "The consistent Leninist policy of industrializing the country by concentrating on the development of heavy industry, and its main branch, the machine-building industry, has brought about deep changes in the structure of RPR [Romanian People's Republic] exports. Machines and equipment are gaining greater importance in export trade."[38]

As a result of this concentration on heavy industry, the composition of Romanian foreign trade has changed. Before 1939, exports of cereals, oil, timber, livestock, and animal derivatives comprised 90 percent of the total. By 1961, machinery and equipment already accounted for 16 percent. In general, an increase in the export of finished products has taken place. Between 1948 and 1958 the proportion of food exports dropped from almost 50 percent to only 15 percent. The current principal imports—industrial machinery, vehicles, machine tools, iron ore, and coal—also reflect the continuing emphasis on industry. In 1986, machinery and equipment exports increased to 32 percent of the total; fuels, minerals, and metals 28 percent; agricultural and foodstuffs 12 percent; and finished products 12 percent.[39]

The economic difficulties resulting from World War II and the subsequent exploitation by the Soviet Union took many years to overcome. Although the country changed sides in August 1944 and fought with the Allies, it was occupied thereafter by the Red Army. Under an armistice agreement with the USSR, Romania paid reparations of $300 million in goods at 1938 prices. Over a period of six years, the Soviet Union took petroleum in considerable amounts for about half of what it would have brought the Romanians on the world market. The total value of reparations actually extracted by the USSR between September 1944 and June 1948 has been estimated at more than $1.7 billion.[40] In order to continue these forced deliveries, several oil companies had to be subsidized by the government at Bucharest.

Soviet occupation forces confiscated all property that had formerly been owned by Germans and Italians, including French, Dutch, and Belgian assets previously expropriated by the Germans. This was in addition to the reparations. By 1946 the USSR owned more than one-third of Romania's industrial and financial enterprises. Some of the seized property formed the basis for Soviet-Romanian joint-stock companies, which were called "Sovroms."

During the period 1946–1947, about 37.5 percent of the national budget had to be committed for the payment of reparations. In the next fiscal year, the amount rose to 46.6 percent.[41] Subsequently, the reparations were reduced but not completely abolished. Only in 1954 did Soviet Premier Georgi Malenkov, in an effort to ease the economic situation and increase voluntary political cooperation by

Romania, announce transfer of Soviet shares in the joint-stock companies to Bucharest. Control, except for that of uranium mining through "Sovromquartz," was handed over to the Romanian communists.

On the whole, the economy of Romania has had a growth rate higher than that of any other East European country. It is claimed that between 1950 and 1959 national income grew by 10.3 percent each year. The officially reported increase averaged 8.5 percent from 1960 through 1964, and the five-year plan for 1966–1970 envisaged an 8 percent annual growth. During 1971–1975 this rate increased to 10 percent. One reason for such an accelerated growth rate, of course, is the low level from which it began. An admitted disparity still exists between the agricultural and the industrial sectors of the economy. By 1970 industrial production had reportedly risen fourteen times over the preceding 30 years compared with only 1.6 times for agriculture. The index for industry during the 1971–1980 period expanded by over 100 percent.[42]

The current decade has not been so successful, with net material product (gross national product) increasing 3.8 percent instead of the planned 7.1 percent during 1981–1985. No physical output targets were published for 1987, although it was claimed that industrial production had gone up by 4.5 percent.[43] One of the most pressing economic problems involves the avowed goal of paying off the foreign debt before 1990.

Agriculture. Although more than one-third of the working population is occupied in the agricultural sector, it accounted for only 14 percent of the national income.[44] The reasons for this include the long-standing peasant opposition to collectivization, the regime's emphasis on industrial investment and neglect of agriculture, high taxation, insufficient mechanization, the continuation of certain backward methods, mismanagement and inefficiency, and droughts. Over the past several years, however, farming has received increased attention.

The primary crops are corn and wheat. In 1963 Romania exported 400,000 tons of wheat to the USSR. The complete socialization of agriculture had been announced the year before, two years ahead of schedule, making Romania the first East European country to achieve this status. The 1986 production of cereals was 30.3 million tons, up from 23 million tons the year before.[45]

Land Reform and Collectivization. An initial land reform act was passed in March 1945. On the basis of this legislation, holdings in excess of 50 hectares and all real property belonging to certain categories of individuals (for example, war criminals and Germans) were expropriated. Land reform had been designed in part to gain the support of the peasants by giving them small private plots. The major long-term objective, however, was the collectivization of agriculture. Gradual pressure on the peasants took the form of compulsory delivery quotas at artificially low prices; state ownership of expropriated agricultural machinery;

socialization of credit institutions, mills, and oil presses; and the 1947 monetary reform, which practically eliminated peasant savings.

Because of resistance, socialization could be carried out only gradually and at different levels. The highest form is the state farm, which is patterned after the *sovkhoz* in the USSR. In this type of enterprise agricultural workers do not share in the profits but are paid wages.

On joining a collective farm, however, a peasant family turns over to the *kolkhoz* its land, farm implements, draft animals, vehicles, and other equipment. The house and a few head of livestock can be retained. A family is given a private garden plot of land ranging from two-thirds of an acre to one acre in size, depending on the quality of soil. After the payment of various expenses, the delivery of compulsory quotas, and the setting aside of funds for investment, the earnings are distributed to the collective farm members by the management. This division is made on the basis of days worked during the year rather than the original contribution of land, animals, and equipment. The number of standard units credited to a member depends on the type of job performed and can total more or fewer than the actual days worked. Many administrators give themselves several times the appropriate number. "In the district of Dobrudja, for instance, the average number of work days per *kolkhoz* member annually was 195, while the chairmen of the *kolkhozes* in this district credited themselves with an average of 711 work days annually."[46]

Because of strong resistance to collectivization, in 1951 the government introduced so-called agricultural partnerships. These involve a less rigid form of association. The peasant has a choice of how much he will contribute, and his share of the profits depends on his contribution and the amount of work he performs. When agricultural partnerships tend to become permanent, higher-level agricultural associations and collective herds are established. In these organizations, cooperation is limited mainly to pooling land for plowing, with the rest of the work done by each individual member. In areas where grazing predominates, collective sheep herds and livestock farms have been established.

The collectivization of agriculture at first proceeded slowly. In late 1957 Bucharest radio announced that 13,065 collective farms had been established.[47] They covered less than one-fourth of the arable land. In June 1960 the third congress of the Romanian Workers' Party adopted a new six-year economic plan. At that time 81 percent of all agriculture was said to be socialized. The largest part consisted of the lowest-level collectives. Only about one-third of the total consisted of *kolkhozes*. In early 1962 it was announced that the goal of 96 percent socialization of agriculture had been reached. In attaining this target, of course, production had been adversely affected. Because of strict controls (some 875,478 communist party members worked in rural areas during 1970) and a low rate of investment, agricultural growth remained lower than capability. Hence, a new law on remuneration for agricultural products went into effect.[48] Small private plots are now also being allocated to state farm workers, as material incentive, within a framework of intensive agricultural development. (See Table 42.)

In his address to the second congress of management councils for socialist agricultural units (19–21 February 1981), Ceausescu proposed that joint state and cooperative agro-industrial councils, established in 1979, be limited to jurisdiction over an average of 20,000 hectares per council, which would make a total of 450 to 500 councils.[49] They are responsible for planning, organizing, and running all agricultural production cooperatives, state agricultural enterprises, and agricultural machinery stations.

Table 42
TYPES OF FARMS IN ROMANIA, 1985

Type	Areas in use (millions of hectares)	Percent of total cultivated area
State agricultural farms	4,466,825	29.7
Agricultural production cooperatives	9,133,234	60.8
(portion of cooperatives that are private plots)	(922,841)	(6.1)
Individual farms	1,420,119	9.5
Total	15,020,178	100.0

SOURCE: [Romania], *Anuarul Statistic al Republicii Socialiste Romania 1986* (Bucharest, 1987), p. 134.

Disastrous shortcomings in agriculture may cause Ceausescu to look for Western assistance. The 1978, 1979, and 1980 harvests did not meet targets, forcing the Romanian leadership to direct more investments into farming. For the first time, the 1981 plan set agricultural growth above that for industry. International Monetary Fund (IMF) loans of $75 million have been obtained for irrigation and drainage systems at the Bucsani-Buzau-Siret-Prut project (total cost estimated at $375 million). Another loan of $80 million helped develop beef and dairy farms as well as processing facilities.[50]

Agricultural policies of the party have created significant economic problems. As with most other East European countries that followed the Soviet model for industrialization, Romanian investment in the agricultural sector (such as construction of fertilizer and tractor factories) has not kept pace with the general growth of the economy. This has made it difficult to maintain a high level of agricultural exports and, at the same time, feed the growing urban population. Food shortages, which have been severe in times of drought or bad weather, continue to cause serious problems for the government and hardships for the population.

Industry. As was the case in agriculture, the nationalization of industry lagged at first. By June 1948, however, most privately owned factories had been taken over by the government. In the following year, the state sector accounted for 85 percent of all industrial production; by 1960, it encompassed 98.8 percent.[51]

As mentioned previously, Romania has been concentrating on the development of heavy industry. Between 1970 and 1975, approximately 58 percent of the total national investment was allocated by plan to this sector of the economy. Both imports and exports are oriented toward industry. In order to increase steel production, it has been necessary to bring large quantities of iron ore, coke, and rolled metals into the country. The trend of imports in machinery and equipment has been toward complete processing plants.

Beginning in 1962, Romania contracted with West European suppliers to build the largest steel-plate mill in the world. A tire factory and two cellulose plants for making paper and related products were obtained from Britain and set up the following summer. A U.S. company was granted a permit in 1965 to construct an oil-cracking plant, and the British helped to set up an ore-processing factory at Galati.[52] Romania's largest trading partner outside the Soviet bloc, the Federal Republic of Germany, has built an iron and steel mill at Hunedoara in the central part of the country. The French installed a winery and a processing plant for sugar beets. Although economic agreements covering the period 1976–1980 were signed with the USSR increasing the reciprocal exchange of goods by about one-third compared with the previous five-year period, it is likely that the Soviet share in Romania's foreign trade will continue to decline. To pay for advanced Western technology and the necessary raw materials, Bucharest depends on exports and credits.

Between 1976 and 1980, approximately 49.1 percent of total national investment was allocated to the industrial sector. During the plan for 1981–1985, however, there were no new investments in industry. Emphasis centered on improving backward agriculture.[53]

Growth rates during 1976–1980 remained relatively stable following a decade of rising ones, demonstrating that even Romania could not be shielded from worldwide economic difficulties. Targets for the 1981–1985 plan were set low, signifying Bucharest's concern over domestic capabilities and the unpredictable international situation. Steadily falling growth rates, a rapidly increasing foreign debt, and widespread food rationing could make the country another Poland, according to a study by Wharton Econometric Forecasting Associates. The report is critical of the IMF decision to extend a $1.46 billion credit to Romania for two reasons. First, the 1986–1990 plan sets the lowest-ever growth targets.

(See Table 43.) Second, the hard-currency debt in early 1988 was estimated at $5 billion.[54] It is discussed below.

In April 1981 Ceausescu gave a report to the congress of trade unions in which he praised the achievements of workers, saying, "Today we are achieving a 48 times higher industrial production and 14 times higher national income than we did before World War II." He also touched on the matter of shortening the average workweek, first by reducing it to 46 hours and then to 44 hours by 1985. Ceausescu mentioned that a ratio of 1:5 exists between the highest and lowest wages. The average outside of agriculture in 1975 was 1,595 lei per month, increasing to 2,238 in 1980, and up to 2,585 by 1985. The average farmer's cash monthly income grew from 571 lei in 1970 to 1,373 in 1980 and increased to 1,620 in 1985.[55]

Table 43
ECONOMIC TARGETS, 1976–1990
(percentage growth)

Index	1976–1980 actual	1981–1985 actual	1986–1990 plan
National income	7.2	4.4	7.6–8.3
Industrial production	10.1	4.0	6.0–6.5
Agricultural production	4.8	2.0	5.4–5.8
Investments	10.9	1.3	1.8–2.5
Foreign trade	16.5	4.7	—

SOURCE: *Business Eastern Europe* 10, no. 23 (5 June 1981), p. 179, no. 30 (24 July 1981), p. 236; Economist Intelligence Unit (EIU), *Country Profile: Romania* (1986–87), p. 13; EIU, *Regional Review* (1986), p. 94.

Once self-sufficient in petroleum, Romania is now a net importer. Annual oil production, which had averaged close to 15 million tons per year, dropped to 12.6 in 1979, and did not reach even 12 million tons in 1980, when consumption was 30 million tons. During that last year, Romania purchased 15 million tons of oil, mostly from OPEC countries, plus 1.5 million tons from the USSR reportedly at OPEC prices and for hard currency. Hard-coal extraction is slowly improving, and coal is now used as a substitute for oil. Natural gas production has begun a slow decline, after a promising increase at the end of the 1970s. (See Table 44.)

One response to the domestic fuel shortage is Romania's ambitious program to build nuclear power plants. An agreement has been signed with a Canadian manufacturer for the Candu nuclear reactor. Construction of the first such plant at Cernavoda on the Danube is under way and scheduled to begin operation in 1985.

Table 44
ROMANIAN FUEL PRODUCTION, 1976–1986

	1976	1977	1978	1979	1986
Petroleum					
(thousand barrels/day)	308	307	288	259	227
Natural gas					
(billion cubic feet)	1,216	1,181	1,190	1,116	940
Hard coal					
(million metric tons)	7.11	7.15	7.42	8.19	8.80

SOURCE: CIA, *Handbook of Economic Statistics 1980* (October 1980), pp. 124, 130–131, *1987* (September 1987), pp. 134, 138–39.

Negotiations for two more Candu-type reactors are in progress. Romania's long-range plan is to build up to sixteen nuclear plants by the year 2000. Ceausescu no longer mentions the previously repeated goal of energy self-sufficiency by 1985. Instead the percentage targets for energy requirements between 1980 and 1990 (in parentheses) are: oil and gas, 40 (5); coal, 40 (44); hydroelectric power, 18 (24); nuclear, 0 (18); and other, 2 (9).[56]

Foreign Trade.   Through direct seizure of certain industries, joint-stock companies, and the CMEA, the Soviet Union openly exploited the Romanian economy for more than a decade. Since 1954, however, Soviet control has progressively lessened. The agreement to sell its interests in industries that were expropriated during the occupation represented a first step in the process of returning the property stolen by Moscow to Bucharest.

The economies of the Soviet Union and Romania parallel each other in certain respects. Both countries are engaged in the process of industrialization, although, of course, at different levels, and both produce substantial agricultural commodities. Consequently they have similar needs, and these requirements are not complementary. The USSR is naturally reluctant to send Romania materials that are in short supply at home.

For many years Bucharest was deprived of an opportunity to obtain foreign exchange because of reparations, expropriation, and arbitrary, as well as discriminatory, prices established by the Soviet Union. It is little wonder that the Romanian communists were anxious to trade on a more equitable basis with capitalist countries. Romania's trade with France almost quadrupled between 1965 and 1974, and its trade with Britain doubled in 1980. Its exchange of goods with the United States for 1976 was expected to surpass $400 million and on 21 November of that year, a ten-year trade agreement was signed by the two countries.[57] Moscow, moreover, does not protest when Bucharest obtains the latest technology from the West.

Imports of coal and iron ore from the Soviet Union have been necessary for the continuing production of steel.[58] Some sources of iron ore have been explored by Romanian trade missions in Algeria, Brazil, India, and the United States, among others. Much emphasis has been placed on the chemical industry because oil, methane gas, coal, salt, and other raw materials are available locally. Romania has imported oil from the Arab states and Iran.

One serious controversy has arisen between the Soviet Union and Romania in connection with the CMEA and economic cooperation. (See Table 45.) Moscow originally wanted Bucharest to concentrate on producing raw materials for the industries of the more developed East European countries, but the shortage of cereals and particularly wheat in the Soviet Union and throughout the bloc in general probably prompted the USSR to press Romania to emphasize agriculture also.

Table 45
ROMANIAN TRADE WITH OTHER COMMUNIST-RULED STATES, 1979 AND 1985
(In millions of lei and percentage of total)

Country	1979		1985	
Albania	212.5	0.2	835.7	0.2
Bulgaria	1,723.8	1.8	7,760.9	2.3
Czechoslovakia	4,072.6	4.4	9,909.9	2.9
China	4,720.9	5.1	13,249.7	3.9
North Korea	324.8	0.3	627.7	0.2
Cuba	178.1	0.2	3,593.6	1.1
East Germany	5,657.0	6.0	16,737.1	4.9
Yugoslavia	1,527.8	1.6	4,519.9	1.3
Mongolia	56.5	0.1	327.2	0.1
Poland	3,025.5	3.2	14,955.6	4.4
Hungary	3,058.8	3.3	8,692.5	2.6
Soviet Union	14,529.8	15.7	74,332.7	21.8
North Vietnam	132.9	0.1	179.2	0.1
	39,221.0	42.0	155,721.7	45.8
Other states	53,037.6	58.0	184,934.9	54.2
Total	92,258.6	100.0	340,656.6	100.0

SOURCE: *Anuarul Statistic al Republicii Socialiste Romania 1980* (Bucharest, 1980), pp. 500–507, *1986*, pp. 286–92.

NOTE: The exchange rate was estimated to be 15.6 lei for one U.S. dollar. (November 1986)

Attempts to make Bucharest accept this role in the CMEA were made by high-ranking Soviet officials who visited Bucharest in person during 1963. Nikolai Podgorny, later president of the USSR, arrived first. Next came Premier Nikita Khrushchev, followed by First Deputy Foreign Minister Vasilii Kuznetsov. A policy statement issued by the Romanian communists almost a year later said that Bucharest favored bringing all communist-ruled states into the CMEA (that is, Albania, China, and Cuba), but that each bloc country should remain sovereign over its own economic affairs and should not be forced by any supranational body to adopt measures against its will.[59] Since then Romania seems to have been successful in retaining the direction of its own economy by always emphasizing equality and noninterference in the affairs of other states.

At the 35th CMEA session at Sofia, Premier Ilie Verdet complained that the Romanian proposal to double trade among member countries during 1981–1985 had been rejected and that turnover would be increased by only 38 percent. He had proposed increasing cooperation "to cover more completely" needs for raw materials, energy, machine tools, and technology and farm products. This will mean expansion of trade with the Soviet Union, the only CMEA partner capable of supplying such requirements. The share of Romania's fuel, mineral raw materials, and metal imports from CMEA amounted to 47 percent in 1970 but dropped to 21 percent ten years later.[60]

Trade agreements with the USSR were signed on 1 July 1981 for the 1981–1985 period. Although total figures were not reported, Romania will deliver a wide range of machinery and equipment, including complex technological equipment for the metallurgical, chemical, and petrochemical industries and various consumer goods. Moscow has agreed to supply Bucharest with cutting machine tools as well as machinery for road construction, agriculture, and shipping. Trade reportedly will double. The two delegations also agreed to collaborate in building a nuclear power plant in the Ukraine that will supply electricity to Romania.[61]

In an effort to modernize its economy and achieve more rapid industrialization, Romania sought and received substantial foreign credits from the West during the late 1960s and 1970s. Because it was exporting petroleum at a time of significant increases in the world price of energy, these investments seemed to be reasonable and secure in the view of Bucharest and its Western creditors. As oil reserves dwindled and the price of energy declined during the 1980s, however, foreign loans became more of a problem. Foreign credits have dried up, and the difficulty of repaying the outstanding debt has increased.

In 1981, the government launched a massive effort to reduce foreign indebtedness, and this has contributed to economic problems. Between 1981 and 1988, Romania's hard-currency debt dropped from an estimated $10 billion to just over $5 billion. Imports from the West were drastically reduced, and exports that earned hard currency or could be exchanged for Soviet oil have increased. During

1986, for example, one-fourth of all meat imported by the Soviet Union came from Romania.

The population has paid a heavy price for Ceausescu's economic dogmatism and crash program to reduce the foreign debt. Severe shortages have resulted in strict rationing of natural gas and other energy during the coldest months of the year.[62] Major city streets are unlighted at night to conserve electricity. Long lines for food are common, and there is little variety in the poor quality available. Meat, fruit, and vegetables are scarce or nonexistent. The shortages have been a fact of Romanian life for most of the 1980s.

Dissent. Unlike the organized and/or traditional opposition groups that exist in Poland and Czechoslovakia, dissent in Romania has assumed three unique forms. The first, intellectual, involving a few individuals or small groups, has not been a serious problem for the regime. By controlling perquisites that are important for intellectuals—the opportunity to be published or to perform, access to consumer products and good housing, the opportunity to travel, and so on—the regime has managed to limit intellectual dissent. Those whose cooperation cannot be won in this manner have generally sought to emigrate. Although the government has not made it easy, the most troublesome intellectual dissent groups continue to exist with regime acquiescence.

The second type of dissent has come from ethnic intellectuals in the former Hungarian areas of Romania (Transylvania). Romania's policy of limiting Hungarian-language schools, theaters, publications, and so on, has created considerable unrest among ethnic intellectuals. Bucharest harshly represses any signs of such nationalist dissent and strictly limits contacts between its Hungarian population and intellectuals in Hungary. Such repression, coupled with emigration to Hungary or the West of the most troublesome among these intellectuals, has managed to keep this aspect of dissent under control. At the same time, however, the communist regime of Hungary has raised the problem of minority treatment with the Romanian government on a number of occasions.[63]

The third type of dissent is spontaneous outburst, usually by a group of workers against repressive conditions. The number is difficult to measure. One such outbreak occurred in 1977, when coal miners in the Jiu Valley stopped work in protest. Ten years later, several thousand workers in Brasov, instead of voting in municipal elections, ransacked the city hall in protest against harsh living conditions.

These spontaneous outbursts bring down tough action against any leaders that may have emerged in the unrest and immediate measures to ameliorate, at least temporarily, whatever conditions sparked the uprising. After the Brasov protests, for example, the military and secret police quickly made several arrests. A mass meeting resulted in pledges of support for party policy and criticism of the plant management. Quick remedial action also included increasing workers' salaries and promises of improvements in the supply of meat and consumer goods.[64]

Church-State Relations.   As in other communist-ruled lands, the churches in Romania are allowed to exist as a temporary evil. Efforts have been made to use them for propaganda and cultural purposes, though these have met with limited success. The mere existence of church organizations is also meant to project an image of religious freedom.

Up to the time when the party gained control of the country, religion played an important part in the life of the people. The Romanian Orthodox church had been the leading and the most powerful religious force before World War I. It continued afterward to be active in both local and state government, but its power gradually declined. In 1921 practically all church lands were expropriated. This measure did not affect the Roman Catholic church as much because it had always been a minority organization.

The communist regime assumed control of all the churches in 1947 and 1948. This was achieved by arrogating to the government all authority over finances, property, and high-level administration; placing in key positions clergy who were subservient to the ruling party; and severing ties with church organizations in foreign countries. As an example, in July 1948 Bucharest abrogated its prewar concordat with the Vatican.

During 1962 the Holy See announced that of the fourteen Catholic archbishops and bishops in Romania, all but one were under arrest. Three years later it was reported that four of the five Catholic bishops remaining in the country had died in prison.[65] Legislation since 4 August 1948 required that all denominations provide the regime's Department of Religious Affairs with inventories of their assets and revenues and that all clergy take an oath of allegiance to the government, pledging to obey and help enforce laws and to defend the state against all enemies.[66] Besides controlling the purse strings and the appointment of personnel in all churches, the Department of Religious Affairs designates the extent and type of catechism that may be taught under church sponsorship.

Apart from such direct techniques, the regime also applies indirect methods to reduce the influence of the churches. Attendance at religious services is not forbidden by law, but mass organizations such as the Union of Communist Youth and the Pioneers schedule activities on Sundays and religious holidays (Easter and Christmas are regular working days in Romania) to make church attendance difficult. The general atmosphere created by the communists discourages participation in religious activities by members of the armed forces and by those holding government positions. The communists have been successful in reducing the influence of the churches, and religious groups no longer pose any significant threat to the regime. Although the constitution, in Article 30, guarantees freedom of religion, in practice it is systematically repressed.

The largest religious denomination has always been Romanian Orthodox, which now has about fourteen million nominal members. Before their forced union with this majority church in 1948, the Eastern-rite Catholics or Uniates represented the next largest group. Roman Catholics are next in size, with about one million members. There are approximately one million Calvinists and about 200,000 communicants of the Lutheran and perhaps 60,000 of the Jewish faiths.[67] The remaining denominations total fewer than 100,000 members. In general, atheistic propaganda among the youth has achieved poor results. Hence, long-term programs were organized in 1976 through so-called "educational brigades" that attempt to shape a "new man."

Before World War II, there existed about sixty recognized religious denominations in Romania. In 1948 a decree entitled Law on Religious Confessions provided official recognition to only fourteen denominations and placed them under close supervision of the government's Department of Religious Affairs. Religious groups frequently protest against the regime's stringent control over their activities but do not have the influence of the Catholic church in Poland or the cohesion of the Czechoslovak priests and, therefore, yield to the regime tactics. In October 1980, five Protestants were arrested for smuggling Romanian- and Russian-language bibles into the country. There were reports that two of them had died, one by suicide and the other after a beating by security police.[68]

In recent years, Romania has had an influx of vocal Christian churches—Baptists, Pentecostals, and others. The government has limited their activities and severely punished some of the leaders, but they continue to function and have found growing support among fundamentalist Christian groups in the United States and elsewhere. Persecution of Protestant churches was an important factor behind the vote in 1987 by the U.S. Congress to deny Romanian foreign trade "most-favored-nation" status.

Foreign Policy. From 1944 until the early 1960s, Bucharest's foreign policy followed that of Moscow. In fact, during this period Romania was perhaps the most loyal of the East European states. In 1947–1948 the Romanians became one of the leading critics of the Yugoslavs just before and some time after the break with the Cominform. Because of Bucharest's loyalty in the struggle against Tito, headquarters of the Cominform were moved from Belgrade to Bucharest. Another indication of loyalty came in 1956 during the Hungarian revolution: when Soviet troops re-established control, the leader of the insurrection was taken to Romania where he was later executed.

After Stalin's death and the rise of Khrushchev to power in the USSR during the mid-1950s, Romanian party leader Gheorghe Gheorghiu-Dej began to take steps that would lead to important economic and political differences with the Soviet Union and to a redefinition of the relationship between the ruling communists and the Romanian people. Initial USSR efforts toward the economic integration of Eastern Europe in the late 1950s and the early 1960s were stubbornly resisted by Gheorghiu-Dej. Although the Soviet proposals had a certain economic rationale, Romania continued to pursue a Stalinist policy of economic nationalism and to proceed with construction of heavy industry projects that Moscow strongly opposed.

The significant differences between the USSR and China in the early 1960s provided Bucharest with the opportunity to expand its autonomy from Moscow in interparty affairs, the high point of which was the April 1964 "Statement" of the Romanian Communist Party (RCP) Central Committee that asserted the sovereignty and independence of each party and affirmed the principle of noninterference of communist parties in the internal affairs of others. This kind of bloc foreign policy allowed the RCP to develop genuine national support.

Such policies were pursued under party boss Gheorghiu-Dej until his death in 1965, and they were extended by his successor, Nicolae Ceausescu. Thus, in 1967–1968, Romania maintained diplomatic ties with Israel, when the rest of the Soviet bloc severed them; established diplomatic relations with West Germany, before the USSR approved *Ostpolitik;* and moved much closer to the nonaligned movement. The Soviet-led invasion of Czechoslovakia in August 1968, which Ceausescu vigorously denounced, marked the apogee of Romanian defiance while emphasizing the limits of such deviance. Although the RCP has continued to pursue an international policy that reflects a degree of autonomy, it has avoided pushing that policy to the point of provoking Soviet military intervention. Because USSR threats and actions have established clear limits, Ceausescu's international policies remain the principal source of his legitimacy with the population.

Despite differences in a number of important foreign policy areas, Bucharest's relations with Moscow and the Soviet communist party remain its first foreign policy priority. Romania seeks to emphasize its sovereignty and play down its bloc military cooperation. Although remaining a member of the Warsaw Pact, Romania's military cooperation has been limited; for example, participation in joint maneuvers has involved only map exercises. In the 1960s Bucharest expanded trade with the West and Third World countries in an effort to minimize economic dependence on the USSR and the countries of Eastern Europe. Romania belongs to the Council for Mutual Economic Assistance (CMEA), yet refuses to participate in many of the joint economic activities of that organization. As Romania's foreign trade problems have mounted during the 1980s, however, exchange with the Soviet Union has substantially increased. In the early 1960s, almost 40 percent of Bucharest's trade was with Moscow; this dropped to about 15 percent in the 1970s and then climbed back to 23 percent in 1986, with further increases projected during the remainder of the decade.

The continuing wariness of the RCP vis-à-vis the USSR could be seen in the attitude toward General Secretary Mikhail S. Gorbachev. In May 1987 he made an official trip to Romania—the last East European country he visited since becoming Soviet party leader in March 1985 but the first by a head of the CPSU since Leonid Brezhnev came to Bucharest in 1976. The delay appears to have been deliberate because Ceausescu also had been the last East European leader in Moscow after Gorbachev's accession to power. Before, during, and after the visit, the Soviet press published critical reports. Gorbachev made frank, though indirect, criticism of Romania's unwillingness to expand cooperation with CMEA and undertake Soviet-style economic reform. The handpicked audience of RCP activists sat in stony silence when Gorbachev described his own policies, and Ceausescu reportedly looked impatiently at his watch.[69]

After the Gorbachev departure, Romania continued its own policies and accepted economic cooperation only when it did not lose control of the process. The party's theoretical journal published an article defending the right to pursue its own development strategy in the face of "globalist theories."[70] Romania continued its selective participation in Soviet–East European meetings: in November, Ceausescu attended the 70th anniversary of the Bolshevik revolution in Moscow yet avoided the 11 December 1987 Warsaw Pact summit in East Berlin at which Gorbachev reported on his meeting with President Reagan.

Romania's next foreign policy priority involves the other communist-ruled countries of Eastern Europe and the Far East. Romania has made a point of developing good relations with all of them, regardless of the Soviet Union. One problem that has caused difficulties with these contacts is the Hungarian minority. Hungary joined Yugoslavia and some West European countries at the Vienna follow-up meetings to the Conference on Security and Cooperation in Europe in a diplomatic initiative that was specifically critical of Romania's policy towards its Hungarian minority.[71]

With the exception of Hungary, contacts between Romania and the other members of the Warsaw Pact followed the pattern of Romania's relations with the Soviet Union, for other East European regimes were anxious not to appear to be more friendly than the USSR. Romanian leaders maintain a regular series of high-level visit exchanges. For example, during 1987, Ceausescu traveled to Bulgaria for meetings with Todor Zhivkov. East German party leader Erich Honecker and Prime Minister Willi Stoph both came to Bucharest on different occasions. Ceausescu also hosted the head of the Yugoslav League of Communists and paid a return visit to Belgrade. The RCP has also pursued a long-standing policy of maintaining cordial relations with nonruling communist and leftist parties. Officials are routinely sent to party congresses around the world, and anniversaries important to even obscure movements elicit a warm message of congratulations from Ceausescu.

After relations with the "socialist countries," Romania places its foreign priorities on the Third World, pursuing a very active policy toward nonaligned countries in an effort to be identified with that group. Ceausescu's favorite method of diplomacy is a personal visit to foreign heads of state, which bolsters his prestige at home and puts him in the spotlight. In 1987, accompanied by his wife, Elena, Ceausescu made a four-nation tour of nonaligned Asian countries—India, Bangladesh, Burma, and Nepal. He made a brief stopover in the Pakistani capital en route to New Delhi to balance the trip to India. A short while later, the Ceausescus were off again, this time for state visits to Angola, Zaire, and Congo/ Brazzaville. That same year, the list of visitors to Bucharest included Somali president Challe Mohamed Siad Barre; Ethiopian president Mengistu Haile Mariam; chairman of the Sudan, Sayed Ahmed el Mirghani; and the president of Burma, U San Yu.

Romania has also pursued friendly ties with both the Arab states and Israel, for the purpose of playing the role of broker in the Middle East conflict. Ceausescu, who received some of the credit for bringing about the Camp David meetings between the leaders of Israel and Egypt in 1978, met with Palestinian and Israeli leaders several times during 1987. During the spring of 1988 the Ceausescus visited Ghana, Liberia, Guinea, and Mauritania.

The third category of countries in Bucharest's hierarchy of foreign policy concerns includes the developed countries of Western Europe and the United States. The Romanian government has carefully sought to balance these relations against its necessarily close relationship to the Soviet bloc. This effort began in earnest during the mid-1960s, after establishment of diplomatic relations with West Germany and the cultivation of closer ties with the United States. It has involved expanded economic as well as political relations. Trade with Western economies increased substantially during the decades of the 1960s and 1970s. The Romanians also pursued economic cooperation with Western businessmen, in an effort to secure investment.

This effort has always centered on a carefully orchestrated balancing act to reassure the Soviet Union. For example, in 1970 just after Bucharest and Moscow signed a new 20-year treaty of friendship, cooperation, and mutual assistance, Ceausescu paid a two-week visit to the United States during which a number of joint economic ventures were concluded and made another visit to the United States in 1973; President Gerald Ford was in Bucharest two years later. In 1978 Ceausescu paid another visit to the United States at the invitation of President Jimmy Carter. The United States throughout the 1960s and 1970s was interested in encouraging Ceausescu's policy of seeking autonomy from the Soviet Union.

In the 1980s, however, the United States gave less attention to Romania for two principal reasons. First, the limits of Bucharest's autonomy from the USSR have been clearly established, and it had gone the limit without provoking Soviet intervention. U.S. policy can help to maintain the status quo, but new developments are not likely. Second, Bucharest's human rights record is appalling, and such considerations have come to play an increasing role in U.S. foreign policy. In 1987, Romania's economic relations with the United States suffered important setbacks for this reason. The U.S. government removed Bucharest from the duty-free Generalized System of Preferences because of disregard for the rights of its workers. During 1987 this probably cost Romania as much as $150 million in lost exports. The second major setback was the bipartisan action of the U.S. Congress to suspend Romania's most-favored-nation (MFN) status for six months and possibly longer. Congress objected to human rights violations, including limitations on religious freedom, restrictions against emigration, and policies toward the Hungarian minority.[72] Romania's trade with the United States during 1986 had given it a surplus of $588 million, with exports of $838.8 million and imports of $250.9 million. U.S. Commerce Department officials estimated that loss of MFN status could cost Romania $300 million a year. This could be particularly difficult because Bucharest is in the midst of a major campaign to reduce its foreign indebtedness. The Romanian reaction was extremely negative and, within a few months, Romania officially notified the U.S. government that it requested an end to its most-favored-nation status.[73]

Conclusion. Since assuming power in 1965, Nicolae Ceausescu has sought to personalize his power. Speeches, interviews, and directives are posed as major sources of insight and truth on foreign and domestic affairs. Leadership of the party and government has become a family affair. Ceausescu's wife, Elena, holding membership in all leading party bodies, is one of three first deputy premiers as well as chairman of the National Council of Science and Technology and reportedly exercises some control over personnel assignments. Their son, Nicu, is a member and secretary of the Grand National Assembly and first secretary of the communist party for Sibiu county. Other relatives of Ceausescu serve in midlevel positions throughout the party and state apparatus.

Ceausescu employs patriotic themes and projects himself as *the* defender of Romanian independence. He is presented to the people as "the human embodiment of Romanian nationalism" and sovereignty and a rallying point for all loyal citizens.[74] Average citizens as well as professional artists are expected to write, compose, and paint in a manner that emphasizes the fusion of nation-party-Ceausescu.

Romanian nationalism, however, is not appreciated by the country's large Hungarian minority. The most publicized condemnation of the regime's minority policy came from a onetime Political Executive Committee candidate member.[75] Ceausescu has dealt with such discontent by calling for improvement in language education, publications, and placement of minority graduates in their native locations. Insisting that the nationality problem in Romania had been essentially solved, he asserts that the lingering controversy is a result of agitation from outside. By blaming elements in Hungary, East and West Germany, Yugoslavia, and elsewhere, Ceausescu has transformed the matter into an issue of Romanian national pride and a focal point for patriotism.

Challenges to Ceausescu's power are either nonexistent or effectively muted to give the appearance of an unopposed leadership. Unexpectedly, however, at the twelfth party congress a strong personal attack against the leader was aired by one of its own founding members, Constantin Pirvulescu, who found himself immediately expelled from the party but only after making public his dissatisfaction with the regime, a sentiment undoubtedly shared by others.[76]

How long opposing views within the party can be kept from surfacing is difficult to tell. Whether or not "Ceausescu's Thoughts" will last after the man himself has gone is also a question for the future. Judging from past personality cults, namely Stalin's, Mao's, and to a lesser extent Tito's, Ceausescu cannot hope for an indefinite extension of his influence. More important and immediate problems exist, however, that must be dealt with over the short-term. First and foremost is the problem of balancing East and West. In the face of mounting economic difficulties, Ceausescu could be pressured into closer alignment with the Soviet Union.[77] Juggling an independent foreign policy, the need for economic reforms, and the country's position within the Eastern bloc will keep Ceausescu and his successors occupied for at least the next decade.

NOTES

1. D. A. Tomasic, "The Rumanian Communist Leadership," *Slavic Review* (October 1961), p. 478.

2. Zbigniew K. Brzezinski, *The Soviet Bloc* (New York, 1962), rev. ed., p. 16. See also Ghita Ionescu, *Communism in Rumania, 1944–1962* (London, 1964), for a complete account of this process.

On the Soviet annexation of Romanian territories, see George Cioranescu, "The Problem of Bessarabia and Northern Bucovina during World War II," RFE, *Background Report,* no. 61 (3 March 1981), Parts I and II.

3. A. V. Mitskevich, *Gosudarstvennyi stroi Rumynskoi Narodnoi Respubliki* (Moscow, 1957), p. 15, discusses the new people's democracy. See also Robert R. King, *History of the Romanian Communist Party* (Stanford, Calif., 1980), p. 190.

4. "Constitution of the Rumanian People's Republic," in Amos J. Peaslee (ed.), *Constitutions of Nations* (The Hague, 1956), 2d ed., vol. 3, p. 251.

5. [Romania], *Constitution of the Socialist Republic of Romania* (Bucharest, 1965), p. 34. See also William B. Simons (ed.), *The Constitutions of the Communist World* (Alphen aan den Rijn, 1980), pp. 312–42, for text and analysis.

6. The party's ninth congress, 19–24 July 1965, adopted the name *Partidul Comunist Roman*. See the article on these changes in *Polityka* (Warsaw), 24 July 1965.

7. The 1965 constitution created a permanent Standing Bureau, attached to the Council of Ministers, that was an inner cabinet for "collectively settling problems which require an urgent solution." It includes the premier, two of three first deputy premiers, four of the

seven deputy premiers and the party general secretary. CIA, *Directory of Romanian Officials* (June 1985), p. 20.

8. *Scinteia,* 19 March 1985.

9. Ceausescu was unanimously re-elected president of Romania by the Grand National Assembly. *Scinteia,* 30 March 1985.

10. See also the law adopted on the organization of the Council of Ministers. *Scinteia,* 18 December 1969, gives the full text.

11. RFE, *East European Leadership List* (15 January 1988) lists ministers and chairmen of these units.

12. *Anuarul Statistic al Republicii Socialiste Romania,* 1986, pp. 12 and 19; CIA, *World Factbook* (1987), p. 205.

13. *Scinteia,* 16 November 1987.

14. The criminal code is discussed in RFE report, by Michael Cismarescu, "The New Rumanian Code on Criminal Procedure or the Limits of Socialist Legality," 24 January 1969.

15. RFE report, by Michael Cismarescu, "The Reform of the Rumanian Judiciary and the Procuratura," 21 February 1969. *Procuratura* prerogatives have been restricted, according to new legislation. See also the Ceausescu speech to Interior Ministry leadership cadres dealing with this, *Scinteia,* 24 December 1976.

16. Randolph L. Braham, *Education in the Rumanian People's Republic* (Washington, D.C., 1963), p. 115. The universities are at Bucharest, Iasi, Cluj, Timisoara, Tirgu Mures, and Craiova. According to *Scinteia,* 26 November 1976, none of them had textbooks for all subjects that are taught.

17. Biographic data on this point are in Tomasic, *Rumanian Communist Leadership,* pp. 480–89.

18. Hugh Seton-Watson, *The East European Revolution* (New York, 1956), p. 90.

19. At the 13th congress (19–22 November 1984), the 3,112 delegates re-elected Ceausescu as general secretary and also elected 265 members and 181 candidates for membership on the Central Committee. Names are listed in *Congresul al XIII-lea al Partidului Comunist Roman* (Bucharest, 1985), pp. 734–39.

20. Tomasic, *Rumanian Communist Leadership,* p. 492.

21. The current statute, with modifications, appeared in *Congresul al XIII-lea al PCR* (Bucharest, 1985), pp. 618–41.

22. RFE report, "The New Rumanian Central Committee," 25 August 1969, contains an excellent analysis.

23. For incumbents in these local organizations, see CIA, *Directory of Romanian Officials,* pp. 55–70.

24. *World Marxist Review* (June 1987), p. 63; CIA, *World Factbook 1987,* p. 205.

25. U.S. Department of State, *Moscow's European Satellites* (Washington, D.C., 1955), p. 12.

26. *Scinteia,* 30 March 1988, gives the same number (200,000) for cadres. Bucharest radio, 2 April 1988; *FBIS-Eastern Europe,* 4 April 1988, p. 37.

27. RFE, *Situation Report,* 7 May 1976.

28. Robert R. King, "Romania," in Richard F. Staar (ed.), *Yearbook on International Communist Affairs: 1988*, p. 305; henceforth, cited as *YICA*.

29. Agerpres dispatch (Bucharest), 7 April 1981. See also RFE, *Romanian Situation Report*, no. 17 (25 November 1980), pp. 1–5.

30. *Keesing's Contemporary Archives* (1987), p. 35,141.

31. According to a Soviet source, "in June 1940 the troops of the Red Army came to the aid of the toilers of Bessarabia." *Kommunist Moldavii* (May 1970), p. 78.

32. CIA, *World Factbook 1987*, p. 205. The decline in number of ethnic Germans is due to emigration. Over the last 20 years the Romanian government has permitted substantial numbers to leave in return for West German economic benefits. A high proportion of remaining Germans reportedly would like to emigrate. Over the last 30 years a large proportion of Jews emigrated to Israel in return for payments to the Romanian regime.

33. Robert R. King, *Minorities Under Communism* (Cambridge, Mass., 1973), pp. 35–44, 82–85, 146–69. An agreement between Bucharest and Budapest should have improved the status of the 1.8 million Hungarians in Transylvania. *Christian Science Monitor*, 5 January 1977. However, this has not occurred.

34. Mitskevich, *Gosudarstvennyi stroi Rumynskoi Narodnoi Respubliki*, p. 43.

35. Ceausescu speech at the tenth party congress. Bucharest radio, 6 August 1969.

36. U.S. Bureau of the Census, *Projections of the Population of the Communist Countries of Eastern Europe: 1975–2000* (Washington, D.C., July 1976), Table 16, p. 27. The annual growth rate totaled 7 percent in 1981. CIA, *World Factbook 1981*, p. 165.

37. Ceausescu interview with *Frankfurter Rundschau*, 23 July 1976.

38. *Probleme economice* (September 1963); translated in *Romanian Press Survey* (15 October 1963). See also *East Europe* (January 1970), pp. 2–8, for reaffirmation of the foregoing.

39. CIA, *World Factbook 1987*, p. 205.

40. Willard Thorp, U.S. delegate to the 1947 Paris peace conference, as cited by Alexandre Cretzianu (ed.), *Captive Rumania* (New York, 1956), p. 51.

41. Brzezinski, *The Soviet Bloc*, p. 125.

42. Michael Cismarescu in *East Europe* (January 1970), p. 5; CIA, *Handbook of Economic Statistics, 1980*, p. 35.

43. Economist Intelligence Unit, *EIU, Regional Review: Eastern Europe and the USSR, 1986*, p. 94; *Scinteia*, 4 February 1988, pp. 1–2. Ceausescu later claimed that net material production had increased by 5.6 percent and agricultural production by 2.3 percent. *Scinteia*, 30 March 1988, pp. 1 and 3.

44. *Quarterly Economic Review* (2d Quarter 1981), p. 16.

45. A. Lukovets (ed.), *Narodnaia Rumyniia segodnia, 1944–1964* (Moscow, 1964), p. 18; EIU, *Country Report: Romania*, no. 1 (1987), p. 17.

46. Wolfgang Oberleitner, "Realities of Agriculture in Rumania," *International Peasant Union Monthly Bulletin* (July–August 1963), p. 19.

47. Cited in *East Europe* (December 1957), p. 51.

48. *Romania Libera,* 7 January 1976. See also *Quarterly Economic Review of Romania, Bulgaria and Albania* (2d Quarter 1981), pp. 9–11, for official response to agricultural failings.

49. Bucharest radio, 19 February 1981.

50. *Business Eastern Europe,* no. 20 (15 May 1981), p. 156.

51. N. Tolkunov (ed.), *Sotsialisticheskii lager* (Moscow, 1962), pp. 293–94.

52. Trade with capitalist states grew from 22.3 percent in 1960 to 34.4 percent of the total in 1979. Cismarescu in *East Europe,* p. 7; *Anuarul Statistic al Republicii Socialiste Romania 1980,* pp. 500–507.

53. *Quarterly Economic Review* (2d Quarter 1981), p. 7.

54. *EIU Regional Review: Eastern Europe and the USSR* (1986), p. 94; BBC, Current Affairs Research Information Service, no. 174 (29 December 1987). A $2.8 billion hard currency trade surplus during 1987 brought about this debt reduction. Communiqué in *Scinteia,* 4 February 1988, pp. 1–2.

55. Bucharest radio, 6 April 1981; *Scinteia,* 25 June 1981.

56. *Business Eastern Europe* 10, no. 29 (17 July 1981), p. 227.

57. RFE, *Romanian Situation Report,* no. 179 (24 June 1981).

58. About 80 percent of Romania's imported iron ore and ferroalloys, half of its coal, approximately 70 percent of its nickel, more than 40 percent of its cotton, and so forth come from the USSR. *New York Times,* 19 April 1970, stressed Romania's almost complete dependence on the Soviet Union for coking coal, which, of course, limited Romanian independence.

59. Agerpres dispatch, *Statement on the Stand of the Rumanian Workers' Party* (Bucharest, 1964), pp. 27–29.

60. *Business Eastern Europe* 10, no. 30 (24 July 1981), p. 237.

61. Agerpres dispatch, 1 July 1981.

62. *Scinteia,* 11 November 1987.

63. RFE, *Hungarian Situation Report,* no. 1, 3, 4 (1987); Budapest television, 6 April 1988, in *FBIS-Eastern Europe,* 7 April 1988, p. 14; *Wall Street Journal,* 18 July 1988, p. 19.

64. *Scinteia,* 12 December 1987; Ibid., 29 June 1988, for another 10 percent increase.

65. Cited by Constantin Visoianu in U.S. Congress, House of Representatives, Committee on Foreign Affairs, 87th Cong., 2d sess., *Captive European Nations: Hearings* (Washington, D.C., 1962), p. 180. For the names and fates of individual bishops see RFE, *Situation Report,* 10 December 1965.

66. See Virgiliu Stoicoiu (comp. and trans.), "Church and State in Romania," in U.S. Senate, Committee on the Judiciary, *The Church and State under Communism* (Washington, D.C., 1965), vol. 2, pp. 4–5, for the oath. *Buletinul Oficial,* no. 103 (15 August 1970), Published Decree no. 334, on the duties of the Religious Affairs Department.

67. According to Chief Rabbi Moses Rosen, there is only one other rabbi left in the country. More than 2,300 Jews were permitted to leave for Israel in 1975 and the same

number in 1976. *Los Angeles Times,* 11 November 1976. A total of 368,000 Jews emigrated between 1946 and 1980. *Viitorul social,* no. 1 (January–February 1981), p. 40.

68. Amnesty International, "Romania," *Briefing Paper,* no. 17 (June 1980), p. 4; RFE, *Romanian Situation Report,* no. 14 (29 June 1981), p. 14.

69. *Izvestiia,* 24 May 1987; *Pravda,* 26 and 27 May 1987. Note the more cordial visit by Supreme Soviet Chairman Andrei Gromyko, discussed in *Lumea,* no. 21 (May 1988).

70. *Era socialista,* no. 11 (10 June 1987), pp. 30–36. See also Agerpres, *National Conference of the Romanian Communist Party: December 14–16, 1987* (Bucharest, 1988), pp. 8–25, for the resolution.

71. *Magyar nemzet* (Budapest), 13 December 1986. For the Romanian response in Vienna, see *Scinteia,* 7 February 1987. Destruction of Hungarian villages in Transylvania is the subject of an editorial in the *New York Times,* 2 July 1988, p. 14.

72. U.S. Congress, House of Representatives, Committee on Foreign Affairs, *United States-Romanian Relations and Most-Favored-Nation (MFN) Status for Romania* (Washington, D.C.: 30 July 1987).

73. *New York Times,* 27 June 1987, 27 February 1988. See ibid., 7 February 1988, p. 4, for visit by the U.S. deputy secretary of state.

74. Robert L. Farlow, "Romania," in M. M. Drachkovitch (ed.), *East Central Europe: Yesterday, Today, Tomorrow* (Stanford, Calif., 1982), pp. 327–48.

75. Karoly Kiraly, "Three Letters to High-Ranking Romanian Communist Party Officials," in *Witnesses to Cultural Genocide* (New York, 1979), pp. 162–78.

76. *Washington Post,* 24 November 1979.

77. For his 70th birthday, 26 January 1988, Ceausescu received the Order of Lenin. *Insight* (2 May 1988), pp. 38–39.

Chapter 8
Socialist Federated Republic of Yugoslavia

Yugoslavia is the only federal state in Eastern Europe and the most heterogeneous country on the continent, with the exception of the USSR. It has been apocryphally described as one political party, two alphabets, three religions, four languages, five nationalities, six republics, and seven bordering states.[1] Even the name Yugoslavia, meaning "land of the southern Slavs" and representing a collective designation for all peoples of Slavic origin who migrated southward across the Danube river during the sixth and seventh centuries A.D., connotes diversity and multiplicity.

GENERAL SURVEY

The establishment of a single country in 1918 resulted from Yugoslavia's geographic location and from a political misunderstanding that the Croats and Slovenes would be joining in a confederation of equals with the Serbs. The territory had served in the past as a passageway or land bridge between Western Europe and Asia. This corridor position influenced the development of the state both positively and negatively. For the most part mountainous, with hills covering about 70 percent of its total area, Yugoslavia comprises six federal republics that fall roughly into line with the geographic features. They are Serbia, Croatia, Slovenia, Bosnia-Herzegovina, Macedonia, and Montenegro. The autonomous regions of Vojvodina and Kosovo-Metohija are located within Serbia.

Corresponding with this geographic division, ethnic groups can be differentiated within the total population of Yugoslavia, which was estimated in 1987 to be about 23.4 million.[2] Table 46 shows the sixteen identifiable ethnic groups, each of which can be found in one or more of the federal republics and autonomous areas. None of the divisions of the country is completely homogeneous.

The five basic languages—Serbian, Croatian, Slovenian, Albanian, and Macedonian—are often treated as only four by joining Serbian and Croatian to form

Table 46
ETHNIC GROUPS IN YUGOSLAVIA, 1987

Nationality	Number (thousands)	Percentage of total
Serbs	8,140,452	34.9
Croats	4,428,005	19.0
Slovenes	1,753,554	7.5
Macedonians	1,339,729	5.7
Montenegrins	579,023	2.5
Moslems	1,999,957	8.6
Yugoslavs	1,219,045	5.2
Albanians	1,730,364	7.4
Hungarians	426,866	1.8
Turks	101,191	0.4
Slovaks	80,334	0.3
Romanians	54,954	0.2
Ruthenes	23,285	0.1
Bulgars	36,185	0.2
Italians	15,132	0.1
Czechs	19,625	0.1
Others and unidentified	1,407,299	6.0
Total	23,355,000	100.0

SOURCES: Figures were calculated on the basis of nationality distribution given in [Yugoslavia], *Statisticki godisnjak Jugoslavije 1987* (Belgrade, 1987), p. 449, which came from the 1981 census.

the Serbo-Croat language. These basic tongues arose from the slow evolution of dialects from a single language, the Old (Church) Slavonic that was spoken at the time when southern Slavs migrated to the Balkan peninsula.

Religion is an important aspect of the diversity that is characteristic of Yugoslavia. About 50 percent of the people are Eastern Orthodox, another 30 percent are Roman Catholic, and more than 10 percent are Muslim, with the remainder belonging to other churches or to no religion.[3] The Orthodox church has strongly identified itself with the Serbian nationality, and the Catholic church, with the Croatians and Slovenes. These alignments have influenced national-istic tendencies and differences that date back to the Middle Ages, when the two groups were under the direct spiritual jurisdiction of Rome. (During mid-August 1970, the Vatican and Yugoslavia resumed diplomatic relations after an eighteen-year break.)

For this reason, the two alphabets are Latin and Cyrillic, corresponding to the East-West religious division. Cyrillic is essentially based on Greek letters, augmented by additional symbols. It is generally used by the Serbs and the Bulgarians (as well as the Russians), who comprise in essence the Eastern Orthodox Slavs. In contrast, the Latin alphabet, supplemented with diacritical marks, is utilized by the Croatians and the Slovenes (as well as the Poles and the Czechs), who comprise the Roman Catholic Slavs. Slovenian can be written only with Latin characters, and Macedonian only with Cyrillic letters.

World War II. Yugoslavia fell early in 1941 to a German invasion. The first guerrilla operations, of the London-supported Chetniks, were headed by Colonel (later General) Draza Mihajlovic. In June of that year Germany's attack on the Soviet Union provided a signal for all communists to support Moscow. Shortly thereafter, a second resistance movement became active in Yugoslavia; Partisans, under the leadership of a mysterious figure known as Tito (the late Josip Broz, leader of the Yugoslav communist party, 1937–1980),[4] began activities against the German occupant. Harsh reprisals became the order of the day. In one case, an entire community of about 7,000 inhabitants was massacred by the Germans. Under Hitler's *Nacht und Nebel* (night and fog) decree, between 50 and 100 Yugoslavs were executed for every German wounded or killed.[5] After initial cooperation in the struggle against the Germans, the forces led by Mihajlovic and Tito engaged in a merciless civil war against each other.

Tito proclaimed the establishment of a de facto government in the fall of 1943 contrary to the wishes of Stalin, who thought the time inopportune. At a small town called Jajce in Bosnia during November, the second session of the Anti-Fascist Council for National Liberation of Yugoslavia proclaimed itself the supreme representative of the peoples and of the state of Yugoslavia as a whole, divested the royal Yugoslav government in exile of its legal rights, forbade King Peter II to return, and decided that the future state should be built on the federalist system.[6]

These moves, combined with British and U.S. favoritism toward the Partisans, led to the abandonment by the West of the Chetnik leader and of the royal government in exile. Western military support and the entry of the Red Army into Yugoslavia during the fall of 1944 allowed the Partisans to seize power.[7] Under pressure from Moscow they established a provisional coalition government.

The coalition provided Tito with 23 Partisan ministers out of 28, and he became premier as well as defense minister. In November 1945 the monarchy was abolished. The establishment of the Federal People's Republic of Yugoslavia followed the promulgation in 1946 of a USSR-type constitution. The last remnant of the former royalist regime faded from the picture when General Mihajlovic was captured and, after a mock trial, executed.[8]

Postwar Developments. The end of the war saw Tito's resistance movement transformed into a constitutional regime. A significant factor that shaped the country was the Yugoslav communists' seizure of power with limited Soviet military assistance and their own armed forces and political cadres. This situation had no parallel in any other East European state that was overrun by the Red Army toward the latter part of World War II. It accounts for the early consolidation of the Yugoslav communist regime and its subsequent conflict with Moscow.

During the period 1945–1949, however, the Federal People's Republic of Yugoslavia was modeled after the USSR in both structure and operation. Its monolithic totalitarianism featured the complete nationalization of industry, centralized economic planning, a single communist-front organization, and the elimination of all opponents.

In the first two postwar years widespread starvation probably would have resulted had it not been for aid from the United Nations Relief and Rehabilitation Administration. Almost simultaneously, reconstruction and nationalization were set into motion, along with a vigorous campaign to collectivize all peasant holdings into producers' work cooperatives, which "ran into passive resistance from the peasantry."[9] The first industrialization drive soon followed.

The planned goals, which were prepared by men with little experience, were too high. The "big leap" involved the hope that rapid conversion could take place from a basically agrarian economy to an industrialized one within five years (1947–1951). The plan anticipated Soviet and other East European support in the form of long-term credits for industrial machinery and equipment. After this economic plan had been set into motion, two developments occurred.

First came unilateral moves by Moscow to extend both its economic and its political domination over Belgrade.[10] These were blocked by Tito. Next the Communist Information Bureau or Cominform—paradoxically suggested by Yugoslav communists themselves—was established in September 1947 by Stalin to keep the satellites under control. Less than a year later, this body passed a resolution condemning and expelling the Yugoslav communist party, anathematizing it as a "traitor" to the Moscow-directed world communist movement. The real reason for the dispute was Stalin's distrust of the leadership in Belgrade.

Tito probably had no desire to challenge Stalin, but the traumatic Cominform experience produced a degree of unity within the Yugoslav party in spite of, or perhaps because of, Soviet pressure. The deteriorating condition of the economy and the faltering of the five-year plan, combined with international isolation, forced Tito reluctantly to turn to the West for aid. The rapprochement with the West, and its resulting economic benefits, surpassed all that Yugoslavia could have anticipated.[11]

Economic Planning. Yugoslavia has a complicated and confusing economy, but it insists on calling itself a socialist state. Industry and commerce involve relatively little private enterprise, yet technically there is no state ownership. A varied type of agriculture, which includes both private and cooperative efforts, is carried on by the peasants. The authoritative journal of the world communist movement adhering to Moscow reported the basic principle of the Yugoslav socialist economy to be "planned guidance."[12] The economy is indeed planned. The state, however, does not administer the various economic enterprises. Its purposes are accomplished by having them operate allegedly under the management of the workers themselves.

Yugoslav economic planning is unlike that of any other communist-ruled country, primarily because the plan is called "indicative" and therefore is not binding. Still, a federal planning bureau is responsible for drawing up the national economic plan. Economic planning takes place simultaneously on all levels, with an attempt at the continuous coordination of efforts among republics, districts, communes, individual enterprises, and economic chambers representing groups of enterprises.

Worker-Management. With the change of policy in the direction of a more decentralized economic system in the early 1950s, the concept of worker-management, and specifically the workers' council, surfaced. According to the latest constitution,[13] which was adopted in February 1974, the system is based on freely associated labor using socially owned means of production, self-management by the working people, and distribution of the social product. In theory the constitution provides every member of a working organization with the guaranteed "right to a personal income and other rights stemming from labor to an amount and volume that ensure his economic and social security." The personal income depends "on the general level of productivity of total social labor and on the general condition prevailing in the environment in which the worker lives."[14]

The working organizations, which are in theory independent and autonomous, may include professionally active individuals who form units that have the same status as those of industrial workers. Any such organization includes the following: a workers' council, which is the basic element, consists of from 15 to 200 members, depending on the size of the enterprise; a management board, usually numbering from three to seventeen persons; and the director or manager of the enterprise, who supervises the business and executes the decisions of the workers' council and other management organs.[15]

All officials are elected from among the employees, with terms of two years for the workers' council and one year for the management board. Although nobody may be elected twice consecutively to the council or more than twice consecutively to the management board, the manager or director may be eligible for additional terms of office. This individual is nominated by the workers' council, after being proposed by an "appointments commission." It is through this commission that state and party control is exercised. In theory, however, the new constitution of 1974 states that self-government in working organizations includes the right of the workers to manage their respective enterprises, either directly or through elected bodies, organize production, and decide about expansion of the enterprise; to distribute income; to regulate working conditions; and to decide to associate with other enterprises.[16] Workers' councils represent one of the features of the Yugoslav system that distinguish it from other communist regimes.[17]

Economic Reform.   Since the mid-1960s, the general economic policy of the ruling party and the government in Yugoslavia has involved a decentralization in decisionmaking. Market forces determine the distribution of investment funds through a price system, including realistic exchange rates. Only plants that are profitable can survive because state subsidies have been eliminated. Voluntary mergers may take place, however. Specific measures aimed at implementing these policies have included a new banking system and the devaluation of the dinar.[18] The foregoing, of course, represent the ideal, which is far from Yugoslav reality.

Despite economic problems such as spiraling inflation and low labor productivity in recent years, decentralization has continued. In 1976, a law on associated labor was in preparation that not only reaffirms self-management but also encourages limited private enterprise on a self-management basis.[19] The anomaly of less economic control and more political control appears to represent a "living Marxist contradiction" in Yugoslavia.

Agriculture.   Yugoslavia has traditionally been a country of farmers, and agriculture represented the most significant branch of the prewar economy. In 1940 about 75 percent of the population lived on the land, but this proportion has been decreasing rapidly. During the most recent census it dropped to 30 percent.[20] Yugoslavia's main goal in agriculture has been to increase production. To achieve this goal, a government policy after the war involved a drive to collectivize the peasantry. The Yugoslav rulers were intelligent enough eventually to confess the failure of forced collectivization and to abandon this approach. A new program in 1953 disbanded most collective farms, with the land being returned to private ownership by the peasants. Compulsory delivery quotas were abolished, a free market for agricultural products was introduced, and the private sale and purchase of land was allowed. Farmers could own up to a maximum of ten hectares (24.7 acres) of land for each household. These concessions caused agricultural production to increase substantially, as Table 47 shows. A constitutional amendment proposed in 1987, if adopted, would expand the ten-hectare limit.[21] The measure is under discussion.

The new policy is oriented toward a gradual socialization of agricultural activities, with increased cooperation between the socialist and private sectors encouraged so that the same goal can be achieved without the use of force. Four basic farm sectors exist today. The private sector predominates, as in 1987 the peasants owned about 84 percent of all agricultural land on almost 2.6 million

Table 47
YUGOSLAV AGRICULTURAL PRODUCTION, 1964–1986
(in thousands of metric tons)

Commodity	1964	1969	1974	1978	1986
Wheat	3,900	4,880	6,282	5,355	4,776
Corn (maize)	6,960	7,821	8,031	7,585	12,526
Sugar beets	2,830	3,636	4,300	5,157	5,599
Sunflower seed	260	390	298	539	449
Potatoes	2,820	3,144	3,127	2,501	2,561
Plums	760	1,292	682	655	721
Meat	679	806	1,012	1,256	1,390
Milk (millions of liters)	2,334	2,723	3,531	4,148	4,536

SOURCES: [Yugoslavia], *Statisticki godisnjak Jugoslavije 1970* (Belgrade, 1970), pp. 129–31 and 135–36, *1975*, pp. 157–59 and 163–64, *1979*, pp. 228–30 and 234–35, *1987*, pp. 240–45; CIA, *Handbook of Economic Statistics* (1987), pp. 198–99.

private farms.[22] The three nonprivate sectors include peasant work cooperatives, which are *kombinats* similar to the Soviet *kolkhozy;* state farms, which are the Yugoslav equivalents of the *sovkhozy;* and general agricultural cooperatives, which are the least regimented.

Peasant work cooperatives are organized, like nonagricultural enterprises, under the worker-management system. They are voluntary, with the land being community owned and farmed. Only 40 of these existed in 1969 throughout the country—a drop from 6,625 in 1948 and 229 in 1959—and their role in production remains small. In 1959 there were 4,803 general agricultural cooperatives, by 1964 the number had decreased to some 2,400, and in 1974 there were only 832. The long-range plan to draw the individual peasant into dependence on the state can be seen from the fact that all government agricultural investments and subsidies are reserved for state farms and general agricultural cooperatives.

By and large, however, the Yugoslav regime has failed in its effort to persuade private entrepreneur farmers to abandon their individual plots and join collectives. The peasants have followed plans of their own. By means of one-year contracts, variations in their annual plowing practices, and adequate fertilization of their land, the peasants are able to circumvent the state.

There are many forms of cooperation between the private sector and the general agricultural cooperatives, but they fall into three basic categories: "rendering services," usually paid in cash by the private individual for the use of machinery, seed, and chemical fertilizers; "joint production," called a higher form of cooperation, in which socialist and private forces join to share proportionately in productive services and goods; and other forms, such as contracts by a cooperative with a private farmer for his expertise, labor, and products.

One method of comparing results in the private and the other two sectors is to examine their yields per hectare. It would appear from government statistics that the greatest yields come from the state farms (or the socialist sector) and the lowest from the private farms. Careful analysis, however, shows major discrimination by the government against the private farms. Private entrepreneurs must pay twice as much for fertilizers as do the others. The socialist and cooperative sectors work the best land and work under the most favorable conditions. Even so, yields are only 2.5 times higher in the socialist sector.

The main objectives in agriculture are, for the private sector, to increase production (in order to remain outside the collectives) and, for the socialist sector, to show a profit. The latter, not infrequently, shows a deficit. This should raise doubts among communist leaders because state farms were created especially to serve as focal points that would attract private farmers, who still cultivate 8.5 million of the 10.7 million hectares in agricultural land.

It is evident that the policy of persuasion has not induced the peasants to join collective farms. Only under the relative freedom of the individual farmer have there been any broadly positive results. This is significant, because nothing goes to the private entrepreneur. Little is provided even for general agricultural cooperatives. As far back as 1969, this situation was described by Executive Bureau member Mika Tripalo as follows: "Our party recognized that uncritical imitation of foreign experiences has hampered not only our economic development but also deteriorated the political alliance with the peasantry which was the strongest army of our revolution."[23]

The "free and voluntary fusion of individual farms" with the socialist sector was seen as the answer to the country's food production problems.[24] Although a much faster development of the socialist sector is more expedient, owing to the fact that average yield per hectare in that sector is greater than among individual farmers, "under present conditions, the one-sided orientation toward a more rapid development of the socialist sector would be very expensive; it would not lead to an increase in production but would, instead, open up many social problems."[25] According to Veselin Djuranovic, reporting to the National Assembly, private farms "had about 83 percent of cultivable land, about 88 percent of livestock, and accounted for over 50 percent of agricultural commodity production."[26]

Industrial Growth and Resource Base.   Yugoslavia has followed Marxist dogma in giving priority to industrialization. Fortunately, the country has been in a comparatively advantageous position to achieve this goal. In contrast to agriculture, the means of industrial production were completely nationalized by the state after the war and have remained so. Primary emphasis has been placed on heavy

industry, mining, electric power, and raw materials in the course of successive
national economic plans. Shifts in policy, however, have prevented industry from
developing evenly.

Results of the 1976–1980 five-year plan point out the gap between the industrial and agricultural sectors. (See Table 48.) Three main objectives for the
1981–1985 plan had been announced: controlled growth, drastic reduction of
investments, and strong export orientation with large cuts in imports. The last is
in response to Yugoslavia's annual trade deficit of more than $2 billion in both
1979 and 1980.[27]

Table 48
YUGOSLAV ECONOMIC INDICATORS, 1976–1990

	1976–1980 Actual	1985 Estimated	1986–1990 Plan
Gross social product	5.7	0.5	4.0
Industrial output	6.9	2.3	4.5
Agricultural output	1.9	<1.0	3.2
Exports (goods and services)	2.9	5.0	5.7
Imports (goods and services)	5.7	5.0	5.3

SOURCES: *Business Eastern Europe* 10, no. 19 (8 May 1981), p. 147; Economist Intelligence Unit,
EIU Regional Review: Eastern Europe and the USSR, 1986, p. 120.

A measure of industrial growth is iron and steel production, which has
increased to become the largest in the Balkans. Transportation, which has lagged
in the past, is being improved. The new Belgrade-to-Bari railroad was completed
in 1976, and construction was begun on a four-lane superhighway linking Yugoslavia and Greece to Western Europe using loans from the European Investment
Bank.[28] The railroad between Shkoder and Titograd opened for freight in August
1986. Surplus unskilled labor in areas too far removed from industrial enterprises
and shortages of skilled manpower represent problems. Both may be solved by
locating new factories in areas that have plentiful labor and by training local
workers in areas where these plants are being constructed.

Yugoslavia is also fortunate in having substantial raw material reserves to
cope with ambitious plans for economic growth. Its mineral resources are abun-
dant, with the exception of coking coal and petroleum. Despite intensive survey-
ing and drilling over a seven-year period, only half of Yugoslavia's oil needs can
be supplied from inside the country. In 1986 Yugoslavia produced 70 million tons
of coal, about 83,000 barrels of oil per day, some 86 billion cubic meters of gas,
and 78 billion kwhr of electricity.[29] The first nuclear plant has been put into
operation at Kalva, near the Bulgarian border, utilizing rich deposits of uranium

from an active mine. A Westinghouse-designed nuclear power station at Krsko in Slovenia was completed late in 1981, two years behind schedule and at a cost of 21 billion dinars (originally set at 9 billion), an overrun of 133 percent.[30] The United States is to provide nuclear fuel until 1990.[31]

Nationalism. Without any doubt, nationalism represents the most important domestic phenomenon in Yugoslavia, closely related to the problem of living standards. On the one hand, antagonism still exists among the various nationalities within the country; on the other, there is the desire for a better life throughout Yugoslavia. The desire certainly exists in the underdeveloped regions of Macedonia and Montenegro as well as in the mountainous parts of Bosnia and Herzegovina, where living conditions have been relatively primitive. One cause for nationalist prejudice appears to be the regime's policy of bringing into better balance the economic development of all regions.

In a report to the National Assembly in 1981, Veselin Djuranovic, president of the Federal Executive Council, addressed this problem, stating that the social plan for 1981–1985 would concentrate on "faster development of economically underdeveloped republics and particularly of the Socialist Autonomous Province of Kosovo, in order to reduce the relative difference which exists in the degree of development between the socialist republics and the socialist autonomous province."[32] Djuranovic called for a more harmonious, even, and stable development of the entire country and for "the equality of all the nations and nationalities of Yugoslavia."[33]

This policy has not been popular, despite the fact that the benefited areas have a more rapidly increasing population, a larger manpower base, and most of the natural resources. One-third of all investments in recent years has gone into these regions; this is twice the amount allocated to the more developed republic of Slovenia. Moreover, production in Slovenia and Croatia has increased more than twice as much as it has in the regions favored by generous regime investments. Serbia was to receive $32 million from the International Finance Corporation for financing small- and medium-sized enterprises, with the provision that 20 percent of the credits be allocated to small private enterprises. On top of that, the World Bank loan of $83 million will go to the Morava district (Serbia) for agricultural and agro-industrial development. The World Bank approved a $110 million loan to finance small- and medium-scale projects: $50 million to Kosovo; $30 million to Bosnia-Herzegovina; $20 million for Montenegro; and $10 million for Macedonia. Between 20 and 30 percent of the Slovene gross national product is diverted to southern republics, which causes resentment.[34]

This nationalist tendency boiling beneath the surface is connected with measures aimed at achieving centralization, which is euphemistically called "integration." Liberal intellectuals object to pressures by party apparatus workers. Their resistance in Slovenia and Croatia is directed against all centralizing measures, which they consider to be violations of nationality rights. The old Croat-Serb dispute also remains an issue, with the Croatians blaming the party (which they have incorrectly identified mainly with Serbia) for the creeping increase in prices that has adversely affected their ability to raise living standards. The share of industries from the underdeveloped areas in the total product for 1980, as against 1950, increased from 6 to 25 percent in Montenegro, from 16 to 42 percent in Bosnia-Herzegovina, from 18 to 41 percent in Macedonia, and from 23 to 35 percent in Kosovo.[35]

Nationality problems have become exacerbated in recent years and have led to crackdowns and the tightening of controls by party and government, as happened in Croatia during 1971–1972. Tension among national groups has been evident in almost every republic. In Kosovo the Albanian Kosovars have become a bone of contention between Yugoslavia and Albania, while the Macedonians are still a problem vis-à-vis Bulgaria. Furthermore, extremist èmigrè groups abroad have added to the differences by propaganda and terrorist acts. There has also been some indication that the Soviet Union is exploiting these problems for its own future advantage.

In March and April 1981 Pristina, the capital of Kosovo autonomous province, as well as two other towns, Prizren and Podnjevo, were the setting for rioting and demonstrations. The demonstrations allegedly began as a protest by students at Pristina University (founded expressly for the Albanian population in Kosovo, it is now the third largest university in the country) against substandard food and poor dormitory conditions but soon grew to include as many as 20,000 demonstrators with demands for better living conditions and full recognition of the Kosovo autonomous province as Yugoslavia's seventh republic. At least 440 persons were purged from the communist party in Kosovo following the riots, including party chief Mahmut Bakali, who was removed after eleven years in office. Bakali was replaced by Veli Deva, 58 years of age, who ten years previously had had to make way for the younger Bakali. A purge of government officials in Kosovo also followed the riots, beginning with the resignation of the provincial president.[36]

According to preliminary reports from the latest census (April 1981), the population of Kosovo province totaled 1,585,000 and was 77.4 percent Albanian, 13.2 percent Serb, 3.7 percent Moslem, 1.7 percent Montenegrin, 0.8 percent Turk, and 3.1 percent unclassified. Economically, it has lagged behind all other regions in Yugoslavia, despite the acknowledgment by former President Tito that "Kosovo should become the concern of Yugoslavia as a whole" and the promise that the other republics would invest more in Kosovo's economy. Rich in natural resources, it has over 50 percent of Yugoslavia's coal deposits and more than 60 percent of the country's lead and zinc reserves, as well as other valuable metals and raw materials. How to exploit these resources, however, and how to use the profits to advance the development of the province remain problems.[37]

By labeling the outbursts of protest in Kosovo as hostile "anti-Yugoslav" actions, the Yugoslav leadership is attempting to put the blame on outside instigation, namely Albanian. Fadil Hodza, a member of the Presidency and of the party Presidium (and an Albanian from Kosovo), delivered a speech in April 1981 to condemn Tirana's provocations and to remind the Kosovars that compared with conditions in Albania their lot was good. The problem is not merely one of Kosovar Serbs comparing themselves with Albanians or with other republics in Yugoslavia. More important, the nationality problem in Kosovo—the antagonism between Albanian and Serb—compounded by economic difficulties, is the type of problem experienced at some time or another by all complex, multinational societies. In this instance, for Yugoslavia the regime's response could prove to be of more lasting importance than the rioting itself. Improvement in the economic situation and/or the establishment of Kosovo as the seventh Yugoslav republic would do much to alleviate the problem but would probably not solve the issue in the long run. Yugoslavia is virtually "pregnant with many large or small Kosovo affairs." Dealing with them all before they can erupt or cause irreparable damage to the nation as a whole is a delicate, ongoing task for the heirs of Tito.[38]

Standard of Living.   Tourism brought in about $1.2 billion during 1980, and contact with the West is relatively free. With the common desire to be better off, a trend toward rising expectations has developed throughout the country. This and the difficulty of finding employment and housing drove more than one million Yugoslav workers abroad in the late 1970s, primarily to the Federal Republic of Germany, France, Austria, and Sweden. During 1978 alone, they remitted $2.8 billion to relatives back home.[39]

As a result of the economic slowdown in Western Europe, Yugoslavia faces the problem of accommodating many of these returning *Gastarbeiter*. The government is attempting to cushion the impact of the returnees by expanding the economy and creating new jobs. Furthermore it is promoting small business and private enterprise to achieve these goals.[40] In 1980 Stane Dolanc contended that the problems of the Yugoslav economy required solutions that "give freer rein to the basic market forces" and the encouragement of small private economic activity. He pointed out that legislation for private enterprises already existed in Slovenia, which made the sector's profits legal and taxable.[41]

Another problem seriously affecting Yugoslavia's standard of living is the rate of inflation within the country. Although during 1976 it had slowed considerably, by 1980 inflation had risen to 40–50 percent.[42] Wages have not kept up with rising prices. To alleviate this problem and to spur economic expansion, the government in 1976 announced a tax reduction on building materials and consumer durables that reduced prices on these commodities by up to 10.5 percent. These measures did not succeed in holding down inflation. By 1980, personal income in real terms fell back to the 1975 level.[43] The Yugoslav standard of living returned to 1967 levels by the fall of 1987, although inflation stood at 146 percent.

Yugoslavia's standard of living is, of course, affected by the extent and availability of education. All children between the ages of seven and fifteen are required to attend school. By 1964 the previously high illiteracy rate had declined to about 21 percent, although it is still "widespread among elderly people and in the villages" and is on the average "three times as high among women as among the men." According to one estimate, among the adults who took postwar reading and writing courses, some 70 percent, 1.5 million persons, reverted to illiteracy. About four-fifths of the population above the age of ten allegedly remained illiterate or had completed at most only four grades of elementary school only a decade ago. By 1987, illiteracy had dropped to 9.5 percent.[44]

The working class in Yugoslavia is probably dissatisfied with the limited access to educational opportunities for its children. Owing to the almost prohibitive cost of housing, food, and school supplies (which has been estimated at 10,000 old dinars per month per student), just one workers' family in four can send its children to a general secondary school. In 1985–1986, there existed 1,568 secondary schools, with about 435,768 students.[45]

STRUCTURE OF GOVERNMENT

The Constitution. The first postwar constitution was proclaimed in January 1946. Its main feature was the establishment of six constituent republics. This was not a genuine federal arrangement because the republics were subordinated in most important matters to the central government. The federal principle remained to a great extent theoretical except that both houses of parliament had equal powers. There were 24 areas of jurisdiction in which the federation possessed exclusive competence, so that residual powers had almost no practical meaning for the republics.

The constitution underwent drastic modifications in January 1953 through a constitutional law, so that it became in effect a new one. Eight of the original fifteen sections were abrogated. It did not cover many important later developments in the political and social system. Hence, at the end of 1960, the Federal Assembly, or parliament, appointed a constitutional commission to prepare a completely new basic law. A preliminary draft was not ready until almost two years later. This third constitution, which had 259 articles, was adopted in April 1963. It received no fewer than 42 amendments in three fundamental changes between 1967 and 1971. Because of these many additions, it was decided to adopt a fourth constitution, which was promulgated on 21 February 1974.

The 1974 constitution[46] has 406 articles and is divided into six fundamental parts, except for the introductory "basic principles." It describes the Socialist

Federated Republic of Yugoslavia, its social system, relations within it as well as the rights and duties of the federation, the organization of the federation, the procedure for amending the constitution, and transitional and concluding provisions. In its exhaustive definition of the social system and government, Yugoslavia's 1974 basic law is the longest and most detailed of all East European constitutions.

On 3 July 1981, the Yugoslav National Assembly adopted eight constitutional amendments aimed at strengthening the collective leadership policy that has evolved since Tito's death. The first amendment officially introduces the term "collective body" into the constitution. The second regulates the various terms of office, with some functionaries holding their posts four years and others only for one. The third amendment specifies that the office of the National Assembly president will be rotated, with incumbents to come from different republics or autonomous provinces. The same applies to presidents of the Federal Chamber and the Chamber of the Republics and Autonomous Provinces. The fourth amendment eliminates the office of president of the republic, which has not existed since the death of Tito. The fifth amendment provides the prime minister with a four-year term and the same with possible re-election for the other members of the federal government. The National Assembly may vote confidence or no confidence in either the prime minister or the entire government, following submission of a government report. The sixth and seventh amendments set terms of office for functionaries in the federal administration and the constitutional court, respectively.[47]

Legislature.   Corresponding to a legislature or parliament is the Federal Assembly, which is divided into two chambers and has a total of 308 members. The Federal Chamber consists of 220 delegates from "self-managing organizations and communities and sociopolitical organizations in the republics and autonomous provinces," while the smaller Chamber of Republics and Autonomous Provinces is composed of delegations from "assemblies of the republics and assemblies of the autonomous provinces."[48]

The primary task of parliament is to discuss and approve legislation in conjunction with any one of the four specialized units: sociopolitical, economic, education and culture, and social welfare and health. Candidates for each of these units are selected by and from the appropriate working organizations. Omer Kurpejovic is president of the Federal Chamber, while Drasko Popovic currently heads the Chamber of Republics and Autonomous Provinces. Marian Rozic is president of the Federal Assembly as a whole.[49]

The Federal Assembly, or parliament, is the only body that is theoretically competent to amend the constitution, pass national laws, adopt federal plans and budgets, call a referendum, ratify international agreements, decide on questions of war and peace, alter the boundaries of Yugoslavia, lay the foundation for internal and foreign policy, and supervise the work of the federal executive and administrative bodies. It elects the president and vice-president of the republic, the president of the Federal Executive Council, and members of the federal courts.

The Federal Assembly has a regular question period during which members may ask for information from government officials. However, legislative proposals by the Federal Executive Council are rarely amended, except in minor ways. The establishment of a joint parliamentary committee with broad powers to investigate expenditures and general policies at all levels, of assembly standing committees with some authority over administration, and of the Constitutional Court may have been conceived to permit the Federal Assembly to act "safely" with more independence. In general, however, the 1974 constitution strengthens the control of the ruling party, as well as the new collective presidency. During 1987 a total of 29 constitutional amendments were proposed.[50]

The Executive.   This branch of the government had been led by Josip Broz Tito, former president of the Socialist Federated Republic of Yugoslavia (SFRY). At the eleventh party congress in June 1978, Tito was elected president for life and the Central Committee Presidium was decreased to fifteen full members and nine ex officio members. Only five Presidium members simultaneously held posts in the State Presidency (Mojsov, Bakaric, Stambolic, Doronjski, and Hodza). Article 26, Section 9, of the party statutes adopted at the eleventh congress provides that "a member cannot at one and the same time perform executive-political functions in the organs of the League of Communists and in the executive organs of the [state] authorities."[51]

Tito died on 4 May 1980 after a long illness. The official announcement praised him "as a visionary, a critic and interpreter of the world." The funeral was attended by 208 delegates from 126 countries, including 121 governments, 68 political parties, four liberation movements, nine international organizations, and six others. Present were four kings, six princes, 31 presidents and ten vice-presidents of republics, eleven presidents of national parliaments, 22 prime ministers and twelve deputy prime ministers, 47 ministers of foreign affairs, and many members of government.

After Tito's death, an entire chapter on "the president of the Republic" (Articles 333–345) had to be removed from the Yugoslav constitution. With termination of that office, the SFRY Presidency "shall exercise all rights and duties vested in it under the present constitution, and the vice-president of the SFRY Presidency shall become president of the SFRY Presidency until the expiration of the term for which he was elected vice-president."[52] The president and vice-president serve one-year terms. Members of the Presidency are elected to five-year terms and may be re-elected only once (Article 324). The State Presidency is to be composed of nine members: one from each of the six constituent republics and the two autonomous provinces, plus one ex officio member. The president's office rotates annually among the eight full members (Articles 313–332).

The introduction of a collective leadership in both party and state, after four decades of powerful one-man rule, has been a long process and one that will continue. Tito had first announced the idea in a speech at Zagreb. The 23-member State Presidency established at that time has since decreased to its present nine-member configuration.[53] Its main functions involve providing executive leadership, appointing civilian and military officials, and carrying out ceremonial duties.

The president of the State Presidency (who is also president of the Council for National Defense) promulgates federal laws by decree, proposes judges for the Constitutional Court, appoints ambassadors, grants pardons, and, if the Federal Assembly and collective presidency are unable to meet, declares war.[54] During hostilities or an immediate threat of war, the president may issue decrees on matters within assembly jurisdiction. These must be submitted to the assembly for approval as soon as it can meet. The president exercises his authority within the restrictions of the constitution and federal law.

The vice-presidency is the second most important position in the country because in the event of a vacancy in the office of president of the Republic (whose incumbent concurrently heads the collective presidency), the vice-president becomes the interim successor. The vice-president serves a one-year term, according to a rotating schedule.

The Federal Executive Council, which is the source of legislative proposals, represents the most important governmental body in terms of day-to-day government operations. It consists of a president, five vice-presidents, and 23 members.[55] The collective presidency proposes a member of the Federal Assembly to be president of the Federal Executive Council; this candidate is then voted upon by the assembly. The incumbent since May 1987 has been Branko Mikulic, who serves as premier. The other council members are elected by the assembly on the recommendation of the premier, with one consideration being that the council reflect the nationality composition of the country.

Local Government.   The decentralization of both political and economic power, which allegedly represents the basis for Yugoslavia's different approach to communism, is nowhere better illustrated than in local government. Broad administrative authority, a degree of autonomy, and extensive citizen participation are major factors in Yugoslavia's claim to have blended democracy with socialism. The basic local unit, which is called a commune, allegedly represents a genuinely new form of government, ''a self-managing sociopolitical community based on the power of and self-management by working class and all working people.''[56]

By 1947 the people's committees had already been established as prime movers in both political and economic affairs. Seven years later, all authority other than that specifically delegated to the federal and constituent republics or autonomous region governments was given to these lowest units of administration. They exist at the level of commune, a subdivision of a district and a city. At district and city levels, these committees are bicameral. Actually there are only two major levels of local government, commune and district, with the district consisting of a number of communes. Larger cities have district status, and smaller ones are governed by special town councils that operate under district or commune authority.

At present the districts hold jurisdiction over broad political matters, such as law enforcement and elections. They are responsible for coordinating activity within their general jurisdiction. But the communes have become key local units that have several primary concerns. One of these is economic, including planning, investments, internal trade, and supervision over economic enterprises. Another concern is municipal services, such as water supply, sewers, streets, and public utilities. A third comprises the area of "social management," that is, citizen control over public activities.

Judicial System. The courts are divided into regular, self-management, and military categories. The federal Supreme Court (a regular tribunal) is the final court of appeal for all others, including military tribunals. Self-management courts, which do not consider criminal cases, mostly arbitrate disputes involving economic enterprises.[57] That the judiciary can be used for political purposes is evident from the case of the dissident author Mihajlo Mihajlov, who was tried and sentenced for political crimes in 1965, 1966, and 1974. Mihajlov was granted amnesty on 2 November 1977, along with 724 other prisoners (of whom 218 were political).

There is no jury trial in Yugoslavia. Economic and regular courts of the first instance and at district levels include both professional and "lay judges"; the latter are citizens legally untrained in law who are elected by people's committees for limited periods. Regular courts at the federal and republic levels consist of professional judges only. In judicial matters as in others, the autonomous regions are served just as the republics are.

The Constitutional Court, which began functioning in 1964, decides on the conformity of laws and other regulations with the constitution and of the laws of the republics with federal law, resolves disputes between sociopolitical committees on the territory of two or more republics, and decides whether any act of a federal agency violates the rights laid down by the constitution.[58] The president and the thirteen judges of this highest tribunal are elected for eight-year terms and may not hold office for more than two consecutive terms.

Elections.   Ordinary voters submit names of candidates for commune, district, autonomous province, republic, and federal assemblies. This procedure takes place every two years by means of "pre-election consultations." The votes of 10 percent of the registered voters in any electoral unit are sufficient to proclaim a candidate. Hence, communist party members attempt to influence the choice and keep down the number of candidates.[59] Once communal assemblies have been constituted in this manner, they subsequently choose from among the candidates who will become deputies to the district, province, republic, and federal legislatures.

All candidates are now elected indirectly by representatives chosen through sociopolitical organizations, economic enterprises, institutions, and government agencies. Deputies to both chambers of the Federal Assembly are elected by commune assemblies (to the Federal Chamber) or by province and republic assemblies (to the Chamber of Republics and Autonomous Provinces).

During the most recent elections, in May 1986, three distinct phases were observed: (1) during December 1985, more than one million delegates were chosen by voters, (2) early in 1986, these delegates elected about 100,000 individuals from their ranks to serve in commune, autonomous province, republic, and federal assemblies, (3) after the May elections the two chambers of the Federal Assembly elected their respective presidents and vice-presidents, the president of the Republic, and the premier.[60] Because the electoral process is confusing, reforms are being debated.

THE RULING PARTY

The movement that controls Yugoslavia today developed from a merger between left-wing social democratic and communist groups. Known initially as the Socialist Workers' Party of Yugoslavia (communist), it was founded at a 1919 unification congress.[61] The name was changed to the Communist Party of Yugoslavia the following year. The new party joined the Comintern and accepted the principles of revolution, the dictatorship of the proletariat, and a Soviet republic as the future form of government.

During elections in November 1920, the communists had the third-strongest party in the country and succeeded in winning 58 out of 417 parliamentary seats. The party was outlawed after an attempt on the life of King Alexander and the assassination in 1921 of the interior minister, Milorad Draskovic; after these events, it lost its unity and became wracked by factional strife. Eventually the Comintern had to intervene actively to solve the conflict between left and right elements.

In 1932 the party's Central Committee was dissolved by the Comintern and Milan Gorkic was appointed leader. Five years later, Stalin began his purge of ranking foreign "comrades" within the Comintern. He was on the verge of dissolving the party in Yugoslavia, as had already been done in Poland, but refrained from doing so, allegedly at the insistence of the Comintern secretary, the Bulgarian Georgi Dimitrov, who offered Tito[62] an opportunity to reorganize the discredited movement. Gorkic was liquidated, and Tito became head of the party.

The Takeover. An agreement signed in 1944 between Tito and Premier Ivan Subasic of the exiled royal Yugoslav government stated that both sides would respect the will of the people with regard to the internal system, that the king would not return until a plebiscite had been held, and that a new legislative assembly would be established by combining Tito's followers in Yugoslavia and some members of the prewar parliament.[63]

The first postwar election for a constituent assembly took place in November 1945. The communist-dominated People's Front provided the only candidates, while the registration of voters was managed by so-called people's committees. As a result, the single list of candidates won 90.48 percent of the vote and all of the seats. This constituent assembly abolished the monarchy and proclaimed a federal people's republic, and the country actually came under communist control.

The ruling party in Yugoslavia at first patterned itself after its Soviet counterpart and wholeheartedly accepted the hegemony of Moscow. No other communist movement adhered more closely to directives from the center than did the Yugoslav.[64] Tito believed that his party, like the Bolsheviks, had come to power after a true revolution. The dispute between Moscow and Belgrade, which finally led to the expulsion of the Yugoslav movement from the Cominform in June 1948, had many causes. The main ones were of a personal and psychological nature, including an underestimation by Stalin of the Yugoslav leadership and particularly of Tito.

The statutes adopted at the party's fifth congress in July 1948 still followed the rules of the Communist Party of the Soviet Union (CPSU). By the time the sixth congress convened in 1952, the Yugoslav communists had withstood Stalin's challenge and were stronger than ever before. Party membership had almost doubled, despite the purge of its pro-Cominform elements. The leaders were convinced that they could advance toward communism in their own way, and this meant deviation from the Soviet model.

Everything possible was done to differentiate the Yugoslav party from the CPSU. At the sixth congress, the party name was changed to the League of Communists of Yugoslavia (*Saveza Komunista Jugoslavije*—SKJ). Aside from distinguishing the Yugoslav party this action proclaimed the country's advancement toward the goal of a communist state. The leadership made it clear, however, that the one-party system would be retained in Yugoslavia. By 1970 specific plans appeared for transformation of the SKJ.[65]

Present Organization. Despite a new name and new statutes, the SKJ still shows considerable similarity to all other communist organizations. It is operated to ensure that a small number of well-disciplined members make the major policy decisions and control all aspects of national life. There can be no fundamental criticism of Marxist-Leninist dogma as it is interpreted by the party, which adheres to the principles of democratic centralism.[66]

The highest SKJ organ, in theory, is the congress, which should convene at least once every five years to hear reports of the statutory Control Commission, amend or adopt the party program, determine the political line, and pass resolutions. The Presidium wields the real power, however. It consists of fourteen members plus nine ex officio members, distributed as follows: eight Serbs, three Croats, three Macedonians, three Slovenes, three Montenegrins, two Albanians, and one Muslim. The eleventh congress was held in June 1978. The thirteenth SKJ congress convened in June 1986, four years after the twelfth and the second since Tito died. Although having an "Alice in Wonderland" quality amid economic chaos, it did serve as a political steam valve. The new president of the SKJ Presidium described the proceedings as characterized by unity and action. The congress, a political and media extravaganza that cost about $1.2 million,[67] did bring about a generational change in leadership from the "Club of 1941."

Tito became president of the party in December 1964; in this capacity he also headed the policymaking Presidium. The social makeup of this body in 1958 was nine workers and six intellectuals. Five possessed university degrees, one was a graduate of a teachers' school, and six could claim only to have attended an elementary school; the rest presumably did not have even that much education.

The Presidium supervises the work of party organizations and oversees the implementation of decisions. In addition, four of its members direct the following specific areas: ideology, organizational development, political propaganda, socioeconomic relations, and international relations. Five other commissions and three standing committees under the Presidium deal with related interests. Seven executive secretaries work under the secretary of the Presidium and act as liaison officers between the top Yugoslav party body and republican or provincial parties. Radisa Gasic was elected secretary in 1986 for a two-year term.[68] (See Table 49.)

The financial records of the party are checked by its Control Commission. The structure of the SKJ in the six republics and two autonomous provinces is similar to that at the federal level.

Membership. Until 1952 the criteria for membership in the communist party of Yugoslavia were the same as those of its Soviet counterpart. A prospective member was required to be eighteen years of age, to have recommendations in writing from two party members (who had been acquainted with him for two years and

Table 49
PRESIDIUM
LEAGUE OF COMMUNISTS OF YUGOSLAVIA (LCY), 1988

Members (14)	Year of birth	Nationality	Year elected	Party office	Government post	Other positions
Brigic, Ivan	1936	Croat	1986			
Ckrebic, Dusan	1927	Serb	1986	President, Social and Economic Commission		
Gacic, Radisa	1938	Serb	1986	Secretary, LCY Presidium		
Korosec, Stefan	1914	Slovene	1986			
Krunic, Bosko	1929	Serb	1986			Member, Socialist Alliance of Working People (SSRN) Presidium
Orlandic, Marko	1935	Montenegrin	1986			
Pancevski, Milan	1935	Macedonian	1986			
Racan, Ivica	1943	Croat	1986			President, Education and Cultural Federation
Renovica, Milanko	1928	Serb	1986	President, Propaganda and Information Commission		Member, SSRN Presidium
Setinc, Franc	1929	Slovene	1986			Member, SSRN Presidium
Siroka, Kolj	1922	Albanian	1986			
Suvar, Stipe	1936	Croat	1986	President, LCY Presidium	Ex officio member, Presidency of Yugoslavia	Chief editor, Socijalizam
Tupurkovski, Vasil	1951	Macedonian	1986	President, Political System and Self-management Commission		
Zarkovic, Vidoje	1927	Montenegrin	1986			

SOURCES: CIA, Directory of Yugoslav Officials (December 1986); RFE, East European Leadership List (15 January 1988), pp. 43–45. Neues Deutschland, 2–3 July 1988, p. 1, for election of Suvar.

Table 50

YUGOSLAV COMMUNIST PARTY MEMBERSHIP, 1937–1988

Year	Number of members	Year	Number of members
1937	1,500	1970	1,111,682
1939	3,000	1974	*ca.*1,100,000
1940	6,000	1976	*ca.*1,400,000
1941	12,000	1978	1,629,082
1945	140,000	1980	1,950,000
1948	448,175	1981	2,041,272
1952	779,382	1983	2,200,000
1956	635,984	1985	2,188,943
1960	898,300	1987	2,150,000
1964	1,030,041	1988	2,099,613
1967	1,046,018		

SOURCES: *Komunist,* 15 October 1964, 6 April 1967, and 20 June 1980; *Borba,* 24 October 1970, 26 February 1975, 18 October 1976, 10 February 1978, and 29 June 1981; Belgrade radio, 19 March 1985, 14 May 1986; *Borba,* 1 January 1987, 1 March 1988, p. 10.

had themselves been members for at least two years), and to submit a written biographic statement. Applications are reviewed by one of the 64,059 basic party organizations and forwarded to the next higher level. If the prospective member proves acceptable, he is placed on probationary status for eighteen months. At the eighth congress these requirements were modified to eliminate written recommendations and probationary status.[69] It appears that membership can be attained now on nomination by workers who are not necessarily party members themselves. The growth of the party's membership is shown in Table 50.

Only one-fourth of the 12,000 members in 1941 survived the war.[70] Thus, more than 95 percent of the 1981 membership joined the party during the preceding 35 years. The significant increase in membership between 1948 and 1952 is indicative of how much Stalin underestimated Tito's strength. The drop that occurred between 1952 and 1956 can be attributed to the confusion created by the new doctrine announced at the sixth congress and by the Milovan Djilas affair. (See the section below on ''reconciliation with the Kremlin.'') Both situations resulted in purges and disillusionment on the part of many members. From the beginning of 1958 through the end of 1964, some 108,236 persons were expelled from the party. Between 1972 and 1979, about 170,000 members left the party either by resignation or expulsion.[71] (See Table 51.)

During the early 1970s purges intensified as a result of nationality problems within certain geographic parts of the country (for example, Croatia) and infiltration by pro-Soviet elements. Although purges have decreased, up to 108,000 members were expelled from the SKJ in 1980, with perhaps 37 percent of these dropped from party roles for political reasons. In January 1981 the SKJ numbered slightly more than two million, after having admitted 199,446 new members during the preceding twelve months. This total had not changed through the end of 1987.[72]

The social composition of the party is shown in Table 52. The fact that, as of the beginning of 1987, workers comprised only 30 percent of the total party

Table 51
PURGES IN LEAGUE OF COMMUNISTS OF YUGOSLAVIA, 1959–1980

Year	New admissions	Expulsions	Voluntary resignations	Total number of members
1959	103,093	14,416	(see note)	935,856
1960	96,176	13,425	(see note)	1,006,285
1961	67,548	14,975	(see note)	1,035,003
1962	26,725	22,655	(see note)	1,018,331
1963	39,362	15,320	(see note)	1,019,013
1964	41,403	10,626	2,273	1,031,634
1965	51,398	12,878	5,762	1,046,202
1966	39,928	13,488	7,640	1,046,018
1967	33,986	11,195	11,182	1,013,500
1968	175,293	14,235	13,363	1,146,084
1969	152,000	11,176	9,447	1,111,628
1970	32,500	←——— 92,601 ———→		1,049,184
1971	47,606	n.a.	8,993	1,025,476
1972	58,262	12,941	14,449	1,009,953
1973	109,150	9,443	5,694	1,076,711
1974	152,673	n.a.	19,134	1,192,461
1975	110,377	n.a.	n.a.	1,302,843
1976	105,724	n.a.	n.a.	*ca.* 1,400,000
1980	199,446	←——— 108,174 ———→		2,041,272

SOURCES: Belgrade radio, 24 January 1970; *Borba*, 19 March 1970. *Druga Konferencija SKJ* (Belgrade, 1972); *Cetvrta Konferencija SKJ* (Belgrade, 1973); *Deseti Kongress SKJ: Dokumenti* (Belgrade, 1974); *Statisticki godisnjak Jugoslavije 1975; Komunist*, 3 June 1971, 28 September 1972, 3 March and 16 June 1975, 25 October 1976; RFE, *Yugoslav Background Report*, no. 7 (20 July 1981), p. 2.

NOTES: Until 1964, members who resigned of their own free will were listed together with those expelled. The 1970 and 1980 figures include both expulsions and voluntary resignations.

Table 52
LEAGUE OF COMMUNISTS OF YUGOSLAVIA, SOCIAL COMPOSITION, 1967–1986

Category	January 1967		June 1976		January 1981		December 1986	
	Number	Percentage	Number	Percentage	Number	Percentage	Number	Percentage
Workers (including peasants in collectives)	355,022	33.9	366,272	28.1	602,176	29.5	624,220	29.6
Peasants (uncollectivized)[a]	77,134	7.4	65,910	5.1	87,774	4.3	73,683	3.5
Intelligentsia	408,378	39.0	542,248	41.8	820,592	40.2	781,483	37.1
Other[b]	96,217	9.3 }	232,274	17.7 }	183,714	9.0	336,912	5.9
Pensioners	74,610	7.1 }			347,016	17.0	155,095	7.3
Students	34,657	3.3 }	96,132	7.3 }			136,650	6.4
Total	1,046,018	100.0	1,302,836	100.0	2,041,272	100.0	2,108,043	100.0

SOURCES: *Komunist*, 6 April 1967; *Vjesnik*, 13 June 1967; *Borba*, 7 January 1979, 29 June 1981, and 1 March 1988, p. 10.

NOTES: [a]This category of peasant in 1946 was 49 percent of the party membership. *Komunist*, 25 May 1967.

[b]Includes members of the armed forces in 1967 through 1986.

membership means that the recommendation of the eleventh party congress "to create a workers' majority in the party" has not been fulfilled.[73] Recent years have seen a constant decline in peasant membership, both in the percentage of the total and in absolute numbers. This can be attributed to the regime's approach toward agriculture and its emphasis on industry. The peasants have become disenchanted with the party because of past attempts to collectivize the farms. Figures for 1986 show that peasants make up only 3.5 percent of total party membership, which is significant considering that 30 percent of Yugoslavia's population (7,450,666 of 22,352,000 inhabitants) lives in the countryside. This means that only 1 percent of all Yugoslav peasants have joined the party. (See Table 53 for a breakdown of party membership by nationality.) On the other hand, the intelligentsia component has remained stable. This is probably a result of the system, which obliges a person to join the SKJ if he or she hopes to acquire a good post after completing his or her higher education. The number of pensioners has been increasing as well; this is characteristic of an "aging" party. In 1981, young people up to age 27 made up 33.1 percent of total party membership.[74]

Table 53
SKJ MEMBERSHIP BY UNIT, 1986

Unit	Number	Percentage
Bosnia-Herzegovina	415,808	19.18
Montenegro	77,763	3.59
Croatia	342,620	15.81
Macedonia	163,318	7.53
Slovenia	126,089	5.82
Serbia	604,716	27.89
Kosovo	200,561	4.64
Vojvodina	228,572	10.54
Army	93,377	4.31
Federal agencies	15,036	0.69
Total	2,167,860	100.00

SOURCE: *Borba*, 25 March 1986.

In Yugoslavia, just as in all other communist-dominated states, control over youth is both a matter of prime importance and a major problem. To supplement the basic education received at school, the Pioneers provide militant political indoctrination. During holidays or free time, participation in volunteer working brigades is encouraged. Yet the young people themselves have prevented the party from exercising tight control and have become disenchanted. This does not necessarily produce direct opposition to communism, but it does involve resistance to rigid conformity.

Of the 3,600,000 members of the Yugoslav Youth Union, in 1980 only 650,000 were party members.[75] Although this is the sole youth movement that is allowed, official figures indicate that only 67.4 percent of those between 15 and 27 in 1980 were members.[76] There is persistent discontent among students and other young people all over Yugoslavia. Only 10 of every 2,000 students were party members in 1980.[77]

Mass Organizations.   The most important mass movement in Yugoslavia is the Socialist Alliance of Working People (SSRN), formerly known as the People's Front, which has thirteen million members. It is composed of both organizations and individuals. To become an SSRN member, an individual must enroll in one of its basic organizations. The purpose is to involve as many people as possible in some type of activity over which the party has control.

The SSRN platform has been designed so that it will be acceptable to practically everyone. A person with a distaste for the principles of the ruling party may find those of SSRN more to his liking. The movement has two fundamental purposes, one political and the other economic.[78] Politically, it helps to influence the masses along the general SKJ line, conducts elections, and on special occasions holds political rallies. The economic purpose consists of assisting in the fulfillment of national economic plans and explaining the need for social change.

The SSRN has an organizational structure similar to that of the ruling party. It extends from the national level down to the commune and is controlled by the SKJ at all levels. Party members are supposed to influence the SSRN by their own efforts and not only through their positions in the communist hierarchy. The president of the SSRN is Ivo Vrandecic, a Croatian, who is serving a one-year term and is eligible for re-election.[79]

The Confederation of Trade Unions in Yugoslavia is another communist-dominated mass organization, which operates as a means for implementing the party's economic policy. Until 1958 labor unions had control over the list of candidates for workers' councils. At that time, out of 220,656 council members there were only 60,012 communists, or 27.2 percent of the total. In individual councils, party membership ranged from 10 percent to 85 percent. Although trade unions no longer control the candidate list, they retain influence within various industrial enterprises, helping the party and the government control factories. In 1980 the trade unions had 5.7 million members.[80] The confederation is headed by Marjan Orozen, who was elected for a one-year term.[81]

Between January 1958 and September 1976 about 2,000 strikes took place in Yugoslavia. Most of these occurred in Slovenia, followed by Serbia, and then

Croatia. An official listing indicates a concentration in metallurgy, with textiles, wood products, and the construction industry following in number of strikes.[82] Both the communist party and the trade unions probably look on strikes as safety valves rather than real threats to the system. During 1980 and the first three months of 1981, some 13,500 Yugoslav workers staged work stoppages because of dissatisfaction at the slowness with which self-management rights were being implemented at their enterprises. By 1987 this escalated to 1,685 strikes involving 288,000 participants.[83]

FOREIGN RELATIONS

Aggressive Postwar Policies. Although provided with extensive wartime military aid by the United States and Britain and disappointed by the failure of the Soviet Union to contribute substantially until the fall of 1944, the new postwar government of Tito openly oriented its foreign policies toward the USSR and considered the capitalist states enemies. Backed by an army that had received delayed aid from Soviet divisions toward the end of the war,[84] communist Yugoslavia attempted to expand its borders. It seems clear that Tito at this time had visions of a Balkan federation led by himself.

An initial argument with Italy concerned the border province of Venezia Giulia, including the port city of Trieste. Populated by a majority of Slavs but ceded to Italy after World War I, the province had been occupied by Partisans in 1945 after the German retreat. The Western Allies subsequently entered the city, but it took nine years to reach a settlement. The Yugoslavs were disappointed by the Soviet failure (1948–1953) to support their claims, and the 1954 agreement was concluded in London without the participation of the USSR. It gave the city of Trieste to Italy and the hinterland to Yugoslavia.

In neighboring Albania, Tito's representatives had advised the newly founded communist party in 1941 and supported the successful guerrilla struggle against Italians and Germans in that country. By establishing joint-stock companies and stationing a few army units in Albania, Yugoslav communists exercised supervision both economically and militarily over their satellite. Imbued with somewhat the same independent spirit as their neighbors, Albanian communists resisted their domination. Annexation by Yugoslavia never took place (although it had previously been suggested by Stalin) because of the Tito regime's 1948 dispute with the Cominform.

Another plan for expansion included Bulgarian and Greek parts of Macedonia adjoining the similarly named republic in Yugoslavia. In August 1947 the Bulgarian communist party agreed to federation at some future date.[85] Tito also influenced the civil war in Greece by re-establishing a Macedonian partisan movement in that country. His plan for consolidating Macedonia was stopped (as in the case of Albania) after the Cominform's expulsion of the Yugoslav communist party in June 1948, together with the termination of the Greek civil war in the following year.

The Tito-Stalin Dispute. Yugoslav communists were completely dedicated to Stalin personally and to the Soviet Union in the early postwar years. This devotion persisted despite several disappointments and differences during the war years and thereafter.[86] Proposals for joint-stock companies, which would have given the USSR control of the Yugoslav economy, were opposed. This was precisely the same procedure that Belgrade had adopted in seeking domination over Albania. Soviet military advisers insisted that the Yugoslav army be remodeled after the USSR example, and brazen intelligence activities were conducted by Soviet representatives in Yugoslavia. Agents were recruited in the army, the government, and even the Central Committee of the Yugoslav communist party.

Relations had already become strained when Tito failed to obey Stalin's summons to Moscow in February 1948. In a series of letters the Yugoslavs were accused by Soviet leaders not only of deviation, arrogance, and ingratitude but even of Trotskyism. (These charges also reopened the matter of the "insult" to the Red Army by Milovan Djilas in 1945 when he complained that Yugoslav women had been raped and murdered by Soviet soldiers.) Yugoslavia's replies, which were always conciliatory, contained pledges of loyalty and suggestions that the Central Committee in the CPSU might be the victim of misinformation. Belgrade offered time and again to prove its loyalty to Moscow. Tito and his colleagues hoped for reconciliation, almost irrationally and to the very end. The Soviets, however, remained adamant and demanded unconditional capitulation.

Failing in his attempt to eliminate Tito with denunciation and expulsion from the Cominform, Stalin turned to direct economic, political, and military pressure. Newspapers were smuggled into the country, and radio broadcasts viciously denounced Tito. Agents from neighboring states infiltrated Yugoslavia to incite national minorities, and an economic boycott was applied by the entire Soviet bloc. In August 1949 the USSR formally declared that it considered the Yugoslav government an enemy. Armed clashes with Soviet satellite troops along the Yugoslav borders became constant occurrences.

Tito Turns West. Reluctantly, Tito looked to the West for help. His economy depended on trade with East European countries and now was in danger of collapse. The Western response was gradual but positive. American-held Yugoslav assets were released, and a trade agreement was signed in December 1948 with Britain. During the following year, negotiations involving trade and a loan from the U.S. Export-Import Bank were completed. In 1950 surplus U.S. grain was sent to alleviate hunger resulting from a serious drought in Yugoslavia.

During the next decade an estimated $3.5 billion worth of assistance came from the West. Nearly half of this was contributed by the United States. As of mid-1962 U.S. economic aid to Yugoslavia amounted to more than $1.5 billion and military assistance to about $719 million. The United Nations Relief and Rehabilitation Administration's help totaled nearly half a billion dollars.[87] An equal amount came from nongovernment charitable institutions such as CARE or in the form of loans from international banks. This provided an annual average of nearly $250 million, which materially assisted in alleviating the foreign trade deficit. (See Table 54 for figures on the adverse balance-of-payments problem.)

Table 54
YUGOSLAVIA'S FOREIGN TRADE, 1970–1986
(in millions of dinars)

Category	1970	1975	1980	1986
Imports	48,857	128,805	411,257	3,108,230
Exports	28,544	88,468	254,086	2,724,204
Total	77,401	217,273	665,343	5,832,434
Balance	−20,313	−40,337	−157,171	−364,026

SOURCE: [Yugoslavia], *Statistical Pocket Book of Yugoslavia 1976* (Belgrade, 1976), p. 80, gives figures for each year between 1961 and 1975; *Quarterly Economic Review* (2d Quarter 1981), p. 10; *Statisticki godisnjak 1987*, p. 572.

One hope of the West had been to bring Yugoslavia indirectly into the North Atlantic Treaty Organization (NATO). A step toward this goal was the treaty of friendship and cooperation signed at Ankara in February 1953 by Yugoslavia, Greece, and Turkey. Several months later, a military pact was concluded by the same three countries. Late the following year and early in 1955, however, Tito toured India and Burma to expound the principles of "active coexistence," equality of nations, and noninterference in the internal affairs of other countries.[88]

Reconciliation with the Kremlin. After Stalin's death, the new Soviet communist party leader, Nikita Khrushchev, realized that the anti-Yugoslav policy represented a liability. The earliest sign of a thaw was the establishment of a Romanian-Yugoslav joint administration over their common part of the Danube River, obviously with Soviet approval. Moscow omitted the usual May Day criticism of Tito in 1953 and proposed that the two countries exchange ambassadors. The offer was accepted. The other satellite countries, one by one, adopted an identical course. Border clashes and subversion virtually ceased, and anti-Tito newspapers and radio stations in neighboring countries were shut down.

Two years later, during May 1955, in full realization of the need to heal the breach, Khrushchev and Premier Nikolai Bulganin journeyed to Yugoslavia. Officially accepting Soviet responsibility for the break between the two countries, Khrushchev, in a speech at Belgrade airport, blamed Lavrenty Beria, the executed secret police chief, for what had happened and asked Yugoslavia's forgiveness.[89] He also proposed the renewal of friendly relations between the two governments and communist parties. In a joint declaration Tito and Khrushchev agreed to respect the sovereignty, independence, integrity, and equality of states; accepted the principle of noninterference, based on the premise that differing forms of social development are solely the concern of each individual country; and condemned aggression as well as political and economic domination.

For his part, Tito supported the USSR in its suppression of the 1956 Hungarian revolt. He had opposed the initial interference, while the local communists were still in control of the situation. After the rebellion got out of hand, however, he considered Soviet intervention to save the country for communism to be the lesser of two evils. In 1957 Tito extended diplomatic recognition to East Germany and, in an essay[90] published abroad, called for the dissolution of NATO and criticized the West for its negative attitude toward Moscow.

At the same time, only limited criticism of communism inside Yugoslavia or of the Soviet Union could be expressed. A good illustration is the case involving Milovan Djilas. Although earlier he had been considered the heir apparent to Tito, Djilas resigned from the communist party in 1954 and subsequently wrote a book entitled *The New Class*. It represents the most devastating and best-known indictment of the communist system. Another book, *Conversations with Stalin*, resulted in his imprisonment for allegedly disclosing "official secrets." After serving part of his sentence, Djilas was released on 31 December 1966. Several years later, regime officials withdrew his passport two days before he had planned to leave for a visit to the United States.[91] Since Tito's death Djilas has increasingly voiced criticism of the existing political system and the new leadership's exaltation of Titoism. In August 1980 a new book by Djilas was published in Vienna in which he disclaims much of Tito's relevance to party history. Djilas's passport has since been returned to him, and he has received permission to visit his son in London during 1988.[92]

The Second Soviet-Yugoslav Dispute. Concerned with unrest throughout Eastern Europe and beset by differences of opinion within his own party leadership, Khrushchev decided it was time to reorganize the Soviet bloc. He prepared and circulated a resolution on communist unity to be presented and signed at Moscow on the 40th anniversary of the 1917 revolution. The document portrayed the world in terms of two uncompromising blocs, with the United States as the "center of world reaction.'' It equated the Soviet bloc with the Warsaw Pact and, in an allusion to the Yugoslavs, declared revisionism to be the greatest danger. Tito was shocked and dismayed. Refusing to attend the anniversary meeting, he sent Edvard Kardelj and Aleksandar Rankovic to Moscow with instructions not to sign the resolution.

The seventh congress of his communist party in April 1958 gave Tito an opportunity to present his version of communism to the world. He circulated drafts of the new party program and in some instances modified it in acquiescence to Soviet objections. The final document[93] represented a formal declaration of Yugoslavia's political and ideological independence. Tito's insistence on retaining the main substance of the draft program resulted in a boycott of the congress by the Soviet communist party as well as its East European allies. Although ambassadors from these countries attended as observers, all except the Polish representative ostentatiously walked out of the congress.[94]

Moscow's attack on Yugoslav revisionism set the tone and the levels of criticism for its supporters to follow. The rift remained moderate in the beginning. Unexpectedly, however, the Chinese communists launched a vitriolic attack, declaring that the Cominform had been correct in its 1948 expulsion of the Yugoslav party.[95] Moscow announced a five-year postponement of its $285 million credit commitment to Belgrade, but no economic blockade or disruption of diplomatic relations followed.

Tito Again Turns West.　　Shortly after the seventh party congress friendship for the United States became official Yugoslav policy. This was claimed not to be based on any requirement for assistance, yet a real need admittedly existed. Tito asked for $100 million in aid during October 1958, and the United States responded with a program encompassing even more.

There were limitations to Yugoslavia's leanings toward the West, as is evidenced by its active support of Fidel Castro even to the point of jeopardizing U.S. assistance. Renewed friendship with the West did not become as intimate as before, nor was the break with the Soviets as serious as the first one. Belgrade could not be convinced that the schism would continue, and Tito privately pictured Khrushchev as the leader of an anti-Stalinist faction that sincerely sought peace with the West. In the same vein, he criticized the administration in Washington for failing to reach an accommodation with the USSR.

Tito next attempted to organize the nonaligned nations with ''third force'' proposals by hosting and addressing a conference of these states that met at Belgrade.[96] This effort brought him dangerously close to a rift with the West. Although the neutralists condemned the existence of all ''blocs,'' their policies approximated those of the USSR in outspoken support for the recognition of East Germany and the seating of Mainland China in the United Nations. There was resentment in Washington when Tito supported the Soviet Union during the Berlin crisis and failed to denounce the USSR's resumption of nuclear testing.

From the first summit meeting of nonaligned countries in 1961 at Belgrade to the time of his death, Tito was inextricably associated with this international movement. That first meeting included only 25 participants, but by the sixth summit conference in September 1979 at Havana, the last in Tito's lifetime, the movement had grown to include some 117 countries. With Tito gone, the seventh conference of the nonaligned in New Delhi (February 1981) was marked by internal disunity and foreign pressure.[97] Yugoslavia also played a substantial role at the eighth summit meeting (1986) in Harare, Zimbabwe.

The Cycle Repeats Itself. After the Sino-Soviet dispute had come into the open at the 22d congress of the Soviet communist party, Tito saw a chance to move closer to Moscow. Despite an amnesty for political prisoners, Milovan Djilas was rearrested in April 1962 because of the imminent publication in English of his book *Conversations with Stalin,* which was critical of the Soviet leadership during and immediately after the war. Because the USSR had split with both Albania and Mainland China, the Yugoslavs showed by this arrest that they desired closer relations.

Beginning with the late 1960s, however, the growing possibility of Soviet interference in the future of Yugoslavia has led the ruling party and regime to take a more sober attitude toward the USSR. This could be seen in Belgrade's condemnation of the Warsaw Pact invasion of Czechoslovakia (August 1968) and its vigorous prosecution of pro-Soviet elements within Yugoslavia during the mid-1970s. The Yugoslav condemnation of Soviet aggression in Afghanistan accentuated further deterioration in relations between Moscow and Belgrade. Despite this, economic relations between the two countries are good. In 1980, they signed a ten-year economic agreement intended to boost trade by at least 60 percent and increase cooperation in such fields as energy, food production, construction, and shipbuilding.[98]

On the other hand, commercial agreements provided for the equivalent of some $26 billion in trade with the USSR during the 1980–1985 period (compared with only $16 billion in the previous five-year period).[99] By contrast, Yugoslavia's trade with the (West) European Economic Community amounted to about 30 percent of its total foreign turnover in 1980, causing it to incur a deficit with the Common Market countries. Trade with the United States is also of importance since U.S. investments have grown over the last several years. The United States now occupies first place as a joint-investment partner with Yugoslavia, an example being the huge $750 million petrochemical complex built by Dow Chemical Company. (See Table 55.)

Typical of problems vis-à-vis the Western world is the present relationship between Yugoslavia and the Federal Republic of Germany. Belgrade has

Table 55
YUGOSLAV FOREIGN TRADE BY AREA, 1979 AND 1986

| | 1979 | | | | 1986 | | | |
| | EXPORTS | | IMPORTS | | EXPORTS | | IMPORTS | |
AREA	(amount)	(percentage)	(amount)	(percentage)	(amount)	(percentage)	(amount)	(percentage)
Developed countries	81.615	44.1	232,868	60.8	991,744	36.4	1,507,428	48.5
Socialist countries	75,003	40.4	97,335	25.5	1,326,913	48.7	1,015,171	32.7
Developing countries	28,852	15.5	52,506	13.7	405,547	14.9	585,631	18.8
Total	185,470	100.0	382,709	100.0	2,724,204	100.0	3,108,230	100.0

SOURCE: *Quarterly Economic Review* (2d Quarter 1981), p. 10; [Yugoslavia], *Statisticki godisnjak Jugoslavije* (1987), p. 321.

NOTE: Amounts are in millions of dinars.

demanded indemnification for Yugoslav war victims and assailed the West Germans for their failure to accept reparation claims. Still, the Federal Republic of Germany remains Yugoslavia's number-one economic trading partner. Despite the obvious benefits from this relationship in the past, about $17.7 billion in debts to Western countries had accumulated by mid-1981 and some $21 billion by the spring of 1988.[100]

Future Developments. The great complexity of Yugoslavia's domestic and international problems and the dominant role one man played since the communists seized power at the end of World War II make predictions about that country hazardous. In the past Tito's leadership and authority were essential in holding the ruling party together, but there is a legitimate question whether Titoism without Tito will prove to be an enduring formula for political cohesion in a diversified country. Yugoslav-Soviet relations have oscillated in the past between extremes of friendship and hostility, and the recent rapprochement between Belgrade and Moscow will be put to another test now that Tito has left the political scene. Disunity among regional communist parties (Serbian, Croatian, etc.), which Tito temporarily overcame, reflects deeper ethnic strivings in that multinational country. The as-yet inconclusive results from experimentation with the decentralized system of workers' self-management, which has from the beginning been incompatible with the one-party rule, represent another unsettling factor. Last but not least, the role the armed forces may play in case of internal disorders after Tito makes the picture even more uncertain.[101]

One should add that more than any other East European country, Yugoslavia has been open to the influence of the West. But this means that popular disposition toward a free political system, beyond the stranglehold of a single party, might also become an element to consider. Therefore, instead of an attempt to predict what will happen, the foregoing enumeration of several basic factors that may shape the future should suffice. The interplay among them will determine the course of events in Yugoslavia.

NOTES

1. U.S. Congress, Senate, Committee on the Judiciary, 87th Cong., 1st sess., *Yugoslav Communism: A Critical Study* (Washington, D.C., 1961), p. 3, prepared by Charles Zalar.

2. CIA, *World Factbook 1987* (Washington, D.C., June 1988), p. 269.

3. Ibid.

4. A special issue on Tito's death appeared in *Yugoslav Facts and Views,* no. 122–23 (May–June 1980), p. 62.

5. Dragoljub Durovic (ed.), *Narodna vlast i socijalisticka demokratija, 1943–1963* (Belgrade, 1964), pp. 22–23.

6. Ibid., p. 56, reproduces the beginning of the proclamation.

7. For an interpretation of Western policy toward the two rival resistance movements, see Walter R. Roberts, *Tito, Mihailovic and the Allies, 1941–1945* (New Brunswick, N.J., 1973).

8. V. N. Durdenevskii (ed.), *Konstitutsii zarubezhnykh sotsialisticheskikh gosudarstv* (Moscow, 1956), pp. 389–408, gives the text in Russian. David Martin (introd.), *Patriot or Traitor: The Case of General Mihailovich* (Stanford, Calif., 1978), 499 pp.

9. Albert Waterston, *Planning in Yugoslavia* (Baltimore, Md., 1962), p. 7.

10. Alex N. Dragnich, *Tito's Promised Land, Yugoslavia* (New Brunswick, N.J., 1954), pp. 290–93. See also Vladimir Dedijer, *The Battle Stalin Lost: Memoirs of Yugoslavia, 1948–1953* (New York, 1971), especially chap. 3.

11. For example, Nikita Khrushchev, when still in power, stated that based "on objective laws, on the teachings of Marxism-Leninism, it is impossible to deny that Yugoslavia appears to be a socialist [i.e., communist] country." Quoted in P. D. Mineev and V. A. Tokarev, *Yugoslaviia* (Moscow, 1963), p. 29.

12. V. V. Zagladin et al., "Yugoslavia Today," *World Marxist Review* (March 1964), p. 66.

13. [Yugoslavia], *The Constitution of the Socialist Federal Republic of Yugoslavia* (Belgrade, 1974), p. 311; henceforth cited as *Constitution*. See also William B. Simons (ed.), *Constitutions of the Communist World* (Alphen aan den Rijn, 1980), pp. 423–578.

14. *Constitution*, pp. 87–90.

15. Mirko Boskovic, *Drustveno-politicki sistem Jugoslavije* (Zagreb, 1963), pp. 121–26.

16. *Constitution*, pp. 84–87, 89.

17. Slobodan Stankovic, "Thirty Years of Yugoslavia's Self-Management System," RFE, *Background Report*, no. 160 (30 June 1980), pp. 2–8, discusses workers' councils.

18. Belgrade decided to devalue the dinar by about 30 percent in 1980. The official rate in November 1986 was 408 dinars to the U.S. dollar. *Vjesnik*, 7 June 1980; CIA, *World Factbook 1987*, p. 270.

19. RFE report (by Slobodan Stankovic), "New Law Encourages Private Enterprise," 12 March 1976.

20. *Borba*, 29 June 1981.

21. During 1980, about 63 percent of the wheat, 62 percent of the barley, 92 percent of the oats, and 97 percent of the rapeseed were produced by private farmers. *Quarterly Economic Review* (1st Quarter 1981), p. 15. Belgrade radio, 4 August 1987; *FBIS-Eastern Europe*, 5 August 1987.

22. *Statisticki godisnjak Jugoslavije 1987*, p. 238; Belgrade radio, 27 March 1988, in *FBIS-Eastern Europe*, 29 March 1988, p. 58.

23. *Vjesnik*, 28 July 1969.

24. *Politika*, 1 July 1980.

25. Ibid., 3 July 1980.

26. Tanjug dispatch, 3 February 1981. Six years later, agricultural workers numbered 2.14 million of the 9.61 million labor force. CIA, *Handbook of Economic Statistics* (1987), pp. 54–55; henceforth, cited as CIA *Handbook*.

27. *Business Eastern Europe* 10, no. 19 (8 May 1981), pp. 147–48.

28. *Christian Science Monitor,* 28 May 1976; RFE report (by Zdenko Antic), "Yugoslavia to Build Highways," 12 March 1976.

29. CIA, *Handbook* (1987), pp. 134, 138, 141.

30. *Quarterly Economic Review* (2d Quarter 1981), p. 15.

31. Richard Nyrop (ed.), *Yugoslavia* (Washington, D.C., 1982), p. 135.

32. Tanjug dispatch, 3 February 1981.

33. Regarding the policy of "equal nations and nationalities," see the speech by Vladimir Bakaric on the occasion of Tito's death, printed in *Yugoslav Facts and Views,* nos. 122–23 (May–June 1980), pp. 15–30.

34. *Quarterly Economic Review* (2d Quarter 1981), p. 17; *New York Times,* 13 July 1987.

35. *Yugoslav Life,* no. 6–7 (June–July 1981), p. 4.

36. Slobodan Stankovic, "The Kosovo Unrest: The Causes and the Consequences," RFE, *Background Report,* no. 97 (April 1981), p. 6; *Frankfurter Allgemeine Zeitung,* 10 June 1981; *New York Times,* 18 July 1981.

37. *NIN,* 10 May 1981; *Kommunist,* 19 October 1979; *Borba,* 14 October 1979.

38. *Borba,* 4 June 1981; *Rilindja,* 28 April 1981; RFE, *Background Report,* no. 145 (18 May 1981), no. 127 (6 May 1981).

39. *Vjesnik,* 8 August 1979.

40. *New York Times,* 24 October 1976, indicates that unemployment would almost reach 1.5 million if all of these workers returned to Yugoslavia. It dropped to 804,000 in 1979. *Indeks,* no. 6 (June 1980).

41. *Financial Times* (London), 20 June 1980, p. 52.

42. *The Economist,* 1 August 1981, p. 52.

43. Zdenko Antic, "Yugoslavia's Economy in 1980," RFE, *Background Report,* no. 26 (4 February 1981), p. 3; *Quarterly Economic Review* (2d Quarter 1981), p. 5.

44. The quotations and estimate of relapse are from Zagladin, "Yugoslavia Today," p. 70; Zagreb radio, 12 February 1966. However, the 1971 census reported that only 15.1 percent of the total population above the age of ten was illiterate and about one-fourth had completed three years of primary school or less. *Statistical Pocket Book of Yugoslavia 1976,* p. 24. For later figures, see CIA, *World Factbook 1987,* p. 269.

45. *Statisticki godisnjak Jugoslavije 1987,* p. 366.

46. *Constitution.* See also Simons, *Constitutions of the Communist World,* pp. 423–578.

47. *Borba,* 4 July 1981.

48. For a description of each chamber's responsibilities, see *Constitutional System of Yugoslavia* (Belgrade, 1980), pp. 109–13.

49. RFE, *East European Leadership List* (15 January 1988), p. 44.

50. Robin A. Remington, "Yugoslavia," in Richard F. Staar (ed.), *Yearbook on International Communist Affairs: 1988* (Stanford, Calif., 1988), pp. 365–66; henceforth, cited as *YICA*.

51. *Kommunist*, 27 March 1978, supplement. See also *Statut Saveza Komunista Jugoslavije* (Belgrade, 1980), pp. 24–25.

52. Simons, *Constitutions of the Communist World,* article 328, p. 554.

53. *Vjesnik*, 23 September 1970. See also Slobodan Stankovic, *The End of the Tito Era* (Stanford, Calif., 1980), pp. 53–77.

54. *Constitution,* pp. 266–67.

55. *Constitutional System of Yugoslavia* (Belgrade, 1980), pp. 116–18, lists the council's powers and duties.

56. Ibid., p. 124. Also pp. 79–84 on communes' rights and duties, resources, and association between communes.

57. *Constitutional System of Yugoslavia,* pp. 70–74, enumerates court jurisdictions.

58. *Constitution,* pp. 286–87.

59. See the discussion of elections by Slobodan Stankovic, "Yugoslavia," in *YICA: 1979,* pp. 99–100.

60. Remington, "Yugoslavia," in *YICA: 1987,* pp. 381–82.

61. See Rodoljub Colakovic (ed.), *Pregled istorije Saveza Komunista Jugoslavije* (Belgrade, 1963), pp. 38–46, on this congress.

62. For a biography of Tito, see U.S. Department of State, Division of Biographic Information, *The Central Leadership of the Union of Communists of Yugoslavia* (Washington, D.C., 1958), p. 19, hereafter cited as *Central Leadership,* and Stankovic, *End of the Tito Era,* pp. 121–22.

63. Robert Lee Wolff, *The Balkans in Our Time* (Cambridge, Mass., 1956), p. 267.

64. Milovan Djilas, *Conversations with Stalin* (New York, 1962), pp. 11–12.

65. The need for transformation from a political party into a political-ideological force, internal SKJ democratization, and broader participation by members in forming and implementing policy were conclusions adopted by the SKJ Presidium and published in *Borba,* 24 April 1970.

66. See the party statute adopted at the eleventh congress, in *Statut Saveza Komunista Jugoslavije* (Belgrade, 1980), p. 128.

67. Remington, "Yugoslavia," in *YICA: 1987,* pp. 381–85.

68. CIA, *Directory,* pp. 3–4, lists incumbents; RFE, *Leadership List* (1988), p. 43.

69. *Komunist,* 15 July 1965; paragraph 1 of statute, in *Osmi Kongres SKJ* (Belgrade, 1964), pp. 236–38.

70. Josef Korbel, *Tito's Communism* (Denver, Colo, 1951), p. 57.

71. *Osmi Kongres SKJ* (Belgrade, 1964), p. 139; *Komunist,* 15 July 1965; *Borba,* 14 June 1980.

72. *Politika,* 16 June 1981; Remington, "Yugoslavia," in *YICA: 1988,* p. 354.

73. *Borba,* 29 June 1981.

74. Ibid.

75. *Borba,* 11 March 1980.

76. Ibid., 21 February 1980; see also Slobodan Stankovic, "Changes in the Yugoslav Communist Youth Federation," RFE, *Background Report,* no. 2 (5 January 1981).

77. *Politika,* 16 December 1980.

78. Boskovic, *Drustveno-politicki sistem Jugoslavije,* pp. 339–47.

79. Remington, "Yugoslavia," in *YICA: 1987,* p. 380.

80. *Neue Zuercher Zeitung,* 23 October 1980.

81. Tanjug dispatch, 2 June 1988.

82. *Vecernje novosti,* 15 May 1976.

83. Ibid., 11 July 1981; Belgrade radio, 2 March 1988, in *FBIS-Eastern Europe,* 3 March 1988, p. 51.

84. Soviet divisions only passed through the northeastern part of the country, but they did assist the Partisans to capture Belgrade. Djilas, *Conversations with Stalin,* pp. 88–89, reports that he discussed with Stalin the 121 reported cases of rape (111 of these also involved murder) and 1,204 registered incidents of looting by Red Army personnel in Yugoslavia.

85. Early in 1948 Stalin turned from his previous opposition and ordered an immediate federation between Bulgaria and Yugoslavia. Djilas, *Conversations with Stalin,* p. 177. It never took place.

86. Milorad M. Drachkovitch, "The Comintern and Insurrectional Activity of the Communist Party of Yugoslavia in 1941–1942," in Drachkovitch and Branko Lazitch (eds.), *The Comintern: Historical Highlights* (New York, 1966), pp. 184–213.

87. Milorad M. Drachkovitch, *United States Aid to Yugoslavia and Poland: An Analysis of a Controversy* (Washington, D.C., 1963), p. 121; *U.S. News & World Report* (8 November 1976), p. 36.

88. Note the speech at Rangoon in Josip Broz Tito, *Selected Speeches and Articles, 1941–1961* (Zagreb, 1963), pp. 172–73.

89. For text of Khrushchev's speech at this meeting and other documents, see CIA, *Key Soviet-Yugoslav Documents* (February 1980), p. 34.

90. Josip Broz Tito, "On Certain International Questions," *Foreign Affairs* (October 1957), pp. 70–72.

91. Belgrade radio, 11 March 1970. See his interview with a reporter from the *Washington Post,* 25 November 1976, in which Djilas urges better relations with the United States.

92. For the English translation, see Milovan Djilas, *Tito: The Story from Inside* (New York, 1980), p. 185; *New York Times,* 20 January 1988.

93. Translated in full in Stoyan Pribichevich (ed. and trans.), *Yugoslavia's Way: The Program of the League of the Communists of Yugoslavia* (New York, 1958).

94. For a discussion of these events and subsequent Soviet-Yugoslav relations, see M. M. Drachkovitch, "Yugoslavia: The Dangers of Political Longevity," in M. M. Drachkovitch (ed.), *East Central Europe: Yesterday, Today, Tomorrow* (Stanford, Calif., 1982), pp. 349–98.

95. *Jen-min-jih-pao* (Peking), 5 May 1958. Just twelve years later, a Yugoslav ambassador arrived in Peking and the Chinese communists appointed an envoy to Belgrade. *New York Times,* 12 August 1970. Since then, friendly relations have developed between the two countries. Mutual trade totaled $29 million in 1976 and by 1979 had expanded to approximately $160 million. *Ekonomska politika,* 6 October 1980.

96. His address is in Tito, *Selected Speeches and Articles,* pp. 388–408.

97. Zdenko Antic, "Yugoslavia Worried About the Future of Nonalignment," RFE, *Background Report,* no. 40 (13 February 1981), p. 2. See also the discussion on nonalignment after Tito in Stankovic, *End of the Tito Era,* pp. 96–98.

98. *Delo,* 26 January 1980; Zdenko Antic, "New Soviet-Yugoslav 10-Year Economic Agreement," RFE, *Background Report,* no. 249 (20 October 1980), p. 3.

99. Ibid., p. 2.

100. The Yugoslav trade deficit with West Germany in 1979 was 3.6 billion DM, but decreased to 2.6 billion DM in 1980. *Politika,* 9 February 1981, p. 2. For debts, see *The Economist,* 1 August 1981, and *Politika,* 25 March 1988, p. 1.

101. On the role of the army after Tito, see Stankovic, *End of the Tito Era,* pp. 34–52 and 112–14.

Chapter 9
Military Integration: Warsaw Pact

The establishment of a multilateral military alliance system in Eastern Europe that was announced by Moscow came ostensibly as a response to West German membership in NATO. The true reason for the Warsaw Treaty Organization (WTO) was probably the USSR's desire to obtain legal justification for stationing its troops in East Central Europe. The pact[1] was initialed in the capital of Poland on 14 May 1955, only one day before the signing of the state treaty in Vienna that restored sovereignty to Austria and obligated Moscow to evacuate its forces from Hungary and Romania within 40 days after the Austrian state treaty had gone into effect. The WTO also provided an additional legal basis for the continued presence of Soviet troops in Poland and the German Democratic Republic (GDR). However, in the case of the GDR, such provision appeared to be superfluous, due to the absence of a peace treaty.

A Soviet declaration[2] at the height of the Hungarian revolution reaffirmed the right of this presence and added that Soviet forces in Poland had the additional justification of the Potsdam agreement. This official statement claimed that no military units existed in any other East European people's democracy—the GDR, which had been proclaimed sovereign in October 1949, apparently did not fall into such a category—and that the Soviet government stood ready to discuss the question of its troops abroad with other signatories to the Warsaw Pact.

The subsequently negotiated status-of-forces treaties with Poland (December 1956), East Germany (March 1957), Romania (April 1957), Hungary (May 1957), and Czechoslovakia (October 1968) all remain in effect today except for the third, which lapsed in June 1958 on the withdrawal of Soviet troops from Romania.[3] These agreements represented the first such arrangements to be made public, although secret accords may have existed in the past. The treaty with East Germany is unique in that it includes a safety clause allowing the USSR to intervene if it finds its own security endangered. Article 18 reads as follows:

> In case of a threat to the security of the Soviet forces which are stationed on the territory of the German Democratic Republic, the High Command of the Soviet

forces in the GDR, in appropriate consultation with the GDR Government, and taking into account the actual situation and the measures adopted by GDR state organs, may apply measures for the elimination of such a threat.[4]

This situation has not changed as a result of the two bilateral friendship, collaboration, and mutual assistance pacts signed in June 1964 and October 1975 between the two countries. (For other treaties, see Table 56.)

Apart from the East German treaty, all the status-of-forces treaties follow a uniform pattern in dealing with the following:

1. The movement of Soviet forces in the host country
2. Jurisdiction over Soviet forces and individual soldiers, members of Soviet military families, and civilian Soviet employees while on the territory of the host country
3. Soviet control and use of military installations on the territory of the host country
4. The jurisdiction of local authorities in civil and criminal matters arising out of, or in conjunction with, the presence of Soviet troops
5. Matters subject to the exclusive jurisdiction of Soviet authorities
6. The settlement of mutual claims.

The inferior status of the GDR can also be seen in certain differences in detail. For example, the treaties with Poland and Hungary omit the article on the basis of which the GDR guarantees to the Soviet Union the use of military and nonmilitary facilities, including transport and communications, that were being used on the date the agreement was signed. Further divergencies exist regarding the movement of Soviet troops.[5] Such movement can allegedly occur in Hungary and Poland only with consent of the host government and with plans made in advance. The GDR agreement provides a general understanding on maneuver areas but says nothing about troop movements. Again, the treaties with Poland and Hungary require the consent of the host governments to changes in the strength of Soviet military formations and to relocation of garrisons, whereas in the treaty with the GDR, only consultation is needed.

The treaty with Hungary is essentially the same as the one with Poland, except that the latter is much more elaborate. For example, its Article 5 reads:

The regulations on entry and exits of Soviet troop units and members of the Soviet armed forces and their families into Poland or from Poland as well as questions concerning types of required documents in connection with their stay on the territory of the People's Republic of Poland will be governed by a special agreement between the contracting parties.[6]

Table 56

EAST EUROPEAN BILATERAL TREATY SYSTEM, 1988

(treaties of friendship, cooperation, and mutual assistance)

	USSR	GDR	Czechoslovakia	Poland	Romania	Bulgaria	Hungary
USSR	—	7 October 1975	6 May 1970	8 April 1965	7 July 1970	14 May 1967	7 September 1967
GDR	7 October 1975	—	17 March 1967	15 March 1967	1 October 1970	7 September 1967	18 May 1967
Czechoslovakia	6 May 1970	17 March 1967	—	1 March 1967	16 August 1970	26 April 1968	14 June 1968
Poland	8 April 1965	15 March 1967	1 March 1967	—	12 November 1970	6 April 1967	16 May 1968
Romania	7 July 1970	1 October 1970	16 August 1970	12 November 1970	—	19 November 1970	24 February 1971
Bulgaria	14 May 1967	7 September 1967	26 April 1967	6 April 1967	19 November 1970	—	10 July 1969
Hungary	7 September 1967	18 May 1967	14 June 1968	16 May 1968	24 February 1971	10 July 1969	—

Sources: Malcolm Mackintosh, *The Evolution of the Warsaw Pact*, Adelphi Papers, no. 58 (London, June 1969), p. 25; *Pravda*, 7 May 1970; *Krasnaia zvezda*, 8 July 1970; East Berlin radio, 1 October 1970; Bucharest radio, 12 November 1970; Sofia radio, 19 November 1970; Bucharest radio, 24 February 1971; Jean-Pierre Brule, "Le Pacte Varsovie a 20 ans," *Est & Ouest* (16–30 April 1975), pp. 2–16; East Berlin radio, 7 October 1975; *The Military Balance 1988–1989* (London, September 1988).

In contrast, the Hungarian treaty simply refers to an agreement on the strength of Soviet troops and the places where they will be stationed.

Finally, the treaty with Poland differs from the other two by introducing a reference (in Article 15) to a special agreement defining "lines of communication, dates, orders, and compensation conditions for transit of Soviet troops and war materiel across the territory of the People's Republic of Poland."

The USSR-Czechoslovak agreement[7] differs from the others in that it is based on the consent of the governments in Bulgaria, Hungary, East Germany, Poland, and Czechoslovakia for some of the Soviet forces already in the country, as a result of the (August 1968) Warsaw Pact invasion. It states that all other military units of WTO allies will be withdrawn over a period of two months and that the temporary presence of Soviet forces "does not violate the sovereignty" of Czechoslovakia (Article 2). However, USSR troops, families, and other civilians are "exempted from passport or visa control when entering, remaining in, or leaving the Czechoslovak Socialist Republic" (Article 4).

A different problem is posed by Albania, which has been outside the bloc since Khrushchev attacked its leadership in October 1961 at the 22d CPSU congress. Although it was not expelled from the Warsaw Pact, Albania refused to attend sessions of its Political Consultative Committee. Since the ouster of Khrushchev two attempts had been made to bring Albania back into active participation, without success. In January 1965 Tirana rejected an invitation, extended by the Polish regime, to attend the seventh meeting of the committee in Warsaw. Exactly one year later, an invitation from the same source proposed that Albania send a delegation to a meeting of communist parties from Eastern Europe and "socialist" countries from Asia to discuss the coordination of military aid for North Vietnam. The following month, the official Albanian news agency published the texts[8] of both the brief invitation and the lengthy refusal. On 13 September 1968, Tirana radio announced Albania's official withdrawal from the WTO because troops of the pact's member states had invaded Czechoslovakia. A week later, Albania protested an alleged concentration of Soviet troops in Bulgaria.

USSR leader Brezhnev informed his party's Central Committee in September 1965 that changes in the military alliance of the pact countries were under consideration. He stated,

> With a view to improving the activity of the Warsaw Treaty Organization, it is necessary to establish within the framework of this pact a permanent and operational mechanism for the evaluation of current problems. The complex international situation forces us to pay special attention to problems of military collaboration with the [other] countries of socialism. A great effort is taking place according to the following plan: standardization of equipment is being implemented, exchange of combat training experience [has been developed], and joint maneuvers are being conducted.[9]

It was not until 17 March 1969, at the Budapest meeting of the WTO's Political Consultative Committee, that certain agreements appeared to implement the "permanent operational mechanism" suggested by Brezhnev. This 110-minute conference agreed to establish a new WTO Defense Council and a Committee of Defense Ministers. (See Chart 1.) Since that time few details have been released on the functioning of these two organs.

The Committee of Defense Ministers reportedly "exchanges experience obtained by the armed forces of member states, coordinates tasks concerning members, and works out proposals serving the effectiveness of joint defenses." The highest military organ of the WTO, the Committee of Defense Ministers, includes the commanding officer of the alliance and his chief of staff, as well as general staff heads from member armed forces. The Convention on the Legal Competence, Privileges and Immunities of the Staff and Other Organs of the United Armed Forces of the Member States of the Warsaw Pact (signed 24 April 1973) is the basis for circumventing both the Political Consultative Committee and the Committee of Defense Ministers. It also permits the USSR to bypass national command authorities of other WTO member states.[10]

CHANGES WITHIN THE WTO

Established from the outset as a highly centralized system, the Warsaw Pact has had only four commanding officers to date. Marshal Ivan S. Konev of the Soviet Union was succeeded in July 1960 by Andrei A. Grechko, who also held that highest military rank in the Soviet armed forces and later became the defense minister. Grechko's successor as WTO commander, Ivan I. Yakubovskii, who was also a marshal of the Soviet Union, died on 30 November 1976. He was replaced on 8 January 1977 by the 55-year-old Soviet chief of staff Viktor G. Kulikov, who was promoted to marshal six days later. There have been five chiefs of staff for the WTO Unified Armed Forces Command, all of them career Soviet officers: Aleksei I. Antonov, who died in office; Pavel I. Batov, who succeeded him in October 1962; Mikhail I. Kazakov, from late 1965 to August 1968; Sergei M. Shtemenko, until his death in April 1976; and, since October 1976, Anatoly I. Gribkov,[11] all generals of the army in rank.

Batov was a Khrushchev man who reportedly strove for rapid integration of pact armed forces along supranational lines. Kazakov commanded Soviet troops in Hungary for four years after the 1956 revolution. He had been in charge of several military districts, most recently the one at Leningrad. His task may have included bringing Eastern Europe into line with Soviet military reorganization. Shtemenko's appointment came only two weeks before the invasion of Czechoslovakia. At one time he had served as Stalin's head of military intelligence, and later he was chief of the general staff in Moscow. Gribkov,

Chart 1 WARSAW PACT STRUCTURE, 1988

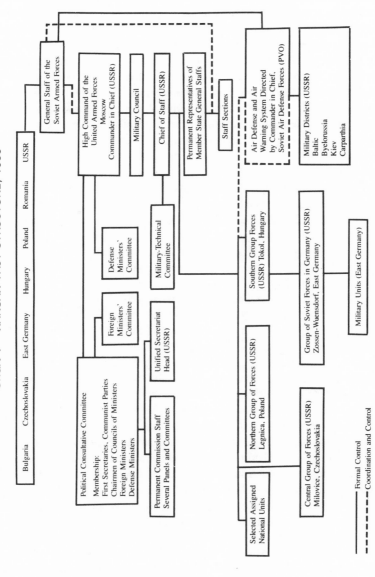

```
Bulgaria   Czechoslovakia   East Germany   Hungary   Poland   Romania   USSR
```

General Staff of the Soviet Armed Forces

Political Consultative Committee
Membership:
First Secretaries, Communist Parties
Chairmen of Councils of Ministers
Foreign Ministers
Defense Ministers

High Command of the United Armed Forces
Moscow
Commander in Chief (USSR)

Military Council

Chief of Staff (USSR)

Permanent Representatives of Member State General Staffs

Staff Sections

Foreign Ministers' Committee

Defense Ministers' Committee

Unified Secretariat Head (USSR)

Permanent Commission Staff Several Panels and Committees

Military-Technical Committee

Air Defense and Air Warning System Directed by Commander in Chief, Soviet Air Defense Forces (PVO)

Military Districts (USSR)
Baltic
Byelorussia
Kiev
Carpathia

Northern Group of Forces (USSR) Legnica, Poland

Central Group of Forces (USSR) Milovice, Czechoslovakia

Southern Group Forces (USSR) Tokol, Hungary

Group of Soviet Forces in Germany (USSR) Zossen-Wuensdorf, East Germany

Military Units (East Germany)

Selected Assigned National Units

———— Formal Control
‑ ‑ ‑ ‑ Coordination and Control

SOURCES: Based on CIA, *Directory of USSR Ministry of Defense and Armed Forces Officials* (Washington, D.C., October 1986), pp. 10–13; IISS, *The Military Balance 1987–1988* (London: Autumn 1987), pp. 46–53; U.S. Department of Defense, *Soviet Military Power, 1988* (Washington, D.C., April 1988), pp. 106–18.

at the age of 57, was transferred from the command of the Leningrad military district.

In 1969, the East European defense ministers joined their Soviet counterpart as members of a new committee of defense ministers, and the East European deputy defense ministers became deputy WTO commanding officers. (See Table 57.) As can be noted from their appointment dates, changes have indeed occurred in the top-echelon military personnel during recent years, with the exception of Bulgaria. One reason may be that many of these defense ministers either received their training in the USSR or have had careers as political commissars rather than as professional military officers. This probably makes them seem more reliable in the eyes of the Soviet leadership and more dependent on advisers sent from Moscow.

Table 57
WARSAW PACT DEFENSE MINISTERS, 1988

Name	Rank	Country	Appointed defense minister
Siwicki, Florian	General of the Army	Poland	November 1983
Vaclavik, Milan	Colonel General	Czechoslovakia	January 1985
Kessler, Heinz	General of the Army	East Germany	December 1985
Milea, Vasile	Colonel General	Romania	December 1985
Dzhurov, Dobri Marinov	General of the Army	Bulgaria	March 1962
Karpati, Ferenc	Colonel General	Hungary	December 1985

SOURCE: RFE, *East European Leadership List* (15 January 1988), pp. 6–41.

On the other hand, a definite rotation system can be seen in the Russian military commands in pact countries where Soviet forces are stationed. The commanders in East Germany, Army General B. V. Snetkov; in Poland, Colonel General I. I. Korbutov; in Hungary, Colonel General A. A. Demidov; and in Czechoslovakia, Lieutenant General E. A. Vorob'ev were identified during 1988 in their positions.[12] These men are not permitted to stay abroad for extended tours of duty, lest they develop an attachment to the local milieu.

Not all the functions of Soviet military commanders are known. They do represent a symbol of USSR power in the four countries involved and they no longer seem averse to publicity. Their photographs appear from time to time in Soviet military newspapers, as do articles by them, and their positions are not concealed. The main contacts between the USSR commanding officers and the regimes in Poland, Hungary, East Germany, and Czechoslovakia are probably the local defense ministers. Representatives of the member countries are stationed at WTO headquarters in Moscow, and routine communications go through them.

Strategic Planning. WTO was at first devised and regarded by the USSR as a defensive alliance, the forward area of which would provide a buffer and absorb an anticipated NATO attack. This attitude, however, has undergone a drastic transformation, resulting in a qualitative buildup of the East European armed forces. The change can be seen from a scenario implemented during quadripartite maneuvers in the German Democratic Republic. Former pact commander Marshal Grechko, in an interview with Tass, stated,

> One must above all note the uniform military doctrine of the socialist countries united in the Warsaw Pact. . . In case of aggression, our armies are ready not to conduct a passive defense but to engage in active military operations, which could be immediately transferred to the territory of the enemy. The armies of the Warsaw Pact countries also adhere to a uniform tactic of battleground action. As to armament, it has been standardized to a considerable degree. . . Consistently, the methods of army training have been almost identical.[13]

The 1965 maneuvers, code named October Storm, included Soviet, East German, Czechoslovak, and Polish military units among the 10,000 troops involved and provided substance for Grechko's remarks. Blue aggressors crossed the GDR border in the southwest and attacked Red defending forces. Concrete plans for such a NATO blitzkrieg supposedly envisage a general direction of attack toward

> Eisenach—Erfurt—Karl Marx Stadt [Chemnitz], as far as the upper reaches of the Neisse [River], then swinging north, in order to wrench the GDR out of the socialist camp within 36 to 48 hours. It was argued [by NATO] that if accomplished facts were created so quickly, a world war could be avoided by, as it were, a police action.[14]

In the course of October Storm, however, the Blue offensive was stopped, and the aggressor, "like a cornered beast," decided to risk all by using tactical atomic warheads. Responding "in greater numbers and with more powerful calibers of nuclear weapons," the Red side struck at the firing potential and troops of the aggressor. Nearly one thousand Polish paratroopers were transported by Antonov-designed AN–22 transports to the drop zone.[15] Their mission included the capture of an airfield near Erfurt and a subsequent attack on the enemy force from the rear.

The Red defenders advanced toward a strategically important bridge that had been identified by reconnaissance as being intact. "In the very last moment, when Blue forces were retreating already, West German workers disarmed a demolition crew and saved the bridge." Marshal Grechko and all of the pact defense ministers attended as observers. The same high-ranking officers witnessed Operation Vltava, which was held in Czechoslovakia during the fall of 1966 with Soviet, East German, Hungarian, and Czechoslovak troops. Some three hundred nuclear warheads of a tactical nature were exploded under simulated conditions by both sides.[16]

Subsequent multilateral maneuvers (see Table 58) also employed large-scale landings from the air that preceded, or occurred simultaneously with, attacks by armored and motorized rifle formations in division strength.[17] These massed forces, moving at speeds of between 70 and 75 kilometers per day, attempted to exploit the element of surprise with the objective of annihilating NATO troops that had survived the initial nuclear strikes.

That this doctrine is of an offensive nature is shown clearly in an article by the GDR's first deputy defense minister, which repeats the remarks of the late Marshal Grechko quoted earlier. Writing in Russian for Soviet military leaders, the East German said,

> The national mission of the NVA [GDR National People's Army] is to be prepared and able to . . . destroy the aggressor on his own territory by decisive, offensive action together with [other] brotherly socialist armies and to assist progressive forces in West Germany to liquidate the imperialist system [in that country].[18]

The fact that Soviet military doctrine is being implemented and that the East European "allies" have a subordinate role in this strategy can be seen from the provision of advanced surface-to-surface missiles capable of carrying nuclear warheads as standard equipment for all WTO armies at present and from Russia's continued insistence on control over these weapons. The modern T-72 battle tank has been deployed in Eastern Europe, and production under license begun in Czechoslovakia.[19]

Decisionmaking.   Only 21 meetings of the WTO Political Consultative Committee took place from 1956 through mid-1988, although 64 meetings should have been convened during this period on the basis of two per year, as the pact statute set forth. Table 59 gives data on the subjects considered at these sessions. The published communiqués deal mainly with issues of propaganda significance, but important questions are no doubt dealt with as well. As an example, the committee meeting held during 25–26 November 1976 at Bucharest issued a draft treaty[20] prohibiting the first use of any nuclear weapons and proposed a freeze on membership in opposing military blocs. It also established a new committee of foreign ministers and broadened the scope of the "unified secretariat."

The 25th anniversary meeting in May 1981 issued a predictable declaration, expressing support for Soviet positions. The declaration in part repeated Soviet proposals for a world treaty on renouncing force, ending the production of nuclear weapons and their gradual reduction, and banning radiological, nuclear, and chemical weapons tests. The WTO also called for the earliest possible convening of a worldwide summit conference to discuss the elimination of international tension and the prevention of war.

During the Political Consultative Committee meeting at the end of May 1987 in East Berlin, all previous Soviet arms control proposals were repeated. In addition, a separate statement proclaimed that Warsaw Pact military doctrine was defensive, that WTO members would never start hostilities or use nuclear weapons first, and that the bloc had no territorial claims in Europe or elsewhere.[21]

Even less is known about the operations of the Military Council, which was established in March 1969. It has held meetings about twice a year, with official announcements mentioning only discussions related to "further strengthening the troops and staff training of Warsaw Treaty states." The meeting at Kiev, for example, discussed "current activity of the Joint Armed Forces and adopted some [unspecified] coordinated recommendations."[22] The latest such gathering (5–8 July 1988) discussed questions pertaining to the current activity of the Joint Armed Forces.

Apart from positions within their own armed forces, no East European military officer heads any top-level WTO organ or command. Air defense for the entire area has been integrated under a Soviet commander who has been, since 1987, General of the Army I. M. Tret'iak, the director of the equivalent armed forces branch in Moscow. The officer in charge of the USSR army, General of the Army Ye. F. Ivanovskii, probably commands the Warsaw Pact ground forces, as he does those of most of the Soviet Union. WTO air and naval units are under Aviation Marshal A. N. Efimov, chief of the USSR's air force, and Fleet Admiral V. N. Chernavin, who commands the Soviet navy.[23]

Despite the fact that no top WTO position is held by any East European, it is probable that at least the defense ministers (all of whom have probably had Soviet training) are given the feeling of participation in decisionmaking. The situation has changed since the time when 32 former Soviet general officers in the Polish army, together with Poland's defense minister, the former Marshal of the Soviet Union K. K. Rokossovskii, returned to Moscow toward the end of 1956 "with the gratitude of the Polish nation." Several, however, remained in high positions in Poland after that date. They included Lieutenant General J. Bordzilowski, first deputy defense minister and chief inspector for training; Major General J. Urbanowicz, third deputy defense minister and chief of political indoctrination; and Vice Admiral Z. Studzinski, ex-navy commander.[24] These three positions were among the more sensitive within the military hierarchy of Poland. They are occupied today by native-born Polish citizens.

Many of the East European officers have attended military schools in the USSR, and this may provide them with a common experience, if nothing else.

Table 58
MULTILATERAL WTO MANEUVERS, 1961–1988

Dates	Code name	Area	Participants
28 September –10 October 1961	Storm	CSSR,* GDR, Poland	CSSR, GDR, Poland, USSR
5–10 October 1962	Baltic/Oder	GDR, Poland, Baltic coast	GDR, Poland, USSR
9–14 September 1963	Quartet	Southern GDR	CSSR, GDR, Poland, USSR
15–20 September 1964	Unnamed	Bulgaria	Bulgaria, Romania, USSR
16–23 October 1965	October Storm	Southwest GDR	CSSR, GDR, Poland, USSR
19–23 September 1966	Vltava	Southwest CSSR	CSSR, GDR, Hungary, USSR
20–27 August 1967	Rodopy	Bulgaria, Romania, USSR, Black Sea	Bulgaria, Romania, USSR
20–30 June 1968	Shumava	Northern Bohemia, CSSR	CSSR, GDR, Hungary, Poland, USSR
24–28 September 1969	Oder/Neisse	Western Poland, GDR, Baltic Sea	CSSR, GDR, Poland, USSR
12–18 October 1970	Brotherhood-in-Arms	GDR	all WTO members (Romanian observers)
13–18 September 1971	Fall Storm	Northern GDR, CSSR	GDR, Poland, USSR
4–16 September 1972	Shield-72	CSSR	CSSR, GDR, Hungary, Poland, USSR; WTO staff
9–16 September 1976	Shield-76	Poland	CSSR, GDR, Poland, USSR
16–19 May 1979	Shield-79	Hungary	Bulgaria, CSSR, Hungary, USSR (Romanian observers)
7–11 September 1980	Brotherhood-in-Arms	GDR, Baltic	all WTO members (Romanian observers)
17 March–7 April 1981	Union-81	CSSR, GDR, Poland, USSR	CSSR, GDR, Poland, USSR

25 September–1 October 1982	Shield-82	Bulgaria, Black Sea coast	all WTO troops (except Romania)
30 May–9 June 1983	Union-83	CSSR, GDR, Poland, Baltic Sea	CSSR, GDR, Poland, USSR
21–22 February 1984	Union-84	Bulgaria, Hungary, Romania (map exercise), USSR, Black Sea	Bulgaria, Hungary, Romania (no troops), USSR
4–10 September 1985	Friendship-85	Baltic coast of Poland	GDR, Poland, USSR
8–12 September 1986	Friendship-86	CSSR, GDR	CSSR, Hungary, USSR
27–31 July 1987	Friendship-87	Poland	GDR, Poland, USSR
8–15 April 1988	Friendship-88	GDR	GDR, Poland, USSR

SOURCES: [Federal Republic of Germany], *Arbeitsgruppe Kriegsbild 2: Wapa Manoever*, through 1979; *Facts on File* (1980), p. 696, (1981), p. 151; *YICA 1982*, p. 526, *1983*, pp. 390–91, *1984*, p. 421, *1985*, p. 384, *1986*, pp. 393–94, *1987*, pp. 401–2, *1988*, pp. 378–80; East Berlin radio, 29 March 1988, in *FBIS–Eastern Europe*, 30 March 1988, p. 18, announcing Friendship-88. Christopher D. Jones, *Soviet Influence in Eastern Europe* (New York, 1981), pp. 301–9; Jeffrey Simon, *Warsaw Pact Forces* (Boulder Colo., 1985), pp. 219–34.

NOTES: *Czechoslovakia.

Bilateral war games and command post exercises regularly took place during the above years, although no multilateral maneuvers apparently occurred in 1973–1975 or 1977–78.

Table 59

WARSAW PACT, POLITICAL CONSULTATIVE COMMITTEE MEETINGS, 1956–1988

Number	Place	Date(s)	Proposals and decisions
1	Prague	27–28 January 1956	*Approved:* Statute for United Military Command; admitted GDR; established Standing Commission and Secretariat
2	Moscow	24 May 1958	*Proposed:* Nonaggression pact with NATO; summit meeting *Approved:* Withdrawal of USSR troops from Romania
3	Moscow	4 February 1960	*Proposed:* Atom-free zone and cessation of nuclear tests
4	Moscow	28–29 March 1961	*Proposed:* Universal disarmament
5	Moscow	7 June 1962	*Discussed:* Albanian refusal to cooperate with WTO
6	Moscow	26 July 1963	*Discussed:* Status of pact armed forces and coordination of training
7	Warsaw	19–20 January 1965	*Discussed:* Possible multilateral nuclear force within NATO and "appropriate countermeasures"
8	Bucharest	4–6 July 1966	*Proposed:* Reduction of tensions through military détente; conference on security in Europe
9	Sofia	6–7 March 1968	*Discussed:* Vietnam conflict; nonproliferation of nuclear weapons
10	Budapest	17 March 1969	*Approved:* Military Council and Committee of Defense Ministers
11	Moscow	20 August 1970	*Approved:* Moscow-Bonn treaty
12	East Berlin	2 December 1970	*Discussed:* European security, Vietnam, Middle East, Guinea
13	Prague	25–26 January 1972	*Approved:* Agenda for conference on peace, security and cooperation in Europe (CSCE); statement on Vietnam
14	Warsaw	17–18 April 1974	*Approved:* Statements on Middle East, Vietnam, mutual force reduction, CSCE
15	Bucharest	25–26 November 1976	*Proposed:* Treaty on no first use of nuclear weapons and freeze on current membership in military alliances (NATO and WTO)

16	Moscow	22–23 November 1978	*Discussed:* Greater military integration in the pact and increased military spending
17	Warsaw	14–15 May 1980	*Proposed:* Conference on military détente and disarmament in Europe
18	Prague	4–5 January 1983	*Proposed:* East/West nonaggression pact
19	Budapest	10–11 June 1986	*Proposed:* Conventional force reductions between Atlantic and Urals
20	East Berlin	28–29 May 1987	*Proposed:* Ban on chemical weapons, Balkan nuclear force zone, effective verification
21	Warsaw	15–16 July 1988	*Proposed:* Peace initiative based on Jaruzelski's plan

SOURCES: U.S. Senate, Committee on Government Operations, 89th Cong., 2d sess., *The Warsaw Pact: Its Role in Soviet Bloc Affairs* (Washington, D.C., 1966), p. 32, on the first seven meetings; *Krasnaia zvezda*, 8–9 July 1966, 10 March 1968, 18 March 1969, 21 August 1970, and 3 December 1970, for others; Lawrence Caldwell, "The Warsaw Pact: Directions of Change," *Problems of Communism* (September–October 1975), p. 5; Moscow radio, 28 November 1976; "Developments in Warsaw Pact Forces," *Strategic Survey* (London, 1980), p. 105; V. F. Mal'tsev (ed.), *Organizatsiia Varshavskogo Dogovora* (Moscow, 1980), pp. 221 and 266; *Pravda*, 7 January 1983, 12 June 1986, 30 May 1987; 17 July 1988.

NOTE: The first PCC general secretary since 1966 was N. P. Firiubin, a USSR deputy foreign minister. Since his death in early 1983, the position has rotated among all WTO members. The current incumbent is Henryk Jaroszek, deputy foreign minister of Poland, according to Moscow radio, 2 March 1988; *FBIS-Soviet Union*, 3 March 1988.

Integration of command obviously requires a single language. Here the chosen one is Russian, a knowledge of which represents a prerequisite for training in the Soviet Union. Bulgarians, Czechoslovaks, and Poles have found Russian relatively easy to learn because of its similarity to their own tongues. It has proven more difficult for East Germans, Hungarians, and Romanians because their languages are not related to the Slavic group. Learning has proceeded rapidly, however, as ignorance of Russian presents an obstacle to obtaining higher military command positions within the armed forces of the individual East European military establishments. Russian expressions have penetrated the military vocabularies of most of the countries within the Soviet bloc.

Execution of Decisions.   The WTO Unified Command, which has its headquarters in Moscow, theoretically correlates and orders the implementation of decisions reached by the representatives of the deputy commanders (that is, of the bloc countries' defense ministers) who make up the staff of this headquarters.

Under the program, the entire East German army and certain other national contingents have been specifically earmarked for WTO service. Although these groups have never been openly identified, it is probable that only elite units are assigned, such as the regiment from the sixth Pomeranian Parachute-Assault Division stationed near Krakow in Poland, which participated in operation October Storm. Its commanding officer, who was at that time 39-year-old Colonel Edwin Rozlubirski, was the subject of a biographic sketch that appeared, along with his photograph, in the daily newspaper of the Soviet Defense Ministry.[25] The twelfth Mechanized Division and a brigade of frontier troops in Poland have also reportedly been assigned specifically to WTO.

The transfer of Soviet troops from the western parts of the USSR to a place outside its borders by any means other than air might have presented some difficulty, although surmountable to be sure, owing to the limited number of interchange points between broad-gauge USSR and standard-gauge East European railroad lines. These points reportedly existed 27 years ago only at Zheleznodorozhny, Brest-Terespol, Przemysl-Medyka, Chop-Zahony, Iasi, and Galati.[26] In the meantime the number of these points must have increased, with a corresponding expansion in machinery for loading and unloading. The construction of secondary railroad links and transmountain lines has been noted. Traffic management is centralized through the Council for Mutual Economic Assistance (CMEA).

In the mid-1960s, CMEA started building a network of automobile expressways to link the major cities in Eastern Europe with Moscow and Kiev.[27] The Permanent Commission for Transportation of the CMEA has the task of coordinating this ambitious scheme. Another project involved the expansion of the 1,900-mile petroleum pipeline that links the Volga-Ural oil fields with Poland, East Germany, Czechoslovakia, and Hungary. All of the WTO members including

Romania are to a great extent dependent on the USSR in this respect, as the next chapter mentions. Oil remains indispensable for moving modern armies, and its delivery from the Soviet Union has facilitated the organization of joint maneuvers.

Credit for the idea of joint maneuvers has been claimed by the communists in Poland:

> Initiated by our [Polish] side, joint field exercises by the armies of Warsaw Pact countries have become permanent. Our troops, staffs, and commands annually train on land, on sea, and in the air with troops, staffs and commands from brotherly armies: the Soviet Army, the Czechoslovak People's Army, and the GDR National People's Army.[28]

It is noteworthy that until Operation Vltava (1966), the Hungarians had never trained with the Czechoslovaks. This may have been due not only to the events of 1956 but also to the fact that about one million ethnic Hungarians lived in Czechoslovakia between the wars and many still reside there. Nationality differences cause friction that could lead to incidents during joint field exercises. Except for Czechoslovaks and Bulgarians, the East European populations have traditionally been hostile to the Russians for good historical reasons. Even so, none of the communist sources mentions any Soviet dissatisfaction with the performance of troops from the bloc countries during maneuvers. On the contrary, the defense minister of Czechoslovakia even applauded the invasion of his own country in August 1968 by "troops from five fraternal states."[29] Such cooperation has extended even to the smuggling of weapons.

The merchant marines of the East European countries have been utilized for the delivery overseas of military equipment. One instance came to light in which the captain of the Bulgarian vessel *Veliko Tirnovo* was fined 5.4 million Lebanese pounds (about $1.75 million) in Beirut for the attempted smuggling of 1,500 automatic rifles. The official Bulgarian news agency argued, "It is a well-known fact that the carrier is not held responsible for the content of the commodities shipped and declared in the bill of lading,"[30] as if the Navibulgare, in owning the ship, were not a state-controlled enterprise.

Although the destination of these rifles (which were possibly intended for Kurds) was not revealed, it is known that Bulgarians had also been selling weapons to royalist forces in Yemen. Some $25 million in Saudi-Arabian gold reportedly had been paid for these weapons, many of which were channeled through the Bulgarian military attaché in Paris. One such shipment was seized by the French when a chartered transport airplane carrying rifles from Belgium landed at Djibouti in former French Somaliland (territories of Afars and Issas).

Czechoslovak weapons have been received clandestinely on Cyprus. Little information can be found about similar arms shipments during the past several years, although submachine guns, ammunition, and grenades from bloc countries were found on Marxist terrorists in Iran. Apart from creating a future dependence for spare parts and bringing in foreign exchange, supplying arms to insurgents contributes to instability, and this in turn creates new communist opportunities to advance Soviet influence throughout the underdeveloped countries of the world. The total value of Warsaw Pact arms transfers during 1982–1986 reached almost $17 billion (not including $86 billion from the USSR).[31]

In addition to facilitating the secret sale of arms, attachés from East European countries also engage in espionage on behalf of the USSR. Three of these men (Monat, Tykocinski, and Kuklinski) defected to the West and have spoken about their experiences.[32] Monat handled reports from all Polish military attachés and forwarded them to Moscow via his office. Tykocinski corroborated the existence of this system and disclosed that for a period of time a career Soviet officer had functioned as chief of Polish military intelligence. Most recently, Kuklinski revealed the extent of USSR influence on the December 1981 proclamation of martial law in Poland.

Another example of military espionage is provided by the extensive operations of East European agents in the Federal Republic of Germany. During 1987 the number of efforts at the recruitment of informants increased only slightly, but many persons were still convicted of high treason or treasonable relations by the federal constitutional court at Karlsruhe and the appellate tribunals in that country. Most of the cases involved GDR intelligence, but Poland, Romania, Hungary, Czechoslovakia, and Bulgaria—not to mention the USSR—all actively engage in espionage.[33]

Soviet Forces in Eastern Europe.   With the exception of Poland and Czechoslovakia, all of the bloc countries have had a so-called Soviet Consultative Group as an element of WTO activity. The rights and privileges of individuals belonging to the group have allegedly remained concealed in various secret agreements. The effectiveness of this operation in Hungary obviously could be guaranteed by the presence of USSR troops. Group members functioned as military advisers.

Before 1956 this Soviet organization in Hungary reportedly controlled both logistics and the armaments industry, with each headed by a deputy defense minister who had a Soviet officer with the rank of colonel as an adviser. The defense minister, his deputies, and these USSR advisers reportedly comprised the "military collegium" in the ministry. The same system applied to the general staff. Each section of the general staff (operations, intelligence, organization and mobilization, military installations, service regulations, military geography, communications, technology and transportation, air force, anti–air defense, civil defense, training, and logistics) included at least one Soviet staff officer as adviser. To each Weapons Inspectorate—armored and motorized troops, air force, communications units, artillery, engineers, ABC (atomic, biological, and chemical) weapons—was attached a Soviet colonel or general and two to four other Soviet officers as assistants.

Similar arrangements supposedly prevailed in the military districts and in each regiment. At the corps level, one senior Soviet officer is said to have controlled operations and the other logistics. It is reported, further, that each of the eleven frontier guard district commands had a Soviet officer and several aides assigned to it and that the entire political indoctrination system within the Hungarian armed forces was directed by a high-ranking USSR officer and six other advisers.[34]

In Bulgaria, on the other hand, Soviet advisory activities were conducted with considerable restraint. Both the main political administration of the armed forces and the military intelligence section may still have Soviet observers. These officers also served as unit advisers, mostly at the division level, although their network had previously extended into the regiments. Each motorized rifle and armored division reportedly had on its staff a Soviet officer with the rank of lieutenant colonel or major under whom four or five others functioned as instructors. Certain armored regiments and operational squadrons of the Bulgarian air force (possibly those assigned to WTO) still have Soviet advisers attached to them.

Among the reasons for these differences between Hungary and Bulgaria was the 1956 revolution in Budapest. There has been nothing comparable in Sofia because the Bulgarians have been consistently loyal to the USSR. Another reason is probably Bulgarian national pride: the people would resent any openly exercised foreign command. A third reason amounts to a corollary of the others. Key positions in the military hierarchy were staffed by natives of Bulgaria who trained as officers in the USSR and resumed their original citizenship on returning home after the war. These officers have included former

Defense minister, Army General Ivan Mikhailov

Chief of the general staff, then first deputy defense minister, later head of the Administrative Organs Department in the Central Committee, Colonel General Ivan Bachvarov, killed in an airplane crash at Bratislava

Commander of the Bulgarian navy and ex-Soviet naval officer, formerly deputy defense minister and chief of civil defense, Admiral Branimir Ormanov

Commandant of the general staff academy, trained as an officer in the USSR and currently chairman of the Committee for Solidarity with Asia and Africa, Colonel General Slavcho Stamenov Trunski

Commander of the Sofia garrison and later head of the Main Political Administration in the armed forces, graduate of both the "Frunze" and the general staff academy in the USSR, currently chief of the ruling party's Central Committee department for social and national security policy, Lieutenant General Velko Ivanov Palin.[35]

In Czechoslovakia, the Soviet advisers for the most part control industries that produce weapons and war matériel for the armed forces of other bloc countries. The use of USSR personnel in training Czechoslovak troops produced an extensive organization called the Soviet Satellite Coordination Command,[36] which preceded the 1955 military system alliance. References have appeared to USSR general officers as representatives of the Joint Supreme Command of the Warsaw Pact armies in the capital cities of member countries, with the exception of Romania.

In Poland it was not necessary to establish a Soviet military mission at all. Some 17,000 USSR officers directed the Polish armed forces after transferring from the Red Army and accepting citizenship in the country to which they had been detailed.[37] Following the change in communist party leadership at Warsaw in October 1956 mentioned above, many of these men returned to the USSR. The functions of those who remained consisted of observing, giving advice, and serving as liaison officers, as well as securing communications with Soviet troops stationed in Lower Silesia (Poland) and East Germany. The situation in the GDR need not be discussed. With approximately nineteen USSR divisions on East German territory, there is no doubt about who remains in control.

By contrast, Romania presents a picture of greater independence from the USSR than does any other bloc state. Military service was reduced to sixteen months in 1964, and since 1966 Bucharest reportedly has balked at permitting WTO maneuvers or even meetings of its Political Consultative Committee to be held in its own country. The Soviet military mission is said to number only two or three men today, compared with fifteen or sixteen in the past. However, staff officers from the USSR and Romania have held map exercises in Bucharest, and the WTO Political Consultative Committee finally did convene its fifteenth session there. Nevertheless, following the November 1978 Political Consultative Committee meeting in Moscow, Ceausescu declared that Romanian troops would never obey foreign commands but only those of their own communist party.[38]

Soviet troops are garrisoned in four of the Warsaw Pact states. In Poland, there is the Northern Group of Forces, with its headquarters at Legnica in Lower Silesia; in Hungary, the Southern Group of Forces, at Tokol near Budapest; in Czechoslovakia, the Central Group of Forces, at Milovice; and in the GDR, the Group of Soviet Forces in (East) Germany, with its headquarters at Zossen-Wuensdorf near East Berlin. The generally accepted figures for these forces outside the borders of the USSR are respectively two, four, five, and nineteen divisions.[39] An approximate one-to-one ratio of armored to motorized rifle divisions among these Soviet units shows a considerably heavier concentration of firepower than prevails in the indigenous East European armed forces. (See Table 60.)

In East Germany, Soviet troops outnumber those permitted the GDR regime by a ratio of almost 3.5 to 1, but in tanks and aircraft the preponderance is

Table 60
DATA ON WARSAW PACT ARMED FORCES, 1987

Country	MANPOWER			EQUIPMENT			EXPENDITURES	
	Army	Air	Navy	Tanks	Combat aircraft (including helicopters)	Vessels (including submarines)	Defense budget 1986 (billion $)	Est. GNP 1985 (billion $)
Bulgaria	105,000	35,000	8,500	1,950	300	86	1,656	40.0
Czechoslovakia	145,000 (80,000)	56,000	—	3,500	468	—	4,426	96.0
East Germany	123,000 (380,000)	40,000	16,000	2,800 (1,600 storage)	407	142	6,865	126.0
Hungary	83,000 (65,000)	22,000	—	1,360	167	—	2,440	48.4
Poland	295,000 (40,000)	88,000	19,000	3,570	687	163	6,874	149.0
Romania	150,000	32,000	7,700	1,430	378	180	1,327	90.0
USSR	1,991,000*	453,000**	451,000	52,000	5,150†	1,960	23,400	1,765.0

SOURCES: International Institute for Strategic Studies, *The Military Balance, 1986–1987* (London, November 1986), pp. 31–54; U.S. Department of Defense, *Soviet Military Power, 1987* (Washington, D.C., March 1987), pp. 91–93. See also Keith Crane, *Military Spending in Eastern Europe* (Santa Monica, Calif., May 1987), especially tables.

NOTES: *Only 565,000 are located in Central and Eastern Europe, as given in parentheses. Total also includes Soviet forces in the western military districts of the USSR proper that would reinforce those deployed against NATO.

**Excluding long-range Air Force

†Tactical only

somewhat less. However, East German armed forces have been equipped with Frog-7- and Scud-B-type ground-to-ground rockets, with the latter employing a guided missile. They are being supplied by the Soviet Union to GDR forces at division and army levels, respectively, and are allocated to the artillery. These weapons have the capability of delivering nuclear warheads over distances of up to 185 miles. It is doubtful that the USSR would allow the East Germans[40] to assume control over atomic warheads, however.

According to a former commander of the Soviet forces in the GDR, after 1965 his troops underwent a process of regrouping. Missile and armored units were added but other types were withdrawn. Russian antiaircraft defense SA-2 batteries were being phased out, but SA-4, SA-6, and SA-8 units remain. The main centers of concentration for Soviet troops since the reorganization are in the area around Suhl in Thueringen, the province of Brandenburg, and territories along the GDR's borders with Czechoslovakia and Poland.

Such regroupings have brought these USSR troops closer to Czechoslovakia, where five Soviet divisions are stationed and where it is important that the uranium mines at Jachymov, Teplice, and Pribram remain protected, as well as those in adjacent East Germany south of Aue. The output of this strategic material goes to the USSR, in amounts that remain secret. The closer disposition of USSR troops to Poland provides for better contact with the two Soviet divisions in Lower Silesia. This will allow for a rapid linkup between forces in the event of other crises, such as those in 1956 and 1968 in which Polish and Czechoslovak troops, respectively, proved unreliable from the communist point of view.

The 1980–1981 crisis in Poland culminated with the indigenous armed forces occupying their own country during mid-December, after proclamation of martial law. The WTO commander in chief made several visits to Warsaw, and Soviet troops carried out extended maneuvers both east and west of Poland, which suggested a capability to intervene if necessary.[41]

The redeployment of USSR forces in East Germany may have been the result of plans for more flexibility in potential countering operations should hostilities break out in Central Europe. These troops had formerly been concentrated along the frontier between East and West Germany in several parallel lines, from Lue-beck in the north to the border with Czechoslovakia at Hof in the south. The new scheme will presumably permit the deployment of Soviet troops in echelons following an east-west direction, with most of them concentrated along the Oder and Western Neisse rivers.[42]

In Hungary, although indigenous forces are almost 25 percent greater than those of the Soviet Union, the USSR maintains a preponderance of two to one in armored divisions and about three to two in aircraft. Besides serving to prevent a repetition of the 1956 rebellion, Soviet troops ensure the delivery of uranium from the Hungarian mines at Pecs. It should be noted, however, that ground-to-ground missiles were displayed at a military parade in Budapest only nine years after the revolution. All of the other Warsaw Pact states have also been equipped with these. In addition, Soviet MIG-21 delta-wing fighter interceptors and Iliushin medium-range bombers belong to the inventories of all East European alliance members.

According to the then first secretary of the Hungarian communist party, Janos Kadar, the presence of Soviet troops is in conformity with domestic as well as international law. Speaking to his parliament, he declared,

> [The USSR armed forces are] an immense help for our people, because if these troops were not here, we would be forced to keep more soldiers under arms at the expense of the living standard, because the fatherland is more important and stronger than the living standard! [Further,] the presence of Soviet troops in Hungary has no internal reason. It depends on the international situation alone . . . We are not afraid of the withdrawal of Soviet troops, but we do not support any unilateral withdrawal, and this is in the interest of the international political situation.[43]

Twelve years ago, in reply to a question regarding Soviet troops, Kadar asserted that a continued USSR presence depended on "the general situation in world politics" and expressed the hope that all foreign troops would be withdrawn in the future.[44]

CHANGES IN SOVIET CONTROL

Penetration by Soviet nationals into the East European military establishments has definitely decreased over the past two decades. For instance, whereas at one time virtually all of the high positions in Poland's armed forces were held by former Soviet officers "fulfilling the duties of Poles," this rarely occurs today. Although it would be difficult to show where the loyalty of these officers lies, the case of K. K. Rokossovskii may be illuminating. He came to Warsaw in November 1949 as defense minister and remained exactly seven years. After that, he returned to Moscow and resumed his rank as marshal of the Soviet Union. Apparently not having lost any seniority, he was made a USSR deputy defense minister, perhaps in reward for services rendered while he was on detached duty in Warsaw.

Military Intelligence in Eastern Europe.   Only sparse information is available about intelligence operations in the WTO countries. Close cooperation, and perhaps even a superior-subordinate relationship, between the counter-espionage establishments of the Soviet Union and one of its client states became evident with the arrest of British subject Greville Wynne jointly by Soviet and Hungarian security services at Budapest and his subsequent trial with Soviet Colonel O. V. Penkovskii in Moscow.[45]

An even more significant and openly admitted role was played by Soviet intelligence during the arrest of plotters against the Bulgarian regime. Communist journalists in Sofia received a briefing on the conspiracy that was "uncovered by Soviet intelligence agents." One of the ten men involved committed suicide. The others, five army officers and four civilians, were sentenced to prison for high treason. In the first announcement of the plot, only three persons were mentioned, and all three had belonged to the "Gavril Genov" partisan detachment during World War II. At least one other had also fought in a guerrilla unit.[46] The fact that most of those tried had been high-ranking military officers on active duty would appear to indicate strong army involvement in the plot.

A further case of collaboration between the Soviet and East European intelligence services appeared in connection with the purge of Aleksandar Rankovic in Yugoslavia. His subordinates in the security apparatus, which he had controlled, were accused of having "too close links" with their Soviet counterparts.[47] Nothing regarding these charges was made public at the subsequent plenum of the Central Committee. It should be recalled, however, that Greville Wynne lost a notebook at a Belgrade hotel that later turned up in Moscow during the trial of Colonel Penkovskii.

Military Production.   As a source of war matériel, the most important geographic area in Eastern Europe is the Czechoslovakia-GDR-Poland industrial triangle. All three states encompass a human pool of skilled technicians, have precision equipment, and possess modern scientific research facilities, especially in nuclear physics. That the USSR hesitates to permit sophisticated military production can be seen from the decision taken at the fourteenth CMEA session that discontinued the East German manufacture of four-engine turbojet aircraft already in the testing stage.[48]

On the other hand, Eastern Europe is of great value to the Soviet Union as a source of uranium in several countries; bauxite for the production of processed aluminum in Czechoslovakia; basic chemicals, rare metals of particular importance for nuclear energy programs, and bismuth mined in association with uranium in East Germany; metallic sodium from a Silesian plant in Poland for the construction of nuclear reactors; cadmium, which is used in regulating the speed of nuclear reactions, in both Poland and the GDR; molybdenum for the production of crucially important matériel in Bulgaria and Poland; and titanium used in nuclear technology and graphite required for nuclear reactors in Poland. It should also be mentioned that the CMEA includes a defense industry commission[49] within its framework, designated as Military-Technology Committee on Chart 1.

PARTY CONTROL OVER THE MILITARY

Political controls by local regimes do not appear to have been altered significantly. The primary party organization, however, does comprise a separate hierarchy. Delegates representing the individual military districts attend national party congresses. The criteria for admission to communist party membership are the same for officers and enlisted men as for civilians. Apparently, it is still a prerequisite for promotion to the rank of colonel that an officer be a member of the ruling party. In all WTO countries, between 80 percent and 90 percent of the regular officers belong to the party or its youth affiliate.[50] This high percentage should not be equated with reliability, which is always difficult to measure.

The only hard figures on defections come from the Federal Republic of Germany, and these involve GDR military personnel who flee across the frontier. For example, some East German battalions of border troops had as many as fifteen successful escape attempts and twenty failures during 1965. A total of 1,850 East Germans soldiers, including 466 border guards, defected in the first five years after the construction of the Berlin Wall.[51]

The Bulgarian military conspiracy mentioned earlier perhaps indicates dissatisfaction in that country with its subordination to the USSR. Soviet decision-makers in a war situation probably would not plan to employ jointly Polish and East German, Czechoslovak and Hungarian, or Romanian and Hungarian troops in actual combat, even though combined maneuvers have taken place over the past several years. In the case of Romania, these have involved command post exercises with maps and no troops.

CHANGES IN POPULAR SUPPORT

Almost 30 years ago researchers at the University of Warsaw polled a representative sample of the city's inhabitants regarding their opinions of the military officer profession as a career.[52] The prestige of the armed forces has probably risen somewhat since then. Compared with the pre-1939 period, however, when officers in the Polish military stood at or near the top of the career scale, at the time of this poll they ranked 14th financially, below lathe operators; 16th in job security, below accountants; and 21st in social prestige, below office supervisors.

Only one similar investigation is known to have been made public about any other East European regime.[53] Apart from this limited indication of changed attitudes, it seems likely that the lack of any tradition in the Soviet bloc has reduced the attractiveness of a military career among officers and enlisted men alike. Communist propaganda classifies the pre-1939 armies in Eastern Europe as either feudal or fascist. The riots in East Germany (1953), the Hungarian revolution (1956) and the events in Poland at the same time (when local units in both states took up defensive positions against the threat of Soviet troop intervention), the complete immobility of Czechoslovak forces (1968), and the refusal of the regular Polish army to fire upon demonstrators (1970, 1976, and 1980–1981) all proved that morale has not been high from the communist point of view.[54]

A recent study concludes that enough functional integration exists, however, to provide military reliability in case of a war with the West. On the other hand, only the senior East European officers have developed attitudinal loyalty toward the USSR. The rank and file, including junior officers, are totally nonreceptive to attitudinal integration.[55]

MUTUAL AND BALANCED FORCE REDUCTIONS (MBFR)

The Warsaw Pact also has performed a valuable function for the Soviet Union in international arms control negotiations. NATO in June 1968 proposed mutual force reductions at the Reykjavik meeting of its foreign ministers. Five years later, on 31 October 1973, negotiations commenced in Vienna. In the West the area affected involves the territories of the Federal Republic of Germany and the Benelux states and in the East Czechoslovakia, East Germany, and Poland.[56] The seven direct NATO participants include Belgium, Canada, West Germany, Luxembourg, the Netherlands, Great Britain, and the United States. The corresponding WTO side has only four: Czechoslovakia, East Germany, Poland, and the USSR. Observer status has been given for the West to Denmark, Greece, Italy, Norway, and Turkey, and for the East, to Bulgaria, Romania, and Hungary.

After almost fifteen years of negotiations, no agreements have been concluded. Talks continue, however, to preserve a channel of communication and to serve as a forum to discuss confidence-building measures. These negotiations are significant as the only existing ones on a bloc-to-bloc basis, helping both sides to maintain cohesion among their allies.

Key issues of disagreement involve (1) data problems, the West arguing that the East underestimates its figures by more than 200,000 men; (2) whether military manpower ceilings should be collective or by individual country; (3) types of forces to be included in the reductions, for example, only ground troops or all categories as favored by WTO; (4) the issue of linkage and a dispute over phases in an agreement; (5) associated measures, to build confidence for eventual verification. Each side blames the other for lack of progress. The USSR claims that the October 1979 announcement of Brezhnev on unilateral withdrawal of 20,000 troops and 1,000 tanks from the GDR, allegedly completed by July 1980, should be considered as a significant reduction and become part of an MBFR agreement. According to an authoritative source, ''the socialist countries have no more important foreign policy task than the active defense of peace and détente and the struggle for a radical improvement in the international atmosphere and the curbing of the arms race."[57]

Parallel with the MBFR talks, representatives of the two alliances began separate meetings in February 1987 to discuss a mandate for a new set of negotiations that would lead to arms reductions between the Atlantic and the Urals. More than one year later, no agreement had been reached on the specific objective or parameters of the new talks, even though the Federal Republic of Germany had presented a proposal for conventional arms stability in the expanded geographic area.[58] These Conventional Stability Talks would replace MBFR.

FUTURE DEVELOPMENTS

Trends and goals remain difficult to project, but it is quite clear that the WTO has changed its emphasis radically from a defensive to an offensive posture. This trend probably will continue, unless Soviet military doctrine itself undergoes a fundamental transformation.

Such a change has been proclaimed by the WTO Political Consultative Committee with a statement on 29 May 1987 proclaiming that (1) Warsaw Pact military doctrine is defensive, (2) member states would never commence hostilities or use nuclear weapons first, and (3) WTO has no territorial claims either in Europe or elsewhere. However, since that time, there has been no attempt by the East to reconfigure its offensive warfare deployments facing NATO.

Over more than three decades from 1956 into 1988, the military equipment and the training of WTO forces have developed consistently in one direction: toward preparation for a war in which it is conceivable to the USSR High Command that nuclear weapons may be used. The Soviet military hierarchy certainly would not knowingly allow an opponent endowed with nuclear warheads to apply the element of surprise and to initiate hostilities. However, increasing attention has been paid to the conventional option: "While working out methods for waging combat under conditions of nuclear war, Soviet military science does not exclude the possibility of combat operations being waged with only conventional weapons."[59]

Soviet military doctrine probably also anticipates a possible conflict in Central Europe within the next decade involving a confrontation between the main forces of NATO and the WTO. Beginning with Soviet strategic nuclear strikes, ground operations would be launched simultaneously by massive armored and motorized rifle divisions in conjunction with airborne units employed on a large scale. These movements, at speeds of up to 75 kilometers per day, would be supported by battlefield nuclear weapons, unless, of course, the conflict remained at the conventional level.

The role of WTO members in such a war can be seen in broad outline even today. For example, Soviet conflict managers are making a concentrated effort to woo Turkey away from the Western alliance. If Greece, where a parallel diplomatic offensive is being carried on by Bulgaria, and Turkey can both be neutralized so that their membership in NATO will become ineffective, the WTO could then concentrate on the main enemy: the Federal Republic of Germany. Such WTO members as Bulgaria, Hungary, and Romania, located in the strategically less important "southern tier" (which are not powerful and not particularly reliable, except for Bulgaria), could be eliminated from the Kremlin's contingency plans.[60]

The Warsaw Pact would then base its military plans on the GDR and Poland as the main allies of the USSR. The continuous barrage of propaganda against the Federal Republic of Germany, especially in Poland, has had the obvious purpose of maintaining a war psychosis that is fed by the fear of a Nazi resurgence and a new *Drang nach Osten*. Since the 12 August 1970 Moscow-Bonn treaty on the renunciation of force, this fear has become muted, but it still exists.

Even so, it is doubtful that Polish or East German troops would be allowed to operate independently in any conflict. As part of Soviet fronts (groups of armies), they would fight with USSR units on both flanks and in the rear. The performance of the WTO will depend ultimately on the specific military situation. Should NATO be dissolved, WTO forces could march to the Atlantic with little or no opposition.[61]

NOTES

1. Boris Meissner (ed.), *Der Warschauer Pakt: Dokumentensammlung* (Cologne, 1962), p. 12. A translation of the Warsaw Treaty into English appears in *United Nations Treaty Series*, CCXIX, Part I, p. 24. N. N. Rodionov et al. (eds.), *Organizatsiia Varshavskogo Dogovora: 1955–1975* (Moscow, 1975), published documents and materials on the WTO, including the treaty.

2. *Pravda*, 31 October 1956.

3. On the withdrawal of Soviet troops from Romania see Guenther Wagenlehner, "Die politische Bedeutung des Warschauer Paktes," *Soldat und Technik* (March 1965), p. 115.

4. Meissner, *Der Warschauer Pakt,* p. 128. For an English translation of the status-of-forces treaties see the RFE report, "Agreements on Soviet Forces Stationed in Czechoslovakia, the GDR, Hungary, and Poland," 24 October 1968.

5. Kazimierz Grzybowski, *The Socialist Commonwealth of Nations* (New Haven, Conn., 1964), p. 205. The most recent Soviet-GDR treaty appears in *Neues Deutschland,* 8 October 1975; the Russian text can be found in *Izvestiia* of the same date.

6. Meissner, *Der Warschauer Pakt,* p. 118. See also Christopher D. Jones, *Soviet Influence in Eastern Europe* (New York, 1981).

7. *Krasnaia zvezda*, 19 October 1968; English translation in RFE report, "Agreement on Soviet Forces," pp. 1–8.

8. Tirana radio, 12 February 1966.

9. *Krasnaia zvezda*, 30 September 1965.

10. For some information on these bodies, see V. I. Menzhinskii (ed.), *Mezhdunarodnye organizatsii sotsialisticheskikh gosudarstv* (Moscow: 1980), pp. 37–38. An analysis of the 1973 convention appears in Jones, *Soviet Influence in Eastern Europe*, pp. 133–37.

11. Gribkov's appointment was broadcast over Moscow radio on 12 October 1976; the announcement also included a short biographic sketch.

12. R. F. Staar, "The Warsaw Treaty Organization," *Current History* (November 1987), p. 359, and current identifications from the Soviet press.

13. Moscow radio, 21 February 1966.

14. Deutschlandsender (East Berlin), 31 October 1965.

15. Warsaw radio, 21 October 1965.

16. "Pr." (Colonel Erich Pruck), "Erkentnisse aus dem Manoever Moldau," *Wehrkunde* (December 1966), p. 662.

17. Graham H. Turbiville, Jr., "Soviet Bloc Maneuvers," *Military Review* (August 1978), pp. 19–34.

18. Admiral Waldemar Werner, "Ten Years of the GDR National People's Army," *Kommunist vooruzhennykh sil* (February 1966), p. 78. See also GDR Defense Minister Heinz Hoffman, "Streitkraefte in unserer Zeit," *Einheit* (March 1976), pp. 354–363.

19. John Erickson, "The Warsaw Pact," in M. M. Drachkovitch (ed.), *East Central Europe: Yesterday, Today, Tomorrow* (Stanford, Calif., 1982). *The Military Balance, 1987–1988* (London, 1987), p. 46.

20. Moscow radio, 26 November 1976, gave the text.

21. V. F. Mal'tsev (ed.), *Organizatsiia Varshavskogo Dogovora: Dokumenty i materialy 1955–1980* (Moscow: Politizdat, 1980), pp. 266–87 and 285–86; *Pravda*, 30 May 1987.

22. Moscow radio, 27 May 1976.

23. Harriet Fast Scott, "Top Leaders of Soviet Armed Forces," *Air Force Magazine* (March 1988), p. 60.

24. Studzinski later became deputy chief of staff for the WTO unified command. *Trybuna ludu*, 8 May 1970. His death was announced by Warsaw radio on 8 March 1976.

25. Yezhi Lentsut [Jerzy Lencut], "The Commander of Airborne Infantry," *Krasnaia zvezda*, 21 August 1965. Another example might be the Fifth Army Corps of Hungary, which in August 1968 helped to invade Czechoslovakia. The late General Shtemenko had stated in "Combat Fraternity," *Krasnaia zvezda*, 24 January 1970, that troop contingents have been allocated by member states for WTO joint armed forces.

26. Hanns von Krannhals, "Leadership Integration in the Warsaw Pact Area," *Military Review* (May 1961), pp. 50–51.

27. Stefan C. Stolte, "Comecon's Nineteenth Conference," *Bulletin of the Institute for Study of the USSR* (May 1965), p. 21.

28. Marshal Marian Spychalski, speech at the fourth congress of the Polish communist party, *Trybuna ludu,* 18 June 1964.

29. Colonel General Martin Dzur, "Loyalty to the Immortal Ideas," *Krasnaia zvezda,* 20 February 1970. The Soviet air force scattered aluminum foil along the Czechoslovak-West German border so that movements of its ground and airborne troops would be difficult to detect by NATO electronic devices. *New York Times,* 13 September 1976.

30. Sofia radio, 2 February 1966.

31. U.S. Arms Control and Disarmament Agency, *World Military Expenditures and Arms Transfers, 1987* (Washington, D.C.: 1988), p. 134.

32. Pawel Monat, with John Dille, *Spy in the U.S.* (New York, 1962), especially pp. 104–12; U.S. House of Representatives, Committee on Un-American Activities, 89th Cong., 2d sess., *Testimony of Wladyslaw Tykocinski* (Washington, D.C., 1966). More recent information has come from Michael Goleniewski in the *Washington Star,* 17 May 1981 and R. J. Kuklinski, "War Against the Nation," in the Polish-language Paris monthly *Kultura* (April 1987), pp. 3–57.

33. Friedrich Zimmermann, *Verfassungsschutzbericht, 1987* (Bonn, Bundesinnenministerium, 1988).

34. Thadaeus Paschta, "Das System der sowjetischen Militaerberater in den Satelliten-staaten," *Wehrkunde* (September 1962), pp. 496–99, is the source for much of the following information. See also F. Rubin, "The Hungarian People's Army," *Journal of the Royal United Services Institute for Defence Studies* (September 1976), pp. 59–66.

35. [United States], *Directory of Bulgarian Officials* (Washington, D.C., August 1969), p. 23; (September 1975), pp. 30–31; (January 1979), pp. 11–17 and 29; (October 1986), pp. 12 and 66. See also names of Bulgarian generals who had fought during World War II in the Soviet army, as given by *Narodna armiia* (Sofia), 23 February 1988, pp. 1 and 3.

36. Krannhals, "Leadership Integration," p. 44.

37. *Zycie i mysl,* no. 10 (October 1964).

38. "Romania–Documents–Events," *Agerpres,* no. 46 (1978), p. 14.

39. International Institute of Strategic Studies, *The Military Balance 1987–1988* (London, September 1987), p. 41. For an order of battle see [Federal Republic of Germany], *Streitkraefte Vergleich 1987: NATO-Warschauer Pakt* (Bonn, December 1987), pp. 47.

40. Teresa Rakowska-Harmstone, Christopher D. Jones, and Ivan Sylvain, *Warsaw Pact: The Question of Cohesion* (Ottawa, November 1984), Phase II, vol. 2, pp. 323–26.

41. As reported by Kuklinski, in "War Against the Nation."

42. In the decade between 1967 and 1977, the USSR added 130,000 men, increased the number of tanks by 40 percent and conventional artillery by 50 to 100 percent in the GDR, according to an interview that NATO commander General Alexander M. Haig, Jr., gave *U.S. News & World Report* (17 January 1977), pp. 35–37. See also *Streitkraefte Vergleich 1987.* Soviet figures for both sides are given by Lev Semeiko, "Once More about Assymetry," *Moscow News,* no. 12 (1988), p. 6.

43. Kossuth radio, 11 February 1965. See Also Charles Fenyvesi, "Hungary 20 Years Later," *New York Times Magazine* (17 October 1976), pp. 32–33, 101–9.

44. *New York Times,* 8 December 1976.

45. Oleg Penkovskiy, *The Penkovskiy Papers* (New York, 1965), pp. 373–75.

46. A discussion of this case appears in John D. Bell, *The Bulgarian Communist Party from Blagoev to Zhivkov* (Stanford, Calif., 1986), pp. 125–26.

47. *New York Times,* 22 July 1966.

48. *Pravda,* 5 March 1961. On Soviet control, see Hans Joachim Berg, "Ursachen, Entwicklung und Auswirkungen der sowjetischen Hegemonialstelling in Warschauer Pakt," *Politische Studien* (May–June 1976), pp. 267–80. See also *Streitkraefte Vergleich 1987,* especially pp. 42–43.

49. Revealed by Prague radio, 17 January 1969. This may have been the Weapons and Equipment Standardization Group to coordinate military technology, mentioned by the Hungarian defense minister Lajos Czinege in *Nepszabadszag,* 10 May 1969.

50. *Krasnaia zvezda,* 11 April 1975.

51. *Soldat und Technik* (April 1966), p. 202. See also *Die Welt* (2 December 1976) on the 30th anniversary of GDR border troops.

52. A. Sarapata and W. Wesolowski, "Evaluation of Occupation by Warsaw Inhabitants," *American Journal of Sociology* (May 1961), pp. 583–85. See also the more recent article by Sarapata, "Social Mobility," *Polish Perspectives* (January 1966), especially table 1, p. 20, regarding the prestige of occupations, including that of army officer.

53. Jaroslav Krejci, *Social Stratification in Postwar Czechoslovakia* (London, 1988), p. 99.

54. A posthumously published article by the former WTO chief of staff indicates that pact troops would be used to suppress "counterrevolutionary activities" throughout Eastern Europe, with the 1968 example of Czechoslovakia specifically listed. S. M. Shtemenko, "Brotherhood Born in Combat," *Za rubezhem* (Moscow), 7–13 May 1976, pp. 6–7.

55. Rakowska-Harmstone et al., *Warsaw Pact,* phase II, vol. 1, p. v.

56. James A. Thompson and Nanette C. Gantz, "Conventional Arms Control Revisited: Objectives in the New Phase," in *A Rand Note* (Santa Monica, Calif., December 1987) N-2697-AF, 17 pp.; Richard F. Staar, "The MBFR Process and Its Prospects," in R. F. Staar (ed.), *Arms Control: Myth versus Reality* (Stanford, Calif., 1988), pp. 47–58.

57. *Pravda,* 6 July 1981.

58. Iu. B. Kashlev, head of Soviet delegation, over Moscow television, 19 February 1988; *FBIS-Soviet Union,* 23 February 1988, p. 9. See also the article by Lothar Ruehl in *Die Welt,* 16 March 1988, p. 6, for the new FRG proposal.

59. Major General I. Ye. Krupchenko et al., *Voennaia istoriia* (Moscow, 1971), p. 345. [Major General] Jan Sejna, *We Will Bury You* (London, 1982), pp. 205.

60. One of these contingency plans reportedly involves the crossing of Austria and the military occupation of Yugoslavia. See the two-part interview with the Czechoslovak defector, Major General Jan Sejna, "Moskaus Aufmarschplaene gegen Oesterreich," *Profil* (Vienna), 14 and 21 February 1974, pp. 39–43 and 29–35. See also his book *We Will Bury You.*

61. Major General Robert Close, who commanded the Belgian Sixteenth Armored

Division in the Cologne area, stated in his *Europe Without Defense?* (New York, 1979), p. 278, that the USSR has the capability of occupying the Federal Republic of Germany within 48 hours. See also Michael Sadykiewicz, "Soviet-Warsaw Pact Western Theater of Military Operations: Organizations and Missions," *A Rand Note* (Santa Monica, Calif., August 1987), N-2569-AF, 174 pp.

Chapter 10
Economic Integration: CMEA

Before World War II most of Eastern Europe's economies could be classified as primarily agricultural. With roughly four-fifths of the population living in rural areas and more than half of the gainfully employed engaged in agriculture, the entire region was almost self-sufficient in food and the small requirement for manufactured goods was met by the limited output. The one exception, Czechoslovakia, did have certain lines of industry that were highly developed. Elsewhere, the growth of a strong industrial working class and of a middle class of private entrepreneurs in the urban centers lagged by comparison.

The military occupation of certain East European states and the transformation of others into Nazi satellites during the war altered the economies in some areas. Under compulsion to turn out matériel for the Wehrmacht and help supply the domestic needs of the Third Reich, the industries of Czechoslovakia, Hungary, and what is today East Germany underwent considerable expansion. Romania served primarily as a producer of agricultural commodities and petroleum. On the other hand, Bulgaria and Poland were allowed to stagnate. All of the countries suffered war damage, but Czechoslovakia emerged with relatively less destruction than the others.[1] All eventually became satellites of the USSR.

For almost a decade after the war the economies of the satellite states remained under the tight control of the Soviet Union. They were even discouraged from developing economic links among themselves. Most major business transactions had to be cleared through Moscow. Following the death of Stalin, however, a change took place. A meeting in March 1954 of the Council for Mutual Economic Assistance (CMEA), also known as Comecon, recommended the coordination of all national economic plans within the bloc. The CMEA, which had been set up by the USSR at the beginning of 1949 as a response to the Marshall plan, had been dormant until then.

The founding communiqué from Moscow indicated that the six charter members included the Soviet Union, Bulgaria, Czechoslovakia, Hungary, Poland, and Romania.[2] Subsequently five other countries were admitted: Albania (1949), East

Germany (1950), Mongolia (1962), Cuba (1972), and Vietnam (1979). At the CMEA council's fifteenth session, in December 1961, Albania's delegate announced that his government would no longer participate in any of the activities. Since that time Tirana has refused to pay its dues to the council and has not been represented at any of the meetings.[3] Yugoslavia applied for and received limited-participant status in 1965 at the nineteenth session of the CMEA council.

In addition, Finland (July 1973), Mexico (August 1975), and Iraq (July 1976) all ratified agreements of cooperation with the CMEA. These do not make them even associate members. Nevertheless, such developments do project an image of an open organization. Observer status has been granted since 1979 to Angola, Ethiopia, Laos, North Korea, and South Yemen and since 1980 to Afghanistan and Mozambique. Nicaragua has been sending observers since 1984.[4]

The date set for beginning the coordination of economic plans by all CMEA members was 1956, but the ensuing revolution in Hungary and related events in Poland during that year disrupted trade and communications over a wide area of the bloc. In the process of re-establishing control and bolstering communist regimes throughout Eastern Europe, the Soviet Union claims to have sent considerable emergency credits into the area.[5] (See Table 61.) By the end of 1958 industry had recovered, by and large, in both Hungary and Poland.

Soviet credits to the East European regimes must be repaid. In addition, the USSR seems to have followed a policy of charging higher than world market prices for certain of its exports into the bloc and of underpaying for commodities imported from this area. Information regarding Soviet credits is based on official statistics that are now being published annually by East European governments. It is apparent that these figures are subject to manipulation in ways other than straight numerical falsification. Propaganda images still represent primary motives for the fabrication of reported economic results. Internal misreporting by subordinate officials contributes to unintentional inaccuracies. Statistical inflation at higher levels magnifies the initial error, especially in agriculture.

It is true that the rapid expansion of industry made possible great increases in the gross national product (GNP) of Eastern Europe.[6] To a considerable degree, however, the increase was achieved by deliberately restricting consumption. The rates of gross investment allegedly reached 25 percent of the national income. Sustained emphasis on heavy industry, especially for defense purposes, and inadequate investments for agriculture have merely accentuated the structural imbalance that has arisen at the expense of the general standard of living.

At the beginning of 1958 indications appeared that the high rate of GNP growth was beginning to decrease. In general, the downward rate of growth for industrial output reflected a similar trend in the Soviet Union. The various five-year plans in most of the East European countries for the years 1961–1965 finally began to include reduced targets in comparison with the previous periods.

Table 61
USSR CREDITS TO EASTERN EUROPE, 1947–1985
(in millions of U.S. dollars)

Country	Years	Credits
Albania	1957–1960	65.0
Bulgaria	1954–1979	1,993.0
Czechoslovakia	1947–1979	14.0
East Germany	1954–1979	990.0
Hungary	1954–1979	348.0
Poland	1954–1981	5,215.0
Romania	1954–1979	123.0
Yugoslavia	1973–1979	848.0
Eastern Europe (all)	1980–1985	30,300.0
Total		39,896.0

SOURCES: Lucjan Ciamaga, *Od wspolpracy do integracji* (Warsaw, 1965), pp. 39–40; Marshall Goldman, *Soviet Foreign Aid* (New York, 1967), pp. 24–25; R. F. Staar (ed.), *1976 Yearbook on International Communist Affairs* (Stanford, Calif., 1976), p. 97; CIA, *Handbook of Economic Statistics, 1980* (Washington, D.C., October 1980), p. 110 (1987), p. 116.

NOTES: The figures do not include credits for defense purposes. Dollar values presumably are derived from official rates of exchange. The USSR claims to have given CMEA members through the end of 1968, "more than 10 billion rubles worth of credits and loans on favorable terms." *Trud,* 14 January 1969; *Narodna Armiia,* 29 January 1970.

In 1980, the USSR extended $4.5 billion in soft- and hard-currency credits to Poland. RFE, *Situation Report,* no. 8 (14 May 1981), p. 20. Repayment of credits equal to four billion dollars, provided Warsaw by other East European governments, has been rescheduled. *New York Times,* 30 August 1981.

The last source (1980–1985) gives a breakdown by year but not by country.

Average increments of national income were now envisaged at 6 or 7 percent a year except in Bulgaria and Romania, where growth rates were to be much higher. Apart from Hungary, the average increase before the decline had been 8 percent annually. Even these more limited targets for 1961–1965 were not attained by most of the countries. (See Table 62 for official figures.)

Although they represent the most industrialized states within the area of Eastern Europe, both the German Democratic Republic and Czechoslovakia suffered from acute economic problems in the first half of the 1960s. During the sixth congress of the Socialist (communist) Unity Party in January 1963 at East Berlin, a substitute seven-year plan was unveiled for the 1964–1970 period. Index figures showed that the preceding plan had been dropped. The new targets for national income, industrial production, and labor productivity were lower than those of the unfinished 1959–1965 plan.

Table 62
GROWTH IN PRODUCED NATIONAL INCOME (1971–1987)

	1971–1987 NATIONAL INCOME (PERCENT CHANGE)					1985 NATIONAL INCOME		1986 NATIONAL INCOME	
	1971–1975	1976–1980	1981–1985	1986	1987	(in billions of dollars)	(percent change)	(in billions of dollars)	(percent change)
Bulgaria	7.9	6.1	3.7	5.5	5.1	61.2	-3.2	6,800	2.2
Czechoslovakia	5.6	3.7	1.8	3.2	2.0	143.9	0.2	9,280	1.2
East Germany	5.4	4.1	4.5	4.3	4.0	187.5	2.4	11,300	2.1
Hungary	6.3	3.2	1.4	0.5	2.0	84.0	-2.4	7,920	1.6
Poland	9.7	1.6	-0.8	5.0	2.0	259.8	0.3	6,930	2.3
Romania	11.3	7.2	4.4	7.0	4.8	137.5	0.5	6,030	5.1
USSR	5.7	4.3	3.6	4.1	2.3	2,356.7	0.2	8,370	3.2
Yugoslavia*	5.9	5.7	0.6	-0.2	2.0	145.0	-0.4	6,220	3.0

SOURCES: *U.N. Economic Survey of Europe in 1985–1986* (New York, 1986), p. 116; CIA, *Handbook of Economic Statistics, 1986* (Washington, D.C., September 1986), p. 40; *1987* (September 1987), pp. 25, 40; *Życie gospodarcze* (Warsaw), No. 12, 1988.

NOTE: *Yugoslavia is only an associate member of CMEA.

A similiar situation had developed earlier in Czechoslovakia, which announced in the middle of 1962 that its five-year plan would be abandoned. After a twelve-month interim period, a new seven-year plan for the years 1964–1970 was introduced, as in East Germany. It is clear that Czechoslovakia, which experienced a 4 percent decline in national income during 1963 and only a 1 percent increase in 1964, had failed to become the show window of Eastern Europe. The aftermath of the August 1968 invasion involved more debts to bolster a faltering economy, and only 1970 could be proclaimed the year of economic consolidation.

FORCED INDUSTRIALIZATION

A basic CMEA document that was adopted by the sixteenth council session laid down authoritative guidelines for the economic integration of industry along the following lines: "Socialist industrialization, with the principal emphasis being placed upon heavy industry and its core, engineering, is the main path toward the elimination of technical and economic backwardness."[7] This belief is basic to most East European communist thinking. The results could be observed in the establishment, at a heavy cost to the populations involved, of modern industries in areas that more often than not remained short of raw materials. Despite the admission of excesses during the early 1950s, heavy industry still leads in investments and, indeed, absorbs the lion's share of each annual budget, with the exception of Hungary and possibly Poland after 1988.

Thus, relatively underdeveloped Bulgaria allocated 38.5 percent of its capital investments during 1949 to industry. Twenty years later the allocation was 48 percent, amounting to more than 2.5 billion leva.[8] In a classic example, Hungary's determination to pursue "extended reproduction" is seen in the fact that 66 percent of that country's output came under the category of producer goods, with the remainder being consumer goods and food. Emphasis continues to be placed on iron and steel facilities as well as on the development of engineering projects, with some differences. Poland planned to triple production at a single Nowa Huta metallurgical complex near Krakow by 1980 to almost nine million tons of steel; this was approximately the amount that was produced in 1965 by the whole country.[9] Still, the country will be forced to rely mainly on the Soviet Union, which provides 76 percent of the iron ore used in Polish industry.

Also importing Russian coal, coke and iron ore, Romania had planned for 1975 a national output of about ten million tons of steel. The Bulgarians, proclaiming the priority of heavy industry in a country without any substantial raw materials base, produced some 1.7 million tons of steel during 1969 at their Kremikovtsi complex. From these few examples it can be seen that the development of basic industry in each country has not been molded to any great extent by supranational considerations. All of the bloc members desire steel mills, but they are not endowed with the varied or substantial raw materials base needed for heavy industry. (See Table 63.)

Still lacking an overall plan, and in most cases distrusting the "international socialist division of labor" principle, most East European states have made only uncertain steps toward commodity specialization despite the CMEA's efforts along these lines since 1960.[10] Efforts and responses have been less than wholehearted. Even bilateral projects are not developing as had been anticipated. Although the basic form of cooperation still remains the all-member approach, two other methods have evolved in practice.

Table 63
SELECTED CMEA INDICATORS, 1986

Product	Total CMEA output	USSR output	USSR percentage of total
	thousand barrels/day		
Crude oil	12,580	11,754	93.4
	million tons		
Iron ore	256.5	250.0	97.5
Pig iron	150.0	114.0	76.0
Steel (crude)	222.0	161.0	72.5
Coal (hard)	742.0	513.0	69.1
Grain	303.0	210.1	69.3
Cement	195.0	135.0	69.2
	billion kwhr		
Electricity	2,080	1,599.0	76.8
	billion cubic feet		
Natural gas	25.9	24.2	93.4
	thousand megawatts		
Nuclear energy	37.3	29.3	78.5

SOURCES: CIA, *Handbook of Economic Statistics, 1987* (Washington, D.C., September 1987), pp. 29, 31, 130, 135, 138, 139, 141, 143, 151–52, 183, 189.

JOINT PROJECTS

The first of the cooperative techniques theoretically involves participation by almost all CMEA members. Such activities as the Friendship oil pipeline, the Peace electric power distribution system, the Brotherhood natural gas pipeline, the pooling of railroad freight cars, the network of expressways, two CMEA banks, and the Intermetal steel community are good examples. The very fact that not all East European countries have availed themselves of the opportunity to join these organizations remains noteworthy in itself. A hard core of six members (the USSR, East Germany, Czechoslovakia, Poland, Hungary, and Bulgaria) appears to be developing within the CMEA that leaves Romania voluntarily on the periphery and Yugoslavia maintaining only affiliated status.

Much publicity has been give to certain ambitious schemes sponsored by the CMEA. During 1981–1985 the Druzhba I pipeline planned to supply 400 million tons of petroleum from the Volga-Ural oil fields[11] to the several East European petrochemical industries. (See Table 64.) The pipeline extends some 1,900 miles from Kuibyshev through Mozyr in the western part of the USSR and Plock, Poland, to the city of Schwedt, East Germany. A branch runs southwest through Brody and Uzhgorod, USSR, and ends at Bratislava, Czechoslovakia, with a spur going south to Szaszhalombatta, Hungary; it has an annual capacity of 105 million tons. Romania also imports petroleum, but neither it nor adjacent Bulgaria contributed toward the cost of the pipeline's construction. The headquarters for the organization is at Moscow, with a Soviet director in charge.[12] More limited in nature is the Soiuz, or Union, natural gas pipeline that, during 1980, delivered approximately 15.5 billion cubic meters of this fuel to Eastern Europe from the USSR.

Table 64

SOVIET EXPORTS OF OIL AND OIL PRODUCTS, 1970–1985

(in millions of tons)

Country	1970	1975	1980	1985
Bulgaria	7.1	11.5	14.5	13.0
Czechoslovakia	10.5	16.0	20.0	15.8
East Germany	9.3	14.9	18.0	15.7
Hungary	4.8	7.6	9.1	6.6
Poland	8.6	13.3	17.4	12.9
Romania	—	—	1.5	1.9
Total	40.3	63.3	80.5	65.9 (estimates)
Soviet exports (percentage of imports)	85.8	81.8	79.0	

SOURCES: U.N. Economic Commission for Europe, "Economic Survey of Europe in 1979," mimeographed prepublication copy dated 31 March 1980, GE 80–41016, p. 101; Moscow radio, 5 June 1980, for promised deliveries to Romania; and *Ekonomicheskaia gazeta,* no. 2 (5 January 1981); Reiner Weichhardt (ed.), *The Soviet Economy: A New Course?* (Brussels: NATO, 1988), p. 138.

NOTE: Soviet sources now provide only the value of these exports in rubles, not millions of tons, for each country.

Romania and Bulgaria participate in the CMEA electric power project Mir, or Peace, which connects with the western Ukraine and specifically the city of Kiev. The first leg of a 750-kilovolt line is part of this grid. The coordinating authority is located at Prague. About eighty billion kilowatt hours of electricity were exchanged during the 1971–1975 five-year planning period.[13] The so-called Iron Gates project, which involves the construction of a hydroelectric power dam and navigation system along 60 miles of the Danube River at a cost of about $400 million, will supply Romania and CMEA-affiliate Yugoslavia with about ten billion kilowatt hours of electricity when completed.

The pooling of railroad freight cars is yet another project, one that was established in 1964 with its main offices at Prague. In 1976 it had some 250,000 units, which transported most of the commodities exchanged within the CMEA area.[14] Joint use of containers for shipping by rail is being established. A network of high-speed expressways will ultimately connect Moscow, Warsaw, and East Berlin; Warsaw and Prague; Warsaw, Krakow, and Budapest; Krakow and Brno; Moscow, Kiev, Bucharest, and Sofia; Kiev and Brno; and East Berlin, Prague, Brno, Budapest, and Bucharest. The CMEA council's Permanent Commission for Transportation is coordinating this ambitious highway project.

A joint operation that is attempting at least in part to emulate Western Europe's highly successful Coal and Steel Community is Intermetal, which was established by a 1965 agreement. Although the signing took place at Moscow, the Soviet Union did not become a charter member; the original signatories were Czechoslovakia, Poland, and Hungary. Subsequently the USSR, East Germany, and Bulgaria joined. With its head offices at Budapest, this organization has the task of modernizing CMEA steel industries and reducing the time required for production and delivery. A noteworthy provision is that Intermetal can pass resolutions that are binding on all members.[15] Perhaps that is why Romania has not become a member officially, although it does participate and benefit from the organization. Neither does the Bucharest regime belong to the CMEA unit formed earlier that directs the production of ball bearings and is administered from Warsaw nor to Interkhim, which coordinates chemical production from headquarters at Halle, East Germany.

Finally, a so-called International Bank for Economic Cooperation is in operation, headed by Vazha G. Dzhindzhikadze. The ten participating CMEA governments contributed a total of 305 million rubles to start banking. (See Table 65.) This capital is in the form of transferable rubles. The CMEA bank settles commercial accounts among member states, largely on a bilateral basis, and also grants credits to member states at 3.5 to 5.0 percent annual interest. It reported a profit of only 500,000 rubles during the first year of operation, presumably from loans, but it claimed to have had its turnover increase over fivefold, from 23 billion rubles during 1964–1965 to 151.3 billion rubles in 1978.[16]

One of the bank's problems has to do with making the transferable rubles

Table 65
CONTRIBUTIONS TO THE INTERNATIONAL BANK FOR ECONOMIC COOPERATION

Country	Capital	Percentage of total
	millions of rubles	
Vietnam	0.9	.03
Mongolia	3	.97
Cuba	4.4	1.40
Romania	16	5.20
Bulgaria	17	5.60
Hungary	21	6.90
Poland	27	8.80
Czechoslovakia	45	14.80
East Germany	55	18.10
Soviet Union	116	38.20
Total	305.3	100.00

SOURCES: *Europa Yearbook 1981*, p. 213.
NOTE: Contribution quotas were based on the volume of exports within the CMEA.

convertible, instead of using them merely as an accounting unit to settle payments among member countries. Although a decision was reached to transform 10 percent of the bank's capital into gold and hard currency, its impact has not affected East-West trade to any noticeable degree. Multiple exchange rates actually exist within the CMEA trading area itself.[17] An International Investment Bank also exists for all CMEA members. Established in 1971, it gave more than two billion transferable rubles in credit to member countries during the first seven years. Disposing of more than one billion rubles, with 30 percent in convertible currency, this bank charges between 3 percent and 5 percent interest on credits over a five- to fifteen-year period. According to board chairman Albert Belichenko, in 1988 the bank was ready to promote joint ventures.[18]

BILATERALISM AND FUNCTIONALISM

The other method of CMEA collaboration is for one member to finance projects on the territory of another. As is the case in bloc ventures overseas, medium-term credits are repayable at a low rate of 2 percent interest. The project is owned by the government on whose territory it has been constructed. Repayment usually follows in the form of deliveries from the project itself or from other sources.

There has been some recognition of the need to distribute the burden of new bilateral investments among more parties than the two that are immediately involved.

Romanian reed cellulose and Bulgarian copper represent examples of raw materials that are extracted and processed with the aid of loans from other CMEA members. Poland has developed its natural resources, coal and sulphur, for bloc needs. Czechoslovakia gave credits to help Polish mining and also for the expansion of iron ore output from Krivoi Rog, USSR. The reason for this, of course, is that Czechoslovakia's economy remains sensitive to and dependent on "outside relations." This euphemism stands for the importing of practically all its necessary raw materials.

An extension of the bilateral arrangements involves the so-called interested party or functional approach, which centers on projects that are of immediate concern to several CMEA members. Joint agreements among Czechoslovakia, Hungary, and Poland have dealt with the ferrous metallurgical industry. Other programs, in which more than two states have participated, include cooperative production of fertilizer and the development of basic fuels. In addition, intergovernmental commissions have been organized for economic and scientific-technical cooperation on a bilateral basis.

Bilateralism can also be illustrated by Polish-Czechoslovak cooperation in manufacturing farm tractors, East German and Polish joint production of high-pressure steam boilers as well as cotton textiles, and the Polish-Hungarian joint stock company called Haldex, which extracts coal from what was formerly scrapped as waste in Poland's mines. Hungary and Bulgaria have also established mixed companies, such as Agromash, for the production of agricultural machinery, as have Czechoslovakia and Bulgaria.

CMEA RELAUNCHED

Soviet leaders belatedly recognized the gathering momentum of West European economic integration and probably decided to give CMEA a new impetus. (See Chart 2.) After the 22d congress of the Soviet communist party in October 1961, the perspective shifted forward to 1980, or a time-span of twenty years. This date was to represent the beginning of a promised transition to communism. As early as March 1961, the CMEA council noted at its fourteenth session in East Berlin that member countries had begun to draw up plans that would reach two decades into the future.

Assuming that the CMEA does increasingly adopt the character of a general staff for bloc plan coordination, its work is likely to be more effective insofar as it refrains from attempts at drastic interference with national economic goals and concentrates on selected areas such as fuel and power. Local approaches to

Chart 2 CMEA ORGANIZATION, 1988

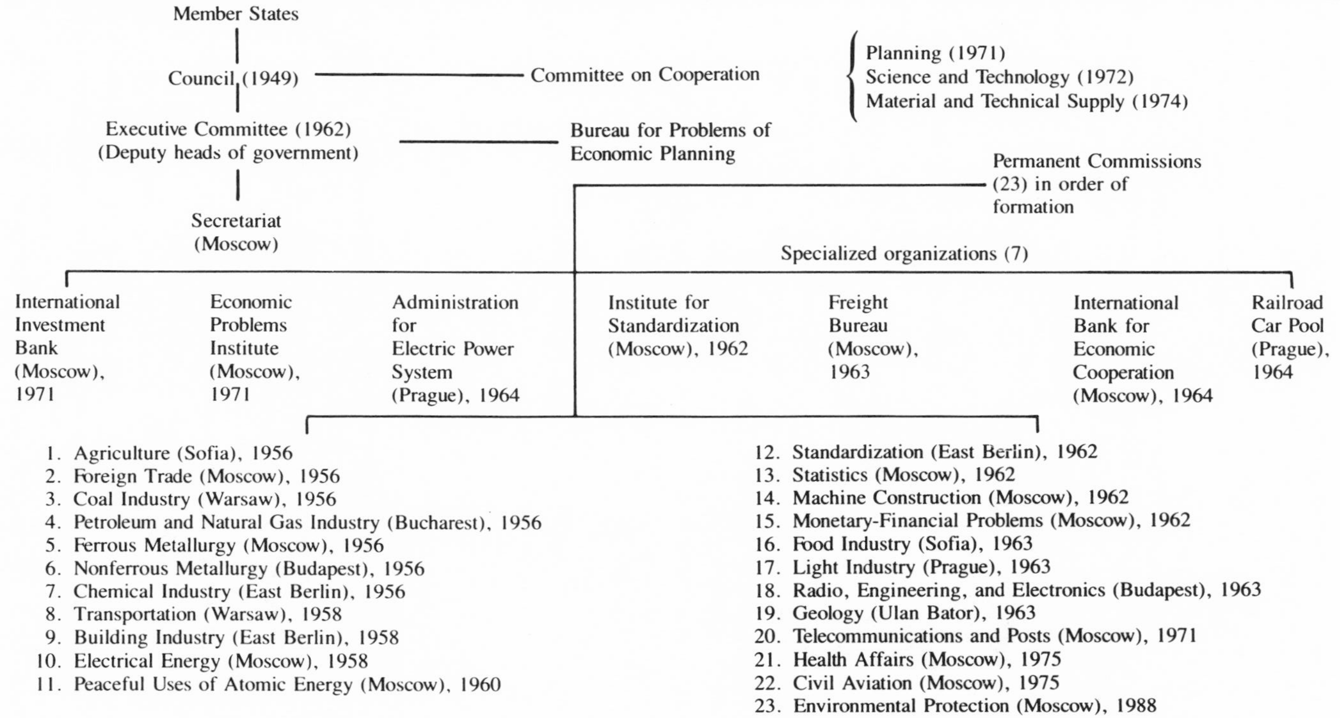

Member States

Council (1949) — Committee on Cooperation

Executive Committee (1962)
(Deputy heads of government)

Bureau for Problems of
Economic Planning

Planning (1971)
Science and Technology (1972)
Material and Technical Supply (1974)

Permanent Commissions
(23) in order of
formation

Secretariat
(Moscow)

Specialized organizations (7)

Economic
Problems
Institute
(Moscow),
1971

Administration
for
Electric Power
System
(Prague), 1964

Institute for
Standardization
(Moscow), 1962

Freight
Bureau
(Moscow),
1963

International
Bank for
Economic
Cooperation
(Moscow), 1964

Railroad
Car Pool
(Prague),
1964

International
Investment
Bank
(Moscow),
1971

1. Agriculture (Sofia), 1956
2. Foreign Trade (Moscow), 1956
3. Coal Industry (Warsaw), 1956
4. Petroleum and Natural Gas Industry (Bucharest), 1956
5. Ferrous Metallurgy (Moscow), 1956
6. Nonferrous Metallurgy (Budapest), 1956
7. Chemical Industry (East Berlin), 1956
8. Transportation (Warsaw), 1958
9. Building Industry (East Berlin), 1958
10. Electrical Energy (Moscow), 1958
11. Peaceful Uses of Atomic Energy (Moscow), 1960
12. Standardization (East Berlin), 1962
13. Statistics (Moscow), 1962
14. Machine Construction (Moscow), 1962
15. Monetary-Financial Problems (Moscow), 1962
16. Food Industry (Sofia), 1963
17. Light Industry (Prague), 1963
18. Radio, Engineering, and Electronics (Budapest), 1963
19. Geology (Ulan Bator), 1963
20. Telecommunications and Posts (Moscow), 1971
21. Health Affairs (Moscow), 1975
22. Civil Aviation (Moscow), 1975
23. Environmental Protection (Moscow), 1988

SOURCES: N. V. Faddeev, *SEV: 1949–1974* (Moscow, 1974), p. 67; RFE report (by Harry Trend), "Comecon's Organizational Structure," Part I, 3 July 1975; RFE report, "An Assessment of the Comecon 30th Session," 23 August 1976; O. A. Chukanov, *Sodruzhestvo stran-chlenov SEV* (Moscow, 1980), p. 146; Moscow radio, 31 March 1988; *FBIS-Soviet Union*, 5 April 1988, p. 4.

industrial development that have already been laid down no longer seem to be challenged. Bulgaria and Romania, for example, are not being asked to remain predominantly agricultural. Bulgarian production of some 120,000 automobiles per year after 1980 had been forecast. During 1986, however, only 18,000 cars were produced.[19]

The Soviet leaders finally must have come to realize that they cannot simply order all of the East European countries to do their bidding. The fact seems to have been recognized that not all CMEA members will "fully exploit the possibilities offered by the international socialist division of labor." Poland has proposed that certain CMEA organs should function above the authority of national sovereignty. Bulgaria and East Germany support this view. Hungary and Czechoslovakia favor reorganization but are against (guardedly, to be sure) any supranational character for the CMEA. Romania sharply opposes any kind of external economic authority, although, under the presence of the debt crisis, it has become more receptive to integration. Perhaps the greatest obstacles are the unwieldy bureaucracies that would have to be integrated.[20]

It was only in the middle of 1964 that delegates to the CMEA executive committee, meeting at Moscow, for the first time exchanged data concerning their broad intentions for the 1966–1970 planning period. At the 1970 session in Warsaw, the coordination of national economic plans was agreed upon. The communiqué[21] spoke about the adoption of concrete measures for the most important branches and types of production during 1971–1975. Subsequent coordination agreements were signed between the Soviet Union and other CMEA member states before the end of the year. The continued primacy of planning and the subordinate role of market relations would appear to indicate Soviet resistance to economic reform; if this is true, it might result in the further strengthening of the USSR's control over Eastern Europe.

One country that is affiliated with CMEA presumably has not gone so far as to reveal its planning to the others. Yugoslavia applied for affiliation in September 1964, and at that time a preliminary agreement was initialed. Ratification did not take place until early the following year, at the nineteenth council session. The limited status allows Yugoslavia to participate in a number of the permanent commissions and to attend council sessions with an advisory vote. The commissions it originally joined were foreign trade, monetary-financial problems, ferrous industry, nonferrous industry, machine construction, chemical industry, and scientific and technological development. It later joined three additional commissions[22] and now belongs to almost all of them.

The affiliated status granted to Yugoslavia may have established a precedent leading to the possible admission of other states to the CMEA. What the Soviet leader had in mind may never be known, for Khrushchev was deposed approximately four weeks after the preliminary agreement with Yugoslavia was reached. In the other direction, he had been responsible in October 1961 for the suspension of Albania from the CMEA. At any rate, it is doubtful that the CMEA will become "an open organization" or that "adequate forms exist for the participation in its work of any country which would join the basic principles of its activity," as its then general secretary declared.[23]

The current Kremlin leadership team probably believes that the economic facts of life are sufficient to keep the CMEA viable. After all, between one-half and more than four-fifths of all intrabloc trade for each East European state (except Albania) is with the Soviet Union. (See Table 66.) Intrabloc trade in 1986 totaled more than 135 billion rubles. Most of these countries also rely on Soviet deliveries of iron ore and coking coal for their steel plants, which are basic to industrial development.[24]

To achieve industrial growth, all of the CMEA members have been adopting rational techniques to a larger or smaller degree, even though many obstacles exist to economic change within the bloc. Slowdowns in growth, warehouses filled with unsold goods of inferior quality, and waste that results from central planning have contributed to a barrage of criticism against the command economy with its regimentation and inefficiency. Although the vested interest of the plant managers often may involve maintaining the status quo, interenterprise cooperative arrangements of various types have begun and probably will expand in the future.

Other obstacles to reform include (1) the lack of stability regarding the economic plans themselves, (2) the contradiction between the slow growth of agriculture and the promises of a higher living standard, and (3) the problems involved in actually drafting specific multiyear economic plans. Many of these problems came out into the open at a meeting of the CMEA council held in July 1976 at East Berlin. (See Table 67 for listing of all the sessions.)

This 30th session ended with agreement on five major sectors that were to be treated as problem areas: fuel, energy, and raw materials; machine building; agriculture and food production; light industry; and transportation. It was also agreed that targets would be established through 1990 and even longer. Joint investments called for nine to ten billion rubles during 1976–1980, with most of the projects located on Soviet territory. They included the construction of a natural gas pipeline from Orenburg, a pulp factory at Ust-Ilimsk, an asbestos mining and enrichment combine at Kiembaevskii, a 750-kilowatt line from Vinnitsa to Albertirsa in Hungary that will become the first leg of a 750-kilovolt network, nickel production in Cuba, and an isoprene rubber plant for Romania.[25] Also mentioned in the communiqué, and probably discussed in great detail, was the topic of East-West trade.

These problems also surfaced at CMEA's thirty-fifth session, although the final communiqué[26] seemed optimistic. It made special mention of achievements under the Comprehensive Program: (1) bilateral and multilateral cooperation and specialization agreements, (2) long-range target programs, and (3) joint investment programs. As had been the case during the previous four sessions,

Table 66
BLOC TRADE BY AREA, 1975 AND 1985 (EXPORTS/IMPORTS)
(percentage of total trade)

	CMEA COUNTRIES		DEVELOPED COUNTRIES		DEVELOPING COUNTRIES	
	1975	1985	1975	1985	1975	1985
Bulgaria	80.0	77.0	9.3	8.5	10.7	14.5
	72.3	72.0	23.6	15.2	4.1	7.8
Czechoslovakia	71.6	80.7	19.8	15.7	8.6	7.3
	69.8	77.0	24.6	15.3	5.6	4.0
East Germany	73.2	66.5	22.4	30.1	4.4	5.4
	66.6	64.5	29.0	28.6	4.4	4.9
Hungary	72.2	54.8	21.4	30.1	6.4	11.3
	66.2	58.6	27.0	38.1	6.8	7.1
Poland	59.9	75.8	31.5	22.4	8.6	6.8
	45.8	70.8	49.3	19.9	4.9	4.3
Romania	46.0	60.9	31.5	n.a.	22.5	n.a.
	43.5	53.3	41.9		14.6	
USSR	60.7	61.1	25.6	25.6	13.7	13.3
	52.4	61.1	36.4	27.9	11.2	11.0

SOURCES: *Statisticheskii ezhegodnik stran-chlenov SEV, 1976* (Moscow, 1976), p. 341; (1986), p. 303.

development of energy resources and the rising cost of imported fuel were discussed. Several multilateral agreements have been signed for oil, gas, electricity, and nuclear power. Under one of them, the USSR is committed to supply electric power to Eastern Europe from 1984 to 2003 at a fixed price.[27]

The first joint investment project in nuclear power is under way at Khmelnitskii in the Ukraine. This 4000-megawatt power station was completed by 1984. Two other 4000-megawatt installations were to be built on Soviet territory.[28] It is hoped that nuclear energy will lessen the dependency on imported petroleum. The USSR has informed Eastern Europe of future cutbacks in the amount of oil that can be supplied. However, long-term agreements that commit the Soviet Union already existed. For instance, the GDR received 18 million tons of oil per year until 1985 from the USSR. During the 1981–1985 five-year period, deliveries from the Soviet Union to Eastern Europe were supposed to total 400 million tons.[29]

The basic reason for the drive toward the expansion of trade with Western Europe and the United States is that all bloc countries require high-grade materials, quality equipment, and technological expertise that remain available only from the outside. Because the CMEA has proven ineffectual for the most part as a device for obtaining these from the USSR, it is probable that the member states will continue along their separate paths in attempting to satisfy their requirements. Romania signed the first 51:49 percent joint-enterprise production agreement with the Federal Republic of Germany.

Even the deep-rooted psychological antipathy of the Poles toward West Germans, for example, has not inhibited the Warsaw regime from negotiating with such companies as Krupp and Grundig. Many joint manufacturing projects already exist. Trade agreements were signed between West Germany and six of the East European countries as far back as 1969, but the Soviet Union still dominates bloc trade with the Common Market as a whole.

The method used by the West Germans is to provide the technological expertise, engineering skills, and capital to begin a project; the partner contributes the site, factory buildings, labor, and raw materials. Machine tools are being produced jointly with Hungary in this manner. Ownership always remains in the hands of the government on whose territory the plant is situated. This is the case with an automobile factory in Poland, estimated to have cost about $40 million, that was established jointly with Fiat of Italy. The coordinating committee in charge of NATO's trade with the bloc countries has indicated that it would even be legal to sell nuclear reactors for peaceful purposes to communist-ruled states.

The main problem in relations of the bloc countries with the West is the increasing amount of foreign debts because of a chronically adverse balance of payments and the necessity to service interest as well as repay credits. At the end of 1986, Eastern Europe alone owed over $100 billion and had available only

Table 67
CMEA SESSIONS, 1949–1988

Session	Date	Place	Principal discussion or action
1	26–28 April 1949	Moscow	Organization and plans for 1949
2	25–27 August 1949	Sofia	Multiyear trade agreements
3	24–25 November 1950	Moscow	Reports on commercial expansion
4	26–27 March 1954	Moscow	Coordination with USSR economic plans
5	24–25 June 1954	Moscow	Priorities for coordination
6	7–11 December 1955	Budapest	Economic plans, 1956–1960
7	18–25 May 1956	East Berlin	Coordination for 1956–1960
8	18–22 June 1957	Warsaw	Permanent commissions
9	26–30 June 1958	Bucharest	"Socialist division of labor"
10	11–13 December 1958	Prague	Chemical industry
11	13–16 May 1959	Tirana	Steel production in 1961–1965
12	10–13 December 1959	Sofia	Charter approval
13	26–29 July 1960	Budapest	Agriculture and 1961–1980 plans
14	28 February–3 March 1961	East Berlin	Cooperation in chemical industry
15	12–15 December 1961	Warsaw	"Socialist division of labor"
16	7 June 1962	Moscow	Executive Committee established
17	14–20 December 1962	Bucharest	Freight-car pool organized
18	25–26 July 1963	Moscow	Plan coordination, 1966–1970
19	28 January–2 February 1965	Prague	Yugoslav associate status approved
20	8–10 December 1966	Sofia	Coordination in 1971–1975
21	12–14 December 1967	Budapest	Mutual interest projects
22	21–23 January 1969	East Berlin	Scientific and technical (S&T) cooperation
23	23–26 April 1969	Moscow	CMEA infrastructure
24	12–14 May 1970	Warsaw	International Investment Bank

25	25–29 July 1971	Bucharest	Comprehensive program
26	10–12 July 1972	Moscow	Cuba accepted as member
27	5–8 June 1973	Prague	Cooperation with Finland approved
28	18–21 June 1974	Sofia	Twenty-fifth anniversary report
29	24–26 June 1975	Budapest	Joint five-year development projects
30	7–9 July 1976	East Berlin	Fifteen-year economic goals
31	21–23 June 1977	Warsaw	Development of domestic energy resources
32	27–29 June 1978	Bucharest	Admission of Vietnam as member; nuclear power development
33	26–28 June 1979	Moscow	Joint projects in energy and fuel production
34	17–19 June 1980	Prague	Multilateral agreements on computer development
35	2–4 July 1981	Sofia	Multilateral integration plans for 1981–1985
36	8–10 June 1982	Budapest	Robots, microprocessors, electronic components, color TV
37	18–20 October 1983	East Berlin	S&T problems
38	12–14 June 1984	Moscow	S&T collaboration; international economic cooperation
39	29–31 October 1984	Havana	Second natural gas pipeline; seventh coordination of economic plans
40	25–27 June 1985	Warsaw	1986–1990 five-year plan; intrabloc trade
41	17–18 December 1985	Moscow	Fifteen-year comprehensive program for S&T
42	10–11 November 1986	Bucharest	Nuclear, electric, thermal power station program through year 2000
43	13–14 October 1987	Moscow	International socialist division of labor, 1991–2005
44	5–7 July 1988	Prague	Restructuring of CMEA

SOURCES: Lucjan Ciamaga, *Od wspolpracy do integracji* (Warsaw, 1965), pp. 209–37; *Zycie Warszawy*, 18–19 December 1966; *Pravda*, 16 December 1967, 24 January 1969; *Ekonomicheskaia gazeta*, 28 April 1969; *Krasnaia zvezda*, 15 May 1970; RFE report, (by Harry Trend), "Comecon's Organizational Structure," 7 October 1975; *Izvestiia*, 10 July 1976; N. V. Faddeev, *SEV: 1949–1974* (Moscow, 1974), pp. 266–73, for a discussion of sessions 1–27; *Facts on File* (9 July 1977), p. 513; *Pravda*, 30 June 1978; L. A. D. Dellin, "Council for Mutual Economic Assistance," in R. F. Staar (ed.), *1980 Yearbook on International Communist Affairs* (Stanford, Calif., 1980), p. 107; *Rude pravo*, 19 June 1980; *Ekonomicheskaia gazeta*, no. 28 (July 1981); *Pravda*, 11 June 1982, 21 October 1983, 15 June 1984, 1 November 1984, 29 June 1985, 19 December 1985, 12 November 1986, 15 October 1987; 8 July 1988.

somewhat more than three billion dollars in foreign-exchange reserves. (See Table 68.) Almost two-thirds of the total indebtedness is owed to private banks in the West.[30]

Table 68
HARD-CURRENCY DEBTS, 1986

Country	Gross Debt[a] (in billions of dollars)	Debt service ratio[b] (percentages)
Poland	33.5	61
USSR	26.6	23
Yugoslavia	19.4	58
East Germany	16.6	32[c]
Hungary	15.1	61
Romania	6.0	29
Bulgaria	4.9	31
Czechoslovakia	4.5	17
Total	126.6	38.9 (average)
CMEA banks[d] (1981)	5.2	
Grand total	131.8	

SOURCES: CIA, *Handbook of Economic Statistics* (Washington, D.C., September 1987), pp. 60 and 75; Organization for Economic Cooperation and Development, *Financial Markets Trends* (Paris, February 1988), p. 20.

NOTES: [a]Equals liabilities to Western governments, commercial banks, suppliers, and other lenders.

[b]Based on exports to non-CMEA countries.

[c]Excluding transactions with West Germany.

[d]International Investment Bank and International Bank for Economic Cooperation, both CMEA agencies. These figures are for 1981.

PROBLEMS IN AGRICULTURE

The dogmatic Marxist belief that farming must involve collective activity, controlled through bureaucratic-industrial methods, has led to the elimination of most of the private entrepreneur farms throughout Eastern Europe. A communiqué issued by the CMEA at its June 1962 meeting in Moscow spoke of the "historic victory" in agriculture by communist-ruled member states (except for Poland and Yugoslavia, which were not then affiliated). The statement, which meant complete collectivization, remains true in ideology and organization only. In production, the collective farm system has been and continues to be for the most part a failure. Its destruction of personal responsibility and incentive has to a large extent alienated the rural population. Routine sessions of the permanent commission for agriculture examine the coordination and collaboration in agricultural production among CMEA members. During 1976–1978, only two multilateral agreements had been signed; in 1979, four; and in 1980, five.[31]

For the millions of collectivized farmers and their families, earnings had been until recently related mainly to the number of labor-days accumulated. This figure was used to calculate each worker's share of the net earnings. It is evident that little incentive existed. Nor was there until recently in the majority of countries any minimum level of earnings on the collective, such as the state farms had provided under their quasi-industrial wage systems. Bulgaria was the first to introduce a scheme for guaranteed labor-day remuneration, providing collective farm workers with a daily minimum of 1.8 leva. Hungary has the "nadudvar" system of monthly payments in cash plus remuneration in kind. Czechoslovakia also makes monthly payments but without any guaranteed minimum. Romania adheres to a rigid labor-day system but offers private plot privileges. In Poland minimum earnings could not make much difference because of the small degree of collectivization. Apart from Poland and Yugoslavia, more than 90 percent of all agricultural land in the bloc countries has been brought into the so-called socialist (collective and state) farm sector. Private plots, although limited in size, retain a disproportionate importance in the economy. This is because of the concentration on labor-intensive, high-value agricultural products.

Even the level of mechanization, which was heralded as the great panacea that would solve most problems, remains far below that of Western Europe. For example, in 1939 Czechoslovakia and France had the same ratio of 1.5 tractors per 1,000 hectares of arable land. More than two decades later, the respective figures were 6 and 26. It is claimed that the East European CMEA member states during the year 1985 alone produced about 114,000 new tractors and grain-harvesting combines.[32] Problems include a lack of spare parts and even a deficiency in technological culture—the general attitude that if a piece of machinery belongs to the government it belongs to everybody, with the result that no particular care is taken of it. In addition, not enough equipment is available to cope with above-average production periods.

Most of this equipment had been owned by the government in Machine Tractor Stations (MTS). Once the Soviet Union began to transform its agricultural system by selling machinery to collective farms, most of Eastern Europe began to do the same. By the end of 1965 all MTS in Hungary had been converted into Tractor Repair Stations, which kept only the heavy tractors and special combines. By 1966 Bulgaria had almost completely phased out the MTS except in hilly areas. On the other hand, Czechoslovakia adopted a dual system: collective farms purchase most of the machinery, but MTS are still operated. Poland abolished the MTS, converting them into repair stations and selling the machinery to collectives. Romania alone has expanded the system, adding to the number of MTS and selling no equipment to farms.

General stagnation continued in agriculture despite these measures. The area could no longer support itself in food, as it had been able to do before the war. After poor harvests, the deficit became greater and more grain had to be imported. This problem was approached in several different ways.

Czechoslovakia and East Germany initially took a harsh line, whittling down the size of private plots as well as the number of livestock allowed and imposing tighter party-state controls over agriculture. The various changes introduced in the organization of Soviet collective and state farms were emulated by these two regimes. Romania announced a proposal for the establishment of cooperative farm unions that would be organized at local, district, and national levels, with congresses meeting every five years and suggesting basic agricultural policy. During 1929–1932 a similar system had existed in the USSR. The Bulgarian communists deliberately strengthened the farmers' incentives, at the expense of the consumers, by raising both government-paid and retail prices for livestock products. Poland announced a shift toward larger state investments in agriculture, although it reversed this policy during the 1980s.

However, because of a deteriorating economic situation, the Warsaw regime announced on 24 June 1976 its intention to raise the cost of food by 70 percent. Spontaneous demonstrations[33] throughout the country forced the government to rescind the proposed measure and to promise that price changes would be introduced only after consultation with workers. At the same time, the Polish regime applied for $200 million in credits with which to purchase agricultural products from the United States. Price increases for meat and other food products during mid-1980 were the main cause of nationwide strikes that led to a general crisis in Poland threatening the legitimacy of the communist regime itself. (See Chapter 6.)

Consumer subsidies, which amounted to approximately 30 percent on retail food sales in Poland, have also been used by other East European states. In Hungary the average government subsidy for one kilogram (2.2 pounds) of pork is 18 forints or almost one dollar and for one kilogram of beef is 26 forints, so that the annual consumption of meat rose to 70 kilograms per person.[34]

TRADE BETWEEN CMEA STATES

CMEA members neither belong to a common market in actual practice nor have they introduced markets domestically. The organization maintains no uniform external tariff and apparently does not aspire to one. Therefore the area cannot be regarded as a single market. Nevertheless, orthodox East European economists insist that the CMEA states strive to increase trade among themselves in preference to commerce with the "capitalist world." This represents an ideological imperative. However, in actual practice, the percentage of trade with nonbloc countries has been expanding for most CMEA members.

Up to now, trade within the CMEA area has been conducted almost entirely within the framework of bilateral agreements. Khrushchev emphasized the need for measures to enhance mutual responsibility within a truly multilateral framework. This has not been achieved, although a communiqué issued following the seventeenth CMEA council session indicated that price adjustments would be made on the basis of average world levels during the preceding five-year period. This system continued until the USSR raised the price of oil in 1974 by 131 percent (Eastern Europe had to pay an additional three billion dollars) and in 1976 by another 8 percent. The previous static five-year average pricing system was replaced as of 1 January 1975 by a movable three-year average, with prices recalculated annually. Five years later, Soviet prices were still 40 percent below those of OPEC.[35] By 1986, however, the cost to CMEA members reached world market levels.

Progress toward effective coordination in trade, however, has been brought about by the USSR. Within the CMEA area commercial exchange increased seven times between 1970 and 1986. (See Table 69.) Between 56 and 78 percent of the foreign trade of each East European state is with the Soviet Union, and the USSR in turn conducts more than 60 percent of its foreign trade within the bloc.

Table 69
TRADE TURNOVER WITHIN THE CMEA AREA, 1970–1986
(in millions of dollars)

Country	1970	1975	1980	1986
Bulgaria	2,836	7,266	14,025	23,160
Czechoslovakia	4,940	11,326	19,994	32,070
East Germany	4,569	13,852	23,460	34,753
Hungary	2,996	8,584	15,085	22,316
Poland	4,494	11,277	20,071	30,045
Romania	1,866	4,320	8,613	12,665
USSR	13,379	31,882	61,623	98,296
Total	35,080	88,507	162,871	253,305

SOURCE: CIA, *Handbook of Economic Statistics 1987* (Washington, D.C., September 1987), pp. 99, 103–4.

With regard to the specialization of production, the East European communist regimes hesitate to surrender their right to engage in particular branches of industry. Nor are the industrially more advanced states necessarily keen to see competitive production established by their more backward neighbors. The Soviet Union has proclaimed its prerogative of strengthening all branches of the economy because of an international duty to build communism. Thus, efforts to achieve a more rational division of labor among the bloc states have been countered by more or less concealed resistance from the threatened producers and by determination of the USSR to proceed along its own path.

The nature of the organization also militates against effective supranational planning. The CMEA council, an advisory body that issues recommendations to member governments, had to wait until the middle of 1962 to acquire an executive committee. Six months later Khrushchev spoke out plainly on the need to establish a joint body that was "empowered to formulate common plans." Developments since that time suggest that the USSR has not yet managed to advance this politically delicate matter beyond some joint planning in limited areas, for example, international economic enterprises and associations. The CMEA committees for cooperation in planning, science and technology, and material and technical supply were all established during the first half of the 1970s (see Chart 2) and represent moves in that same direction.

The communiqué issued after the July 1981 CMEA session left open the possibility of convening a summit meeting in early 1982 at which questions of structural reform and new programs would be worked out. Romanians were especially interested in such a meeting, where they would ask for more help in technology and raw materials.[36]

It seems that evermore grandiose plans are being made, like the Collective Concept for the International Socialist Division of Labor in the Years 1991–2005, elaboration of which was agreed on at the 43rd (extraordinary) session of CMEA in Moscow. That meeting also decided to assist the less-developed non-European member countries of Cuba, Mongolia, and Vietnam, which have been a continuing burden for the USSR.[37]

Regardless of whether these future proposals are implemented, it may not be possible to solve the many economic problems of Eastern Europe unless closer relations are developed with Western Europe and the United States. Regional integration may have become obsolete, as recent trends toward an international monetary system and a world economy indicate. Finally, it behooves the East European members of the CMEA to become postindustrial societies as rapidly as possible, or they will continue to remain far behind their West European counterparts.[38]

NOTES

1. In 1945, however, Czechoslovak industry was producing at only half its 1937 level. V. I. Morozov, *Soviet ekonomicheskoi vzaimopomoshchi* (Moscow, 1964), pp. 80–81.

2. Text in Alexander Uschakow, *Der Rat fuer gegenseitige Wirtschaftshilfe* (Cologne, 1962), p. 86. The 1959 CMEA charter has been translated into English by Michael Kaser,

Comecon (London, 1967), 2d ed., pp. 235–46. It was amended in 1962, 1974, and again in 1979. For the 1979 amendment, see Harry G. Trend, "Communique of the 33rd Comecon Council Session," RFE, *Background Report,* no. 150 (3 July 1979) and V. I. Menzhinskii, *Mezhdunarodnye organizatsii sotsialisticheskikh gosudarstv* (Moscow, 1980), p. 62.

3. Lucjan Ciamaga, *Od wspolpracy do integracji* (Warsaw, 1965), p. 17.

4. Richard F. Staar (ed.), *Yearbook on International Communist Affairs: 1985* (Stanford, Calif., 1985), p. 377.

5. Poland allegedly received the equivalent of $420 million (mainly in rubles) and Hungary about $285 million during the 1956–1957 period. Ciamaga, *Od wspolpracy do integracji,* pp. 39–40.

6. Actually GNP, as used here, refers to the growth of the net material product excluding services (government administration, legal, passenger transportation, etc.) that do not directly affect production.

7. Quoted from "Fundamental Principles of the International Socialist Division of Labor," *Pravda,* 17 June 1962.

8. Sofia radio, 24 January 1970.

9. [Poland], *Maly rocznik statystyczny 1966* (Warsaw, 1966), table 7, p. 64.

10. By 1980, member countries had concluded about a hundred multilateral and over a thousand bilateral specialization agreements. O. A. Chukanov, *Sodruzhestvo stran-chlenov SEV* (Moscow, 1980), p. 76.

11. *Die Wirtschaft* (East Berlin), as cited by Hamburg radio, 19 January 1981.

12. By the end of 1976 a new 290-kilometer pipeline called Druzhba II connected Uzhgorod with Szaszhalombatta and gave Hungary ten million tons of oil a year. *Ekonomicheskaia gazeta,* no. 2 (5 January 1981), p. 20.

13. In 1986, nuclear power-generating capacity exceeded 37,300 megawatts in CMEA countries. CIA, *Handbook of Economic Statistics, 1987* (Washington, D.C., October 1987), p. 143.

14. *Krasnaia zvezda,* 16 July 1976.

15. N. V. Faddeev in *Izvestiia,* 27 March 1970.

16. Chukanov, *Sodruzhestvo stran-chlenov SEV,* p. 85.

17. RFE report (by Harry Trend), "The Labyrinth of Intra-Comecon Exchange Rates," 30 August 1976.

18. Chukanov, *Sodruzhestvo stran-chlenov SEV,* pp. 85–86. For the less-developed member states, interest rates are discounted. Cuba pays only 2 percent and Mongolia 0.5 percent annual interest. Moscow radio, 21 February 1988; *FBIS-Soviet Union,* 22 February 1988, p. 4, on credits for Soviet joint venture members.

19. [Bulgarian Communist Party], *Directives of the Eighth Congress of the People's Republic of Bulgaria in the Period of 1961–1980* (Sofia, 1963), p. 36; CIA, *Handbook of Economic Statistics, 1987,* p. 179.

20. *The Economist* (London), 24 July 1976.

21. *Pravda,* 15 May 1970.

22. Belgrade radio, 11 August 1969.

23. Interview in *Journal Export* (Belgrade), quoted by Zagreb radio, 26 December 1965. A few years later, however, the CMEA was called the first "socialist" collective organization by this same man. *Izvestiia*, 27 March 1970. See N. V. Faddeev, *SEV: 1949–1974* (Moscow, 1974), p. 375. The current general secretary, since 1983, is Viacheslav V. Sychev. *Pravda*, 30 March 1988.

24. CMEA, *Statisticheskii ezhegodnik* (1987), pp. 305–6.

25. *Ekonomicheskaia gazeta*, 2 August 1976: *Pravda*, 20 November 1976. For details on these projects, see Chukanov, *Sodruzhestvo stran-chlenov SEV*, pp. 26–27 and 194–95.

26. *Ekonomicheskaia gazeta*, no. 28 (July 1981), pp. 13–14.

27. Cam Hudson, "CMEA Joint Investments in Soviet Nuclear Power Stations," RFE, *Background Report*, no. 11 (20 January 1981).

28. *Pravda*, 26 January 1981.

29. *Die Wirtschaft*, cited by Hamburg radio, 19 January 1981. They totaled only 338, according to A. S. Burov, p. 141.

30. See V. Sobell, "Eastern Europe's Debts," *RAD Background Report*, no. 50 (22 March 1988), pp. 4.

31. *Selskaia zhizn'*, 21 December 1980.

32. *Statisticheskii ezhegodnik stran-chlenov SEV 1986*, p. 208.

33. Seven workers at the Ursus tractor plant went on trial in Warsaw under article 220 of the penal code, which envisages sentences from five years in prison to death. *The Observer* (London), 18 July 1976.

34. CMEA meat production during 1986 totaled 29 million tons, or 3.3 million above 1980. CIA, *Handbook of Economic Statistics, 1987*, p. 198. See also Nancy J. Cochrane, "The Private Sector in East European Agriculture," *Problems of Communism* (March–April 1988), pp. 47–53.

35. *Die Wirtschaft*, cited by Hamburg radio, 19 January 1981.

36. RFE, *Romanian Situation Report*, no. 15 (31 July 1981), pp. 13–15.

37. *Pravda*, 15 October 1987, p. 4.

38. In 1976, a proposal by the CMEA requesting most-favored-nation treatment by the European Economic Community (EEC) was rejected, although negotiations continued. The EEC prefer the continuation of trade links with individual Soviet bloc states. On 9 June 1988 an agreement was signed at Moscow establishing official relations between the EEC and CMEA. *Pravda*, 10 June 1988.

Chapter 11
Intrabloc Political Relations:
Unity in Diversity

The experiment of maintaining a single organization, the Communist Information Bureau—Cominform—to control Eastern Europe politically from Moscow existed less than nine years. It is doubtful that this instrument could have been used at all after the death of Stalin. The only eyewitness account of the Cominform's establishment tells how Andrei Zhdanov proposed that its weekly newspaper be called *For a Lasting Peace, For a People's Democracy.* This political slogan was treated as a joke, especially by the Italians and the French. Only after Zhdanov had explained that he was voicing Stalin's suggestion did the laughter cease.[1]

This organizational meeting took place during 22–27 September 1947 at Szklarska Poreba (the former Bad Schreiberhau) in the part of Silesia that Poland had annexed with Soviet support at the end of World War II. Representing the host country's communist party was Wladyslaw Gomulka, who also signed the original Cominform manifesto denouncing the Marshall Plan and condemning the United States as "an arsenal of counterrevolutionary tactical weapons."[2] The other delegates came from the remaining East European parties (except for the Albanian) as well as from those in Italy and France, where it was assumed that the communists would be in power shortly.

The second meeting took place at the beginning of 1948 in Belgrade, where Cominform headquarters functioned for a brief period. The third, which was held at Bucharest on 28 June 1948, issued the communiqué excluding the Yugoslav communist party from the organization. A fourth meeting, held at Budapest toward the end of 1949, devoted its time to planning a world drive for signatures to a so-called peace manifesto.[3] After that, little could be accomplished and the Cominform had been all but forgotten until April 1956, when it was dissolved, apparently as part of the price for reconciliation between Belgrade and Moscow.

The abolition of the Cominform, the existence of which had manifested itself during its last few years only by publication of the weekly newspaper, left a vacuum in the Soviet bloc. Coinciding with what has become known as de-Stalinization, this act seems to have had a further purpose, that of helping to transform the image of East European leaders so that they would appear not as Moscow agents but as respectable "national communists." (It should be noted that this term has never been used in official Soviet or East European terminology.) Khrushchev had launched the de-Stalinization process with his secret speech in February 1956 to the twentieth CPSU congress.[4] After hearing about Stalin's crimes vis-à-vis domestic as well as foreign party members, this elite gathering could surmise that future relations with member states in the East European "commonwealth of nations" would follow a new course.

Whatever may have motivated Khrushchev to repeat his denunciation of Stalin publicly at the 22d CPSU congress in October 1961, sweeping changes in Eastern Europe did not materialize. The simple fact of the matter was that many regimes would have fallen if full-fledged de-Stalinization had been implemented. The same has continued to be true since then. Most of the leaders in power as of mid-1988 had been at one time or another ardent supporters of Stalinist techniques, and some might even yet like to revert to them. Hence, by and large, de-Stalinization was restricted to changing the names of streets and cities, taking down statues of Stalin, including the five-ton monument in Prague that had been made from a solid piece of marble, and removing the mummies of Stalin and Gottwald from their mausoleums. Nothing has come, however, of Khrushchev's proposal to erect a monument in Moscow to perpetuate the memory of comrades who fell victims to arbitrary rule.[5]

Khrushchev's successors (L. I. Brezhnev, Iu. V. Andropov, and K. U. Chernenko) did little to change relations between the metropole and Eastern Europe. It remained for Mikhail S. Gorbachev, when he gave the main address at the 70th anniversary of the Bolshevik revolution, to enunciate six binding principles for relations between the CPSU and other ruling communist parties.[6]

1. Unconditional and total equality
2. Responsibility of the ruling party for its own domestic affairs
3. Concern for the general cause of communism
4. Respect for achievements in other bloc countries
5. Voluntary cooperation
6. Strict observance of peaceful coexistence

Whether the foregoing will be translated into practice may depend on Gorbachev's ability to maintain his position as CPSU general secretary.

EAST EUROPE'S LEADERS

The men controlling the communist regimes within the Soviet bloc, even those in Albania and Yugoslavia, share many characteristics. They are almost all hard-core apparatus workers, professional revolutionaries who reached the top posts after having served in less responsible positions when their parties were banned by the prewar or World War II governments. They have all proven themselves to be dedicated communists, some of them in "capitalist" prisons and even in their own postwar jails. (See Table 70.)

Ramiz Alia,[7] first secretary of the Albanian Labor Party (ALP), is a Gheg whose parents immigrated from Kosovo after World War I. He served as political commissar for a brigade and later a division in World War II. Elected to the ALP Central Committee (1948), the Politburo (1956), and the Secretariat (1961), he has also been general secretary of the youth movement, education minister and, most recently, president of the country (1982).

At that time (1982), ALP leader Enver Hoxha designated Alia his deputy and heir apparent. Despite elimination of other Ghegs from top party positions over the years by the Tosks, who dominate the military and security, Alia's election to first secretary on 13 April 1985 took place smoothly after the death of Hoxha. The new leader improved on his predecessor, when 100 percent of the electorate voted in parliamentary elections on 1 February 1987.

Bulgaria's leader, Todor Zhivkov,[8] spent the war years in his own country, like others, in the communist underground. Here, however, the resemblance ends. Born into a peasant family, Zhivkov completed only a few years of elementary school. Between 1936 and 1941 he may have been in Moscow undergoing training; there is a gap in his biography for this period. In 1952 Zhivkov succeeded the notorious "little Stalin," Vulko Chervenkov, as a member of the new collective leadership in Bulgaria. He has consistently followed the Moscow line and rivals his East German colleague in this respect. In power 36 years as party leader, Zhivkov holds the record for length of service among East European regime leaders. He has maintained this post by eliminating all potential rivals.

The leader in Czechoslovakia is Milos Jakes,[9] also of peasant extraction, although an electrician by training. He joined the communist party immediately after World War II, rising to head the youth movement during the early 1950s, after which he spent three years at the Higher Party School in Moscow. As chairman of the Central Control and Audit Commission, he directed the purge that expelled 460,000 Dubcek supporters from the party after the August 1968 Soviet invasion. He succeeded 75-year-old Gustav Husak on 17 December 1987 as general secretary and will probably be willing to collaborate with the USSR to the same extent he did some twenty years earlier.

Among all East European leaders, Erich Honecker of the German Democratic Republic for a long time had no choice but to remain the most submissive in his relations with the Soviet Union. Born of communist parents in Saarland, he joined the party's youth organization at ten and later received training at Moscow's international school. Honecker spent a full decade in a Nazi prison for illegal activities but survived to become chairman of the East German communist youth

Table 70

EASTERN EUROPE'S COMMUNIST LEADERS, 1988

Country	Leader's name and party position	Year of birth	Father's occupation	Joined communist party	Profession	Years in jail	Spent World War II	Years in USSR	Government post	Became member of party Politburo
Albania	Alia, Ramiz First Secretary, 1985–	1925	Unknown	1943	None	None	Albania	None	Chairman, People's Assembly (president)	1956
Bulgaria	Zhivkov, Todor General Secretary 1954–	1911	Peasant	1932	Printer	None	Bulgaria	1936–1941?	Chairman, State Council (president)	1951
Czecho-slovakia	Jakes, Milos General Secretary, 1987–	1922	Peasant	1945	Electrician	None	Czechoslovakia	None	None	1977
East Germany	Honecker, Erich General Secretary 1971–	1912	Coal miner	1929	Roof tiler	1935–1945	Germany	1930–1931; 1956–1957	Chairman, State Council (president)	1950

Hungary	Grosz, Karoly General Secretary, 1988–	1930	Worker	1945	Printer	None	Hungary	None	Prime Minister	1985
Poland	Jaruzelski, Wojciech First Secretary 1981–	1923	Land-owner	1947	Army officer	None	USSR	1941–1945	Chairman, State Council (president)	1971
Romania	Ceausescu, Nicolae General Secretary, 1965–	1918	Poor peasant	1936	None	1936–1939; 1940–1944	Romania	None	Chairman, State Council (president)	1954
Yugoslavia	Krunic, Bosko President of the Presidium, 1987–1988*	1929	Middle class	1946	Lawyer	None	Yugoslavia	None	Member, Presidium SSRN	1986

SOURCES: RFE, *Eastern Europe's Communist Leaders*, 5 vols. (Munich, 1966), with 1988 identifications from the press; *Drustveno-politicke zajednice* (Belgrade, Interpress, 1968), vol. 1, p. 222. Guenther Buch (comp.), *Namen und Daten* (Berlin, 1973), p. 120; Boris Lewytzkyj and Juliusz Stroynowski (eds.), *Who's Who in the Socialist Countries* (New York, 1978), pp. 264, 413–14; *YICA: 1983*, pp. 247–48; *Pravda* 18 December 1987; RFE, *East European Leadership List* (15 January 1988), pp. 3–4.

*Yugoslavia has a rotating leadership system, with each Presidium member serving as president for a one-year term. Bosko Krunic was elected in June 1987 and succeeded by Stipe Suvar the following year. See Table 49.

movement and in 1948 a member of the SED Central Committee. After training in the USSR, he took over defense and security affairs for the party in February 1958, when he was appointed to the Secretariat. His elevation to first secretary came in May 1971, and in October 1976 he was elected State Council chairman, or chief of state.[10] It appears that Honecker has firm control of the leadership post, evidenced by his re-election at the eleventh SED congress (April 1986). He continues to steadfastly support the Moscow line in both domestic and foreign policies. Examples include his support for Soviet aggression in Afghanistan and for crushing the Solidarity movement in Poland. During September 1987, Honecker finally was allowed to visit West Germany.

Another man who has spent almost his entire life in the service of communism is Karoly Grosz,[11] the first East European leader to have spent his entire career under a communist regime. He began as a printer and then graduated from a university and the central party school. His party assignments have included supervision of radio and TV, director of Agitprop, first secretary for Budapest, and, since 1984, prime minister. In 1985 he became a Politburo member. Only the future will tell whether this new general secretary can solve the economic problems. By the later 1980s, Hungary was in the midst of a three- to six-year stabilization period, to be followed by ten to fifteen years of full development. The standard of living has dropped in recent years so that Czechs, and in many ways East Germans, are probably better off than Hungarians.

The fall from power of Stanislaw Kania on 18 October 1981 made General of the Army Wojciech Jaruzelski party leader in Poland. This career officer comes from the intelligentsia, spent part of World War II as a worker, and then in 1943 joined the Polish armed forces being organized in the USSR. He served in military reconnaissance, commanded a motorized division after the war, headed political indoctrination, became chief of staff, and in 1968, defense minister. On 11 February 1981, he was named prime minister, a post he later relinquished. Jaruzelski provided the strength that Kania had lacked, and he does have a constituency in the officers' corps of the Polish armed forces.[12] With the proclamation of martial law on 13 December 1981, the military took over direct administration of the country. In recognition of his services in suppressing the Solidarity trade union movement and restoring communist rule, Jaruzelski stood on top of Lenin's tomb in Moscow with Zhivkov, Honecker, and Ceausescu during the 70th anniversary of the Bolshevik Revolution, reviewing the military parade.

The most independent leader in the bloc is Nicolae Ceausescu of Romania. Like others, he experienced imprisonment under the precommunist government of his country. Always advancing to more important party positions, Ceausescu spent the war in Romania and most of this time in jail. His contacts with the Soviet Union have included repeated visits ever since 1957, when he attended the 40th anniversary celebration of the Bolshevik Revolution. Even so, no delegation from Bucharest went to Moscow for the 1–5 March 1965 meeting of communist parties that was intended as a preliminary to a world conference. The Albanians and the Chinese also refused to attend. On the other hand, Ceausescu was host to the Warsaw Pact and CMEA sessions during July 1966 in Romania. He also attended the June 1969 world communist conference in Moscow and the June 1976 meeting of European party chiefs in East Berlin. Ceausescu hosted a Warsaw Pact session the end of November 1976 at Bucharest and attended the 70th anniversary of the Bolshevik Revolution in Moscow. Gorbachev came to Bucharest in May 1987, the last among all WTO capitals that he visited.[13]

The situation in Yugoslavia presents a unique predicament. The leadership, since Tito's death in May 1980, has attempted to implement his policy of collective leadership. Tito had established a revolving presidency plan for both party and state. On the surface, this policy has worked smoothly. The current party president, Bosko Krunic,[14] is serving a one-year term (1987–1988), after which a successor will be selected from among the fifteen-member Presidium. In reality, however, criticism is being voiced within the party that this system has been ineffective. Major changes did not occur at the thirteenth party congress during June 1986.[15]

Unity in Diversity. As the foregoing sketches show, the backgrounds of these eight communist leaders suggest that they could be difficult for the USSR to manipulate. Interestingly enough, it was a communist from outside the bloc who coined the somewhat misleading term "polycentrism" for a policy that had already been put into practice six years earlier by Tito.[16]

Palmiro Togliatti, then general secretary of the Italian communist party, is credited with having used the term in 1956. While Stalin was still alive, this man was among the most obedient among prominent foreign communists. In 1964, however, during a vacation at Yalta, he wrote a memorandum that was intended to represent the basis for discussions with Khrushchev. These never took place because Togliatti died. His body and the memorandum were taken back to Italy.

Brezhnev, who was at that time the Soviet heir apparent, represented the CPSU at Togliatti's funeral in Rome. He first learned of the memorandum there and attempted to have it suppressed. Although it probably never would have appeared if Togliatti had lived, the new Italian communist leadership under Luigi Longo eventually decided to publish it.[17] *Pravda* carried a translation five days later, without comment. Subsequently the presses of most other East European communist parties also printed the memorandum. Many of its ideas, of course, had already surfaced before that time in one way or another.

Togliatti maintained that the Soviet bloc had been developing a "centrifugal tendency," that is, that the individual parties had been moving away from the centralized control exercised by Moscow. He went on to express opposition to any proposal for again creating organizations like the Comintern (1919–1943) or the

Cominform (1947–1956). Togliatti rebuked the USSR and the communist-ruled states in Eastern Europe for their slowness in, and resistance to, "overcoming the regime of restrictions and suppression of democratic and personal freedom introduced by Stalin." Finally, he asserted: "one must consider that the unity one ought to establish and maintain lies in the diversity and full autonomy of the individual countries."[18]

If Khrushchev had acquiesced in the translation and publication of the Togliatti memorandum, this might have meant that his policy toward Eastern Europe would have included an effort to modify the master-servant relationship existing under Stalin. His goal appeared to be the introduction of more flexible contacts with the various communist parties, whereby common policies might be reached by means of discussion, although the USSR would still maintain the decisive voice because of its power position. A most important aspect of his plan was economic integration, that is, a supranational division of labor through the CMEA. This grand design failed for various reasons, including the half measures that Khrushchev allowed, the unexpected strength of nationalism, the effects of incomplete de-Stalinization, and the impact of the Soviet dispute with China.

Ever since the dissolution of the Cominform, the day-to-day business of handling relations among the various bloc communist parties has been conducted through special units within the Central Committee apparatus of each organization. (See Table 71.) Mikhail Suslov, then chief ideologist for the CPSU, indicated early in 1964 that international discipline no longer involved orders "from above" but that it had become voluntary.[19] The most that he and Khrushchev seem to have regarded as attainable among the communist-ruled countries was an international

Table 71
RELATIONS AMONG PARTIES IN EASTERN EUROPE, 1988

Country	Individual responsible	Position
Albania	No relations with other East European parties or CPSU	
Bulgaria	Stanishev, Dimitur	Secretary
Czechoslovakia	Bilak, Vasil	Presidium member and secretary
East Germany	Axen, Hermann	Politburo member and secretary
Hungary	Szuros, Matyas	Secretary
Poland	Czyrek, Jozef	Politburo member and secretary
Romania	Stoian, Ion	Political Executive Committee candidate, member and secretary
Soviet Union	Med'vedev, Vadim A.	Secretary
Yugoslavia	Orlandic, Marko	Presidium member

SOURCE: RFE, *East European Leadership List* (15 January 1988), pp. 5–42.

system of "democratic centralism" in party relations, wherein the minority would accept the decisions of the majority.

FALL OF KHRUSHCHEV AND AFTER

Togliatti had dealt with deficiencies of communist interstate relationships, and the manner in which Khrushchev was dismissed enhanced the impact of his memorandum. The nuances of the slogan "unity in diversity" can be observed very well in the various reactions to the *Pravda* editorial explaining the change of leadership at Moscow.[20] Even the most obedient among the East European regimes had finally come to the realization that they should not believe everything that Khrushchev's successors proclaimed.

Thus the fall of Khrushchev at first caused general bewilderment across almost the whole of Eastern Europe. Whereas previous changes of this kind had been accepted without hesitation by all communists, there was now comment that included questioning and, in many cases, even criticism. Demands for more detailed explanations of why Khrushchev had been deposed continued, and the new Soviet leadership found itself compelled to state its case in Moscow to delegations from a number of communist parties. Some of these explanations could be taken care of during the traditional anniversary celebration of the Bolshevik Revolution. It is not known from the communiqués issued at various times whether the delegations were satisfied with the results of these talks, however.

Khrushchev had scheduled a preparatory conference of 26 communist parties from Eastern and Western Europe to be held in Moscow on 15 December 1964. The conference was to draw up an agenda for a world congress of representatives from the international communist movement. A high-level Chinese delegation headed by Chou En-lai attended the anniversary celebrations in the USSR during early November and probably influenced the new Soviet leaders to postpone the preparatory conference until the following spring. Finally, it was scheduled for 1–5 March 1965.

Only eighteen of the parties invited sent delegations, and another one sent an observer, so the gathering became merely a "consultative meeting," which meant that it could make no binding decisions. The Albanians, Romanians, and Yugoslavs refused to attend. The communiqué[21] on the meeting, issued five days after it was over, dropped for the time being and for all practical purposes the idea of holding a world congress but left open the possibility of having one sometime in the future, providing conditions changed.

The USSR under Khrushchev and his successors has been unable to supply Romania's needs in full and thus has not been able to respond satisfactorily with economic pressure to that country's occasional defiance. Romania's struggle for economic independence has been closely related to the process of limiting Soviet political influence. For a brief period Bucharest even suspended publication of the *World Marxist Review* in the Romanian language. When publication was resumed, the journal came out with reduced content and the specific deletion of articles that might endanger Bucharest's neutrality in the Sino-Soviet dispute[22] or contradict its position on other political and economic matters.

Certain East European leaders are, to some extent, exploiting feelings of nationalism to obtain some identification with the people. In the case of Romania, this has led to an overtly anti-Soviet attitude. On the other hand, Jaruzelski in Poland has had to discourage the deep feelings of hostility on the part of the Polish people against Russians in general and Soviet communists in particular.[23] Since 1967, and perhaps even before that, Bulgarian communists have been paying lip service to nationalism. The East German regime in the mid-1970s began to play the "national" theme. More recently, it has even been willing to distance itself from Moscow.

In all the East European countries except Bulgaria and Czechoslovakia, the people (in contrast to their rulers) for good historical reasons have been traditionally antagonistic toward the colossus in the East. The Germans fought against the Russians in both world wars. The same is true of the Hungarians, even though many of them may have done so reluctantly. During World War II, the USSR forced Romania to cede Northern Bukovina and Bessarabia. The people of Poland, steeped as they are in history, remember that Russia (both czarist and communist) participated in all six dismemberments of their country: 1772, 1793, 1795, 1939, and 1945. Nor have they forgotten the suppression of revolts in the nineteenth century, the mass deportations that followed the Hitler-Stalin pact, the massacre of prisoners of war in Katyn Forest, or the failure of the Red Army to assist in the 1944 Warsaw uprising against the Germans.[24] No sweeping generalization could cover isolated Albania and multinational Yugoslavia, but popular feeling in those two countries has hardly ever risen above distrust or indifference toward the Soviet Union.

At the leadership level, opposition surfaced to a limited extent at a meeting of representatives from 29 communist parties from both East and West Europe during 29–30 June 1976. It had taken sixteen preliminary sessions over a period of twenty months to hammer out a document that would be acceptable to all. The final text, entitled *For Peace, Security, Cooperation and Social Progress in Europe*, did not include the term "proletarian internationalism," which is understood to mean CPSU pre-eminence. This omission was achieved by the West European parties, with support from the Romanians and Yugoslavs. The other East European leaders did not oppose Moscow's supremacy, at least not at that conference.

Although the communist parties in many of the West European states can safely oppose Soviet domination, this certainly is not true for those in Eastern Europe. For countries like Czechoslovakia, East Germany, Hungary, and Poland, the so-called Brezhnev Doctrine remains in force. Their regimes are fully aware of the prevailing power relationships; namely, that the Soviet Union can intervene with its armed forces anywhere in the bloc if it considers communist rule to be threatened.

A summit meeting of bloc party leaders was held at Moscow during 4–5 December 1980 to discuss problems in Poland and consider possible courses of action to counter so-called antisocialist forces in that country. The final communiqué expressed the participants' confidence that the Poles would overcome their crises and that Polish workers would "assure the country's development along the socialist path." It added, however, that "the Polish people can firmly count on the fraternal solidarity and support of the Warsaw Treaty countries."[25] All seven party leaders of the Warsaw Pact member states were present, accompanied by their domestic security and military advisers. Although many similarities existed between this summit and the 1968 ones dealing with Czechoslovakia, the results were quite different. Warsaw was given a chance to solve its internal problems.

Gorbachev ruled out any possibility of a future world congress of communist parties when he stated that "the days of the Comintern, of the [Com] Informburo, and even of binding international conferences, have passed."[26] If one can believe that the six principles he specified in November 1987 for relations between the CPSU and other ruling parties (listed at the beginning of this chapter) will be implemented, then perhaps the East European regimes may indeed become more than satrapies.

CONFLICTS WITHIN EASTERN EUROPE

Whatever may be their unarticulated reservations about the Soviet Union, the East European peoples have many traditional enmities among themselves. The image of East Germany is affected by the painful memories in other countries of Nazi occupation or domination during World War II. Although the communist regimes attempt to divert these feelings westward against the Federal Republic of Germany, much of the hatred for all Germans still remains, some of it going back to before the war. It has been especially prevalent in Czechoslovakia since the Munich crisis of September 1938 and in Poland as a result of its occupation by Prussia/Germany from 1796 to 1918, as well as by Nazi Germany during World War II, which resulted in the death of six million Polish citizens.

Minority Problems. The most important potential area of bloc conflict involves the Hungarians in the territory of Transylvania that was acquired by Romania. Discrimination against these people was intensified after the 1956 uprising in Hungary, when the possibility of contagion seemed imminent. Budapest had made no public effort to intercede on behalf of this minority, but behind-the-scenes efforts existed. Hungarians, even within the communist party, feel strongly about the repression of their kinsmen across the border. In 1987 the Budapest government finally raised the issue at the Conference on Security and Cooperation in Europe talks at Vienna.

Czechoslovakia too has its Hungarian minority and is pursuing a process of integration. For example, a Slovak communist party weekly stated that the "participation of workers and collective farmers of Hungarian nationality in the country's economic upsurge will depend on the extent to which they can master Czech and Slovak technical literature as well as on expertise in their respective fields."[27] It is noteworthy that bus lines between Czechoslovakia and Hungary were not opened until 1964 and that the bridge over the Danube between the two countries at Esztergom had not been rebuilt over thirty years after it was destroyed at the end of World War II.

The best illustration of minority problems can be found in Yugoslavia, with its many nationalities. Bulgaria has persistently maintained that the majority of inhabitants in the Yugoslav federal republic of Macedonia are of Bulgarian ethnic origin. For their part, the Yugoslavs have protested Bulgaria's recent official policy of denying that there is a sizable number of Macedonians living within its borders.[28] Officially, formal relations exist between the two countries, but they are not friendly. More than 1.7 million Albanians live inside Yugoslavia.

Internal Nationality Problems.   Two of the East European countries, Czechoslovakia and Yugoslavia, are faced with the question of how to foster and preserve unity among their different ethnic groups without erasing national identities. The two states have not existed long enough to change the fundamental individualism of their minority components. The Slovaks remember their brief separate statehood during World War II, and even the communists are proud of the 1944 uprising against the Germans in Slovakia. After the war local autonomy was granted, but resentment flared in 1960 when the Board of Commissioners, which symbolized that self-rule, was dissolved under the new "socialist" constitution.

The dismissal during 1963 of two notorious Stalinists of Slovak extraction only contributed to further demands for the restoration of autonomy. The fact that the new premier, Jozef Lenart,[29] had formerly been president of the Slovak National Council suggests that the government wished to appear to have made a concession. The powers of the National Council were increased, and this culminated in a federation on 1 January 1969. However, there has been a gradual erosion of the federal system, and this process could involve curtailment of Slovak autonomy.

The problems in Yugoslavia are more complex. The general domestic relaxation of the late 1960s led to a revival of nationalism within the individual republics that Belgrade could not leave unchecked. Thus the latest Yugoslav constitution (1974) re-emphasized the federalist nature of the state, while the nationalist-inclined party leadership in Croatia underwent a purge during 1971–1972. Official policy centers on the Titoist system of workers' self-management within a decentralized framework; this system allegedly permits each nationality to solve its problems and guarantee its own interests. The riots in Kosovo during 1983 and continuing turmoil there, however, suggest that the system does not work.

Nationality most assuredly will play a part in the leadership succession. The fact that Tito was a Croatian may have been insignificant, but this is not the case with regard to his successors. However, since the collective presidency includes eight members, with one from each of the federal republics and the autonomous regions, ethnic balance is important. The results of the thirteenth party congress (June 1986), and specifically the makeup of the new party authorities, emphasize this point again.

Conflicts Among States. The governmental system that is now in operation throughout Eastern Europe was imposed on those countries against the wishes of the vast majority of their populations. This basic conflict between the people and their rulers exploded into riots during 1953 in Czechoslovakia and especially East Germany and into demonstrations three years later in Poland and a simultaneous full-scale revolution in Hungary.[30] Poland experienced riots at the end of 1970, during the summer of 1976 because of food prices, and on the occasion of the growing power of Solidarity, which led to martial law from 13 December 1981 to 22 July 1983. Other conflicts at the intrabloc level have involved Yugoslavia and Albania with the USSR since 1948 and 1961, respectively. These two countries broke away completely from the Soviet bloc. However, Yugoslavia has improved its relations significantly with other East European states, maintains close economic ties within the CMEA, and supports many basic tenets of Soviet foreign policy. The most successful case in which independence is being asserted concerns Romania and dates back in its overt form about 25 years. But even in that instance Bucharest has attempted to make an accommodation with Moscow rather than to challenge it openly. However, the plan to provide a socialist system in Czechoslovakia "with a human face" led to the August 1968 invasion of that country by neighboring Warsaw Pact troops. On the whole, differences in both politics and economics exist among the East European regimes themselves, affecting their relations with the Soviet Union but not threatening Moscow's pre-eminence.

Although intervention by Soviet armed forces crushed the revolution in Hungary, apart from the initial postrevolt terror in that country, there has been no return to the Stalinist type of government that precipitated the uprising. Kadar soon demonstrated firmly the impossibility of any alternative to the communist regime, and it seems that the population has indeed come to terms with this reality.[31] This situation is reinforced by the presence of four Soviet divisions that are temporarily garrisoned in Hungary. Although these forces pose a sensitive problem, Kadar has indicated openly that they will remain as long as they are needed. The same can be said of Czechoslovakia, where Husak and Jakes have repeatedly thanked the USSR leadership for saving communism in that country.

No Soviet troops have been stationed in Romania since 1958, and it is perhaps because of this situation that the communist regime in Bucharest dares to exploit nationalist sentiments domestically. There has been a deliberate attempt to underemphasize the role the Red Army played at the end of the war in establishing the present system. Compulsory study of the Russian language was discontinued in secondary school, and the Soviet names of streets in Bucharest were changed in the early 1960s. This trend reached a high point in 1964 with the publication of previously unprinted notes by Karl Marx on Romanian history of the late eighteenth and early nineteenth centuries; these notes indicted czarist policies and accepted the Romanian claim to Bessarabia. Further, Romanian party leaders and historical journals have criticized Comintern interference in party affairs during the interwar period. Romania's right to independence and sovereignty has been asserted repeatedly.[32]

As these developments have been taking place in various East European countries, bringing some internal relaxation and even some attempts at asserting a certain degree of independence vis-à-vis the Soviet Union, one of the bloc states has remained more rigid until recently. East Germany's position will continue to be unique because it is part of a divided country. Honecker must counter all independent tendencies and prevent domestic relaxation to avoid ferment and agitation for union with the much larger and wealthier Federal Republic of Germany. This has also been the reason behind his successful drive for diplomatic recognition of the German Democratic Republic as a sovereign state in its own right.

Initial agreements to establish West German trade offices in Poland, Romania, Hungary, Bulgaria, and Czechoslovakia made the East German regime uneasy. Negotiations by the Krupp combine for economic cooperation and joint enterprises in Eastern Europe certainly have political as well as economic overtones. Obviously, a growing trade with Bonn would make the other bloc partners less sensitive to the needs of Pankow. That is why East German propaganda stressed the danger of subversive activities by the trade missions and raised the specter of economic blackmail by the West. This campaign subsided when the trade missions became embassies.

On the other hand, Yugoslavia has always supported East Germany and extended de jure recognition to that regime despite the sanctions applied by West Germany under the former Hallstein Doctrine, whereby Bonn claimed to speak for all Germans. Until early 1967 it would not exchange ambassadors with any government recognizing the GDR. Attitudes by the bloc toward Yugoslavia have varied, depending on the behavior of Moscow. During two periods, 1948–1955 and 1958–1962, Tito found himself ostracized. By December 1962, however, when he visited the USSR, Khrushchev personally conceded that Yugoslavia was indeed a socialist country. The following month, a Yugoslav communist delegation traveled to East Berlin to attend another bloc party's congress for the first time since its expulsion from the Cominform. The extent of rapprochement with the USSR could be measured during the March 1988 visit by Gorbachev to Belgrade.[33]

All but one of the East European governments now accept Yugoslavia as a member of the ''socialist camp,'' even though it does not belong formally to the Soviet bloc. Albania continues to denounce its communist neighbor, although it has come to the realization that it needs a strong Yugoslavia to stand as a buffer between Soviet military might and its own borders. The reasons for this continued hostility include the fear of possible domination and the presence of a sizable Albanian minority in Yugoslavia whose number equals nearly 57 percent of the total population inside the borders of Albania itself. Toward the end of 1960, at the conference of 81 communist parties in Moscow, Enver Hoxha attacked the Soviet Union and accused it of attempting to starve Albania into submission. In the spring of the following year, the USSR and Czechoslovakia stopped aid to Tirana, which over the preceding thirteen years had amounted to more than one billion rubles; by the end of the summer all bloc experts and technicians had left Albania.

At the 22d CPSU congress, Khrushchev openly attacked the Albanian leadership for resorting to force and arbitrary repression. Diplomatic relations between the two countries were severed in December 1961 at the instigation of Moscow. After that time Albania stopped sending representatives to any CMEA or Warsaw Pact meetings (withdrawing from the latter after the 1968 military occupation of Czechoslovakia). The other bloc countries reduced their ranking diplomatic representatives to the levels of chargé d'affaires. The Romanians, however, have maintained relatively friendly relations with the Tirana regime. In recent years, especially since the death of Hoxha, contacts with other East European states have improved.

Sino-Soviet Dispute. Apart from the conflicts between the USSR and individual countries within Eastern Europe, as well as among the latter states themselves, the Sino-Soviet dispute had made an impact on the bloc due to the differing attitudes toward this rift. Ideologically, of course, the communist parties of all these countries except for Albania, Romania, and Yugoslavia never wavered in their support of Moscow. Besides proclaiming its neutrality, Romania attempted to mediate the quarrel by dispatching delegations to Peking and Moscow. Bucharest was definitely against any excommunication of China and remained opposed to a world conference that might precipitate such a move. The leaders of Bulgaria, Czechoslovakia, East Germany, and Poland supported the Soviet position as being correct both doctrinally and in the tactics used to handle the differences.[34] Over the past several years, every one of the East European bloc leaders has visited Beijing in anticipation that the CPSU general secretary Gorbachev may follow suit.

THE LIMITS OF RELAXATION

It would seem logical that the attainment of some freedom from Soviet control throughout Eastern Europe should be connected with a loosening of the totalitarian control exercised by each regime on the population concerned. That this is not necessarily true can be seen from the example of Albania, which has been de facto outside the bloc since the end of 1961 when the USSR severed diplomatic and party relations with that country. The leadership in Tirana continues its harsh rule and, hence, will not be treated in this section.

Among the other bloc countries, three have long delayed an internal détente for various reasons, including the fact that some of the leaders could not overcome their Stalinist backgrounds. In Czechoslovakia, the nationalism of the Slovaks and a general intellectual ferment precipitated disputes within the leadership that led to the ouster of Novotny. His successor, Dubcek, introduced reforms, but these were cut short by the 1968 Soviet-led invasion. East Germany has not experienced any relaxation to speak of, and it recently "celebrated" the 27th anniversary of the Berlin Wall.[35] Domestic policy in Romania has vacillated between strict internal control and limited liberalization, with control being the more recent, in sharp contrast to its assertions of independence within the CMEA and the Warsaw Pact.

Major differences can be seen between the two countries that played principal roles in attempts at defiance of the Soviet Union during 1956. Kadar, who was put into power in Hungary by the USSR and served its interest by betraying the government of Imre Nagy, has tried to obtain the support of the population and, by and large, has relaxed domestic conditions. Gierek, conversely, on whom so much hope was placed in Poland after December 1970, pursued policies that led the country (after ten years) to political stagnation, economic bankruptcy, and his expulsion from the party.[36]

Despite some changes, the communist regimes in Eastern Europe remain more similar than different. Not one of them has indicated an intention to abandon one-party rule or the centrally planned economy. Regardless of the speculation engendered by some of its behavior, even Romania will not leave the CMEA or the Warsaw Treaty Organization. It is true that the secret police are less in evidence throughout the bloc, but detailed card files on persons suspected of antiregime feelings are most certainly being maintained. Last but not least, the October 1981 ouster of Kania in Poland served to remind the average citizen that change in the top leadership in Eastern Europe may come suddenly and at the instigation of the USSR.

Repressive policies do not seem to have affected the numerical strength of the various communist parties. If anything, membership has increased. Until 1969 Czechoslovakia claimed the highest proportion of party members in relation to the total population.[37] East Germany and Romania have that distinction today. In other bloc countries this proportion ranges from 4.7 percent to 10.9 percent (see Table 72). Drives to increase membership alternate with purges, which are conducted periodically in connection with the exchange of party cards, so that the movement can cleanse itself.

In the meantime a trend has developed, beginning in Hungary and spreading throughout Eastern Europe, toward professional qualifications rather than party

Table 72
EASTERN EUROPE AND USSR, BASIC DATA, 1988

Country	Population	Communist party membership (percentage of total population)		Elections (percentage of vote and number of seats)
Albania	3,085,985	147,000	(4.7)	100.0 (1987); all 250 Democratic Front
Bulgaria	8,960,749	932,055	(10.4)	99.9 (1986); all 400 Fatherland Front
Czechoslovakia	15,581,993	1,705,490	(10.9)	99.9 (1986); all 350 National Front
East Germany	16,610,265	2,234,386	(13.5)	99.9 (1986); all 500 National Front
Hungary	10,613,000	870,992	(8.2)	98.9 (1985); all 352 Patriotic Front
Poland	37,726,699	2,130,000	(5.9)	78.8 (1985); all 460 National Unity Front
Romania	22,936,503	3,640,000	(15.9)	97.8 (1985); all 369 Front of Socialist Unity
USSR	284,008,160	19,037,946	(6.8)	99.9 (1984); all 1,500 CPSU-approved
Yugoslavia	23,430,830	2,168,000	(9.2)	70.0* (1986); all 308 Socialist Alliance

SOURCES: "Register of Communist Parties," in Richard F. Staar (ed.), *Yearbook on International Communist Affairs (YICA): 1988*, pp. xxi–xxii.

NOTE: *In 1982, that was the percentage of nomination meetings that accepted lists of candidates prepared in advance by the authorities. Robin Remington, "Yugoslavia," *YICA: 1987*, p. 383.

service as the basis for determining who shall occupy certain positions in the economy and public administration. The resulting conflict between the young (by and large nonpolitical) cadres and the old party members, who lack any training in management, is becoming intensified. The need of economic reform is closely connected with this trend and with the differing attitudes espoused by the young managerial elite and the party apparatus workers. Most of the regimes in the bloc now realize that progress cannot be achieved without a more realistic pricing system, at least some decentralization, and appropriate incentives for workers. Even Hungary and Poland have relaxed economic controls in important ways.

These developments have been accompanied by more contacts with the West, even in the case of regimes that have maintained the tightest control over their own populations. Although tourism is recognized as a major source of foreign exchange, Western visitors are still thought to represent a danger from the ideological point of view. In the opposite direction, Bulgaria, Czechoslovakia, East Germany, and Romania have strict regulations on foreign travel by their citizens, and currency restrictions are probably the main reason why it is also difficult for others to obtain passports.

Perhaps the threat of Western ideological "corruption" caused the reimposition of harsh controls on cultural life in Eastern Europe. Throughout the area, it seemed that the early 1960s represented the beginning of greater freedom for writers. This could be observed in Czechoslovakia, Hungary, Poland, and particularly Yugoslavia. After that time, journals were closed down, editorial boards changed, and some individuals indicted. The well-publicized cases of Polish philosophy professor Leszek Kolakowski and Yugoslav university instructor Mihajlo Mihajlov are especially pertinent; Kolakowski has been expelled from the Polish communist party and is now at Oxford, and Mihajlov, after being in and out of prison, has resided in the United States during the past several years.

Although a certain degree of relaxation came back to Eastern Europe during the mid-1980s, it is strictly limited and subject to sudden reversal. If developments in the Soviet Union may serve as a rough model, we should anticipate a struggle for power within the communist parties of the individual countries as soon as, or even before, the current leaders pass from the scene. It is not unlikely that one or more of these key individuals may follow in the footsteps of Khrushchev and be overthrown by a palace coup.

What Will the USSR Do?   The future of intrabloc relations will depend primarily upon the new Soviet leadership under Mikhail S. Gorbachev. The invasion of Czechoslovakia carried a warning to all other East European regimes against close bilateral dealings with the Federal Republic of Germany. It is not inconceivable, however, that the new group of Soviet leaders might decide in the future to purchase a West German exit from NATO by agreeing to the same status for East

Germany, that is, by having it withdraw from the Warsaw Pact and establishing some kind of neutral status for it.

If these moves materialize during the early 1990s, as part of a new overall European settlement, relations within the Warsaw Treaty Organization (WTO) will undergo modification. A decision may be reached to separate the WTO's political functions from its military ones. The appointment of a civilian Soviet government official as Warsaw Pact general secretary, a post always held before by the chief of staff (a career military officer), might represent a move in this direction. The Foreign Ministers' Council may also provide the East European representatives with a greater feeling of participation in the decision-making process.

On the other hand, eventual USSR military withdrawal from East Germany would probably necessitate strengthening the Soviet garrisons in Poland, Czechoslovakia, and Hungary. As compensation, the USSR might allow the rotation of WTO ground, air, navy, and air-defense commands among qualified senior officers from these three countries. Candidates could be selected from the graduates of the war college in Moscow. Their first deputies, however, would certainly be Soviet officers functioning as control agents. None of this will happen, however, if the next USSR leadership consists of hard-liners.

The economies of the East European countries will probably also remain dependent to a considerable degree on Soviet raw materials, especially petroleum, iron ore, and cotton. Some problems within the CMEA can be solved if and when an intrabloc convertibility of currencies is implemented. The long-range viability of the CMEA, however, will require closer relations with Western Europe. Poland and Romania, not to mention CMEA-affiliated Yugoslavia, are already members of the General Agreement on Tariffs and Trade (GATT). Such moves have paved the way for receiving hard-currency loans from the West. However, the Soviet Union has warned against running up enormous debts to Western banks.

Following the July–August 1981 meetings between Brezhnev and individual party leaders from Eastern Europe, the CPSU Politburo issued a communiqué that specifically mentioned Poland and provided guidelines for all Moscow-controlled communist regimes:

Adherence to Leninist norms in party activities

Strengthening links with the masses

Perfecting socialist democracy

Conducting a realistic economic policy, without excessive indebtedness to capitalist states

Educating workers in the spirit of internationalism

Manifesting revolutionary vigilance

Resolutely rebuffing antisocialist forces[38]

Each of these governments was then admonished to consider not only its own interests but also those of its "friends and allies."

Any true détente must be limited, however, by domestic as well as external considerations. The common desire on the part of all communist regimes is to remain in power, and they do not now and never have held this position by the will of the people they rule. This, then, is the broad framework within which the communist systems operate: they cannot permit complete freedom of expression, and their choice of policies is limited by the ideological straitjacket of Marxism-Leninism. Perhaps the only hope for Eastern Europe must be sought in the long-range process governing the development of human society, which in fact represents communism's invincible enemy.[39]

NOTES

1. Eugenio Reale, *Nascita del Cominform* (Rome, 1958), p. 51. For the predecessor organization see the research guide by Witold S. Sworakowski, *The Communist International and Its Front Organizations* (Stanford, Calif., 1965).

2. Guenther Nollau, *Die Internationale* (Cologne, 1959), pp. 196–96.

3. *For a Lasting Peace, For a People's Democracy,* 1 July 1948 and 29 November 1949.

4. U.S. Senate, Committee on the Judiciary, 85th Cong., 1st sess., *Speech of Nikita Khrushchev Before a Closed Session of the XXth Congress of the Communist Party of the Soviet Union on February 25, 1956* (Washington, D.C., 1957), 66 pp.

5. *Pravda,* 29 October 1961; translation in Charlotte Saikowski and Leo Gruliow (eds.), *Current Soviet Policies IV* (New York, 1962), p. 198.

6. Cited by Vladimir Kusin in *RAD Background Report,* no. 220 (Munich: RFE, 13 November 1987). Full speech in *Pravda,* 3 November 1987.

7. Nikolas A. Stavrou, "Albania," in *Yearbook on International Communist Affairs: 1983* (Stanford, Calif., 1983), pp. 247–48; henceforth, cited as *YICA.*

8. RFE, *Eastern Europe's Communist Leaders: Bulgaria* (Munich, 1966), vol. 4, pp. 34–37; Borys Lewytzkyj and Juliusz Stroynowski (eds.), *Who's Who in the Socialist Countries* (New York, 1978), p. 702.

9. Biography appeared in *Pravda,* 18 December 1987, p. 1, and *World Marxist Review* (February 1988), p. 70.

10. Branko Lazitch and Milorad M. Drachkovitch, *Biographical Dictionary of the Comintern* (Stanford, Calif., 1986), pp. 181–82; Lewytzkyj and Stroynowski, *Who's Who in the Socialist Countries,* p. 224; ADN dispatch, 13 October 1980.

11. *New York Times,* 23 May 1988, p. A-5.

12. *Trybuna ludu,* 20–21 July and 19 October 1981.

13. RFE, *Eastern Europe's Communist Leaders: Rumania,* vol. 3, pp. 19–22. See also his biography in the *New York Times,* 15 October 1970; Lewytzkyj and Stroynowski,

Who's Who in the Socialist Countries, p. 95; and Robert R. King, "Romania," in *YICA: 1988*, pp. 304–12.

14. His biography appeared in *Drustveno-politicke zajednice* (Belgrade, 1968), p. 222.

15. Robin L. Remington, "Yugoslavia" in *YICA: 1988*, pp. 354–71.

16. Even the Yugoslavs adopted this term, as can be seen from a lecture by Milenko Markovic at the Institute for Study of Workers' Movements, over Belgrade radio, 5 February 1965.

17. The memorandum appeared first in *Rinascita*, 5 September 1964.

18. Ibid., points 33 and 34.

19. *Pravda*, 3 April 1964.

20. Ibid., 17 October 1964.

21. *Krasnaia zvezda*, 10 March 1965.

22. In an article published by *Pravda*, 19 April 1970, Ceausescu implied that Romania would not support the USSR in a war against China, because the Warsaw Pact applies only to Europe.

23. R. F. Staar, "Soviet Policies in East Europe," *Current History* (October 1981), pp. 317–20, 342–43.

24. J. K. Zawodny, *Death in the Forest: The Story of the Katyn Forest Massacre* (Notre Dame, Ind., 1962), pp. 235, and his *Nothing But Honour: The Story of the Warsaw Uprising* (Stanford, Calif., 1977), pp. 69–70.

25. TASS dispatch, 5 December 1980, for communiqué; see also Robert L. Hutchings, *Soviet-East European Relations: Consolidation and Conflict, 1968–1980* (Madison, Wis., 1983), pp. 314.

26. Moscow television, 4 November 1987; *FBIS-Soviet Union*, 4 November 1987.

27. *Predvoj*, 19 January 1961.

28. Postwar censuses in Bulgaria showed 500,000 Macedonians in 1946, 180,000 in 1956, only 8,000 in 1965, and none at the end of 1975; *Vjesnik* (Zagreb), 11 January 1976, called this "statistical assimilation." Ten years later, only 2.5 percent of the Bulgarian population was identified as Macedonian in CIA, *World Factbook, 1987* (Washington, D.C., June 1987), p. 35.

29. Lenart subsequently became first secretary in the communist party of Slovakia. RFE, *East European Leadership List* (15 January 1988), p. 8. Lenart lost this position on 8 April 1988.

30. Ferenc A. Vali, *Rift and Revolt in Hungary* (Cambridge, Mass., 1961), especially pp. 358–80.

31. See editorial, "Twenty Years Ago," in *Nepszabadsag*, 4 November 1976, and the *New York Times*, 5 November 1986, for the 30th anniversary.

32. For an example, see *Revista de Filozofie*, no. 2 (March–April 1981), cited in RFE, *Romanian Situation Report*, no. 14 (22 July 1981), pp. 2–3. See also *Scinteia*, 27 May 1987, on Gorbachev's visit to Bucharest.

33. Gorbachev's address before the Yugoslav parliament appeared in *Pravda*, 17 March 1988, pp. 1–2.

34. Speeches given at the 1969 world conference of communist parties in Moscow were broadcast over radio stations in Warsaw, 6 June 1969; East Berlin, 9 June 1969; Sofia, 10 June 1969; and Prague, 12 June 1969.

35. However, during the first eight months of 1987 more than 866,000 GDR citizens were allowed to visit West Germany. *Neues Deutschland* (East Berlin), 9 September 1987.

36. Jan B. de Weydenthal, *The Communists of Poland* (Stanford, Calif., 1986), rev. ed., pp. 147–82.

37. During 1970, however, an exchange of party identification cards took place that led to a substantial decrease in membership. *Rude pravo,* 23 September 1970.

38. *Pravda,* 23 August 1981.

39. See Charles Gati, ''The Unsettled Condition of Eastern Europe,'' in Henry S. Rowen and Charles Wolf, Jr. (eds.), *The Future of the Soviet Empire* (New York, 1987), pp. 41–52.

Selected Bibliography

Albania

[Albania]. *40 Vjet Shqiperi Socialiste*. Tirana: 8 Nentori, 1984. 158 pp .

———. *History of the Party of Labour of Albania, 1966–1980*. 2d ed. Tirana: 8 Nentori, 1981. 327 pp .

———. *An Outline of the People's Socialist Republic of Albania*. Tirana: 8 Nentori, 1978. 177 pp.

———. *Twenty Years of Socialism in Albania*. Tirana: Naim Frasheri, 1964. 127 pp.

———. *Vjetari Statistikor i Republika Popullore te Shqiperise 1965–1981*. Tirana: Drejtoria e Statistikes, 1966–1982.

Alia, Ramiz. *Report to the 9th Congress of the Party of Labor of Albania*. Tirana: 8 Nentori, 1986. 214 pp.

Bardhoschi, Besim, and Kareco, Theodor. *The Economic and Social Development of the People's Republic of Albania During Thirty Years of People's Power*. Tirana: 8 Nentori, 1974. 247 pp.

Biberaj, Elez. *Albania and China: A Study of an Unequal Alliance*. Boulder, Colo.: Westview Press, 1986. 180 pp.

Cami, Foto. *Constitution of Triumphant Socialism*. Tirana: 8 Nentori, 1980. 153 pp.

Dilo, Jani I. *The Communist Party Leadership in Albania*. Washington, D.C.: Institute of Ethnic Studies at Georgetown University, 1961. 20 pp.

Dodic, Lazar. *Historischer Rueckblick auf die Stellung Albaniens im Weltkommunismus*. Trittau/Holstein: Juergen Scherbarth, 1970. 142 pp.

Fournial, Georges (preface). *Le Proces des espions parachutes en Albanie*. Paris: Editions Sociales, 1950. 201 pp.

Halliday, Jon, ed. *Memoirs of Enver Hoxha*. London: Chatto and Windus, 1986. 394 pp.

Hamm, Harry. *Albania: China's Beachhead in Europe*. London: Weidenfeld & Nicolson, 1963. 176 pp.

Hoxha, Enver. *Selected Works*. 59 vols. Tirana: 8 Nentori, 1969–1988.

Kessel, Patrick. *Les Communistes albanais contre le revisionnisme: De Tito a Krouchtchev, 1942–1961: Textes et documents*. Paris: Union Generale d'editions, 1974. 426 pp.

Lange, Klaus. *Grundzuege der albanischen Politik*. Munich: Rudolf Trofenik, 1973. 129 pp.

Logoreci, Anton. *The Albanians: Europe's Forgotten Survivors*. London: Victor Gollancz, 1977. 230 pp.

Lorenz, Lothar. *Volksrepublik Albanien*. Giessen: Aschenbach, 1974. 204 pp.

Marmullaku, Ramadan. *Albania and the Albanians*. London: C. Hurst, 1975. 178 pp.

Myrdal, Jan, and Kessle, Gun. *Albania Defiant*. New York: Monthly Review Press, 1976. 185 pp.

Omari, Luan. *The People's Revolution and the Question of State Power in Albania*. Tirana: 8 Nentori, 1986. 230 pp.

Pano, Nicholas C. *The People's Republic of Albania*. Baltimore, Md.: Johns Hopkins University Press, 1968. 185 pp.

Pollo, Stafanaq. *The History of Albania: From Its Origins to the Present Day*. London: Routledge & Kegan Paul, 1981. 322 pp.

Prifti, Peter R. *Albania Since 1944*. Cambridge, Mass.: MIT Press, 1978. 311 pp.

Russ, Wolfgang. *Der Entwicklungsweg Albaniens*. Meisenheim am Glan: Anton Hain, 1979. 350 pp.

Shehu, Mehmet. *Der Kampf um die Befreiung Tiranas*. Tirana: 8 Nentori, 1980. 131 pp.

Skendi, Stavro, ed. *Albania*. New York: Praeger, 1956. 389 pp.

Thomas, John I. *Education for Communism: School and State in the People's Republic of Albania*. Stanford: Hoover Institution Press, 1969. 131 pp.

Toennes, Bernhard. *Sonderfall Albanien*. Munich: Oldenbourg, 1980. 512 pp.

[United States]. Central Intelligence Agency, *Directory of Albanian Officials*. Washington, D.C.: Directorate of Intelligence. June 1985, CR 85–10668. 91 pp.

Bulgaria

Bell, John D. *The Bulgarian Communist Party: From Blagoev to Zhivkov*. Stanford: Hoover Institution Press, 1986. 202 pp.

Bernov, Iu. V., and Cherneiko, G. A. *Narodnaia Respublika Bolgariia: spravochnik*. Moscow: Politizdat, 1974. 127 pp.

Bidinskaia, L., ed. *Istoriia Bolgarskoi Kommunisticheskoi Partii*. Moscow: Gospolitizdat, 1960. 392 pp.

Bogomolov, O. T., chief ed. *Narodnaia Respublika Bolgariia*. Moscow: Nauka, 1983. 333 pp.

[Bulgaria]. *Constitution of the People's Republic of Bulgaria*. Sofia: Foreign Languages Press, 1964. 33 pp.

————. *Dvanadeseti kongres na Bulgarskata kumunisticheska partiia: Dokladi i resheniia*. Sofia: Partizdat, 1981. 238 pp.

————. *Information Bulgaria: A Short Encyclopaedia of the People's Republic of Bulgaria*. New York: Pergamon Press, 1985. 976 pp.

————. *Konstitutsiia na Narodna Republika Bolgariia*. Sofia: Nauka i Izkustvo, 1971. 64 pp.

————. *Problems of the Transition from Capitalism to Socialism in Bulgaria.* Sofia: Bulgarian Academy of Sciences, 1975. 365 pp.

————. *Statisticheskii ezhegodnik, 1969–1981.* Sofia: Gosudarstvennoe Upravlenie Informatsii, 1970–1982.

————. *Statisticheskii godishnik na Narodna Republika Bulgariia, 1986.* Sofia: Tsentralno statistichesko upravlenie, 1987. 683 pp.

Cherneiko, G. A., et al., eds. *Narodnaia Respublika Bolgariia.* Moscow: Nauka, 1974. 175 pp.

Dellin, L. A. D., ed. *Bulgaria.* New York: Praeger, 1957. 457 pp.

Devedjiev, Hristo H. *Stalinization of the Bulgarian Society, 1949–1953.* Philadelphia: Dorrance, 1975. 216 pp.

Dobrin, Bogoslav. *Bulgarian Economic Development Since World War II.* New York: Praeger, 1973. 185 pp.

Economist Intelligence Unit. *Country Profile, 1986–87: Bulgaria, Albania.* London, The Economist, 1986. 39 pp.

Evans, Stanley George. *A Short History of Bulgaria.* London: Lawrence & Wishart, 1960. 254 pp.

Feiwel, George R. *Growth and Reforms in Centrally Planned Economies: The Lessons of the Bulgarian Experience.* New York: Praeger, 1977. 345 pp.

Ganchovski, Nedelcho. *Georgii Dimitrov.* 2 vols. Moscow: Politizdat, 1979.

Ganov, Banko. *Dimitur Blagoev.* Sofia: Narodna prosveta, 1978. 163 pp.

Kabakchiev, Khristo Stefanov. *Dimitur Blagoev i partiinata na tesnite sotsialisti.* Sofia: Partizdat, 1979. 395 pp.

Kostov, Pavel, et al., ed. *Materiali po istoriia na Bulgarskata Komunisticheska Partiia (1944–1960).* Sofia: Izdatelstvo na BKP, 1961. 195 pp.

Lampe, John R. *The Bulgarian Economy in the Twenthieth Century.* London: Croom Helm, 1986. 245 pp.

Litavrin, G. G., ed. *Kratkaia istoriia Bolgarii.* Moscow: Nauka, 1987. 568 pp.

Markov, Georgi. *The Truth That Killed.* New Haven, Conn.: Ticknor & Fields, 1984. 280 pp.

McIntyre, Robert. *Bulgaria: Politics, Economics and Society.* London: Francis Pinter, 1988. 200 pp.

Michev, Dobrin, et al. *Georgi Dimitrov: Biografiia.* Sofia: Partizdat, 1982. 663 pp.

Moser, Charles A. *Dimitrov of Bulgaria: A Political Biography of Dr. Georgi M. Dimitrov.* Thornwood, N.Y.: Caroline House, 1979. 360 pp.

[United States]. Central Intelligence Agency, *Directory of Bulgarian Officials.* Washington, D.C.: Directorate of Intelligence, October 1986, LDA86–12408. 137 pp.

Zhivkov, Todor. *Za partiinoto stroitelstvo: dokladi, rechi, statii.* 3 vols. Sofia: Politizdat, 1978.

Czechoslovakia

Benes, Edward. *Memoirs of Dr. Edward Benes.* London: Allen & Unwin, 1954. 364 pp.

Brisch, Hans, and Volgyes, Ivan, eds. *Czechoslovakia.* Boulder, Colo.: East European Quarterly, 1979. 239 pp.

Bugajski, Janusz. *Czechoslovakia: Charter 77's Decade of Dissent.* New York: Praeger, 1987. 118 pp.

Bystrina, Ivan. *Narodnaia demokratiia v Chekhoslovakii.* Moscow: Gosiurizdat, 1961. 265 pp.

Cerny, Jan, and Cervenka, Vaclav, comps. *Statni obcanstvi CSSR.* Prague: Orbis, 1963. 196 pp.

[Czechoslovakia]. *The Constitution of the Czechoslovak Socialist Republic.* Prague: Orbis, 1964. 70 pp.

————. *Statisticka rocenka CSSR, 1986.* Prague: Statni Nakladatelstvi Technicke Literatury, 1986. 695 pp.

Dawisha, Karen. *The Kremlin and the Prague Spring.* Berkeley: University of California Press, 1984. 426 pp.

Epifanov, M. P., ed. *15 let svobodnoi Chekhoslovakii.* Moscow: IMO, 1960. 191 pp.

Faye, Jean Pierre. *Prague: La Revolution des conseils ouvriers, 1968–1969.* Paris: Seghers-Laffont, 1978. 285 pp.

Golan, Galia. *Reform Rule in Czechoslovakia: The Dubcek Era, 1968–1969.* Cambridge, Eng.: Cambridge University Press, 1975. 349 pp.

Gottwald, Klement. *Vybor z dila.* 2 vols. Prague: Svoboda, 1971.

Hajek, Jiri. *Dix ans apres Prague, 1968–1978.* Paris: Editions du Seuil, 1978. 203 pp.

Horsky, Vladimir. *Prag 1968: Systemveraenderung und Systemverteidigung.* Munich: Koesel, 1975. 534 pp.

Hruby, Peter. *Fools and Heroes: The Changing Role of Communist Intellectuals in Czechoslovakia.* Oxford, Eng.: Pergamon Press, 1980. 265 pp.

Kalvoda, Josef. *Czechoslovakia's Role in Soviet Strategy.* Washington, D.C.: University Press of America, 1978. 382 pp.

————. *The Genesis of Czechoslovakia.* Boulder, Colo.: East European Monographs, 1986. 673 pp.

Kaplan, Karel. *The Communist Party in Power.* Boulder, Colo.: Westview Press, 1987. 231 pp.

————. *The Short March: The Communist Takeover of Power in Czechoslovakia, 1945–48.* London: C. Hurst, 1985. 240 pp.

Korbel, Josef. *The Communist Subversion of Czechoslovakia: 1938–1948.* Princeton, N.J.: Princeton University Press, 1959. 258 pp.

Krechler, Vladimir, ed. *Prirucni slovnik k dejinam KSC.* 2 vols. Prague: Nakladatelstvi Politicke Literatury, 1964.

Kuhn, Heinrich, comp. *Biographisches Handbuch der Tschechoslowakei.* Munich: Robert Lerche, 1969.

Kusin, Vladimir V. *From Dubcek to Charter 77.* New York: St. Martin's Press, 1978. 353 pp.

Loebl, Eugen. *My Mind on Trial.* New York: Harcourt Brace Jovanovich, 1976. 235 pp.

Mamatey, Victor S., and Luza, Radomir, eds. *A History of the Czechoslovak Republic, 1918–1948*. Princeton, N.J.: Princeton University Press, 1973. 534 pp.

Mlynar, Zdenek. *Nachtfrost: Erfahrungen auf dem Weg vom realen zum menschlichen Sozialismus*. Cologne: Europaeische Verlagsanstalt, 1978. 366 pp.

Pachman, Ludek. *Was in Prag wirklich geschah: Illusionen und Tatsachen aus der Aera Dubcek*. Freiburg: Herder, 1978. 127 pp.

Paul, David W. *Czechoslovakia: A Profile of a Socialist Republic at the Crossroads of Europe*. Boulder, Colo.: Westview Press, 1981. 186 pp.

Pech, Stanley Z. *The Czech Revolution of 1948*. Chapel Hill: University of North Carolina Press, 1969. 386 pp.

Piekalkiewicz, Jaroslaw A. *Public Opinion Polling in Czechoslovakia, 1968–1969: Results and Analysis of Surveys Conducted During the Dubcek Era*. New York: Praeger, 1972. 330 pp.

Precan, Vilem. *Die sieben Jahre von Prag, 1969–1976*. Frankfurt/Main: Fischer, 1978. 253 pp.

Reiman, Pavel, ed. *Dejiny Komunisticke Strany Ceskoslovenska*. Prague: Statni Nakladatelstvi Politicke Literatury, 1961. 710 pp.

Rice, Condoleezza. *The Soviet Union and the Czechoslovak Army, 1948–1983: Uncertain Allegiance*. Princeton, N.J.: Princeton University Press, 1984. 303 pp.

Riese, Hans-Peter, ed. *Since the Prague Spring*. New York: Vintage Books, 1979. 288 pp.

Rupnik, Jacques. *Histoire du parti communiste Tchecoslovaque*. Paris: Fondation Nationale des Sciences Politiques, 1981. 257 pp.

Shawcross, William. *Dubcek*. New York: Simon & Schuster, 1971. 317 pp.

Sik, Ota. *Das kommunistische Machtsystem*. Hamburg: Hoffmann & Campe, 1976. 357 pp.

Simecka, Milan. *The Restoration of Order: The Normalization of Czechoslovakia, 1969–1976*. London: Verso, 1985. 167 pp.

Skilling, H. Gordon. *Charter 77 and Human Rights in Czechoslovakia*. Winchester, Mass.: Allen & Unwin, 1981. 363 pp.

―――. *Czechoslovakia's Interrupted Revolution*. Princeton, N.J.: Princeton University Press, 1976. 924 pp.

Stepanek-Stemmer, Michael. *Der wahre Dubcek: Woran der Prager Fruehling scheiterte*. Cologne: Ellenberg, 1978. 182 pp.

Suda, Zdenek. *Zealots and Rebels: A History of the Ruling Communist Party of Czechoslovakia*. Stanford: Hoover Institution Press, 1980. 412 pp.

Taborsky, Edward. *Communism in Czechoslovakia, 1948–1960*. Princeton, N.J.: Princeton University Press, 1961. 628 pp.

―――. *President Edvard Benes Between East and West, 1938–1948*. Stanford: Hoover Institution Press, 1981. 299 pp.

[United States]. Central Intelligence Agency, *Directory of Czechoslovak Officials*. Washington, D.C.: Directorate of Intelligence, May 1985, CR 85–12102. 166 pp.

Valenta, Jiri. *Soviet Intervention in Czechoslovakia 1968: Anatomy of a Decision*. Baltimore, Md.: Johns Hopkins University Press, 1979. 208 pp.

Vidnianskii, S. V. *Konsolidatsiia profsoiuznogo dvizheniia v Chekhoslovakii, 1969–1975*. Kiev: Naukova dumka, 1979. 209 pp.

Vladislav, Jan, ed. *Vaclav Havel or Living in Truth*. London: Faber & Faber, 1987. 315 pp.

Zinner, Paul E. *Communist Strategy and Tactics in Czechoslovakia*. New York: Praeger, 1963. 264 pp.

German Democratic Republic

Baerns, Barbara, ed. *Die DDR in Deutschland*. Cologne: Wissenschaft & Politik, 1986. 119 pp.

Baske, Siegfried, ed. *Bildungspolitik in der DDR, 1963–1976*. Wiesbaden: Harrassowitz, 1980. 493 pp.

Behr, Wolfgang. *Bundesrepublik Deutschland-Deutsche Demokratische Republik: System-vergleich*. Stuttgart: Kohlhammer, 1979. 203 pp.

Bentley, Raymond. *Technological Change in the German Democratic Republic*. Boulder, Colo.: Westview Press, 1984. 296 pp.

Beyme, Klaus von, and Zimmerman, Hartmut, eds. *Policymaking in the German Democratic Republic*. New York: St. Martin's Press, 1983. 401 pp.

Biermann, Wolfgang. *Demokratisierung in der DDR*. Cologne: Wissenschaft & Politik, 1978. 170 pp.

Buch, Guenther, comp. *Namen und Daten: Biographien wichtiger Personen der DDR*. 3d rev. ed. West Berlin: Dietz, 1982. 384 pp.

Buxhoeveden, Christina von. *Gewissenschaft und Politik in der DDR*. Cologne: Wissenschaft & Politik, 1980. 301 pp.

Childs, David. *The GDR: Moscow's German Ally*. 2d rev. ed. Winchester, Mass.: Unwin Hyman, 1988. 384 pp.

Dennis, Mike. *German Democratic Republic: Politics, Economics and Society*. London: Pinter, 1988. 223 pp.

Deutsches Institut fuer Wirtschaftsforschung Berlin. *Handbuch DDR-Wirtschaft*. 4th ed. Reinbek bei Hamburg: Rowohlt, 1984. 439 pp.

Dornberg, Stefan, chief ed. *Aussenpolitik der DDR*. East Berlin: Staatsverlag der DDR, 1979. 240 pp.

Dulles, Eleanor Lansing. *The Wall: A Tragedy in Three Acts*. Columbia: University of South Carolina Press, 1972. 105 pp.

Edwards, G. E. *GDR Society and Social Institutions*. London: Macmillan, 1985. 244 pp.

Erbe, Gunter, et al. *Politik, Wirtschaft und Gesellschaft der DDR*. Opladen: Westdeutscher Verlag, 1979. 421 pp.

Federal Republic of Germany. *Der Staats- und Parteiapparat der Deutschen Demokratischen Republik*. Bonn, 1986. 54 pp.

———. *Materialen zum Bericht zur Lage der Nation im geteilten Deutschland, 1987*. Bonn: Bundesministerium fuer Innerdeutsche Beziehungen, 1987. 819 pp.

————. Bundesministerium fuer gesamtdeutsche Fragen. *SBZ von A bis Z.* 11th ed. Bonn, 1969. 832 pp.

————. *SBZ von 1945 bis 1954.* 3d ed. Bonn, 1961. 324 pp.

————. *SBZ von 1955 bis 1958.* Bonn, 1961. 594 pp.

————. *SBZ von 1959–1960.* Bonn, 1964. 317 pp.

Foster, Thomas M. *Die NVA: Kernstueck der Landesverteidigung der DDR.* Cologne: Markus-Verlagsgesellschaft, 1983. 414 pp.

————. *The East German Army: Second in the Warsaw Pact.* 2d ed. London: Allen & Unwin, 1980. 310 pp.

Freiburg, Arnold. *Kriminalitaet in der DDR.* Wiesbaden: Westdeutscher Verlag, 1980. 370 pp.

Fricke, Karl Wilhelm. *Opposition und Widerstand in der DDR.* Cologne: Wissenschaft & Politik, 1984. 254 pp.

————. *Zur Menschen- und Grundrechtssituation politischer Gefangener in der DDR.* Cologne: Wissenschaft & Politik, 1986. 255 pp.

[German Democratic Republic]. *The Constitution of the German Democratic Republic of 1968, as Modified in 1974.* East Berlin: Staatsverlag der DDR, 1974. 56 pp.

————. *Der Grundvertrag.* East Berlin: Staatsverlag der DDR, 1973. 224 pp.

————. *Directives Issued by the 19th Congress of the SED for the Five-Year Plan for the GDR's National Economic Development, 1981–1985.* East Berlin: Zeit im Bild, 1981. 196 pp.

————. Institut fuer Hochschulbildung. *Das Hochschulwesen der DDR: Ein Ueberblick.* East Berlin: Deutscher Verlag der Wissenschaften, 1980. 259 pp.

————. Ministerium fuer Auswaertige Angelegenheiten. *Die Organisation des Warschauer Vertrages: Dokumente und Materialien, 1955–1985.* East Berlin: Staatsverlag der DDR, 1985. 336 pp.

————. *Statistical Pocket Book of the German Democratic Republic, 1987.* East Berlin: Staatsverlag der DDR, 1987. 160 pp.

————. *Statistisches Jahrbuch der DDR, 1955–1987.* East Berlin: Deutscher Zentralverlag, 1956–1988.

————. *Zehnter Parteitag der SED im Palast der Republik in Berlin, 11–16 April 1981.* 2 vols. East Berlin: Dietz, 1982.

————. SED. Politbuero. *Tagung, 1975–1980.* East Berlin: Dietz, 1980. 190 pp.

Gradl, J. B. *Anfang unter dem Sowjetstern: Die CDU 1945–1948 in der sowjetishchen Besatzungszone Deutschlands.* Cologne: Wissenschaft & Politik, 1981. 208 pp.

Groschoff, Kurt, ed. *Die Landwirtschaft der DDR.* East Berlin: Dietz, 1980, 470 pp.

Haase, Herwig E. *Entwicklungstendenzen der DDR: Wirtschaft fuer die 80er Jahre.* West Berlin: Osteuropa Institut, 1980. 115 pp.

Hackel, Renate. *Katholische Publizistik in der DDR, 1945–1984.* Mainz: Matthias Gruenewald, 1987. 163 pp.

Hacker, Jens, et al. *Die nationale Volksarmee der DDR in Rahmen des Warschauer Paktes.* Munich: Bernard & Graefe Verlag, 1980. 238 pp.

Hartwig, Juergen, and Wimmel, Albert. *Wehrerziehung und vormilitaerische Ausbildung der Kinder und Jugendlichen in der DDR.* Stuttgart: Seewald, 1979. 207 pp.

Heidenheimer, Arnold J. *The Governments of Germany.* 2d ed. New York: Crowell, 1966. 254 pp.

Heinrich, Wolfgang. *Das unverzichtbare Feinbild: Hasserziehung in der DDR.* Bonn: Hohwacht, 1981. 111 pp.

Herrmann, Friedrich-Georg. *Der Kampf gegen Religion und Kirche in der sowjetischen Besatzungszone Deutschlands.* Stuttgart: Quell, 1966. 142 pp.

Hindrichs, Armin. *Die Buergerkriegsarmee: Die militanten Kampfgruppen des deutschen Kommunismus.* 2d ed. West Berlin: Arani, 1964. 174 pp.

Honecker, Erich. *Reden und Aufsaetze.* East Berlin: Dietz, 1987. 467 pp.

————. *Report to the Central Committee of the Socialist Unity Party of Germany, to the 11th Congress of the SED.* East Berlin: SED, 1986. 109 pp.

Klein, Fritz. *Friedliche Koexistenz: Erfahrungen—Chancen—Gefahren.* East Berlin: Akademie Verlag, 1987. 300 pp.

Klein, Margarete Siebert. *The Challenge of Communist Education: A Look at the German Democratic Republic.* New York: Columbia University Press, 1980. 174 pp.

Krisch, Henry. *The Democratic German Republic.* Boulder, Colo.: Westview Press, 1985. 105 pp.

Kul'bakin, V. D., ed. *Istoriia G.D.R., 1949–1979.* Moscow: Nauka, 1979. 535 pp.

Leonhard, Wolfgang. *Child of the Revolution.* Chicago: Regnery, 1958. 447 pp.

Lippmann, Heinz. *Honecker: Portraet eines Nachfolgers.* Cologne: Wissenschaft & Politik, 1971. 272 pp.

Lueers, Hartwig. *Das Polizeirecht in der DDR.* Cologne: Wissenschaft & Politik, 1982. 156 pp.

Mampel, Siegfried. *Die sozialistische Verfassung der Deutschen Demokratischen Republik: Text und Kommentar.* Frankfurt/Main: Metzner, 1982. 1364 pp.

McAdams, A. James. *East Germany and Detente.* New York: Cambridge University Press, 1985. 233 pp.

McArdle, Arthur W., and Boenau, Bruce. *East Germany: A New Nation under Socialism?* Washington, D.C.: University Press of America, 1984. 364 pp.

McCauley, Martin. *The German Democratic Republic Since 1945.* London: Macmillan, 1983. 282 pp.

Meyer, Michel. *Freikauf: Menschenhandel in Deutschland.* Vienna: Paul Zsolnay, 1978. 218 pp.

Nawrocki, Joachim. *Bewaffnete Organe der DDR.* West Berlin: Holzapfel, 1979. 206 pp.

Noll, Fritz. *Ueber Schwerter und Pflugschare: Der DDR-Friedensbewegung.* Neuss: Plambeck & Co., 1982. 141 pp.

Plischke, Elmer. *Contemporary Government of Germany.* 2d ed. Boston: Houghton Mifflin, 1969. 248 pp.

Prokop, Siegfried. *Uebergang zum Sozialismus in der DDR.* East Berlin: Dietz, 1986. 420 pp.

Rossmann, Gerhard, et al., eds. *Geschichte der Sozialistischen Einheitspartei Deutschlands.* East Berlin: Dietz, 1978. 676 pp.

Ruetz, Michael. *Im anderen Deutschland: Menschen in der DDR.* Munich: Artemis, 1979. 124 pp.

Scharf, C. Bradley. *Politics and Change in East Germany.* Boulder, Colo.: Westview, 1984. 219 pp.

Schneider, Eberhard. *The GDR: The History, Politics, Economy and the Society of East Germany.* London: C. Hurst, 1978. 121 pp.

Shabalin, A. Ia., ed. *Germanskaia Demokraticheskaia Respublika.* Moscow: Nauka, 1983. 358 pp.

Socialist Unity Party of Germany. *Direktive des XI. Parteitages des SED zum Fuenfjahrplan fuer die Entwicklung der Volkswirtschaft der DDR in den Jahren 1986 bis 1990.* East Berlin: Dietz, 1986. 125 pp.

————. *Dokumente und Materialen der Zusammenarbeit zwischen der Sozialistischen Einheitspartei Deutschlands und der Kommunistischen Partei der Sowjetunion, 1980 bis 1985.* East Berlin: Dietz, 1986. 640 pp.

Starrels, John M., and Mallinckrodt, Anita M. *Politics in the German Democratic Republic.* New York: Praeger, 1975. 350 pp.

Surman, Rolf. *Die Muenzenberg-Legende.* Cologne: Boehlau, 1983. 307 pp.

Thalheim, Karl Christian. *Die wirtschaftliche Entwicklung der beiden Staaten in Deutschland.* Opladen: Leske, 1978. 142 pp.

Ulbricht, Walter. *Ausgewaehlte Reden und Aufsaetze.* East Berlin: Dietz, 1979. 342 pp.

[United States]. Central Intelligence Agency, *Directory of East German Officials.* Washington, D.C.: Directorate of Intelligence, August 1987, LDA 87–12937. 181 pp.

Weber, Hermann. *DDR: Grundriss der Geschichte, 1945–1981.* Hannover: Fackeltraeger, 1982. 242 pp.

Weber, Hermann, and Oldenburg, Fred. *25 Jahre SED: Chronik einer Partei.* Cologne: Wissenschaft & Politik, 1971. 160 pp.

Weichelt, Wolfgang, et al. *Der Staat im politischen System der DDR.* East Berlin: Staatsverlag der DDR, 1986. 400 pp.

Wilhelmi, Jutta. *Jugend in der DDR: Der Weg zur "sozialistischen Persoenlichkeit."* West Berlin: Holzapfel, 1983. 141 pp.

Woods, Roger. *Opposition in the GDR under Honecker, 1971–85.* London: Macmillan, 1986. 267 pp.

Zimmermann, Friedrich. *Verfassungsschutzbericht, 1987.* Bonn: Der Bundesminister des Innern, 1988.

Zimmermann, Hartmut, ed. *DDR Handbuch.* 2 vols. Cologne: Wissenschaft & Politik, 1985.

Zitzlaff, Dietrich. *DDR-Jugend heute.* Stuttgart: Metzler, 1986. 153 pp.

Hungary

Andorka, Rudolf, and Bertalan, Laszlo, eds. *Economy and Society in Hungary.* Budapest: Karl Marx University, 1986. 331 pp.

Balogh, Sandor. *Parlamenti es Partharcok Magyarorszagon, 1945–1947*. Budapest: Kossuth Konyvkiado, 1975. 631 pp.

Berend, Ivan R., and Ranki, Gyorgy. *The Hungarian Economy in the Twentieth Century*. New York: St. Martin's Press, 1985. 336 pp.

Delaney, Robert F., ed. *This Is Communist Hungary*. Chicago: Regnery, 1958. 260 pp.

Egorov, Iu., ed. *Kadar Janos: Izbrannye statii i rechi, 1957–1960 gody*. Moscow: Gospolitizdat, 1960. 643 pp.

Feher, Ferenc, and Heller, Agnes. *Hungary 1956 Revisited*. Winchester, Mass.: Allen & Unwin, 1983. 174 pp.

Fejto, Francois. *Memoires de Budapest a Paris*. Paris: Calmann-Levy, 1986. 323 pp.

Friss, Istvan, ed. *Essays on Economic Policy and Planning in Hungary*. Budapest: Corvina, 1978. 279 pp.

Gadney, Reg. *Cry Hungary!: Uprising 1956*. London: Weidenfeld & Nicholson, 1986. 180 pp.

Gati, Charles. *Hungary and the Soviet Bloc*. Durham, N.C.: Duke University Press, 1986. 244 pp.

Grothusen, Klaus-Detlev, ed. *Ungarn*. Goettingen: Vandehoeck & Ruprecht, 1987. 781 pp.

Hajdu, Tibor. *The Hungarian Soviet Republic*. Budapest: Akademiai Kiado, 1979. 172 pp.

Hare, Paul; Radice, Hugo; and Swain, Nigel, eds. *Hungary: A Decade of Economic Reform*. Winchester, Mass.: Allen & Unwin, 1981. 257 pp.

Held, Joseph, ed. *The Modernization of Agriculture: Rural Transformation in Hungary*. New York: Columbia University Press, 1980. 508 pp.

Helmreich, Ernest C., ed. *Hungary*. New York: Praeger, 1957. 466 pp.

Hungarian Socialist Workers' Party. *A Magyar Szocialista Munkaspart XI. kongresszusa 1975. Marcius 17–22*. Budapest: Kossuth Konyvkiado, 1975. 247 pp.

———. *A Magyar Szocialista Munkaspart XII. kongresszusanak jeguzokonyve: 24–27 March 1980*. Budapest: Kossuth Konyvkiado, 1980. 544 pp.

———. *The 13th Congress of the Hungarian Socialist Workers' Party: 25–28 March 1985*. Budapest: Corvina, 1985. 291 pp.

[Hungary]. Central Statistical Office. *Statisztikai evkonyv, 1987*. Budapest: Kozponti Statisztikai Hivatal, 1987. 493 pp.

———. *Statistical Pocket Book of Hungary, 1969–1988*. Budapest: Statistical Publishing House, 1969–1988.

Kadar, Janos. *Sotsializm i mirovoi revoliutsionyi protsess*. Moscow: Mysl, 1978. 350 pp.

Kiraly, Bela, and Jonas, Paul, eds. *The Hungarian Revolution of 1956 in Retrospect*. New York: Columbia University Press, 1978. 157 pp.

Kiraly, Bela; Lotze, Barbara; and Dreisziger, Nandor F., eds. *The First War Between Socialist States: The Hungarian Revolution and its Impact*. New York: Brooklyn College Press, 1984. 608 pp.

Kopacsi, Sandor. *In the Name of the Working Class: The Inside Story of the Hungarian Revolution*. New York: Grove Press, 1986. 304 pp.

Kopeczi, Bela. *Kulturrevolution in Ungarn.* Budapest: Corvina, 1978. 404 pp.

Kovaly, Heda, and Kohak, Erazim. *The Victors and the Vanquished.* New York: Horizon, 1973. 274 pp.

Kovrig, Bennett. *Communism in Hungary: From Kun to Kadar.* Stanford: Hoover Institution Press, 1979. 525 pp.

Lommax, Bill, ed. *Eyewitness in Hungary: The Soviet Invasion of 1956.* Nottingham, Eng.: Spokesman, 1980. 183 pp.

Molnar, Miklos. *De Bela Kun a Janos Kadar: Soixante-dix ans de communisme hongrois.* Paris: Fondation Nationale des Sciences Politiques, 1987. 335 pp.

————. *A Short History of the Hungarian Communist Party.* Boulder, Colo.: Westview, 1978. 136 pp.

Paloczi-Horvath, George. *The Undefeated.* Boston, Mass.: Little Brown, 1959. 305 pp.

Radvanyi, Janos. *Hungary and the Superpowers: The 1956 Revolution and Realpolitik.* Stanford: Hoover Institution Press, 1972. 197 pp.

Robinson, William F. *The Pattern of Reform in Hungary: A Political, Economic and Cultural Analysis.* New York: Praeger, 1973. 467 pp.

Szoboszlai, Gyorgy. *Politics and Public Administration in Hungary.* Budapest: Akademiai Kiado, 1985. 485 pp.

Toma, Peter A. *Socialist Authority: The Hungarian Experience.* New York: Praeger, 1988. 180 pp.

Toma, Peter A., and Volgyes, Ivan. *Politics in Hungary.* San Francisco: Freeman, 1977. 188 pp.

[United States]. Central Intelligence Agency. *Directory of Hungarian Officials.* Washington, D.C.: Directorate of Intelligence, July 1987, LDA 87–12233. 130 pp.

Vali, Ferenc A. *Rift and Revolt in Hungary: Nationalism Versus Communism.* Cambridge, Mass.: Harvard University Press, 1961. 590 pp.

Vasary, Ildiko. *Beyond the Plan: Social Change in a Hungarian Village.* Boulder, Colo.: Westview Press, 1987. 308 pp.

Volgyes, Ivan. *The Hungarian Soviet Republic, 1919: An Evaluation and a Bibliography.* Stanford: Hoover Institution Press, 1970. 90 pp.

————. *Hungary: A Profile.* Boulder, Colo.: Westview Press, 1981. 128 pp.

Poland

Andrews, Nicholas G. *Poland, 1980–81: Solidarity versus the Party.* Washington, D.C.: National Defense University Press, 1985. 351 pp.

Barecki, Jozef, ed. *Rocznik polityczny i gospodarczy, 1981–1983.* Warsaw: Panstwowe Wydawnictwo Ekonomiczne, 1984. 464 pp.

Bingen, Dietrich, ed. *Polen, 1980–1984: Dauerkrise oder Stabilisierung?* Baden-Baden: Nomos, 1985. 401 pp.

Black, Jonathan. *Militaerseelsorgen in Polen.* Stuttgart: Seewald, 1981. 173 pp.

Black, J. L., and Strong, J. W. *Sysyphus and Poland.* Winnipeg, Canada: Ronald P. Frye & Co., 1986. 191 pp.

Blazynski, George. *Flashpoint Poland.* New York: Pergamon Press, 1979. 416 pp.

Boyes, Roger, and Moody, John. *The Priest Who Had to Die.* London: Victor Gollancz Ltd., 1986. 204 pp.

Brzeski, Andrzej, ed. *Raport o stanie narodu i PRL: Dokumenty.* Paris: Instytut Literacki, 1980. 221 pp.

Burda, Andrzej. *Parliament of the Polish People's Republic.* Wroclaw: Ossolineum, 1978. 174 pp.

Castellan, Georges. *Dieu garde la Pologne.* Paris: Robert Laffont, 1981. 302 pp.

Centre for Research into Communist Economies. *Poland: Stagnation, Collapse or Growth?* London: Pika Print Ltd., 1988. 100 pp.

Ciechocinska, Maria K., and Graham, Lawrence S., eds. *The Polish Dilemma: Views from Within.* Boulder, Colo.: Westview Press, 1986. 300 pp.

Coutouvidis, John, and Reynolds, Jaime. *Poland: 1939–1947.* Leicester, Eng.: Leicester University Press, 1986. 393 pp.

Curry, Jane Leftwich, ed. and trans. *The Black Book of Polish Censorship.* New York: Random House, 1984. 433 pp.

Danecki, Jan, ed. *Toward Poland "2000": Problems of Social Development.* Wroclaw: Zaklad Narodowy Imienia Ossolinskich, 1980. 281 pp.

Davis, Norman. *Heart of Europe: A Short History of Poland.* Oxford, Eng.: Clarendon Press, 1984. 511 pp.

Dobieszewski, Adolf, and Golebiowski, Janusz W. eds. *PZPR (1948–1978).* Warsaw: PWN, 1978. 316 pp.

Dziewanowski, Marian K. *The Communist Party of Poland: An Outline of History.* 2d ed. Cambridge, Mass.: Harvard University Press, 1976. 419 pp.

Erard, A., and Zygier, M., eds. *La Pologne: Une societe en dissidence.* Paris: Maspero, 1978. 195 pp.

Golebiowski, Janusz W., and Gora, Wladyslaw, eds. *Ruch robotniczy w Polsce Ludowej.* Warsaw: Wiedza Powszechna, 1980. 646 pp.

Gomulka-Wieslaw, Wladyslaw. *Przemowienia.* 11 vols. Warsaw: Ksiazka i Wiedza, 1957–1969.

Gora, Wladyslaw. *PZPR (1948–1978).* Warsaw: MON, 1978. 191 pp.

Groth, Alexander J. *People's Poland: Government and Politics.* San Francisco: Chandler, 1972. 155 pp.

Grot-Kwasniewski, Jerzy. *Society and Deviance in Communist Poland: Attitudes Toward Social Control.* New York: St. Martin's Press, 1984. 210 pp.

Grzelak, Edward. *U podstaw polityki wyznaniowej.* Warsaw: Ksiazka i Wiedza, 1980. 225 pp.

Hahn, Werner G. *Democracy in a Communist Party: Poland's Experience since 1980.* New York: Columbia University Press, 1987. 368 pp.

Holzer, Jerzy. *Solidaritaet*. Munich: C. B. Beck, 1984. 441 pp.

Kanturkova, Eva. *My Companions in the Bleak House*. Woodstock, N.Y.: Overlook Press, 1987. 314 pp.

Karpinski, Jakub. *Countdown: The Polish Upheavals of 1956, 1968, 1970, 1980*. New York: Karz Publishers, 1982. 214 pp.

Krannhals, Hanns von. *Der Warschauer Aufstand 1944*. Frankfurt/Main: Bernard & Graefe, 1962. 445 pp.

Kwiatkowska-Viatteau, Alexandra. *Katyn, l'armee polonaise assassinee*. Brussels: Editions "Complex," 1982. 175 pp.

Lammich, Siegfried. *Der "Popieluszko-Prozess."* Cologne: Wissenschaft & Politik, 1985. 108 pp.

Lauen, Harald. *Polen nach dem Sturz Gomulkas*. Stuttgart: Seewald, 1972. 260 pp.

Letowski, Janusz, ed. *Administration in People's Poland*. Wroclaw: Zaklad Narodowy Imienia Ossolinskich, 1980. 276 pp.

Lipski, Jan Jozef. *KOR: History of the Workers' Defense Committee in Poland*. Berkeley: University of California Press, 1985. 560 pp.

Mackiewicz, Jozef. *Katyn: Ungesuehntes Verbrechen*. Frankfurt/Main: Possev Verlag, 1983. 244 pp.

Malcher, George C. *Poland's Politicized Army: Communists in Uniform*. New York: Praeger, 1984. 287 pp.

Mason, David S. *Public Opinion and Political Change in Poland, 1980–1982*. New York: Cambridge University Press, 1985. 256 pp.

Maziarski, Jacek, et al. *The Polish Upswing, 1971–75*. Warsaw: Interpress, 1975. 151 pp.

Mikolajczyk, Stanislaw. *The Rape of Poland: Pattern of Soviet Aggression*. New York: McGraw-Hill, 1948. 309 pp.

Misztal, Bronislaw, ed. *Poland After Solidarity*. New Brunswick, N.J.: Transaction Books, 1985. 167 pp.

Monat, Pawel, with Dille, John. *Spy in the U.S.* New York: Harper & Row, 1962. 208 pp.

Monticone, Ronald C. *The Catholic Church in Communist Poland*. Boulder, Colo.: East European Monographs, 1986. 227 pp.

Moody, John. *The Priest and the Policeman: The Courageous Life and Cruel Murder of Father Jerzy Popieluszko*. New York: Summit Books, 1987. 251 pp.

Mynarek, Hubert. *Zwischen Gott und Genossen: Als Priester in Polen*. West Berlin: Ullstein, 1981. 312 pp.

[Poland]. *Concise Statistical Yearbook of Poland, 1969–1988*. Warsaw: Central Statistical Office, 1969–1988.

———. *Polskie dane statystyczne, 1987*. Warsaw: Glowny Urzad Statystyczny, 1987. 101 pp.

———. *Rocznik statystyczny, 1955–1987*. Warsaw: GUS, 1955–1987.

Polish United Workers' Party. *VII Zjazd PZPR*. Warsaw: Ksiazka i Wiedza, 1975. 315 pp.

———. *VIII Zjazd PZPR*. Warsaw: Ksiazka i Wiedza, 1980. 262 pp.

————. *IX Zjazd PZPR.* Warsaw: Ksiazka i Wiedza, 1983. 1,167 pp.

Polonsky, Antony, and Druker, Boleslaw, eds. *The Beginnings of Communist Rule in Poland.* Boston: Routledge & Kegan Paul, 1980. 180 pp.

Pomian, Krzysztof. *Pologne: Defi a l'impossible? De la revolte de Poznan a "Solidarite."* Paris: Editions Ouvrieres, 1982. 235 pp.

Potel, Jean-Yves. *Strike Scenes in Poland.* New York: Praeger, 1982. 320 pp.

Rachwald, Arthur. *Poland Between the Superpowers.* Boulder, Colo.: Westview, 1983. 154 pp.

Raina, Peter. *Poland 1981: Towards Social Renewal.* London: Allen & Unwin, 1985. 472 pp.

————. *Political Opposition in Poland, 1954–1977.* London: Arlington Books, 1978. 584 pp.

Sanford, George. *Military Rule in Poland.* New York: St. Martin's Press, 1986. 298 pp.

————. *Polish Communism in Crisis.* New York: St. Martin's Press, 1983. 250 pp.

Schaff, Adam. *Polen heute.* Vienna: Europaverlag, 1984. 236 pp.

Simon, Maurice D., and Kanet, Roger E., eds. *Background to Crisis: Policy and Politics in Gierek's Poland.* Boulder, Colo.: Westview, 1981. 418 pp.

Slomczynski, Kazimierz, and Krause, Tadeusz K. *Class Structure and Social Mobility in Poland.* White Plains, N.Y.: M. E. Sharpe, 1979. 211 pp.

Slomczynski, Kazimierz, and Krause, Tadeusz K., eds. *Social Stratification of Poland.* Armonk, N.Y.: M. E. Sharpe, 1986. 189 pp.

Spasowski, Romuald. *The Liberation of One.* San Diego, Calif.: Harcourt Brace Jovanovich, 1986. 704 pp.

Staar, Richard F. *Poland: Sovietization of a Captive People.* Westport, Conn.: Greenwood Press, 1975. 300 pp.

Staniszkis, Jadwiga. *Poland's Self-Limiting Revolution.* Princeton, N.J.: Princeton University Press, 1984. 352 pp.

Swidlicki, Andrzej. *Political Trials in Poland, 1981–1986.* London: Croom Helm, 1988. 426 pp.

Szymanski, Albert. *Class Struggle in Socialist Poland.* New York: Praeger, 1984. 265 pp.

Szymanski, Leszek. *Candle for Poland: 469 Days of Solidarity.* San Bernadino, Calif.: Borgo Press, 1982. 128 pp.

Taras, Ray. *Ideology in a Socialist State: Poland 1956–1983.* New York: Cambridge University Press, 1984. 299 pp.

————. *Poland: Socialist State, Rebellious Nation.* Boulder, Colo.: Westview, 1986. 200 pp.

Toch, Marta [pseud.]. *Reinventing Civil Society: Poland's Quiet Revolution, 1981–1986.* New York: U.S. Helsinki Watch Committee, 1986. 101 pp.

Touraine, Alain, et al. *Solidarity. The Analysis of a Social Movement: Poland.* New York: Cambridge University Press, 1983. 203 pp.

Unger, Peter. *Die Ursachen der politischen Unruhen in Polen im Winter 1970/71.* Berne: Herbert Lang, 1975. 287 pp.

[United States]. Central Intelligence Agency. *Directory of Polish Officials*. Washington, D.C.: Directorate of Intelligence, April 1987, LDA 87–10997. 178 pp.

Voronkov, V. I., et al. *Polskaia Narodnaia Respublika: spravochnik*. 3d ed. Moscow: Politizdat, 1984. 124 pp.

Walesa, Lech. *A Way of Hope*. New York: Henry Holt & Co., 1987. 325 pp.

Weber, Wolfgang. *Solidarnosc, 1980–1981, und Perspektive der politischen Rewolution*. Essen: Arbeiterpresse Verlag, 1987. 124 pp.

Weydenthal, Jan B. de. *The Communists of Poland: An Historical Outline*. rev. ed. Stanford: Hoover Institution Press, 1987. 272 pp.

––––––. *The Polish Drama, 1980–1982*. Lexington, Mass.: Lexington Books, 1983. 351 pp.

Wieczorek, Mieczyslaw. *Armia Ludowa: powstanie i organizacja, 1944–1945*. Warsaw: MON, 1979. 371 pp.

Woodall, Jean, ed. *Policy and Politics in Contemporary Poland: Reform, Failure, Crisis*. London: Frances Pinter, 1982. 200 pp.

Wozniuk, Vladimir. *From Crisis to Crisis: Soviet-Polish Relations in the 1970s*. Ames: Iowa State University Press, 1987. 176 pp.

Zagajewski, Adam. *Polen, Staat im Schatten der Sowjetunion*. Reinbeck bei Hamburg: Rowohlt, 1981. 207 pp.

Zamoyski, Adam. *The Polish Way*. New York: Franklin Watts, 1988. 422 pp.

Zawodny, J. K. *Death in the Forest*. Notre Dame, Ind.: University of Notre Dame Press, 1962. 235 pp.

––––––. *Nothing but Honour: The Story of the Warsaw Uprising, 1944*. Stanford: Hoover Institution Press, 1978. 328 pp.

Romania

Amburtsumov, E. A., and Bogomolov, O. T., chief eds. *Sotsialisticheskaia Respublika Rumyniia*. Moscow: Nauka, 1984. 368 pp.

Bobango, Gerald J. *The Emergence of the Romanian National State*. Boulder, Colo.: East European Quarterly, 1979. 311 pp.

Braham, Randolph L. *Education in the Rumanian People's Republic*. Washington, D.C.: U.S. Government Printing Office, 1963. 222 pp.

Braun, Aurel. *Romanian Foreign Policy Since 1965*. New York: Praeger, 1978. 218 pp.

Ceaucescu, Ilie, ed. *War, Revolution and Society in Romania: The Road to Independence*. Boulder, Colo.: Social Science Monographs, 1983. 198 pp.

Ceaucescu, Nicolae. *Romania on the Way to Completing Socialist Construction: Reports, Speeches, Articles*. 15 vols. Bucharest: Meridiane, 1969–1979.

Cioranescu, George. *Bessarabia: Disputed Land Between East and West*. Munich: Ion Dumitru Verlag, 1985. 372 pp.

Cretzianu, Alexandre, ed. *Captive Rumania: A Decade of Soviet Rule*. New York: Praeger, 1956. 424 pp.

Croghan, Martin J., and Croghan, Penelope P. *Ideological Training in Communist Education: A Case Study of Romania*. Washington, D.C.: University Press of America, 1980. 201 pp.

Funderburk, David B. *Pinstripes and Reds: An American Ambassador Caught Between the State Department and the Romanian Communists, 1981–1985*. Washington, D.C.: Selous Foundation Press, 1987. 226 pp.

Ghermani, Dionisie. *Die nationale Souveraenitaetspolitik der Rumaenien*. 2 vols. Munich: Oldenbourg, 1981.

Goma, Paul. *Le Tremblement des hommes: Peut-on vivre en Roumanie aujourd'hui?* Paris: Seuil, 1979. 329 pp.

Graham, Lawrence S. *Romania, a Developing Socialist State*. Boulder, Colo.: Westview, 1982. 136 pp.

Ionescu, Ghita. *Communism in Rumania, 1944–1962*. London: Oxford University Press, 1964. 378 pp.

King, Robert R. *History of the Romanian Communist Party*. Stanford: Hoover Institution Press, 1980. 190 pp.

Nelson, Daniel N. *Romania in the 1980s*. Boulder, Colo.: Westview, 1981. 313 pp.

Orlik, I. I., et al. *Sotsialisticheskaia Respublika Rumyniia*. Nauka, 1974. 190 pp.

Pacepa, Ion Mihai. *Red Horizons: Chronicles of a Communist Spy Chief*. Chicago: Regnery Gateway, 1987. 446 pp.

Pascu, Stefan, ed. *Die Unabhaengigkeit Romaeniens*. Bucharest: Editura Academiei RSR, 1978. 285 pp.

Potapov, Vladimir Il'ich. *Sotsialisticheskaia Respublika Rumyniia: spravochnik*. 3d rev. ed. Moscow: Politizdat, 1984. 141 pp.

[Romania]. *Anuarul Statistic al Republicii Socialiste Romania, 1969–1987*. Bucharest: Directia Centrala de Statistica, 1969– 1987.

———. *Congresul al XII-lea al Partidului Comunist Roman: 19–23 Noiembre 1979*. Bucharest: Editure Politica, 1981. 933 pp.

———. *Congresul al XIII-lea al Partidului Comunist Roman: 19–22 Noiembre 1984*. Bucharest, 1985. 767 pp.

———. *Constitution of the Socialist Republic of Rumania*. Bucharest: Meridiane, 1965. 35 pp.

Shafir, Michael. *Romania: Politics, Economics and Society*. London: Francis Pinter, 1985. 232 pp.

Tontsch, Guenther H. *Das Verhaeltnis von Partei und Staat in Romaenien*. Cologne: Wissenschaft & Politik, 1985. 201 pp.

Tsantis, Andreas C., and Pepper, Roy. *Romania, the Industrialization of an Agrarian Economy Under Socialist Planning*. Washington, D.C.: World Bank, 1979. 707 pp.

Turnock, David. *The Romanian Economy in the Twentieth Century*. London: Croom Helm, 1986. 296 pp.

[United States]. Central Intelligence Agency. *Directory of Romanian Officials*. Washington, D.C.: Directorate of Intelligence, June 1985, CR 85–10667. 145 pp.

Yugoslavia

Alexander, Stella. *Church and State in Yugoslavia Since 1945*. New York: Cambridge University Press, 1979. 351 pp.

Bacic, Hrvoje, et al. *Constitutional System of Yugoslavia*. Belgrade: Jugoslovenska stvarnost, 1980. 133 pp.

Beloff, Nora. *Tito's Flawed Legacy*. London: Gollancz, 1985. 287 pp.

Bertsch, Gary K. *Values and Community in Multinational Yugoslavia*. New York: Cambridge University Press, 1976. 160 pp.

Borowiec, Andrew. *Yugoslavia After Tito*. New York: Praeger, 1977. 122 pp.

Boskovic, Mirko. *Drustveno-politicki sistem Jugoslavije*. Zagreb: Naprijed, 1963. 365 pp.

Clissold, Stephen. *Djilas: The Progress of a Revolutionary*. New York: Universe Books, 1983. 352 pp.

Clissold, Stephen, ed. *Yugoslavia and the Soviet Union, 1939– 1973: A Documentary Record*. New York: Oxford University Press, 1975. 318 pp.

Colakovic, Rodoljub, ed. *Pregled istorije Saveza Komunista Jugoslavije*. Belgrade: Institut za Izucavanje Radnickog Pokreta, 1963. 571 pp.

Dedijer, Vladimir. *The Battle Stalin Lost: Memoirs of Yugoslavia, 1948–1953*. New York: Viking, 1971. 341 pp.

———. *Jugoslovensko-Albanski odnosi, 1939–1948*. Belgrade: Borba, 1949. 227 pp.

Djilas, Milovan. *Conversations with Stalin*. New York: Harcourt Brace & World, 1962. 211 pp.

———. *The New Class*. New York: Praeger, 1957. 214 pp.

———. *Rise and Fall*. San Diego, Calif.: Harcourt Brace Jovanovich, 1985. 424 pp.

———. *The Story from the Inside*. New York: Harcourt Brace Jovanovich, 1980. 185 pp.

Doder, Dusko. *The Yugoslavs*. New York: Random House, 1978. 256 pp.

Dragnich, Alex N. *Tito's Promised Land, Yugoslavia*. New Brunswick, N.J.: Rutgers University Press, 1954. 337 pp.

Dunn, William M., and Obradovic, Josip. *Workers' Self-Management and Organizational Power in Yugoslavia*. Pittsburgh, Pa.: University of Pittsburgh Press, 1978. 448 pp.

Duzevic, Stipe, chief ed. *Tenth Congress of the League of Communists of Yugoslavia*. Belgrade: Komunist, 1975. 210 pp.

Gibianskii, L. Ia. *Sovetskii Soiuz i novaia Iugoslaviia, 1941–1947*. Moscow: Nauka, 1987. 204 pp.

Grlickov, Aleksandar, ed. *Privreda Jugoslavije, 1947–1977*. Belgrade: Provredni pregled, 1978. 273 pp.

Kardelj, Edward. *Reminiscences*. London: Blond & Briggs, Ltd., 1982. 279 pp.

————. *Tito and Socialist Revolution of Yugoslavia*. Belgrade: Socialist Thought & Practice, 1980. 275 pp.

Kolisevski, Lazar. *Aspects of the Macedonian Question*. Belgrade: Socialist Thought & Practice, 1980. 250 pp.

Lovric, Ivan. *The Delegate System of Yugoslavia*. Belgrade: Kommunist, 1977. 199 pp.

Lydall, Harold. *Yugoslav Socialism: Theory and Practice*. New York: Clarendon Press, 1986. 302 pp.

Markovski, Venko. *Goli Otok: Island of Death*. Boulder, Colo.: East European Monographs, 1984. 229 pp.

Martin, David, ed. *Patriot or Traitor: The Case of General Mihailovich*. Stanford: Hoover Institution Press, 1978. 499 pp.

Micunovic, Veljko. *Moscow Diary*. Garden City, N.Y.: Doubleday, 1980. 474 pp.

Mihajlov, Mihajlo. *Underground Notes*. 2d rev. ed. New Rochelle, N.Y.: Caratzas Brothers, 1982. 206 pp.

Mojsov, Lazo. *Dimensions of Non-Alignment*. Belgrade: Jugoslovenska Stvarnost, 1981. 281 pp.

Nikiforov, L. A., and Ostrovidov, Iu. P. *Sotsialisticheskaia Federativnaia Respublika Iugoslaviia: spravochnik*. Moscow: Politizdat, 1985. 127 pp.

Nyrop, Richard F. *Yugoslavia*. Washington, D.C.: U.S. Government Printing Office, 1982. 336 pp.

Palmer, Stephen E., and King, Robert R. *Yugoslav Communism and the Macedonian Question*. Hamden, Conn.: Archon Books, 1971. 247 pp.

Rajovic, Radosin, chief ed. *Jugoslovenski savremenici: Ko je ko i Jugoslaviji*. Belgrade: Hronometar, 1970. 1208 pp.

Ramet, Pedro, ed. *Yugoslavia in the 1980s*. Boulder, Colo.: Westview, 1985. 355 pp.

Roggemann, Herwig, ed. *Die Verfassung der SFR Jugoslawien*. West Berlin: Berlin Verlag, 1980. 288 pp.

Seroka, Jim, and Smiljkovic, Rados. *Political Organizations in Socialist Yugoslavia*. Durham, N.C.: Duke University Press, 1986. 321 pp.

Sirc, Ljubo. *The Yugoslav Economy Under Self-Management*. New York: St. Martin's Press, 1979. 270 pp.

Stankovic, Slobodan. *The End of the Tito Era*. Stanford: Hoover Institution Press, 1981. 168 pp.

Sussman, Leonard, moderator. *Yugoslavia: The Failure of "Democratic Communism."* New York: Freedom House, 1987. 89 pp.

Tito, Josip Broz. *Selected Speeches and Articles, 1941–1961*. Zagreb: Naprijed, 1963. 460 pp.

[United States]. *The Central Leadership of the Union of Communists of Yugoslavia, Elected at the Seventh Congress, April 22–26, 1958*. Washington, D.C.: Department of State, Division of Biographic Information, 1958. 67 pp.

————. Central Intelligence Agency. *Directory of Yugoslav Officials*. Washington, D.C.: Directorate of Intelligence, December 1986, CR85–16320. 207 pp.

[Yugoslavia]. *Constitutional System of Yugoslavia.* Belgrade: Jugoslovenska stvarnost, 1980. 133 pp.

———. *Drustveno-politicke zajednice.* Vol. 1. Belgrade: Interpress, 1968. 353 pp.

———. *Eleventh Congress of the League of Communists of Yugoslavia.* Belgrade: Kommunist, 1978. 240 pp.

———. *Statisticki godisnjak Jugoslavije, 1970–1987.* Belgrade: Savezni zavod za Statistiku, 1970–1987.

———. *Ustav Sotsijalisticke Federativne Republike Jugoslavije.* Belgrade: Sluzbeni List SFRJ, 1974. 200 pp.

Vucinich, Wayne S., ed. *Contemporary Yugoslavia.* Berkeley: University of California Press, 1969. 441 pp.

Wilson, Duncan. *Tito's Yugoslavia.* Cambridge, Eng.: Cambridge University Press, 1980. 269 pp.

Warsaw Pact

Close, Robert. *Europe Without Defense?* New York: Pergamon Press, 1979. 278 pp.

Crane, Keith. *Military Spending in Eastern Europe.* Santa Monica, Calif.: Rand Corporation, May 1987, R–3444–USDP. 104 pp.

Czimas, Michael. *Der Warschauer Pakt.* Bern: Schweizerisches Ost-Institut, 1972. 152 pp.

Gac, Stanislaw. *Geschichte der polnischen Armee.* East Berlin: Militaerverlag der DDR, 1978. 342 pp.

Gosztony, Peter, ed. *Zur Geschichte der europaeischen Volksarmeen.* Bonn-Bad Godesberg: Hohwacht, 1976. 270 pp.

Holloway, David, and Sharp, Jane M. O., eds. *Warsaw Pact: Alliance in Transition?* Ithaca, N.Y.: Cornell University Press, 1984. 229 pp.

International Institute for Strategic Studies. *The Military Balance, 1987–1988.* London: September 1987. 246 pp.

Johnson, A. Ross. *East European Military Establishments: The Warsaw Pact Northern Tier.* New York, Crane Russak, 1982. 182 pp.

Jones, Christopher D. *Defending Socialism In Eastern Europe: Political Autonomy, Military Intervention and the Warsaw Pact.* New York: Praeger, 1980. 350 pp.

———. *Soviet Influence in Eastern Europe: Political Autonomy and the Warsaw Pact.* New York: Praeger, 1981. 322 pp.

Lee, William T., and Staar, Richard F. *Soviet Military Policies Since World War Two.* Stanford: Hoover Institution Press, 1986. 263 pp.

Lewis, William J. *The Warsaw Pact: Arms, Doctrine and Strategy.* New York: McGraw-Hill, 1982. 471 pp.

Mal'tsev, V. F. *Organizatsiia Varshavskogo Dogovora: dokumenty i materialy, 1955–1980.* Moscow: Politizdat, 1980. 296 pp.

Marcinkowski, Adam. *Uklad Warszawski: Problemy dzialalnosci politycznej.* Krakow: Agencia Wydawnicza, 1986. 248 pp.

Meissner, Boris, ed. *Der Warschauer Pakt: Dokumentensammlung*. Cologne: Wissenschaft & Politik, 1962. 204 pp.

Nelson, Daniel N. *Alliance Behavior in the Warsaw Pact*. Boulder, Colo.: Westview, 1986. 134 pp.

————. *Soviet Allies: The Warsaw Pact and the Issue of Reliability*. Boulder, Colo.: Westview, 1984. 273 pp.

Oldberg, Ingmar, ed. *Unity and Conflict in the Warsaw Pact*. Stockholm: Swedish National Defense Research Institute, 1984. 158 pp.

Orlik, I. I., ed. *Vneshniaia politika stran Varshavskogo dogovora: pervaia polovina 80-kh godov*. Moscow: Nauka, 1986. 319 pp.

Rakowska-Harmstone, Teresa; Jones, Christopher D.; and Sylvain, Ivan. *Warsaw Pact: The Question of Cohesion*. 3 vols. Ottawa: Department of National Defence, 1981–1984.

Ratajczyk, Leonard. *Historia wojskowosci*. 2d ed. Warsaw: MON, 1980. 613 pp.

Remington, Robin A. *The Warsaw Pact: Case Studies in Conflict Resolution*. Cambridge, Mass.: MIT Press, 1973. 268 pp.

Rodionov, N. N., et al. eds. *Organizatsiia Varshavskogo dogovora, 1955–1975*. Moscow: Politizdat, 1975. 192 pp.

Sadykiewicz, Michael. *Soviet-Warsaw Pact Western Theater of Military Operations: Organization and Missions*. Santa Monica, Calif.: Rand Corporation, August 1987, N–2596–AF. 174 pp.

Simon, Jeffrey. *Warsaw Pact Forces: Problems of Command and Control*. Boulder, Colo.: Westview, 1985. 246 pp.

Staar, Richard F., ed. *Arms Control: Myth vs. Reality*. Stanford: Hoover Institution Press, 1988. 211 pp.

[United States]. Central Intelligence Agency, *Directory of USSR Ministry of Defense and Armed Forces Officials*. Washington, D.C.: Directorate of Intelligence, October 1986, LDA 86–11907. 46 pp.

————. Department of Defense, *Soviet Military Power: An Assessment of the Threat, 1988*. Washington, D.C.: The Pentagon, May 1988. 175 pp.

————. Arms Control and Disarmament Agency, *World Military Expenditures and Arms Transfers 1987*. Washington, D.C.: U.S. Government Printing Office, March 1988. 147 pp.

Volkogonov, D. A., ed. *Armii stran Varshavskogo Dogovora: spravochnik*. Moscow: Voenizdat, 1985. 223 pp.

Wiener, Friedrich. *Soldaten im Ostblock*. Munich: Lehmanns Verlag, 1972. 208 pp.

Woerner, Manfred. *Streitkraeftevergleich 1987: NATO-Warschauer Pakt*. Bonn: Bundesministerium der Verteidigung, 1987. 47 pp.

CMEA

Adam, Jan. *Employment and Wage Policies in Poland, Czechoslovakia and Hungary since 1950*. New York: St. Martin's Press, 1985. 251 pp.

Bogomolov, O. T., chief ed. *Upravlenie vneshneekomicheskoi deiatel'nostii sotsialisticheskikh stran.* Moscow: Nauka, 1979. 320 pp.

Budkin, V. S. *Internatsionalizatsiia sotsial'noekonomicheskogo razvitiia evropeiskikh stran-chlenov SEV.* Kiev: Naukova dumka, 1987. 246 pp.

Burenin, V. A. and Potapov, V. I. *Organizatsiia upravleniia vneshne-ekonomicheskimi sviaziami SSSR.* Moscow: Mezhdunarodnye otnosheniia, 1987. 96 pp.

Burov, A. S. *Ekonomicheskoe sotrudnichestvo SSSR so stranami sotsializma.* Moscow: Mezhdunarodnye otnosheniia, 1987. 303 pp.

Chukanov, O. A., ed. *Nauchno-tekhnicheskoe sotrudnichestvo stran SEV: spravochnik.* Moscow: Ekonomika, 1986. 288 pp.

Ciamaga, Lucjan. *Od wspolpracy do integracji: Zarys organizacji i dzialalnosci RWPG w latach 1949–1964.* Warsaw: Ksiazka i Wiedza, 1965. 250 pp.

Council for Mutual Economic Assistance. *CMEA: Figures, Facts, Arguments.* Moscow: CMEA Secretariat, 1983. 56 pp.

———. *SEV: voprosy i otvety.* Vol. 2. Moscow: Upravlenie delami sekretariata SEV, 1986. 47 pp.

———. *Statisticheskii ezhegodnik stran-chlenov SEV, 1987.* Moscow: Finansy i statistika, 1987. 462 pp.

Danilenko, V. M. *Sotrudnichestvo SFRIU so stranami-chlenami SEV.* Kiev: Naukova dumka, 1987. 111 pp.

Faddeev, N. V. *Sovet ekonomicheskoi vzaimopomoshchi.* 2d ed. Moscow: Ekonomika, 1969. 263 pp.

Flavien, Jean, and Lajoinie, Andre. *L'Agriculture dans les pays socialistes d'Europe.* Paris: Editions Sociales, 1976. 288 pp.

Fomin, V. N. *SEV i drugie mezhdunarodnye organizatsii.* Moscow: Nauka, 1983. 174 pp.

Gumpel, Werner. *Sozialistische Wirtschaftssysteme.* Munich: Guenter Olzog Verlag, 1983. 223 pp.

Jeffries, Ian. *The Industrial Enterprise In Eastern Europe.* New York: Praeger, 1981. 165 pp.

Karcz, Jerzy F. *The Economics of Communist Agriculture: Selected Papers.* Bloomington, Ind.: International Development Institute, 1979. 494 pp.

Kaser, Michael. *Comecon: Integration Problems of the Planned Economies.* 2d ed. London: Oxford University Press, 1967. 279 pp.

Koeves, Andras. *The CMEA Countries in the World Economy.* Budapest: Akademiai Kiado, 1985. 247 pp.

Konstantinov, Iu. *Den'gi v sisteme stran SEV.* Moscow: Finansy, 1978. 288 pp.

Koval'chak, Hryhorii I. *Pol'skaia Narodnaia Respublika v sodruzhestve stran-chlenov SEV: ekonomicheskii ocherk.* Kiev: Naukova dumka, 1980. 197 pp.

Lehar, Bohumil. *Rada vzajemne hospodarske pomoci, 1949–1979.* Prague: Svoboda, 1978. 138 pp.

North Atlantic Treaty Organization. *The CMEA Five-Year Plans (1981–1985) in a New Perspective: Planned and Nonplanned Economies.* Brussels: Economics and Information Directorates, 1983. 309 pp.

―――. *Economic Reforms in Eastern Europe and Prospects for the 1980s: Colloquium, 16–18 April 1980, Brussels.* New York: Pergamon Press, 1980. 320 pp.

―――. *The Economies of Eastern Europe and their Foreign Economic Relations.* Brussels: Economics and Information Directorates, 1987. 363 pp.

Pecsi, Kalman. *The Future of Socialist Economic Integration.* Armonk, N.Y.: M. E. Sharpe, 1981. 189 pp.

Pekshev, Iu. A. *Dolgosrochnye tselevye programmy sotrudnichestva stran-chlenov SEV.* Moscow: Nauka, 1980. 190 pp.

Schaefer, Henry W. *Comecon and the Politics of Integration.* New York: Praeger, 1972. 218 pp.

Schoenfeld, Roland, ed. *RGW-Integration und Suedosteuropa.* Munich: Oldenbourg, 1984. 298 pp.

Shastitko, V. M., chief ed. *Mezhdunarodnyi rynok SEV v usloviiakh integratsii.* Moscow: Politizdat, 1980. 237 pp.

Sinetskii, B. I. *Vneshnetorgovye operatsii: organizatsiia i tekhnika.* Moscow: Mezhdunarodnye otnosheniia, 1987. 112 pp.

Staar, Richard F., ed. *The Future Information Revolution in the USSR.* Washington, D.C.: Crane and Russak, 1988. 216 pp.

[United States]. Central Intelligence Agency. *Handbook of Economic Statistics, 1987.* Washington, D.C.: Directorate of Intelligence, September 1987, CPAS 87–10001. 242 pp.

―――. Congress. Joint Economic Committee, 99th Cong., 1st–2d sess. *East European Economies: Slow Growth in the 1980's.* 3 vols. Washington, D.C.: U.S. Government Printing Office, 1985–86.

Vienna Institute for Comparative Economic Studies. *Comecon Foreign Trade Data, 1986.* London: Macmillan Press, 1988. 551 pp.

Zloch-Christy, Iliana. *Debt Problems of Eastern Europe.* Cambridge, Mass.: Cambridge University Press, 1987. 220 pp.

Intrabloc Relations

Adam, Jan. *Wage Control and Inflation in the Soviet Bloc Countries.* London: Macmillan, 1979. 243 pp.

Allen, Richard V., ed. *1968 Yearbook on International Communist Affairs.* Stanford: Hoover Institution Press, 1969. 1,165 pp.

Andren, Nils, and Birnbaum, Karl E., eds. *Belgrade and Beyond: The CSCE in Perspective.* Rockville, Md.: Sijthoff & Noordhoff, 1980. 180 pp.

Aslund, Anders. *Private Enterprise in Eastern Europe.* New York: St. Martin's Press, 1985. 294 pp.

Brzezinski, Zbigniew K. *The Soviet Bloc.* Cambridge, Mass.: Harvard University Press, 1960. rev. ed. New York: Praeger, 1961. 467 pp.

Butler, William E., ed. *A Source Book on Socialist International Organizations.* Alphen aan den Rijn: Sijthoff & Noordhoff, 1978. 1,143 pp.

Commission on Security and Cooperation in Europe. *Five Years After Helsinki.* Washington, D.C.: Government Printing Office, 1980. 341 pp.

Connor, Walter D. *Socialism, Politics, and Equality: Hierarchy and Change in Eastern Europe and the USSR.* New York: Columbia University, 1979. 389 pp.

Curry, Jane L., ed. *Dissent in Eastern Europe.* New York: Praeger, 1983. 227 pp.

Dahm, Helmut. *Der gescheiterte Ausbruch: Entideolisierung und ideologische Gegenreformation in Osteuropa (1960–1980).* Baden-Baden: Nomos, 1982. 938 pp.

Davisha, Karen, and Hanson, Philip, eds. *Soviet-East European Dilemmas: Coercion, Competition, and Consent.* New York: Holmes & Meier, 1981. 226 pp.

Djordijevich, Dimitrije, and Fischer-Galati, Stephen. *The Balkan Revolutionary Tradition.* New York: Columbia University Press, 1981. 271 pp.

Drachkovitch, Milorad M., ed. *East Central Europe: Yesterday, Today, Tomorrow.* Stanford: Hoover Institution Press, 1982. 400 pp.

———. *United States Aid to Yugoslavia and Poland: Analysis of a Controversy.* Washington, D.C.: American Enterprise Institute, 1963. 124 pp.

———. *Yearbook on International Communist Affairs, 1966.* Stanford: Hoover Institution Press, 1967. 766 pp.

Dunn, Dennis J. *Detente and Papal-Communist Relations, 1962–78.* Boulder, Colo.: Westview, 1979. 216 pp.

Durdenevskii, V. N., ed. *Konstitutsii evropeiskikh stran narodnoi demokratii.* Moscow: Gosiurizdat, 1954. 183 pp.

Economist Intelligence Unit. *EIU Regional Review: Eastern Europe and the USSR, 1986.* London: The Economist, 1986. 124 pp.

Eidlin, Fred H. *The Logic of "Normalization."* New York: Columbia University Press, 1980. 278 pp.

Fischer-Galati, Stephen, ed. *The Communist Parties of Eastern Europe.* New York: Columbia University Press, 1979. 393 pp.

———. *Eastern Europe in the 1980s.* Boulder, Colo.: Westview, 1981. 291 pp.

Furtak, Robert K. *Die politischen Systeme der sozialistischen Staaten.* Munich: Deutsches Taschenbuch, 1979. 242 pp.

Gerner, Kristian. *The Soviet Union and Central Europe in the Post-War Era.* Lund: Swedish Institute of International Affairs, 1984. 238 pp.

Gorbachev, M. S. *Izbrannye rechi i stat'i.* Vol. 4. Moscow: Politizdat, 1987. 511 pp.

Gorbanevskaia, Natalia. *Nous dissidents: La Dissidence en U.R.S.S., Pologne, Allemagne de l'Est, Tchecoslovaquie.* Paris: Editions recherches, 1978. 254 pp.

Gromyko, A. A., ed. *Diplomatiia stran sotsializma.* Moscow: MO, 1980. 431 pp.

Gyorgy, Andrew, and Kuhlman, James A., eds. *Innovation in Communist Systems.* Boulder, Colo.: Westview, 1978. 294 pp.

Hacker, Jens. *Der Ostblock: Entstehung, Entwicklung und Struktur, 1939–1980.* Baden-Baden: Nomos, 1983. 900 pp.

Hammond, Thomas T., ed. *The Anatomy of Communist Takeovers*. New Haven, Conn.: Yale University Press, 1975. 664 pp.

Hazan, Baruch A. *The East European Political Systems*. Boulder, Colo.: Westview, 1985. 396 pp.

Horak, Stephan M., and Blanke, Richard. *East European National Minorities, 1919– 1980: A Handbook*. Littleton, Colo.: Libraries Unlimited, 1985. 274 pp.

Hutchings, Robert L. *Soviet-East European Relations: Consolidation and Conflict, 1968– 1980*. Madison: The University of Wisconsin Press, 1983. 314 pp.

Kalenichenko, P. M., and Kolesnik, V. P. *Granitsa druzhby i mira*. Lvov: Vishcha shkola, 1980. 156 pp.

Kende, Pierre, and Pomian, Krzysztof. *1956 Varsovie-Budapest: La Deuxieme revolution d'octobre*. Paris: Editions du Seuil, 1978. 262 pp.

Kertesz, Stephen P., ed. *East Central Europe and the World: Developments in the Post-Stalin Era*. Notre Dame, Ind.: University of Notre Dame Press, 1962. 386 pp.

King, Robert R. *Minorities Under Communism: Nationalities as a Source of Tension Among Balkan Communist States*. Cambridge, Mass.: Harvard University Press, 1973. 326 pp.

Klein, George, and Reban, Milan J., eds. *The Politics of Ethnicity in Eastern Europe*. New York: Columbia University Press, 1981. 279 pp.

Kuhlman, James A., ed. *The Foreign Policy of Eastern Europe*. Leyden: A. W. Sijthoff, 1978. 302 pp.

Lazitch, Branko, and Drachkovitch, Milorad M. *Biographical Dictionary of the Comintern*. rev. ed. Stanford: Hoover Institution Press, 1986. 532 pp.

Lendvai, Paul. *The Bureaucracy of Truth: How the Communist Governments Manage the News*. Boulder, Colo.: Westview Press, 1981. 285 pp.

Lewis, Paul G., ed. *Eastern Europe: Political Crisis and Legitimation*. New York: St. Martin's Press, 1984. 202 pp.

Linden, Ronald H. *Communist States and International Change. Yugoslavia and Romania in Comparative Perspective*. Winchester, Mass.: Unwin Hyman, Inc., 1987. 240 pp.

Linden, Ronald H., ed. *The Foreign Policies of Eastern Europe*. New York: Praeger, 1980. 319 pp.

Lovenduski, Joni, and Woodall, Jean. *Politics and Society in Eastern Europe*. Bloomington: Indiana University Press, 1987. 474 pp.

Mensonides, Louis J., and Kuhlman, James A., ed. *The Future of Inter-Bloc Relations in Europe*. New York: Praeger, 1974. 214 pp.

Menzhinskii, V. I. *Mezhdunarodnye organizatsii sotsialisticheskikh gosudarstv*. Moscow: Politizdat, 1980. 256 pp.

Narkiewicz, Olga A. *Eastern Europe, 1968–1984*. London: Croom Helm, 1986. 273 pp.

Pelikan, Jiri, and Wilke, Manfred. *Menschenrechte: Ein Jahrbuch zu Osteuropa*. Reinbek bei Hamburg: Rowohlt, 1977. 477 pp.

Petrenko, F. F., chief ed. *Partiinoe stroitel'stvo v sotsialisticheskikh strankh*. Moscow: Politizdat, 1980. 535 pp.

Radio Free Europe. *East European Leadership List.* Munich, 15 January 1988. 42 pp.

―――. *Eastern Europe's Communist Leaders.* 5 vols. Munich, 1966.

Radu, Michael. *Eastern Europe and the Third World: East vs. South.* New York: Praeger, 1981. 376 pp.

Rakowska-Harmstone, Teresa, ed. *Communism in Eastern Europe.* 2d ed. Bloomington: Indiana University Press, 1984. 391 pp.

―――. *Perspectives for Change in Communist Societies.* Boulder, Colo.: Westview, 1979. 194 pp.

Reale, Eugenio. *Nascita del Cominform.* Rome: Mondadori, 1958. 175 pp.

Rowen, Henry S., and Wolf, Charles, Jr., eds. *The Future of the Soviet Empire.* New York: St. Martin's Press, 1987. 368 pp.

Saikowski, Charlotte, and Gruliow, Leo, eds. *Current Soviet Policies IV: The Documentary Record of the 22nd Congress of the Communist Party of the Soviet Union.* New York: Columbia University Press, 1962. 248 pp.

Scherer, John L., ed. *USSR Facts & Figures Annual.* Vol. 11. Gulf Breeze, Fla.: Academic International Press, 1987. 383 pp.

Schulz, Donald E., and Adams, Jan S., eds. *Political Participation in Communist Systems.* Elmsford, N.Y.: Pergamon Press, 1981. 334 pp.

Sejna, Jan. *We Will Bury You.* London: Sidgwick & Jackson, 1982. 205 pp.

Seton-Watson, Hugh. *The East European Revolution.* New York: Praeger, 1956. 406 pp.

Shevtsova, L. F. *Soiuznicheskie partii v politicheskoi sisteme stran sotsializma.* Moscow: Nauka, 1978. 178 pp.

Shoup, Paul. *The East European and Soviet Data Handbook: Political, Social, and Developmental Indicators.* New York: Columbia University Press, 1981. 481 pp.

Shumikin, N. F., chief ed. *Sotsializm i sovremennyi mir.* Kiev: Vyshcha shkola, 1987. 344 pp.

Simon, Jeffrey. *Cohesion and Discussion in Eastern Europe.* New York: Praeger, 1983. 235 pp.

Simon, Jeffrey, and Gilberg, Trond. *Security Implications of Nationalism in Eastern Europe.* Boulder, Colo.: Westview, 1986. 327 pp.

Simons, William B., ed. *The Constitutions of the Communist World.* Alphen aan den Rijn: Sijthoff & Noordhoff, 1980. 644 pp.

Sodaro, Michael J., and Wolchik, Sharon L., eds. *Foreign and Domestic Policy in Eastern Europe in the 1980s.* New York: St. Martin's Press, 1983. 192 pp.

Staar, Richard F. *Long-Range Environmental Study of the Northern Tier of Eastern Europe in 1990–2000.* McLean, Va.: Research Analysis Corp., 1970. 252 pp.

―――. *USSR Foreign Policies After Detente.* 2nd rev. ed. Stanford: Hoover Institution Press, 1987. 308 pp.

Staar, Richard F., ed. *Aspects of Modern Communism.* Columbia: University of South Carolina Press, 1968. 416 pp.

―――. *Yearbook on International Communist Affairs, 1969–1988.* Stanford: Hoover Institution Press, 1969–1988.

Strashun, B. A.; Topornin, B. N.; and Shakhnazarov, G. Kh., eds. *Konstitutsii sotsial-isticheskikh gosudarstv.* 2 vols. Moscow: Iurizdat, 1987.

Stroynowski, Juliusz, ed. *Who's Who in the Socialist Countries of Europe: Albania, Bulgaria, CSSR, GDR, Hungary, Poland, Romania, Yugoslavia.* 3 vols. New York: K. G. Saur, Inc., 1988.

Sugar, Peter. *Ethnic Diversity & Conflict in Eastern Europe.* Santa Barbara, Calif.: ABC Clio, 1980. 553 pp.

Svanidze, K. N., chief ed. *Konferentsiia kommunisticheskikh i rabochikh partii evropy (29–30. VI. 1976).* Moscow: Politizdat, 1977. 296 pp.

Swearingen, Rodger, ed. *Leaders of the Communist World.* New York: Free Press, 1971. 632 pp.

Sworakowski, Witold S., ed. *World Communism: A Handbook, 1918–1965.* Stanford: Hoover Institution Press, 1971. 576 pp.

Szajkowski, Bogdan, ed. *Marxist Governments: A World Survey.* 3 vols. London: Macmillan, 1981.

Tampke, Juergen. *The People's Republics of Eastern Europe.* New York: St. Martin's Press, 1983. 178 pp.

Tang, Peter S. H. *The Twenty-Second Congress of the Communist Party of the Soviet Union and Moscow-Tirana-Peking Relations.* Washington, D.C.: Research Institute on the Sino-Soviet Bloc, 1962. 141 pp.

Terry, Sarah Meiklejohn. *Soviet Foreign Policy in Eastern Europe.* New Haven, Conn.: Yale University Press, 1984. 375 pp.

Thomson, James A., and Gantz, Nanette C. *Conventional Arms Control Revisited: Objectives in the New Phase.* Santa Monica, Calif.: Rand Corporation, December 1987, N–2697–AF. 17 pp.

Toekes, Rudolf L., ed. *Opposition in Eastern Europe.* Baltimore, Md.: Johns Hopkins University Press, 1979. 306 pp.

Triska, Jan F., and Gati, Charles, ed. *Blue Collar Workers in Eastern Europe.* Winchester, Mass.: Allen & Unwin, 1981. 320 pp.

United Nations. *Statistical Yearbook 1980.* New York: Department of Economics and Social Affairs, 1981. 914 pp.

[United States]. Central Intelligence Agency. *The World Factbook 1987.* Washington, D.C., June 1987, CPAS WF87–001. 290 pp.

————. Congress. House Committee on Foreign Affairs, 87th Cong., 2d sess. *Captive European Nations: Hearings.* Washington, D.C., 1962. 377 pp.

————. House Committee on Un-American Activities, 87th Cong., 1st sess. *Who Are They?* 9 parts. Washington, D.C., 1957–1958.

————. Senate Committee on Foreign Relations, 81st Congress, 1st sess. *A Decade of American Foreign Policy.* Senate Document 123. Washington, D.C., 1950. 1,381 pp.

————. Senate Committee on the Judiciary, 85th Cong., 1st sess. *The Church and State Under Communism.* 9 vols. Washington, D.C., 1964–1966.

————. Senate Committee on the Judiciary, 89th Cong., 2d sess. *A Study of the Anatomy of Communist Takeovers.* Washington, D.C., 1966. 70 pp.

————. Senate Committee on the Judiciary, 87th Cong., 1st sess. *Yugoslav Communism: A Critical Study.* Washington, D.C., 1961. 387 pp.

————. *Speech of Nikita Khrushchev Before a Closed Session of the XXth Congress of the Communist Party of the Soviet Union.* Washington, D.C., 1957. 66 pp.

————. Department of Commerce, Bureau of the Census. *Projections of the Population of the Communist Countries of Eastern Europe, 1975–2000.* Washington, D.C., 1976. 51 pp.

————. Department of State, Bureau of Intelligence and Research. *World Strength of the Communist Party Organizations.* Washington, D.C., 1973. 182 pp.

[USSR]. *Narodnoe khoziaistvo SSSR v 1986 g.* Moscow: Statistika, 1987. 862 pp.

Volgyes, Ivan. *Politics in Eastern Europe.* Chicago: Dorsey Press, 1986. 368 pp.

Volgyes, Ivan, ed. *The Peasantry of Eastern Europe.* Elmsford, N.Y.: Pergamon Press, 1979. 192 pp.

————. *Social Deviance in Eastern Europe.* Boulder, Colo.: Westview, 1978. 198 pp.

Voss, Eugen, ed. *Die Religionsfreiheit in Osteuropa.* Zollikon: G–2–W Verlag, 1984. 272 pp.

Waedekin, Karl Eugen. *Agrarian Policies in Communist Europe.* Totowa, N.J.: Allanheld & Osmun, 1982. 324 pp.

Wolchik, Sharon L., and Meyer, Alfred G., eds. *Women, State and Party in Eastern Europe.* Durham, N.C.: Duke University Press, 1985. 366 pp.

Wolff, Robert Lee. *The Balkans in Our Time.* Cambridge, Mass.: Harvard University Press, 1956. 618 pp.

Yedlin, Tova, ed. *Women in Eastern Europe and the Soviet Union.* New York: Praeger, 1980. 320 pp.

Zagladin, V. V., and Kiselev, G. A., eds. *Politicheskie partii: spravochnik.* Moscow: Politizdat, 1986. 382 pp.